Two week loan
Benthyciad pythefnos

Please return on or before the due date to avoid overdue charges
*A wnewch chi ddychwelyd ar neu cyn y dyddiad a nodir ar eich llyfr os
gwelwch yn dda, er mwyn osgoi taliadau*

SCANDINAVIAN ARCHAEOLOGY

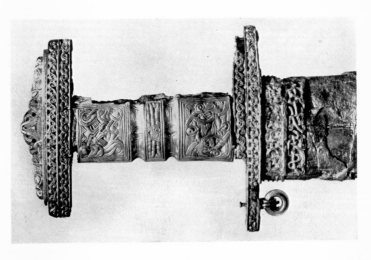

b. The handle of a sword, bronze gilt and set with garnets. 7th century, from Valsgärde, Uppland

a. The handle of a sword adorned with gold and silver. 6th century, Snartemo, Norway

SCANDINAVIAN ARCHAEOLOGY

BY

HAAKON SHETELIG

PROFESSOR OF ARCHAEOLOGY
BERGEN MUSEUM

AND

HJALMAR FALK

LATE PROFESSOR OF GERMANIC PHILOLOGY IN THE
UNIVERSITY OF OSLO

TRANSLATED BY

E. V. GORDON

SMITH PROFESSOR OF ENGLISH LANGUAGE
AND GERMANIC PHILOLOGY IN THE
UNIVERSITY OF MANCHESTER

OXFORD
AT THE CLARENDON PRESS
1937

OXFORD UNIVERSITY PRESS
AMEN HOUSE, E.C. 4
London Edinburgh Glasgow New York
Toronto Melbourne Capetown Bombay
Calcutta Madras
HUMPHREY MILFORD
PUBLISHER TO THE UNIVERSITY

PRINTED IN GREAT BRITAIN

PREFACE

THIS book has been produced by the happy collaboration of an archaeologist and a philologist. Its theme is the ancient Norse culture, which we know partly through tangible remains and partly through the oldest Norse literature. Division of the work was a necessity, since the different materials in the two fields of study call for quite different methods. But not for different presentation: what gives the book its value is that both authors, however unlike as scholars, are working each in his own field with a common aim, to make the life of ancient times live again for our generation. The truth is that Professor Shetelig is something more than an archaeologist, and the late Professor Falk was something more than a philologist. They have both refused always to be confined within the narrow limits of the specialist, and each in his own way has been at pains to make his science serviceable to other disciplines; both have an eye for effective synthesis when researching into the culture of the past.

It would be superfluous to give to an English public interested in history any account of Professor Shetelig's work in archaeology. I will mention only two points. He has written time after time on the archaeology of his country, unpartnered, and he has never repeated himself. He is constantly at work to reveal some new interest in his material. He is possessed by the restlessness of the true investigator, which impels him to be searching always for a fresh view of his material, gained by some new approach. The other point is a detail, but it is an important detail. Professor Shetelig is the author of a volume much prized in Norway, the first volume of the great *Life and History of the Norwegian People* (published only in Norwegian).

Professor Falk I have called a philologist, but this word is far from comprehending all his widespread researches. He was in addition a literary and textual scholar who mastered the surviving Old Norse literature in its entirety—the Edda, the poetry of the scalds, and the sagas. In the philological field, together with Professor Torp, he produced the standard works on Norse etymology, among others the great *Etymological Dictionary of the Norwegian and Danish Languages* (issued also in a German edition). In Falk the etymologist becomes an explorer of cultural history: through his extraordinarily comprehensive knowledge of the history of the word he was able to reveal what words have to tell of the society that used them. As early as 1900 he wrote a little book bearing the significant title *Words as a record of culture* (*Kulturminder i Ord*). And this philologist worked through the whole of the rich Norse literature and wrote scholarly monographs on what is actually said there about various forms of Old Norse life and activity— on ships, weapons, costume, and much else. Every statement that came from his pen was supported by citations from the old writings, and all his evidence had to satisfy the strict demands of modern linguistic science, and pass the tests of morphological and semantic analysis. His work was the fruit of a rich matured learning and a warm interest both in the life that was lived in ancient times and in the various survivals of its forms and customs in out-of-the-way districts of Norway.

We can accordingly look to this book to give the right orientation to the results of research. In scope it covers periods from the remotest antiquity, when men were pushing forward into lands where the great ice-sheet of the glacial age had only lately retreated and yielded ground for settlement—when Scandinavia was still a Greenland, with inland ice and a coastal strip—right down to the turbulent centuries of the viking age, when heathendom and Christendom were locked in a desperate struggle, and historic Scandinavia appeared with a West European civilization.

The prehistory of the North is thus far from being an even and continuous growth from the native basis alone. Accessions from the leading cultures of Europe can be observed all through the prehistoric periods. Let me mention just one such influence, the great cultural activity betokened by the introduction of writing (in runes) into the North a few centuries after Christ. The disputed question of the origin of the runes Professor Shetelig has set in its historical background, and he has given it a highly original and attractive treatment. In Professor Falk's contribution, which comprises chapters XVIII–XXIII—all the rest of the book is by Professor Shetelig—the weighty chapter on 'Religion' is worthy of special attention. Its content could not be better described than by this one word: it is not mythology, not religious history in the usual sense; its nature can only be expressed by a word of deeper signification.

There is another fortunate circumstance in the making of this book to which I would like to call attention. It has been translated by a scholar, Professor E. V. Gordon of Manchester University, who is excellently versed in the Old Norse language and literature. In various places he has supplemented Professor Falk's account with notes, where he has found reason to mention the latest discussions of material points. In the same way Professor Shetelig has made it his care to see that significant archaeological material which first became available after Professor Falk's death has not passed unnoticed in chapters XVIII–XXIII, and in various ways he has been at pains to ensure full harmony between the philological and archaeological treatment of the same factual evidence.

There is one matter not immediately evident from the title of the book, which is worth mentioning. Norse culture in the viking period should not be looked at in isolation. In particular, we must not omit to look westward across the North Sea. English and Irish cultural influences are easy to trace in Scandinavia at the beginning of the historic period. But there was also an influence in the reverse direction, as is well known. The most vivid impression of this is given in the chapter on 'Seafaring'. There was a time when the Scandinavian peoples were the teachers of all western Europe on the sea. Many an English (and French) word is shown in this chapter to have been derived from Norse. Here we have a striking demonstration of the valuable results which collaboration between philology and history can give.

Thanks are due to those whose names are indicated on pages xi–xvii and also to the authorities at the National Museum of Copenhagen, the State Antiquary of Sweden, the National Museum of Finland, the University Museum of Antiquities at Oslo, and the Museums of Bergen, Stavanger and Trondheim, for the use of illustrations.

MAGNUS OLSEN

OSLO,
April 1936.

CONTENTS

x CONTENTS

LIST OF PLATES

xii LIST OF PLATES

LIST OF TEXT-FIGURES

A NOTE ON THE TERMINOLOGY

IN general the current terminology of English archaeological literature has been employed in this translation and in particular the
technical terms found in the British Museum guides to prehistoric
antiquities. Some terms may, however, need explanation to readers
not versed in Scandinavian pre-history. Among the general terms it
should be noted that 'Norse' is the equivalent of 'Scandinavian', and
therefore distinct from 'Norwegian': these terms correspond respectively to *nordisk* and *norsk* in the authors' manuscript, and to *nor-
disch* and *norwegisch* in German. A similar distinction is made
between 'Germanic', which refers to the whole group of Teutonic
peoples, and 'German', which has its normal limited sense. 'The
north' in this book usually refers to the Scandinavian north, but is
less precise in its application than 'Scandinavia': it comprehends
Scandinavia proper and the immediately neighbouring lands. 'Scandinavia' is more comprehensive than 'the Scandinavian peninsula',
and includes Denmark and the adjacent islands. Finland and Iceland are regarded as Scandinavian lands, but not as part of Scandinavia.

To make the precise application of the terms clear, the equivalent
in French or German is often added in brackets, as on page 19:
'pick-axes (*pics*) and flake-axes (*tranchets*)', or, if the thing referred
to is peculiarly Scandinavian, the Old Norse or modern Scandinavian
name may be added.

Among the technical terms used one is entirely new: 'flake-axe'.
This word was a happy coinage of Professor Shetelig's, and was
gratefully accepted by the translator as handier and more suitable
than the older 'shell-mound axe'. The term 'beaker' is used throughout in its general use of 'drinking-vessel with a wide mouth', 'drink-
ing-bowl', and never with the specialized sense given to it by some
archaeologists with reference to certain vessels of the bronze age.
'Dwelling-site' or 'dwelling-station' refers (as commonly in archaeological writings) to a place once occupied by a prehistoric settlement.
The term does not imply the existence of dwelling-houses on the site.

Apart from the bibliographical references, Scandinavian names are
given in traditional English form, whenever there is one still in use,
as Denmark, Copenhagen, Zealand (Danish *Sjælland*), the Skaw
(Danish *Skagen*), &c. Some of the letters in the Scandinavian words
and names quoted may be unfamiliar to English readers and therefore call for comment. In Old Norse ǫ represents an open *o*-sound,
and may be pronounced like the *o* in *not* (though it was really a sound

between the *o* in *not* and the *u* in *but*) ; þ had the sound of *th* in English *thin* ; ð had that of *th* in *then*. The acute accent indicates length. In modern Norwegian and Danish *ø* is like *ö* in Swedish or German; Norwegian and Swedish *å*, Danish *aa*, has a sound like the vowel heard in English *broad*; Norwegian and Danish *æ* is like *ä* in Swedish and German, and may be either short or long. In Old Norse, however, *æ* was always long. The final -*r* in many Old Norse names and nouns is the ending of the nominative singular. This ending is usually omitted when the name or word is anglicized: thus 'Ólafr' is found when given as an Old Norse form, but 'Olaf' in ordinary English use. The numerous Old Norse terms used in the later chapters will be best understood with the aid of a dictionary; the most convenient for English readers are Cleasby and Vigfusson's large *Icelandic-English Dictionary* and the smaller *Old Icelandic Dictionary* by Geir Zoega.

ABBREVIATIONS

Aarb. f. nord. Oldk.   Aarbøger for nordisk Oldkyndighed og Historie

Dan.	Danish	OE.	Old English
dial.	dialect	OFr.	Old French
Du.	Dutch	OFris.	Old Frisian
Eng.	English	OGaul.	Old Gaulish
Fr.	French	OHG.	Old High German
Ger.	German	OIr.	Old Irish
Got.	Gothic	OLG.	Old Low German
Gr.	Greek	ON.	Old Norse
Ir.	Irish	ONorw.	Old Norwegian
Lith.	Lithuanian	ORuss.	Old Russian
ME.	Middle English	OSax.	Old Saxon
Med. Gr.	Medieval Greek	OSlav.	Old Slavonic
Med. Lat.	Medieval Latin	OSw.	Old Swedish
MHG	Middle High German	Run.Got.	Runic Gothic
MLG.	Middle Low German	Run.N.	Runic Norse
Mod. Icel.	Modern Icelandic	Run.Sw.	Runic Swedish
n.	footnote	Russ.	Russian
Norw.	Norwegian	Sansk.	Sanskrit
ODan.	Old Danish	Swed.	Swedish

I

GEOLOGICAL CONDITIONS AND THE EARLIEST SETTLEMENTS IN SCANDINAVIA

A LIMIT is set to our knowledge of human culture in Scandinavia by the great quaternary glaciations which covered the whole of northern Europe. During the period of greatest severity an unbroken sheet of ice was spread out over an immense area extending from the North Cape to the Carpathians, from Ireland to Ural. Every form of life must inevitably have ceased, and at the same time the masses of ice obliterated every trace of any older habitation that might conceivably have existed in the more favourable climate of the preceding periods.

The varying phases of the ice age present a history of extreme vicissitudes. It can be made out with certainty that several great glaciations followed one after another, interrupted by inter-glacial periods, when the ice receded; but the geological interpretation is difficult and often desultory, because each new ice age effaced the traces of the preceding inter-glacial period over an extensive area. Most is known about the last inter-glacial period, through the recent researches carried out in Denmark and the neighbouring part of northern Germany.[1] In the oldest strata which follow immediately upon a glaciation, the vegetation is Arctic, characterized by Arctic mosses, bear-berry (*Dryas octopetala*), several kinds of Polar willows (*Salix herbacea* and others), dwarf birch (*Betula nana*), &c. Next follows a period of great forests of birch and red fir, which again are succeeded by West-European forest-trees, first and foremost the oak, but together with it an extensive intermixture of elm, lime, yew, and holly. At that time a kind of elephant, probably the mammoth, lived in the Danish forests; also deer, Irish elk, and beaver. In the succeeding period conifers again prevail, at first mainly spruce, later red fir mingled with birch. Finally, these forests are completely displaced by Arctic dwarf birch,

[1] Knud Jessen and V. Milthers, 'Stratigraphical and Palaeontological Studies of Interglacial Freshwater Deposits in Jutland and North-west Germany', *Danmarks geologiske Undersøgelse*, II Række, no. 48 (København, 1928). See especially the admirably abstracted summary, p. 336.

which is in turn succeeded by a poor, purely Arctic flora. A new ice age is approaching.

We can safely assume that the other Scandinavian regions underwent corresponding changes of climate during the last inter-glacial period, even though there is no such reliable documentation of the evidence available there as in Denmark. From Norway and Sweden important discoveries of fossils can be cited, bones of mammoth and musk-ox believed to date from the last inter-glacial period. It is a point of special interest that the mammoths are found in high-lying valleys in the interior of the peninsula, as at Våge, near Otta, and in Jämtland, and musk-oxen as far north as Trøndelag.[1] The Scandinavian inland ice had therefore melted away completely, and the peninsula had a flora and a fauna which might well afford conditions suitable for human habitation. Here, then, is a possibility which we shall see later has a certain theoretical interest, but at the same time it must be emphasized that up to the present no trace of an inter-glacial population has been found either in the Scandinavian peninsula or in Finland. Similarly, the highest authority on this problem as it appears in Denmark has made certain that traces of inter-glacial man are completely absent there, in spite of the rich and luxuriant growth of plant and animal life under the most favourable climatic conditions.

The last great glaciation which descended from the Scandinavian highland was more limited in extent than those preceding it. The inland ice had its southern limit in Mecklenburg; it covered the whole of Scandinavia, the Baltic lands, and the neighbouring parts of Russia. This North-European ice age must have resembled the present ice age in Greenland. The very surface of the ice, with peaks of rock projecting above it, the extent of the inland ice, and the Polar Sea surrounding it, were much the same. But even at the greatest extent of the last glaciation Jutland still had an unbroken shore in the west free from ice, and the same conditions are attested in many stretches along the western coast of Norway.[2] Thus even during

---

[1] G. Frödin, *Ett par nyare svenska mammutfynd.* Svenska geologiska Föreningens Förhandlingar, 1916. It is also possible that these mammoths date from the early post-glacial period; in that case the mammoth must have survived the last ice age in Scandinavia.

[2] Sven Ekman, *Djuvärldens Utbredningshistoria på Skandinaviska Halvön* (Stockholm, 1922), p. 397 f.; Rolf Nordhagen, *Brædæmte sjøer i Sunndalsfjel-*

this severe Arctic period the Scandinavian coasts on the North Sea may have offered possibilities of human habitation under almost the same conditions as the Eskimos enjoy in Greenland. This possibility has assumed considerable significance in the study of the oldest forms of Norse culture.[1]

Eventually the time came when the last great sheet of ice melted away and the Scandinavian lands came to light again in the form which had been impressed upon them by these great movements, with the same surface and soil as they have had ever since. It is still possible to trace the stages as the ice limit receded from the west and south towards the north and east. During the progress of the melting definite periods are distinguished: the Daniglacial period, when the ice receded from Jutland almost to Øresund; the Gothiglacial period, when the extent of the ice was further limited by a retreat from Skåne to the middle of Sweden; and the Finiglacial period, when the ice came to a halt in the north of Sweden, in Jämtland. The Swedish geologist G. de Geer even succeeded in working out an exact chronology of the periods which elapsed while the ice melted away from Skåne to Jämtland. De Geer's method was to count the layers of clay deposited annually as they were left by the water from the melting inland ice, and his results are now generally accepted. In this way it can be shown that it took some 3,000 years for the edge of the ice to retreat from Skåne to the middle of Sweden. At that stage there was a pause in the melting; then it began again, the ice receding at the rate of 300 to 400 metres a year. At the end of another 2,000 years the ice had been pushed back to the northernmost districts of the peninsula, with its border in Jämtland. From an examination of other geological factors it has also been possible to bring this computation into contact with historical chronology, and thus establish that it is now about 14,000 years since the last glaci-

dene, kvartærgeologiske og botaniske iagttagelser, 1929. In these works it is pointed out that the flora and fauna of the high mountains may have survived the last ice age along the coast in western Scandinavia. The same is possibly true of the mammoths mentioned above. During recent years fresh discoveries of mammoths have been noted from the suburbs of Oslo, from Romerike and Otta.

[1] The whole problem is exhaustively studied in the recent book by Rolf Nordhagen, *De senkvartære klimavekslinger i Nordeuropa og deres betydning for kulturforskningen,* Instituttet for Sammenlignende Kulturforskning, serie A, vol. xii (Oslo, 1933).

ation extended all the way to Zealand and Skåne. Geological computation thus affords a clear chronological survey of the whole prehistoric period in the north.

The ground left by the ice consisted of barren morains, stony clay, and sandbanks, but gradually it was covered by an Arctic vegetation such as is now characteristic of the tundra in the north of Russia—bearberry (*Dryas*) and dwarf birch (*Betula nana*); and the animal life which first appears has the same character, namely, reindeer, wolf, Alpine hare, ptarmigan, and lemming. Later came scrub and small woods of birch and low red fir; elk, bears, and beavers then followed. We come again to the period when Norse lands begin to offer conditions capable of supporting human habitation.

The search for the earliest traces of man in northern Europe has been a peculiarly fascinating task, since that area had been exposed to the full effects of the successive glaciations. We know, of course, that during these same periods western Europe and central Europe had a population which passed through the first stages of material and spiritual culture before and during the period of the last great ice age in the north. There should, then, be a possibility of coming upon the oldest Norse antiquities in a secondary stratum left behind in the loose material which the ice scraped along with it from Scandinavian ground. In a single instance it has been thought that flint implements of that age were found in deposits from the ice age at Kiel in Holstein.[1] These were flints, rolled and ground like all the other loose pieces in the same stratum, and they must therefore have come to the place where they are now found through the movement of the ice from the north. By comparison with other deposits it can be proved that these flints originally belonged to the Baltic region. The pieces in question are simple fragments with a little rough chipping; some of them have one side shaped like a primitive cutting-edge, while others are pointed like weapons of war or tools for boring. Otherwise the forms are accidental and various, as in eolithic implements generally. They are indeed subject to all the doubt which attaches to eolithic work: a few experts have recognized them as genuine eoliths, but others think they were produced entirely by the play of natural forces. They

[1] Fr. Richters, *Nordische Urfaustkiele*, 43. Bericht der Senckenbergischen Naturforschenden Gesellschaft, 1912, Frankfort a. M.

are mentioned here because they point at least to a possibility of tracing the oldest stage of human culture in Scandinavia. Proof is obviously not established by a single isolated discovery, which, moreover, is much disputed. More extensive and sustained researches into this problem are needed; up to the present this source has contributed nothing to Scandinavian archaeology of sufficient importance to deserve further attention.

A better impression is made by a find in Jutland, which, even though it is as yet similarly unique and isolated, seems nevertheless to be free from doubt. It is the roughly chipped implement of flint (see Pl. 1) found by a geological survey near Harebjerg in Jutland. This flint lay 7 metres deep in the untouched inter-glacial stratum and was covered by gravels which had mostly been deposited during the last ice age.[1] To judge from the photograph this piece is fashioned with a technique resembling the Mousterian in France and England, and must be assigned to a period before the last great glaciation of Scandinavia. Yet the discovery brings nothing else to light but this meagre fact; and a single isolated object cannot give any picture of a culture as a whole.

The great Swedish archaeologist Oscar Montelius attempted to trace the oldest habitation in another way, when he devoted one of his last works to these early and dark periods of Scandinavian pre-history.[2] From the classification of the finds as they are arranged in the museums Montelius picked out a certain group of large, rough, flint articles, which could not be given a place in any of the later periods of the stone age. They were oval, approximately almond-shaped implements, fashioned by simple chipping from a piece of flint which was roughly similar in shape: often pieces, large or small, of the original calcium crust still remained on the surface of the flint, but the edge had been sharpened by more careful, finer chipping. These implements were rather massive and heavy, and they were

---

[1] Anathon Bjørn, 'Noen norske stenaldersproblemer', Norsk geologisk Tidsskrift, x, 1928, p. 55; Therkel Mathiassen, 'Primitive Flintredskaber fra Samsö', Aarb. f. nord. Oldk., 1934, p. 43, footnote 2. According to Mathiassen the flint of Harebjerg is rather atypic, and the conditions of the discovery not absolutely reliable.

[2] O. Montelius, 'Palaeolithic Implements found in Sweden', The Antiquaries Journal, i, p. 98.

associated by their common shape, which was constant, and by the uniform method of treating the flint. This is, in a few words, the character which Montelius claimed for his special group.

In the development of this theory the flint which Montelius regarded as decisive was a typical specimen of the almond-shaped type, found in the peat under Järavallen in Skåne. Järavallen is a huge gravel-bank, formed along the shore during the great post-glacial rise of the sea in the stone age; this is known to geologists as the *litorina* subsidence or the *tapes* subsidence (see below, p. 10). The gradual sinking of the land here, moreover, is marked by geological finds in several strata. At the highest point of the gravel-bank there is a dwelling-site from the later stone age; deeper in the bank flint of a more primitive character is deposited, certainly from the period of the middens, and finally the almond-shaped flint was found in the peat below the gravel.[1] Montelius accordingly concludes that the date of the almond-shaped flints must be moved back correspondingly. From consideration of the shape of these Scandinavian flints he classed them with the well-known West-European flint weapons of the Solutrean culture, shaped like a laurel leaf in a pointed oval with the greatest width roughly at the middle. These are often excellently worked and show the palaeolithic technique in flint work at its highest point; but rougher pieces can also be found, and it would be possible to find examples that are not superior to the best Norse work. By this association with the Solutré culture we reach a point of time which falls within the last period of the ice age, probably after the culmination of the last glaciation in Scandinavia. We should probably not meet with any insuperable obstacle in natural conditions if we assumed a first settlement on the ice-free coasts of Denmark, Skåne, and the west of Sweden and Norway. Montelius accordingly assigned the almond-shaped flints to the first period of the melting of the great ice, to De Geer's Daniglacial period.

But Montelius's interpretation of the almond-shaped flints is

[1] For details of the whole find see: Knut Kjellmark, 'En stenåldersboplats i Järavallen vid Limhamn', *Antikvarisk Tidskrift för Sverige*, xvii, no. 3, 1905; Otto Rydbeck, 'The Changes of Level of the Stone Age Sea and the Earliest Settling of Man in Scandinavia', *Bulletin de la Société Royale des Lettres de Lund*, 1927–8.

PLATE 1

Flint implement of palaeolithic type, found
under deposits of glacial gravels at Harebjerg,
Jutland. After Bjørn

As a background for the study of the post-glacial stone age in Scandinavia a survey of the varying natural conditions must first be given, including both the topographical results of the rising and sinking of the land and the changing climatic periods. In the early post-glacial period the whole of southern Scandinavia was considerably higher above the sea than it is now. Even at the beginning of the post-glacial forest period a great part of the North Sea was solid land, including a large extension from the present shore-line of south-west Jutland. The Danish isles were joined by solid land to Skåne and northern Germany, and the western and southern parts of the Baltic were dry land continuing the north German lowland. The Baltic was cut off from the sea as a vast fresh-water lake, and its surface stood 20 or 30 metres higher than the sea. This was the ancylus lake, as it is called from the river limpet *Ancylus fluviatilis*, which then lived in the Baltic lake. The ancylus lake covered a great part of the central Swedish lowland and had its outlet from there to the Cattegat.

The most southerly part of the Norwegian coast was also higher than now. On the other hand the central parts of the Scandinavian peninsula were considerably lower than their present level. The lowest point of the sinking was reached during the melting of the last remaining sheet of the great inland ice; in the interior of the country the land sank to about 250 metres lower than it now is, around Oslo to about 220 metres lower, at the mouth of Oslofjord to about 160 metres lower. At Trondhjemsfjord the deepest subsidence was to a point 200 metres below the present level. But on the western side of the peninsula the difference from the present elevation was much smaller: in the district around Bergen the general level was about 60 metres below the present elevation, and around Ålesund about 40 metres below. The results of the subsidence were much more clearly marked in the topographical changes. To the east, in Oslofjord, the sea may have covered large areas which are now land, and similarly on the Baltic coasts; but the west coast on the whole was steep and high and so kept essentially the same coast-line during the subsidence as it has had ever since.

The ensuing rise of the land has a special significance for the investigator of Scandinavian settlement, since the various stages in the rise also fix definite levels in the periods of cultural development. The study of this interrelation has been especially fruitful in the east of Sweden, where the nature of the ground caused areas of considerable extent to be raised out of the sea during the older cultural periods. It can be shown that the older types of culture had their geographical limits along certain lines of elevation, and that the settlement expanded as more land rose out of the sea. In Oslofjord, where the rise was very great, similar investigations again produced plentiful results. Even on the west coast, where the rise was comparatively slight, and where much smaller areas were freed from the sea, certain levels are of great importance in grouping the older and later forms of culture. The post-glacial rise of the land provides a fixed scale by which the periods of archaeology can be measured and checked over the whole of Scandinavia. The old coast-lines give the interrelation of culture and elevation in each separate district with absolute certainty. For example, the dwelling-site at Ramsjö in the Stockholm district belongs to the kitchen-midden period, and the former coast-line is now 40 metres above the sea; another dwelling-site at Torslunda is two thousand years later, and its coast-line is little more than 20 metres above the sea. In the Lofoten group of islands in the north of Norway the highest 'flint-places' date from the earliest part of the stone age, lower dwelling-sites containing Nøstvet forms are contemporary with the Danish kitchen middens, and still lower are Arctic slate articles from the neolithic period. We shall often have occasion to refer to this relationship in the following pages.

Another means of determining the periods geologically is provided by the various periods of vegetation after the ice age. In the ancylus period fir was the usual forest-tree in Denmark, mingled to some extent with birch and poplar; towards the end of this period the earliest traces of oak, elm, and lime appear. The climate was continental and became gradually milder; at the end of this climatic period the temperature, at least in summer, was about as high as at the present time. The beginning of the warm post-glacial period thus falls in the latter part of the ancylus age. This period with a relatively warm and dry climate is known to geologists as the boreale period; it corresponds roughly to the period of Maglemose culture.

After this the rise of the land was interrupted by a very

considerable subsidence of the whole of the Scandinavian area, a subsidence which on the Baltic shore is generally known as the *litorina* subsidence (from the periwinkle *Litorina litorea*), but on the Norwegian coasts it is called the *tapes* subsidence (from the shell-fish *Tapes decussatus*). The Sound and the Belts were opened out wider and deeper than now, so that the Baltic lake became an arm of the sea; its waters, moreover, were somewhat salter than at present. The climate was damp and oceanic, producing a vigorous growth of bog-plants. In the south of Scandinavia the fir was completely superseded by oak and other foliiferous trees. In Norway the oak was then found at its greatest extent in the lowland, while heavy forests of fir spread over the highland plateaus up to 1,250 metres above the sea. Perpetual snow and ice were no longer found in Scandinavia. This is the Atlantic period, with a humid warm climate, and it coincides roughly with the midden period of the stone age.

In the following subboreale period the climate became drier again, but the summer temperature was still higher than it is now. In Denmark the beech begins to make an appearance. It was possibly at this point that a new subsidence took place in Scandinavia and Finland. This period corresponds fairly closely to the later neolithic period and the bronze age in the history of civilization. Finally, a second damp period followed, the subatlantic period, when there was a vigorous growth of bog-plants and the summers were cooler. The earlier warmth-loving animals disappeared or became very rare. On the Scandinavian peninsula the highest points of the mountains were again covered with perpetual snow and ice. This period belongs in the main to the prehistoric iron age. In this era the rise of the land ceased in western Scandinavia, but the Baltic coasts continued to rise gradually above the sea, just as in later historical times up to the present day.

The climatic developments which are sketched here in barest outline are to a large extent common to the whole Scandinavian territory. But it is obvious, from the great extent of Scandinavia north and south and east and west, that the effects of the climatic changes must have varied considerably in the several districts, according to the latitude of the locality, its distance from the sea, and its elevation. Yet the interchange of warmer and cooler summers, of dry and humid climate, of the sea's advance and retreat, must everywhere have followed the same order and shared the same reciprocal relations. This has formed the basis of a collaboration between natural science and archaeology which has proved most fruitful in ascertaining the relation between the geological periods and the development of human culture. Moreover, the natural conditions are obviously factors of the greatest importance in determining the manner of life and the distribution of the earliest population in the north.[1]

[1] I may here indicate individual works which expound the contributions of natural science on these problems. O. Gunnar E. Erdtman, 'Pollenanalytische Untersuchungen von Torfmooren und marinen Sedimenten in Südwest-Schweden', *Arkiv för Botanik*, vol. xvii, no. 10 (Stockholm, 1921); Erik Granlund, 'Landhöjningen i Stockholmstrakten efter människans invandring', *Geologiska Föreningens i Stockholm Förhandlingar*, vol. l, p. 207 (Stockholm, 1928); Wilhelm Ramsay, 'Nivåförändringar och Stenåldersbosätning i det Baltiska Området', *Fennia*, vol. xlvii, no. 4 (Helsingfors, 1926), with a summary in German.

II

THE EARLIEST TRACES OF POST-GLACIAL HABITATION IN THE NORTH. THE LYNGBY CULTURE. RÅÖ AND VARBERG. THE FLINTS FROM FOSNA AND KOMSA

WITH the aid of the geological criteria described in the preceding chapter we are now able to trace the habitation of man in the north back to the beginning of the post-glacial era. The researches of recent years have produced a succession of surprising discoveries in this field, and have revealed a completely new aspect of the problems surrounding the earliest immigration into Scandinavian territory. Even from the time when the edge of the great ice-sheet still lay in Holstein and near Lübeck, undoubted traces have been discovered of men who approached very near to the borders of the ice. At Schlutup, in the neighbourhood of Hamburg, pieces of worked reindeer horn have been found in a stratum which is characterized by high Arctic vegetation and by reindeer and Irish elk as the principal species of animals. From the same period comes a split flint found during the excavation of the Kaiser Wilhelm canal in Holstein, likewise in a setting of late glacial flora and fauna. In both of these places the finds are merely isolated single pieces which do not give any picture of culture or manner of life, but they are nevertheless complete proof of the presence of men at a time when the ice had not long departed.

From somewhat later in the same period come the more extensive finds known by the name of the locality, near the Schaalsee.[1] The Schaalsee finds are not characterized geologically, since the flints are found for the most part on the surface of morains of the last glaciation; yet the flint work in itself gives an impression of extraordinarily high antiquity.

[1] G. Schwantes, 'Nordisches Paläolithikum und Mesolithikum', *Mitteilungen aus dem Museum für Völkerkunde in Hamburg*, xiii (Hamburg, 1928). See further Julius Andree, 'Beiträge zur Kenntnis des Norddeutschen Paläolithikums und Mesolithikums', *Mannus-Bibliothek*, vol. lii (Leipzig, 1932). In *Geschichte Schleswig-Holsteins*, Band i, Lieferung 1 (1935), Schwantes describes the recent discovery at Meiendorf, a site which has yielded large collections of worked bone and horn of reindeer.

Noteworthy are the heavy cores and the coarse thick flakes of irregular form, showing traces of use, either entirely without special shaping or partially chipped into the form of scrapers. A typical form is the very large pointed hand-axe made from suitably large flakes, chipped at one end to a point, to provide a handle; also gravers (*burins*), borers, and scrapers of various forms. The technical treatment of the flints is in general reminiscent of early Mousterian. G. Schwantes, who has rendered distinguished service in these researches, believes that the Schaalsee culture represents the oldest phase of human habitation in these parts of northern Germany. As representing the next phase the same investigator describes the flint finds from Ahrensburg and Lavenstedt near Altona, a group which shows a much more highly-developed stage in the treatment of flint. Thick flakes were still in use as hand-axes and scrapers, but there is also a rich variety of regularly shaped slender flakes and many small implements fashioned from such flakes, scrapers and borers and gravers of all the various forms. As a specially characteristic form the small flake-points with a tang are most notable, the 'one-edged' arrowheads, which play an important part in the oldest Norse stone age. The Ahrensburg culture as a whole is, undoubtedly, nearly related to the late palaeolithic, to forms from Aurignac and La Madeleine. Schwantes considers this phase to be most nearly related to the early Tardenoisian in western Europe, and he considers that the Lyngby culture in Denmark is its direct continuation. It is concluded from the character of the flints that Ahrensburg must be reckoned the earlier and Lyngby the later stage of one and the same culture. The Ahrensburg series of finds belongs to a period when northern Germany still had a subarctic climate like that of present-day Finmark, while Lyngby carries us forward to the time when forests were beginning to grow in Jutland.[1] These researches around Hamburg provide the best starting-point for a survey of the earliest culture found on Scandinavian ground.

The first period in which we can distinguish beyond all doubt traces of a population in Norse lands, and in which we can also

[1] G. Schwantes, loc. cit., pp. 164–5, gives a table showing the early cultural phases mentioned here parallel with the contemporary geological periods.

obtain some idea of the conditions of culture, is the early post-glacial period; the forests had then begun to appear, but the reindeer still remained in southern Scandinavia. In the clay strata from this period, both in Denmark and Skåne, pieces of reindeer horn are occasionally found which have been worked by man. The most characteristic form is a kind of axe-like weapon of reindeer horn, in shape very like a hoe, and as a rule fitted with a small sharp blade of flint.[1] The classic find is an axe made in this way from reindeer horn (see Pl. 2), which was found on the shore under the cliff at Nørre-Lyngby in Jutland, and most investigators have assumed that it must have been lying in the very old post-glacial deposits in the cliff, though there is no direct proof of this. Later a careful geological survey of the strata in the cliff was carried out, and a simple arrowhead of flint was found in its proper place in the deposit, so that its age was determined geologically: it must be roughly contemporary with bones of reindeer, ptarmigan, Alpine hare, beaver, and other varieties of animals from a slightly deeper stratum in the cliff.[2] The fauna thus gives a rather Arctic impression, though the beavers indicate that there must have been woods not far away. Reindeer much prefer ground that is free from woods, but they can also adapt themselves to life in woodland. It is shown by other finds, too, that reindeer still lived in Denmark at the beginning of the afforestation, but died out in the period when fir forests prevailed, the period known in the history of civilization as that of the Maglemose culture. The axes of reindeer horn are thus limited by various tests to the early post-glacial period and to the first stage of afforestation in Scandinavia.

The Lyngby arrowhead was a simple triangular blade of flint, split off with a single blow and chipped into a point to fasten to the shaft. Montelius has classed it with a well-known form belonging to the Solutré culture in France, but the shape is hardly characteristic enough to afford in itself evidence of the date. It is much more important that this kind of arrow-

[1] First described by Sophus Müller, *Aarbøger for nordisk Oldkyndighed*, 1896, p. 304; Georg F. L. Sarauw, ibid., 1903, p. 303.

[2] A. Jensen and V. Nordman,' Ferskvandslagene ved Nørre-Lyngby klint', *Danmarks geologiske Undersøgelse*, II Række, no. 29 (København, 1915). Cf. Montelius, 'Palaeolithic Implements found in Sweden', *The Antiquaries Journal*, i.

PLATE 2

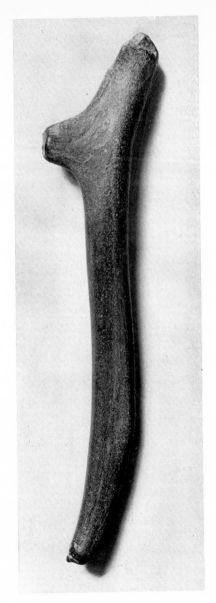

Axe of reindeer horn. Nørre-Lyngby,
Jutland. After Brøndsted

head was apparently widespread in the earliest period of Norse culture. A specimen from Kristiansund in Norway can be dated geologically in a correspondingly early period, a second comes from Zealand, a third from Holstein. Further, other simple split pieces of flint are known from corresponding geological strata.

It is this series of finds that represents the Lyngby culture, which derives its name from the first find, described above; and in recent years it has attracted considerable attention.[1] It must be admitted that the remains of this culture up to the present have occurred in widely separated places, and they are all isolated finds in deposits of clay and marl belonging to the early post-glacial period. No trace of dwelling-sites has yet been discovered. Yet these scattered evidences are sufficient proof that men were living at the same time as the reindeer during the early post-glacial period in the north-east of Germany and the south of Scandinavia, and probably also along the coasts of Norway washed by the North Sea and the Atlantic. We must suppose that they were hunting tribes who pressed forward and took possession of the regions which were first freed by the melting of the ice of the last glaciation, and we perceive that this happened at the same time as the first scattered appearance of forest-trees on the limits of the vanishing Arctic vegetation.

The culture of this group of tribes, moreover, is very poorly represented. Except for small flint arrowheads, the only items to be reckoned here are rude bone harpoons of the Magdalenian type, though found on Norse ground, and, first and foremost, the characteristic axe-like weapons of reindeer horn. These are something new, unknown among palaeolithic types; they have, indeed, been adduced as the decisive criterion which provides a dividing line between the palaeolithic and neolithic periods.[2] They are, moreover, quite different from the so-called 'cere-

---

[1] Gunnar Ekholm, the works cited above. G. Schwantes, 'Das Beil als Scheide zwischen Paläolithikum und Neolithikum', *Archiv für Anthropologie*, N.F., xx; id., *Die Bedeutung der Lyngby-Zivilisation für die Gliederung der Steinzeit* (Hamburg, 1923); also *Die Germanen, Volk und Rasse* (München, 1926); Wolfgang La Baume, *Zur Kenntnis der frühesten Besiedelung Nordostdeutschlands*, Elbinger Jahrbuch, 1924; O. Rydbeck, 'Aktuelle Steinzeitprobleme, 1. Die älteste Bevölkerung des Nordens', *Bulletin de la Société Royale des Lettres de Lund*, 1933–4 (Lund, 1934), p. 162.

[2] Schwantes, *Das Beil als Scheide zwischen Paläolithikum und Neolithikum* cited above.

monial staves' (*bâtons de commandement*) of the Magdalenian culture. On the other hand the earliest hunters in the north are obviously descended from an older palaeolithic population; some investigators have assumed that they must have come from central Europe, from the south or south-east, but one cannot help thinking that they have some connexion with the late palaeolithic peoples in western Europe, even though no certain link between them can be pointed out at present. The first reindeer hunters are not separated by any great period of time from the Magdalenian period in France.

The find at Lyngby comes from semi-Arctic surroundings in Jutland, though at the beginning of the forest growth, that is, from the time of the hardy foliiferous trees—the period of poplars in Denmark. As the climate became milder, these poplar woods were succeeded by red fir. From the transition between these two periods comes a single find which gives a characteristic glimpse into this early and little known stage in the history of northern settlement. This is the urox from Vig.[1] In a small bog in Zealand a skeleton of an urox was found which had been hunted and wounded with small flint arrows before it was drowned in the sea, on the spot where it was now found covered with peat. It must have been a hot chase, and the urox had taken to swimming to escape. The arrows have a very primitive form, made from quite accidentally formed chips of flint, which are sharpened by hewing obliquely from the point. The urox lay in the transitional stratum between the poplar and fir strata of the bog, and hence can be dated from the beginning of the fir period.

The history of human habitation on the Scandinavian peninsula can now be introduced with the highly remarkable discoveries which have been made in quite recent years on the west coast of Sweden at Råö and Varberg in North Halland.[2] In both places worked flints were found embedded in a stratum of marine clay

---

[1] N. Hartz and Herluff Vinge, 'Om Uroxen fra Vig', *Aarb. f. nord. Oldk.*, 1906, p. 225.

[2] Nils Niklasson, *Råö och Varberg*. Ett bidrag till Kännedomen om bosät-ningen i Sverige under senglacial tid. Arkeologiska studier tillägnade H. K. H. Kronprins Gustaf Adolf, utgivna av Svenska Fornminnesföreningen (Stock-holm, 1932).

which was covered by later strata; they lay about 4 metres below the present surface of the ground, which is here about 7 metres above the sea-level. The clay had been deposited at a depth of about 15 to 20 metres in the sea, and it contains shell-fish which live in Arctic conditions (*Macoma calcarea* and *Saxi-cava arctica*). By means of the scale representing the rise of the land the period can be fixed within the years 10000–9000 B.C., corresponding to the Gothiglacial stage in the melting of the inland ice. The edge of the ice lay very near the west coast of Sweden at that time.

The flints were a secondary deposit in the clay of the sea bottom, and must have been washed out by the waves from the dwelling-stations on the shore close by. The pieces show an extraordinarily primitive treatment of the flint. There are practically no definitely established types of designed forms, only pieces split at random and made usable by a minimum of chipping. The flints can be distinguished according to their use as scrapers and hollow scrapers, planes, gravers, borers, hand-axes, pointed chopping-tools, &c. In spite of the rudimentary technique, in their form and appearance a close relationship with the late palaeolithic flint work stands out clearly, especially with Aurignacian, and likewise with the palaeolithic types in Finmark, of which we shall say more later.

The material which has been obtained up to the present from Råö and Varberg is still too limited to afford grounds for any elaborate analysis, but the discoveries have nevertheless revealed an entirely new view of the earliest population on the Scandi-navian coasts. There is now complete proof that men lived on the west coast of Sweden under definitely Arctic conditions, under the shadow, almost, of the inland ice. To these have been added, still more recently, new finds from Østfold on the east side of Oslofjord.[1] The most important are very old dwelling-stations in Sponvik near the town of Halden, lying on the former coast-line of a period considerably anterior to the *tapes* sub-sidence. The material which has been collected here consists in the main of roughly chipped flints without distinct form of any implement, though it is possible to distinguish among them a core-plane, a type which is of palaeolithic origin. A group of

---

[1] Anathon Bjørn, 'Nye stenaldersfund fra Østfold og Telemark', *Universi-tetets Oldsaksamling Årbok*, iv, 1930; ibid., 1932, p. 1 f.

other flint-places at still higher levels, on the average about 100 metres above the coast-line of the *tapes* subsidence, are believed to date from the earliest post-glacial period, when the district of Oslofjord had a subarctic climate, and so presented roughly the same conditions as we met at Lyngby in Jutland. Investigations at Oslo are still in an initial stage and at the present moment do not afford sufficient basis for a complete account. Yet they have already given sufficient indication for us to expect important new discoveries which will throw light on the earliest immigration after the ice age.[1]

Important evidence is also supplied by a series of dwelling-stations along the west and north-west coasts of the land, the so-called 'flint-places' of Norway, representing a civilization which has been given the name of Fosna culture.[2] The flint-places are still not fully and finally investigated, but it is certain that they are the oldest remains of habitation along the western coast of the Scandinavian peninsula, and represent a culture of very ancient origin. The flint-places are dwelling-stations on open ground; often a site was chosen in a small valley which afforded shelter on the side where the wind was usually strongest, and preferably also in some sort of flat and level meadowland, which as a rule was very near the shore of the time or on the shore itself. This shows that the site was always chosen with an eye to a good landing-place. Such a situation, unprotected from an extremely rainy climate, was especially unfortunate for the preservation of any organic materials that might be left in the dwelling-station; it is evident that remains of meals and articles of bone and horn have been washed away so completely that a proper deposit of organic remains is almost never found in these dwelling-stations. Even of the ashes there is very little, though fire-places and burned flint are found, showing clearly where the fires were kindled. The flints alone, then, are all that remains of what accumulated during human occupation of the place.

It is the flints which determine the character of the finds. A vast number of them were cut in the dwelling-stations, but most

---

[1] A. Nummedal, 'Et stenaldersfund i Ski', *Norsk geologisk Tidsskrift*, x (Oslo, 1929), p. 474.

[2] The name is taken from the sites at Kristiansund where the first important discoveries came to light. See Anathon Bjørn, 'Studier over Fosna-Kulturen', *Bergens Museums Årbok*, 1929.

of them were not formed as any definite implement. Formless split pieces preponderate, chips and waste from chipping; a great number of these pieces were used, however, for cutting and scraping, whenever they had a useful sharp edge. Actual implements are comparatively rare and few. These great numbers of formless pieces of flint are a feature which the flint-places share with other primitive habitations in Scandinavia, as is also the quality of the flint, a rather coarse variety of grey or grey-white colour. The types of implements comprise pick-axes (*pics*) and flake-axes (*tranchets*), as a rule rather small and unfinished—these two types occurring comparatively rarely—and also small flat scrapers of flint, carinated planes, cores (*nuclei*) with handles, characteristic gravers (*burins*), and, finally, micro-liths of various forms. The technique and forms as a whole have a very archaic character and are undoubtedly related in many respects to late palaeolithic and early mesolithic work; the complete collection has a character that is decidedly older than the kitchen-midden culture in Denmark and the Nøstvet culture in Norway. The dating of the Fosna culture is still much disputed; the flints themselves cannot determine the absolute period, since forms of great antiquity might yet be regarded as relics of a much earlier period, especially here in a distant border of the European sphere of culture. The determination of the date is further exceedingly difficult be-cause all articles of bone and horn have disappeared, and we also lack remains of fauna and flora which might establish a relation to the post-glacial vegetation periods. The only possibility is, then, a geological dating based on the raising of the land, which is marked by the old shore-lines of the flint-places. Here, too, we meet with very complicated problems, but it is thought to be demonstrable by this means that the flint-places go back to a time before the ancylus period.[1] From

[1] A. Nummedal, 'Om Flintpladsene', *Norsk geologisk Tidsskrift*, viii. 89 f., especially p. 127; summary in English, p. 140. But a caution must be given against the writer's conclusion that the flint-places are contemporary with the late Magdalenian culture in western Europe. See also Anathon Bjørn, 'Studier over Fosna-Kulturen,' *Bergens Museums Årbok*, 1929, Hist.-ant. række, no. 2, pp. 6–8. At Kristiansund a number of flint-places are situated along the former shore-lines about 44 metres above the present level of the sea. In the same localities the shore of the ancylus period can be traced at an elevation of about 30 metres, and thus the flint-places by their higher elevation are referred to the more remote part of the post-glacial raising of the land.

archaeological indications also this is felt to be a probable conclusion. It remains only to add that the culture of the flint-places covers a very long period.

In spite of the meagre yield of ancient materials, the Fosna flint-places are of unusual interest, because they prove the extension of habitation along the Scandinavian shores of the North Sea in the earlier post-glacial period. They are now known from Bergen northwards into the coast of Helgeland north of Trondhjem. In recent years similar discoveries have also been made in the most northerly regions of Scandinavia, on the coasts of Finmark facing the Arctic Ocean. This group has been given the name of 'Komsa culture' in scientific litera-ture, and it is represented by a considerable number of dwelling-stations in the districts of Alta and Porsanger. Here, too, the implements preserved are exclusively of stone, some of quartz and some of dolomite flint; this latter kind of stone has the same technical properties as flint of cretaceous formation, but, regarded geologically, it is of quite different origin. Thus already at this early age we have an interesting example of the adapta-tion of local raw material. The technical treatment of the flint has a character which corresponds in every particular to palaeolithic work, and, what is most surprising of all, investi-gators believe that in some collections from a single site, where the flints must have been in use contemporaneously, they have forms which belong to widely separated periods of the early stone age in western Europe, from Mousterian to the end of the Magdalenian. According to the latest pronouncement by Dr. Johannes Bøe, the mystery is explicable if we suppose that the Komsa culture was originally based on Mousterian types and technique, but was gradually enriched by Aurignacian and Magdalenian influences.[1] It is certain that we have to do with very ancient forms.

The final study of the material has not yet been published,[2]

[1] Johs. Bøe, 'Funde von paläolithischem Charakter in Finnmark', *Bergens Museums Årbok*, 1932, Historisk-antikvarisk række, no. 3.

[2] The investigation is under the direction of 'Instituttet for Sammenlignende Kulturforskning' in Oslo, and is being carried out by A. Nummedal, who has given a preliminary communication in the *Norsk geologisk Tidsskrift*, ix. 43 f. (Oslo, 1927). See also Anathon Bjørn, 'Nogen norske Stenaldersproblemer', *Norsk geologisk Tidsskrift*, x, 1928, p. 54. Since this chapter was first written a full description of the sites and the materials collected up to 1926 has been published by A. Nummedal, *Stone Age Finds in Finnmark*, Instituttet for

and we are therefore unable to give a more thoroughgoing
account of this most northerly group of Europe's early stone
age. The geological conditions indicate that it may go back to
the oldest post-glacial period. The group consists of dwelling-
stations along the old coast-lines of the Arctic Ocean, and the first
few years' researches have already established that a primitive
population lived at that time along the whole north coast of
Norway as far as the boundary with Finland. In the preliminary communications about the finds it is indicated that many
features point to relationship with the palaeolithic stone age in
Siberia and Mongolia. It has further been stated that we must
reckon with a possible invasion of eastern palaeolithic people
through northern Russia, and that one branch of this stem may
have left its traces in the Fosna culture of the flint-places southward along the west coast of Norway. In all this new problems
are raised, and their solution will require much serious work;
but, whatever the final result may be, it must be said that the
excavations in Finmark in recent years have produced most
interesting discoveries. The boundaries of the early European
stone age have been pushed northward to the uttermost edge
of the continent.

The few and scattered discoveries of remains from the earliest
Norse stone age which have been surveyed in this chapter, in
Jutland, on the west coast of Sweden and in Oslofjord, in
western and northern Norway, are spread over a very long period
of time, something like two or three thousand years at least.
They do not permit of any discussion of the course followed by
the first immigration, nor of any final classification of the culture
from its character. Yet, inconclusive as these flints are, they
afford reliable evidence that men found their way to the Scandinavian coasts, following closely upon the retreating ice, as soon as

Sammenlignende Kulturforskning, series B, xiii (Oslo, 1929), with lii plates.
A final complete publication of all the discoveries up to 1934 is being prepared
by Johs. Bøe, to be issued in 1936 in the same series under the title *Le Finmar-
kien, Matériaux pour servir à l'étude de la civilisation humaine dans l'extrême
Nord de l'Europe.* Recently Rolf Nordhagen has assigned the Komsa stations
to a space of time covering the late glacial and the early post-glacial period.
See *De senkvartære klimavekslinger i Nordeuropa og deres betydning for kulturforskningen,* 1933, p. 109.

the natural conditions offered any possibility of maintaining life. In these earliest post-glacial times there can be no question of any other than an extremely sparse population. We might take as a parallel the present-day Arctic regions of Canada, where the Eskimos live scattered over immense areas, with distances of several months' journey over the wilderness separating the various small groups.

THE BONE AGE OF MAGLEMOSE

THE oldest known dwelling-sites that give a complete picture of primitive civilization in the north come from the time when the great fir forests had spread over southern Scandinavia and the Danish isles were connected by solid land with Jutland, Skåne, and northern Germany.[1] Five dwelling-sites are known, all in the bogs of Zealand; two of them are in Maglemose, which has given its name to the whole period of this culture, one in Sværdborg Moss, and two near Holmegaard.[2] All these bogs were lakes at that time, and the dwelling-sites stood on low points of land or on small islands which were under water in winter and therefore bare of trees, but were above the surface in summer and lay as open marshy meadows in the woods. In the summer[3] they were extremely attractive hunting-stations by lakes which had an abundant bird life; the lakes were girt with brushwood of alder and birch, and immense fir trees rose up on all sides. From one of the dwelling-sites a wooden oar is preserved, showing that these people moved about the lake in boats. The remains of meals in the dwelling-sites show clearly what forms of animal life afforded subsistence to the hunters of that time. The most important were urox, elk, and hart, then the roe, wild swine, bear, and wolf; of smaller animals, otter, beaver, fox, badger, martin, wild cat, squirrel, porcupine, and marsh tortoise. The list of birds comprises the eagle, heron, crane, swan, wood-grouse, grey goose, various ducks and cormorants; of fish none were ever eaten but the pike. The only domestic animal was the dog. Apart from meat and fish hazelnuts were eaten in great quantity; seeds also were gathered from the yellow water-lily (*Nuphar luteum*), which are very

---

[1] Knud Jessen, *The Composition of the Forests in Northern Europe in Epipalaeolithic Times*, Danske Videnskabernes Selskab. København, 1935.

[2] Georg F. L. Sarauw, 'Ein steinzeitlicher Wohnplatz im Moor bei Mullerup auf Seeland', i–ii, *Prähistorische Zeitschrift*, iii–iv (Leipzig, 1911 and 1914); K. Friis Johansen, 'En Boplads fra den ældste Stenalder i Sværdborg Mose', *Aarb. f. nord. Oldk.* (København, 1919); H. C. Broholm, 'Nye Fund fra den ældste Stenalder, Holmegaard og Sværdborgfundene', *Aarb. f. nord. Oldk.*, 1924.

[3] The hunters, of course, retired to other places during the winter, when the bogs were flooded.

nutritious. The seeds of water caltrops (*Trapa natans*) were like-wise eaten by the early stone-age people in the south of Sweden.

The excavations have produced a rich harvest of antiquities, which can be counted in thousands from each of the dwelling-sites. The inventories of these antiquities give evidence of a common civilization in all essentials, though each locality has its own definite characteristics too: in each find occur types which do not appear in any of the others. The finds supplement each other, and together they give a very complete picture of a predominantly hunting culture. Among the implements the articles of bone are the chief centre of interest. Bones of the larger mammals, together with hartshorn and elkhorn, were used to make nearly all the implements and weapons needed for hunting and fishing, and the material was worked with a skill and experience that bear witness to an old and robust tradition. A characteristic example is provided by the slender points of bone (pins and awls), which were always made from the metatarsal bone of hart or elk, with a definite, wholly characteristic technique identical with that of corresponding palaeolithic implements from France; the same technique is manifest, for example, in the pieces from the cave of La Madeleine, except that there the bone material is from the reindeer and wild horse. Articles of bone and horn are in general so prevalent that in the north the period has often been given the name of 'the bone age'.

It is a very rich hoard of bone articles that has come to light in the Danish investigations just mentioned. There are smooth, slender points of bone, round or flat-sided; bone points re-sembling harpoon heads, with small barbs, identified for the most part as spearheads (Pl. 3); hooks of bone or hartshorn of simple primitive form without barbs; bone arrowheads with small sharp pieces of flint inserted into each side, generally known as 'fowling arrows'. Axes of hartshorn are very common, and very often have a blade formed from a piece of flint (as in Pl. 3), or from a tusk of a wild boar, and fitted into the haft. A rarity is a big bone of an elk or an urox adapted as an axe. Almost all the axes have the primitive characteristic of adze-hafting, with the blade set at an angle with the haft. Next on the list are chisels of bone and hartshorn, peculiar pointed thrusting weapons of horn, hammers, and clubs of bone. Animals' teeth with holes bored in them were worn as ornaments,

PLATE 3

a. Harpoon-heads from Sværdborg. After Friis Johansen

b. Axe of hartshorn from Sværdborg.
After Broholm

c. A figure of a bear, carved in amber, from a bog at
Resen, Jutland. After Sophus Müller

and once a pendant of amber was found. This is a group which comprises highly developed forms of their kind, but they are also very definitely limited, in accordance with the few and simple needs involved in the life of the time. It must also be remembered that we have a very incomplete picture of the equipment then in use, since articles of wood have rarely survived. Exceptionally favourable conditions are necessary for wood to be preserved for any long period, and yet we know from modern peoples still living in a state of nature what an extraordinarily large part wood plays as material in primitive work. Wood must similarly have played a large part in the Maglemose culture, but only extremely rare specimens of wooden articles are extant. From Holmegaard pointed weapons of wood, used as throwing-spears, are known, two clubs of wood, and a piece of an oar. From the somewhat later find at Brabrand, which will be described farther on, spears, boomerangs, and a paddle for a canoe are preserved. This is indeed a very brief glimpse of the use of wood, which must have been employed, beyond all doubt, for every possible purpose. It must suffice to remark that many of the bone points, horn axes, and the like were fastened to wooden handles.

Bone, horn, and wood thus provided the raw materials for all kinds of weapons and implements, but the shaping of these materials was undoubtedly accomplished by means of flint. Practically speaking, no other kinds of stone were worked, and even of flint a certain quality of grey or black exclusively; no yellow or brown flints are found. An extraordinary amount of flint was used in the dwelling-sites; in the excavation at Sværdborg over 100,000 pieces of flint were counted which had been hewn on the spot. But most of these are irregular chips which were only the waste of the hewing. Of distinct and undoubted implements only a few forms are found. Among these are included forms which should more properly be called blades; they were split from the block of flint by a single blow in the form of long flakes with parallel sharp edges, so that they could be used without further dressing for cutting and shearing. By further shaping of the blades knives, scrapers, and augers were produced. Typical of this period is the little flat scraper of flint which resembles closely the small round scrapers of the French Azilian culture. Among the blocks which were the raw material for the production of flakes and blades one special form stands out which is usually known as a 'core with handle', in Denmark it is characteristic of the bone age, and it is fairly general in the late palaeolithic age of western Europe. The same is true of another form, the carinated planes (*grattoirs carénés*), which likewise appear in this Scandinavian culture. Specially characteristic, however, is the rich production of pygmy flints, microliths, very small, sharp, and finely shaped pieces of flint of geometrical forms, triangular, rhomboid, &c. (see Fig. 1); they

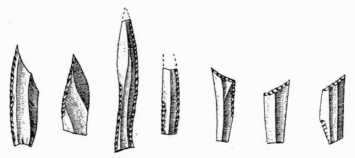

FIG. 1. Pygmy flints, Maglemose. *After Sarauw.*

are found in great numbers at Sværdborg, as well as in other Danish dwelling-sites. It is not certain what their proper use was, very probably to fasten as barbs on the sides of fish-spears and bone arrowheads. The microliths are a feature which associate the Maglemose culture with the West-European Tardenoisian culture; and the Tardenoisian falls in the transition between the palaeolithic and neolithic periods.

The flint work as a whole in this period has a very primitive character: its forms are very little developed. Of the larger implements there are the two types, the pick-axe (*pic*) and the flake-axe (*tranchet*), both with an edge formed by the meeting of two facets of flint. Neither grinding nor polishing was ever applied. The pick-axe was made from the flint block itself by chipping away the superfluous mass until the piece took form, while the flake-axe was made of thick flakes which had been split from the block. The two different forms are naturally of the same definite technique of production (see the illustrations, Pl. 4 below). In the Maglemose period they are both produced only in small dimensions, never above medium size; they are always roughly hewn and of somewhat haphazard form. Most of them are intended to be set as a blade in an axe of bone or hartshorn. The flint was hewn with a rounded block of flint or another stone used as a hammer; more rarely tines of hartshorn were also used as 'fabricators' for finer treatment of the flint by pressure. Apart from the pygmy flints, the microliths, the flint work is on the whole rough and little developed. The art of pottery was completely unknown. As in the French Magdalenian and Azilian cultures, the handwork in the Maglemose culture was concentrated around the use of bone and hartshorn; these materials were treated with great proficiency, and importance was attached to finished and distinctive workmanship in the production. Axes of hartshorn were ground on flat slabs of sandstone, and bone points and similar weapons were given a fine polish.

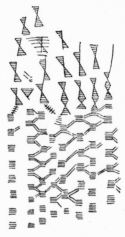

FIG. 2. Ornament of incised lines on a pointed horn weapon from Horsens Fjord. *After Broholm.*

In this bone work we meet with the first decorative art in Scandinavia. It should be mentioned that one of the axes of reindeer horn from the Lyngby period has a small group of incised lines on it, but they are made in such a haphazard and rude manner that they can hardly be reckoned as decoration. In the Maglemose group, on the other hand, decoration of the bone articles was quite usual, always very simple geometrical patterns composed of lines and dots. They are straight lines crossed by short, thick, transverse strokes, or zigzag lines, herring-bone patterns, or rows of small holes bored into the bone. Some are more complex, such as the various combinations of tri-angles, square panes as on a chessboard, or a network of hexa-gons as in a honeycomb (Fig. 2). Figures of animals are rarely found: only two harts on an axe of elkhorn from Skåne (Fig. 3), and a fish on an axe of elkhorn from Zealand. These pictures must, undeniably, be reminiscences of the ice-age art in western Europe, which is very poorly represented in the Maglemose culture compared with the astonishing richness of late palaeo-lithic art. Of sculpture only one small isolated piece is known, a representation of a bear worked in amber and ornamented with lines (Pl. 3).

The known finds of dwelling-sites from the Maglemose period are located, as has been mentioned, in the interior of Zealand.

FIG. 3.   Drawing of incised lines on an axe of hartshorn from Ystad.
After Montelius.

They reveal a hunting life in summer on lakes surrounded by great forests. The picture is filled out by a considerable number of scattered finds of harpoons, bone points, fowling arrows, &c., found singly in the bogs and along river-courses and lakes where hunting was carried on. These are traces of the hunting and fishing carried on in the fir forests of the ancylus period, also directly evidenced in a find on the island of Falster; a skeleton of an elk was found in a bog together with a broken harpoon-head of bone. In a bog in Skåne a harpoon head of bone was found stuck through the skeleton of a large pike. On several bone-points corrosion of the surface indicates that the weapon had pierced a fish which escaped with the point sticking in it We can now, in a general way, construct a complete and lively conception of this early hunting culture in the south of Scandinavia, but at the same time we must remember that in any picture which we form of this period the details must always be very incomplete. We know only the dwelling-sites and finds of the interior, because the coasts of that period now lie sunk beneath the sea. We have every reason to think that the Danish hunting people of that time knew how to profit by the rich resources of the sea-coast, and that their equipment for this purpose was somewhat different from that of the inland dwelling-sites; but of this we can never gain any comprehensive information. It is only in the north of Norway that we find coastal dwelling-sites of this time still on dry land; but their evidence is limited, in that flint alone remains preserved in them, while the bone articles have not survived to our time.

This Maglemose civilization, as has been mentioned, has its classical representation in the dwelling-sites on Zealand, which have been brilliantly studied by Danish archaeologists. It has been indicated in the preceding pages that this culture is nearly related in many ways to the late palaeolithic culture in western Europe. In both we have a 'bone culture', and they show striking similarities in their essential features; this was, indeed, pointed out in the first instance in the classical and basic description of Maglemose.[1]

On the other hand it has been argued that the whole of this Norse bone age had its most important parallel eastwards, in north Germany and the Baltic lands, and some have accordingly sought the origin of the whole Norse group in the palaeolithic people of south-eastern Europe. But the connexion vanishes at essential points; nor has the attempt to find the source of the bone culture still farther east, in Russia and Siberia, been at all successful. In the eastern region, in Brandenburg, East Prussia, Poland, and Esthonia, the bone culture is found in a later stage than in Scandinavia, enriched with new, more recent forms, known especially from the finds near Kunda in Esthonia.[2] The Kunda culture, as it is called, is doubtless related, but it is later than that of Maglemose, and the similarly related finds from the River Pernau in Esthonia

[1] Sarauw, *Prähistorische Zeitschrift*, loc. cit.; *Aarbøger for nordisk Oldkyndighed og Historie*, 1903.

[2] The German and Baltic culture is admirably presented by G. Schwantes, 'Nordisches Paläolithikum und Mesolithikum', *Mitteilungen aus dem Museum für Völkerkunde in Hamburg*, xiii (1928), p. 159.

and from the neighbourhood of Lake Ladoga show a culture that is even later. Some have tried to connect the whole of this series, including Maglemose, to form a special Baltic culture-group. But it should not be forgotten that contemporary and corresponding forms of bone articles are also found in western Europe, in Belgium, France, England, and Scotland.[1] There are typical forms such as bone harpoons and pieces of hartshorn to be fitted on to axe-heads; and there is further a certain type of ornament in lines arranged in zigzags, in triangles, or with a long line crossed by shorter strokes; and finally the decoration by means of small holes drilled into the bone, which we know from Sværdborg. M. l'Abbé Breuil, the highest authority on the early stone age in western Europe, has also taken these pieces as evidence of a connexion with the Maglemose culture. The finds have been few up to the present, but it must be remembered that exceptionally favourable conditions are needed for bone articles to be preserved in dwelling-sites on open ground. It must now be recognized that western Europe had a bone culture corresponding to that in Denmark.

Striking parallels can also be found in the work in stone: small round scrapers which are known in both Azilian and Tardenoisian cultures, and, above all, the microlith work, which was developed in very similar forms in Denmark and in western Europe. The connexions with the west are quite as close as with the eastern region, especially Poland, where some have sought the origin of the Norse microliths. But the eastern association should not therefore be wholly discounted; on that side also parallel phenomena may be observed.

To summarize all factors which throw light on the bone age in Denmark, it may be said that the Maglemose culture has its roots in the palaeolithic culture. From the preceding age traces of early reindeer hunters are known on Norse ground, and the Lyngby culture is marked by an important innovation, axes of reindeer horn, with or without blades of flint, a device which was unknown to the palaeolithic peoples. Tradition from this time was undoubtedly one of the elements in the complex which formed the bone age in the north. But new factors find their way in from the later West-European groups, the Azilian and

---

[1] Latest comparison by Erik Westerby, *Stenaldersbopladser ved Klampenborg* (København, 1927), pp. 153 ff.; summary in French, pp. 213–14.

Tardenoisian cultures, and possibly also from the eastern side of central Europe. The developments are intelligible enough, if it is borne in mind that the north after the ice age would not suddenly become repopulated; the immigration began in a small way, in small groups, and increased gradually during a long period. During the whole of the early stone age new additions came regularly from the peoples of the south-west, south, and east; the Norse area accordingly kept pace with the gradual modifications of West-European culture, though at the same time it retained its own special character in great part, since the western influence came in gradually and insensibly. In brief, it may be said that the bone age as we know it from Maglemose is a late continuation of palaeolithic culture on Norse ground, during the period of the fir forests in Denmark.

At the present day it is only in Zealand that we know the culture of that period from dwelling-sites which have preserved their rich store of bone articles complete; otherwise remains of this period in Scandinavia must be looked for either in scattered and accidental finds of single objects, or in dwelling-sites on open ground, where the unfortunate conditions of preservation have left only the meagre indications which can be given by the worked flint alone. Specially characteristic of this culture is the wide distribution of bone points with barbs. They are found in all parts of Denmark, in the islands (including Bornholm) and in Jutland.[1]

In Skåne and western Sweden the period is also well represented in isolated finds of characteristic forms, bone points, harpoons, fowling arrows, hartshorn axes and—a specially significant form—the so-called 'netting-sticks', an implement of uncertain use which belongs to the period of Maglemose culture.[2] Finds occur more sporadically farther north in Sweden as far as Jämtland. In two places dwelling-sites also are found resembling the Danish ones, namely, in Råbelöv Lake in Skåne and at Hästefjorden in Dalsland. It is of importance that the ornament of the time is also found in Skåne: the axe of elkhorn from Ystad with pictures of animals, an axe of hartshorn from

[1] K. Friis Johansen, 'En Boplads fra den ældste Stenalder i Sværdborg Mose', *Aarb. f. nord. Oldk.*, 1919, pp. 226–7; Sophus Müller, 'Sønderjyllands Stenalder', ibid., 1913, p. 170.

[2] Sune Lindqvist, *Nordens Benålder och en Teori om dess Stenåldersraser* (Rig 1918, Stockholm).

Höganäs with squares and lines, a netting-stick from Järavallen with ornamentation of drilled holes. The last two are geologically fixed in the ancylus period, as are other isolated finds, such as a netting-stick from Östergötland.[1] It is thus placed beyond all doubt that there were settlements in Sweden in the same period as the Maglemose people lived in Denmark. From Finland also some scattered antiquities from this time have been found, though they are probably more nearly related to south Baltic culture than to Scandinavian.[2]

In Norway the position is in no doubt. A netting-stick of elk-bone was found in Oslo, deposited in clay from the ancylus time, and scattered finds of bone points, fowling arrows, and harpoons bear witness to the spread of the bone culture over a wide extent of territory. Also a great number of the Fosna flint-places are referred, geologically, to the ancylus period and are thus contemporary with the Maglemose civilization of Denmark.

This is the period of culture which has been called the bone age in Scandinavia. In Denmark the bone culture has a rich and interesting representation in the great dwelling-sites of Maglemose, Sværdborg, and Holmegaard, situated by former lakes in the fir forests of the period. In Norway we assign to the same period a long series of flint-places along the coast to the west and north, and we can trace the population of the time otherwise through isolated finds of characteristic antiquities. This period is essentially the same as that called the ancylus period by geologists, or, from the climatic condition, the boreale period, as described earlier. The characteristic civilization which marks the bone age lasted at least to the end of the boreale period and into the transition to the next climatic period. The most important geological change which was a factor at that time was the interruption of the post-glacial rise of the land by a second subsidence of the Scandinavian land-masses, from which changes in climatic and hydrographic con-

[1] See Lindqvist, loc. cit.; Otto Rydbeck, 'Stenåldershavets nivåföränd-ringar och Nordens äldsta Bebyggelse', with an English summary ('The Changes of the Level of the Stone Age Sea and the Earliest Settling of Man in Scandinavia'), *Bulletin de la Société Royale des Lettres de Lund*, 1927–8.

[2] E. Hyppä, 'Geologische Altersbestimmung des steinzeitlichen Netzfundes von Korpilakti', *Suomen Museo*, xl, 1933 (Helsinki, 1934). See also the bone implement of Kunda type, illustrated in *Finska Fornminnesföreningens Tidskrift*, xxxii (1922), plate ii. 4.

ditions resulted (see p. 10). It has been proved that the forms of the bone age were still in full use during the rise of the sea to higher coast-lines.

At Klampenborg, near Copenhagen, several dwelling-sites have been found in which careful excavation has made it possible to follow the whole transition period down to the lowest point of the subsidence.[1] The settlement was connected with the sea by a fjord which existed in former times, but is now a peat-bog; and it is possible to see how the coast-line, on which the dwelling-sites stood, shifted as the sea encroached upon the land. The same impression is given by the flora of the period, which in the oldest strata is marked by a mixture of fir and oak, and in the later by oak almost entirely. We thus stand midway in the transition between the boreale and Atlantic vegetation periods. The most sustained researches were carried out on Bloksbjerg, a little hill which was an island in the fjord in the early stone age. Here many objects of antiquity were found. These are sometimes the old well-known forms—bone harpoons, fowling arrows with flint edges and other bone points, carinated planes (*grattoirs carénés*), graving tools (*burins*), microlithic flints; but new articles also appear as a sign that we are in a later period than the dwelling-sites of Maglemose and Sværdborg. Firstly it may be mentioned that the flake-axe of flint is now much more prominent, as are the picks and choppers of flint. Then something quite new appears, axes made of various kinds of volcanic rock, both rounded axes with a thick neck and the flatter form related to the Limhamn type, and finally, pieces of simple pottery, which was completely unknown in the Maglemose civilization. These new articles are actually characteristic of the midden period in Scandinavia, as we shall show in the next chapter. Thus we see in the dwelling-sites of Klampenborg how the tradition of the bone age is met by new cultural forms, which afterwards develop gradually into leading forms; and similarly in the flora of these dwelling-sites we are enabled to see the transition from fir forests to oak. The investigation at Klampenborg has thus been of great importance in solving a problem long under discussion among Scandinavian archaeologists, namely, the true relation between the two culture periods

[1] Erik Westerby, *Stenaldersbopladser ved Klampenborg* (Kjøbenhavn, 1927); with a summary in French.

of Maglemose and Ertebølle, between the bone age and the age of the kitchen middens.

A corresponding position is occupied by a dwelling-site at Viste, near Stavanger in Norway.[1] It was found in the cave named Svarthåla, where the settlement had left a layer of refuse about half a metre thick. This layer consisted for the most part of shells from the shell-fish eaten by the occupants; but among them were other remains of meals, bones of animals, birds, and fish, ashes from the fires, fire-places here and there, together with more or less damaged implements of bone, horn, and stone. In the flora the oak is prominent, and among the animals the wild pig and the weasel, which show that the climate of Norway was then somewhat milder than it is now. Among the implements from Viste bone articles are the most prominent, and they are strikingly reminiscent of the Maglemose culture. We have pieces of harpoons with barbs, several forms of fowling arrows with flint edging, bone hooks of smooth slender shape, without barbs; also a rude little axe of hartshorn, and possibly a fragment of an axe of elkhorn. On the whole the bone articles predominate, while the work in flint is less developed. Some scrapers and augers were found, two flake-axes (*tranchets*), a number of small flakes, &c. So far the Viste find is very nearly related to the Maglemose group, but new features also appear which point to a later time. Pottery was found there, pieces of simple pots, most nearly related in kind to the earthenware vessels from the kitchen middens in Denmark; also fragments of ground axes of trap and a little piece of slate, the edge of which was used for grinding. The axes are of the type we call 'round axes', a form which was also found at Klampenborg, and is likewise attested continuously from the older part of the kitchen-midden period onwards. The Viste find is thus later than Maglemose; it shows the bone-age culture mixed with new elements which herald the arrival of the next period of culture.[2]

[1] A. W. Brøgger, 'Vistefundet, en ældre stenalders kjøkkenmødding fra Jæren', *Stavangers Museums Årshefte*, 1907, ii, and ibid., 1910, v; *Naturen* (Bergen, 1910), p. 332; Helge Gjessing, *Rogalands Stenalder* (Stavanger, 1920), p. 147.

[2] There has been a certain amount of disagreement about the absolute dating of the Viste find, but it is certainly right to put it in the kitchen-midden period, as was done by Brøgger already in the first description of the find.

IV

THE KITCHEN-MIDDEN PERIOD

THE term 'Danish kitchen middens' is a designation which has long since become classic in archaeological literature and recognized internationally. The kitchen middens or shell-mounds—or refuse heaps as they are also called—are primitive dwelling-sites which lie along the coast-lines of the early stone age in north-eastern Denmark, and they are specially character-ized by the great masses of shells which are heaped up as the refuse from meals. They have been one of the most important sources for the study of the early stone-age civilization in Scandi-navia, and it is with good reason that the whole of this period has taken its name from them. They can only be described briefly here, with references to literature which is generally accessible.[1]

The kitchen middens always lay quite near the shore of the period, preferably in sheltered bays, along deeply indented fjords, and commonly at the foot of a slope which gave shelter from the wind. Many of the dwelling-sites lie above the highest shore-line, while others have evidently been exposed to the wash of the waves; they thus afford evidence that this popula-tion lived both in the last part of the post-glacial subsidence and in the beginning of the ensuing rise of the land in north-eastern Denmark. This is fully corroborated by a fortunate find in Brabrand Lake near Aarhus.[2] The dwelling-site in this instance was situated at the end of a landlocked and sheltered fjord, and it is possible to mark off as clearly as on a rule the point where the culture of the kitchen middens begins—a con-siderable time before the lowest point in the subsidence of the land was reached; and we can see that it continues without a break for a long time after the land had begun to rise again. Here, then, we find a chronology of the kitchen middens which is as accurate as we can expect when a period of culture has to

[1] Lord Avebury, *Prehistoric Times*, 7th ed. (London, 1913); Sophus Müller, *Vor Oldtid* (København, 1897), pp. 7 ff.; A. P. Madsen, Sophus Müller and others, *Affaldsdynger fra Stenalderen i Danmark* (København, 1900).

[2] Thomas Thomsen and A. Jessen, 'Brabrand-Fundet fra den ældre Sten-alder', *Aarb. f. nord. Oldk.*, 1906.

be dated from geological indications. The geological relation also explains the peculiar limitations of the middens' present positions; these we shall now proceed to describe.

The kitchen middens appear as huge masses of shells heaped up as the refuse from meals. The heaps measure in length up to 150 metres, and in thickness up to something over 2 metres. The greater number of the shell-fish which were eaten were oysters (*Ostrea edulis*) and cockles (*Cardium edule*), as well as mussels (*Mytilus edulis*) and periwinkles (*Litorina litorea*). The people continued to live on the shell-heaps, which were constantly added to; and they formed an excellent preserving-cover over everything that was left there during the daily life of the place. Bones of wild animals and fish are found in the heaps, fire-places and remains of fires, here and there skeletons of the dead who were buried in the refuse, implements of flint, bone, and hartshorn, the waste material from the manufacture of implements, and pieces of rude earthen pots. Thanks to the elaborate and exemplary researches carried out by the National Museum in Copenhagen, the civilization of the kitchen middens was brought to light complete in every particular. It was a population of hunters and shell-fish eaters that left us the kitchen middens. They existed entirely on hunting, fishing, and the gathering of shell-fish, and their only domestic animal was the dog. The culture exhibited by the implements and their technique is very primitive, but it has a definite and typical character which occurs most fully developed in the dwelling-site at Erte-bølle. In archaeological literature the whole group is often called the Ertebølle culture, which in a more precise application may be taken to denote the older phase of the kitchen-midden period.

In their manner of life and their subsistence the people of the kitchen middens had essentially the same conditions as we know in the Maglemose period, even though the natural conditions were different. With the subsidence of the land the Baltic was opened out as an immense arm of the sea with much salter water than at the present time. As a result the wealth of the coast returned again in the form of oysters and other edible shell-fish. The fir forests were replaced by oak; the elk and urox practically disappeared, and the red deer now ranked first among the wild animals. The industry and the implements also assume a different character; in particular flint now comes much more into the foreground as the most important material, while bone no longer has such a prominent part as before. The 'bone age' is succeeded in the kitchen middens by the first real 'flint age'. Flint is the principal material for implements, and in all dwelling-sites worked flint is found in great quantities. The flint was shaped exclusively by chipping, and the most characteristic of the implements are two types of primitive axes, the pick-axe (*pic*) and the flake-axe (*tranchet*), both types which are known earlier, but now appear definitely formed for the first time; and they now increase so greatly in size and number that they must be reckoned as leading types. The pick-axe was made from the block of flint itself by hewing away the superfluous part until the piece took form, while the flake-axe was made from thick flakes which had first been split from the block. The two different forms are thus naturally and definitely of the same technique in their production. The flake-axes are wider and flatter, often having projecting corners to the edge; the pick-axe is long and slender, often comparatively thick, with a short edge and a convex edge-line. Pointed choppers are also found which have a three-cornered cross-section. Still more flint implements are found: sharp blades, scrapers, borers, and others, all produced with a definitely developed technique and in definite forms. Especially significant of this trend of culture are the chisel-shaped arrowheads which are made from slender blades; they take the place of the microliths of the older period. No true microlithic work appears in the kitchen middens.

It is now flint which steadily becomes more and more the basis of the material culture and is the object of an intensive technical treatment designed to exploit all its possibilities as a material, while the work in bone diminishes in importance. There was still, of course, some work in bone and hartshorn, as such work is known right through the whole of the stone age; but we no longer find the larger, artistically made implements, harpoons, fowling arrows with flint edges, and large pointed weapons. The work in bone is now restricted to smaller and simpler articles, pins and bodkins, small comb-formed tools, daggers made from the bigger bones, and knives from the tusks of wild boar. The axe of hartshorn appears in a new form, in that the hole for the shaft passes through a projecting side-piece; and another innovation is the flaking tool known as a 'fabricator', that is, a tine from a hart's antler with the point cut squarely off. It was undoubtedly used as an implement for flaking flint by pressure. Of wooden articles from this period only a few pieces from the dwelling-site at Brabrand Lake are known, namely, a piece of an ashen bow, a throwing-spear of maple, and some points which resemble boomerangs, but might also be regarded as prongs of fish-spears.

Apart from the supreme importance of the flints, the culture of the middens is marked by two other momentous innovations. These are the technical use of varieties of volcanic rock, and the potter's art. From various rocks, such as trap, gneiss, granite, and porphyry, the same forms are produced as in the flake-axes and pick-axes of flint, and in addition a wholly new form which was unknown in flint, the rounded axe with a circular cross-section. In these kinds of stone a completely new technical treatment also was employed. Firstly, there is the grinding of the stone, which is not much needed with flint. Such close-grained and hard varieties of rock, it is true, by splitting alone give an imperfect kind of edge similar to flint, but at the same time it is much easier to grind these kinds of stone, and the process had long been known from the work in bone and hartshorn. Ground axes of stone are found in the kitchen middens very early, while grinding of flint first became an established practice in the later neolithic period. 'Pecking' (*piquetage*) is likewise a new method which was little used with flint, but was naturally resorted to in dealing with fine-grained rock. The process is this: the material is struck repeatedly with a sharp-edged stone, and the surface is gradually worn away until the piece assumes the form desired. In early times it was primarily the rounded axe (Pl. 4) which was produced in this way, while during the following phase of the stone age the process was brought into universal use.

An equally important advance is marked by the art of pottery, which at this period is seen in the first stage of its inception. Two principal forms are prevalent, a rude pot with the edge bent outward (Pl. 5), and an oblong open bowl. The mode of production was most primitive: the vessel was made of narrow strips of clay, each of which was coiled round on itself in a rising spiral and joined to the end of the next strip; the edges in contact were pressed together with the fingers. Decorations

PLATE **4**

a. Pick-axe of flint. After Brøndsted
b. Flake-axe of flint. After Hans Kjær

c. Rounded axe, produced by the 'pecking' method. After Shetelig

PLATE 5

Clay pot from a kitchen midden. After Brøndsted

appear on these pots only in the simplest form, made by the impression of a pin or nail.

On the whole the artistic activities which can be traced in the culture of the middens is poor, undoubtedly retrograde compared with the older work from Maglemose. The care evident in the finely outlined patterns of lines on the older bone articles is absent in the work of the middens: these patterns were replaced by careless crisscross and zigzag lines, roughly scratched, and a little rare ornamentation of drilled holes. No figured ornament is known. It seems that in this respect the kitchen middens were already leading up to the later Danish stone age, so conspicuous in technical development, but poor in true art.

The distribution of the kitchen middens in Denmark is marked by characteristic limits which are due to geological causes. In Zealand and the north of Jutland the ancient coast-lines of this period lie higher than the present shore, and consequently the dwelling-sites are here found correspondingly elevated, and are now some distance from the sea. In the southern half of Denmark, on the other hand, the old coasts have now sunk under the sea, just as in the north of Germany. There were naturally many kitchen middens in this region which were washed away by the surf and waves. In the parts where the old coast-lines do not lie at any great depth, it is to be expected that antiquities from the submerged dwelling-sites will be washed up along the shore in large numbers, and at greater depths they may be discovered in the dredging of modern harbour construction, as, for example, in the free harbour of Copenhagen. It has also been found that a dwelling-site under the sea may become accessible for excavation when a shallow bay is dammed up and drained. This happened at Vaalse Vig in Falster, where there was a dwelling-site that yielded an unusually rich harvest. These coast-finds (as they are called) of Denmark complete our conception of the distribution of population at this period. But the population was not associated exclusively with the coasts and the sea; rich dwelling-sites are also found by the lakes and bogs in the interior of the country. One of the most significant finds of the period is the 'lake-find' at Vestre Ulslev on Laaland, where excavation brought to light some 5,000 articles of antiquity. The remains of the meals here in this inland place have a somewhat different character from those on the coast; by the lakes edible shell-fish are absent, but in their stead are found quantities of shells of hazel-nuts, which formed an important part of the food supply. Hunting and fishing, being the most important occupations, were, of course, common to the whole population during the whole of the period.

A problem which has been much discussed by Scandinavian archaeologists in recent years is the relation between the Maglemose civilization and the kitchen middens in Denmark. Differences between the two groups are so obvious that many investigators have concluded that we have to reckon with an immigration of a new people as bearers of the new form of culture; that, in other words, there is a break in the continuous development between these groups.[1] Emphasis has been laid on the fact that precisely the most characteristic forms of the bone-age culture, such as harpoons, fowling arrows, and netting-sticks, have completely disappeared in the middens; so also have the implements connected with certain methods of hunting, trapping, and fishing, the spheres in which a primitive culture is normally extremely conservative. On the other hand, the Danish investigators have always held that there is a natural connexion, that the later culture arose from the earlier by a series of gradual changes,[2] and they have pointed out that a few of the old forms appear occasionally in the kitchen middens. The recent important discoveries in the dwelling-places at Klampenborg have also shown that the harpoons and other primitive types of the bone age were in use at a period which can be dated geologically as contemporary with the kitchen-midden period; and these old types are there found side by side with new elements, earthen vessels and axes of volcanic rock, which are distinctive of the later culture. It is thus clear that the civilizations of the two periods

[1] See especially Sune Lindqvist, *Nordens Benålder och en Teori om dess Stenåldersraser* (Rig, Stockholm, 1918); Shetelig, *Primitive Tider i Norge* (Bergen, 1922), pp. 118 ff.

[2] K. Friis Johansen, 'En Boplads fra den ældre Stenalder i Sværdborg Mose', *Aarb. f. nord. Oldk.*, 1919, p. 235; Erik Westerby, *Stenaldersbopladser ved Klampenborg* (København, 1927); H. C. Broholm, 'Langøfundet: En Boplads paa den ældre Stenalder paa Fyn.', *Aarb. f. nord. Oldk.*, 1928, p. 129, especially pp. 189–90.

were in contact with each other during the period which is marked by the great post-glacial subsidence.

This, then, is the situation at Klampenborg, quite different from that in the dwelling-site at Brabrand, which goes back to an equally ancient time, towards the end of the period of fir forests. Yet there at Brabrand precisely those forms are absent from first to last which are the most important, the leading types of the Maglemose period. At Brabrand it can be seen that the flint culture of the middens was developed gradually, until the people by degrees secured a complete mastery over flint as a material for implements. But the origin was not in the life of the bone age. The dwelling-site at Brabrand shows clearly that the typical midden culture was developed upon a different basis from that of Maglemose. This, of course, does not prevent the two forms from meeting and crossing within a limited period which constitutes a transition. In the opinion of the present writer the natural explanation is provided by the assumption that the new culture seen for the first time at Brabrand was produced by the coming of a new people who introduced new potentialities. At that remote period one obviously cannot assume a large collective invasion giving a new character to the country at a single stroke; among the early hunting peoples the migrations must have been accomplished in small bands, which always left room for older surviving forms by the side of the new: but the new forms would gradually prevail and oust or assimilate their predecessors. Comparison of Klampenborg and Brabrand gives precisely this picture of two different groups still existing side by side. But the dwelling-sites at Klampenborg are an exceptional survival; the culture of the bone age had practically passed away in Denmark, and almost all traces of it had been obliterated from the kitchen-midden culture as a whole. On the Scandinavian peninsula we shall see that the situation was different: there we find strong reminiscences of the oldest culture running right through the whole of the stone age. This gives us ground for believing that the special conditions in Denmark had special causes. It is there that the new impulses are first perceptible which eventually produced a fundamental change in the culture of all Scandinavia.

Of the new features which distinguish the kitchen-midden

period from the Maglemose period there are in the first place larger and stronger implements of stone; it is a macrolithic culture, compared with the preceding microlithic work.[1] In Denmark it is flint which predominates, and the same types of flint implements were adopted and made in Sweden and Norway too. Pick-axes and flake-axes are prominent in Skåne, where there was, of course, close contact with the neighbouring land of Zealand, and the same forms have another centre farther north on the west coast of Sweden, in the southern part of the province of Bohuslän.[2] It has been established that the flint culture must have arisen here from direct connexions across the Cattegat with the north of Jutland. Here, it is true, no typical kitchen middens are found; but a large number of dwelling-sites are known from the same geological level as the Danish kitchen middens, and they are undoubtedly from the same archaeological period. A new feature which appears is a more extensive use of hard volcanic rocks, also known in Denmark, but, in relation to flint, in a completely subordinate position. Even at this early time implements of such stone are much more prevalent in Skåne. We find rounded axes, produced by the pecking method, which are already well known to us from Brabrand and Klampenborg (Pl. 4). Another form is the Limhamn type, a rather broad flat axe, roughly hewn and finished by grinding, which, however, does not remove all marks of hewing. This type is prominent in the south of Sweden and on Gotland. Farther north another new type appears, which in Sweden is named after the place Lihult in Bohuslän, in Norway after Nøstvet near Oslo. The Lihult or Nøstvet type—they are different names for one and the same form—is a long thick axe, always very slender and having as a rule a convex edge-line. In the west of Norway we meet with a special variation of this form, which has been named the Sigersvoll type; it is longer, and its neck tapers to a point. As a type of implement the Nøstvet axe is identical with the flint pick-axe in Denmark, but it is adapted to a different material. It is to be noted especially that these kinds of

[1] C. A. Nordman, 'Den yngre Stenåldern i Mellan-, Väst- och Nordeuropa' in *De förhistorika Tiderna i Europa*, ii. 31 (Stockholm, 1927).
[2] Arvid Enqvist, *Stenåldersbebyggelsen på Orust och Tjörn* (Uppsala, 1922); Sarauw and Alin, *Götaälvsområdets Fornminnen* (Göteborg, 1923).

rock require grinding and were ground, while grinding of flint was still unknown.

The Nøstvet axe more than any other form is the leading type of this cultural phase on the Scandinavian peninsula, and there was a natural cause for this. The peninsula had no adequate natural source of flint which could form the basis of a flint culture like that in Denmark, and it was therefore necessary to find other material to satisfy the new demand of the time for strong implements. Something was known earlier about the adaptation of hard volcanic rocks, but it now became the most important raw material. It is evident that in each district the best local material available was employed. In the dwelling-places on Oslofjord it has been observed that the Nøstvet axes are made from a great variety of rocks, as, for example, hornblende, quartz porphyry, syenite porphyry, and close-grained trap; but the material was always very hard and of close and fine grain. It is evident that the best material was sought in gravel-banks from the ice age: in morains especially a rich and varied choice of every kind of usable stone is found.[1] In some places, even at this early period, the population knew how to quarry rock from solid mountains. On the island Bømlo on the west coast of Norway we have an example of how the industry of this period employed a homogeneous and superior trap from local quarries, which can still be seen.[2] As stones for hammering in the process of hewing naturally rounded boulders were used, of sizes varying from the very small up to a weight of several kilograms. They were often splintered or split, since the volcanic rock is closer in grain than flint and consequently must be treated with heavier blows when it is hewn. Axes were ground on flat slabs of sandstone, which are found in large numbers on the dwelling-sites and work-places.

In the whole of the Scandinavian peninsula varieties of volcanic rock are thus the prevailing material for stone implements, though they were not the only commonly used material. Flake-axes and pick-axes of flint appear practically everywhere that stone axes are found, though they are, by comparison, the

[1] A. W. Brøgger, 'Økser av Nøstvettypen', *Norges geologiske Undersøkelse*, no. 42 (Kristiania, 1905).

[2] H. Shetelig, 'L'Industrie néolithique de la Norvège', *Bergens Museums Årbok*, 1922–3, Hist.-ant. rekke, no. 4.

exceptions. For small tools such as knives, augers, scrapers, and the like, flint is constantly used and in great quantity; but rock-crystal, quartz, quartzite, and similar stones were also used for these same purposes. It is significant that already at this period slate began to be used in the north-west of Norway as the material for broad flat spear-points.[1] Very little is known of the articles of bone such as are found together with typical forms of the Lihult or Nøstvet group, since the dwelling-sites are unsheltered and all organic materials have disappeared. The find at Viste near Stavanger which was mentioned earlier belongs to this time, and it shows that in Norway harpoons of bone and hartshorn were still in use, as well as bone arrows with flint edging and other forms which were an inheritance from the Maglemose period. These same ancient types are found scattered in isolated finds in many places in Norway and Sweden, sometimes in geological conditions which point to a later time, sometimes showing variations in form proper only to a later time.[2] We thus have evidence that these greatly time-honoured methods of hunting, fowling, and fishing were still in use on the Scandinavian peninsula at the end of the stone age,[3] whereas in Denmark they had been abandoned already by the kitchen-midden period. On the Scandinavian peninsula the manner of life was thus more conservative, less disturbed by foreign influence. On the peninsula the new culture is limited essentially to the development of stone implements; pottery is rare and the hunting life retains its old forms. This difference, moreover, is a strong argument in favour of the assumption that the culture of the kitchen middens in Denmark received its character from an immigration, which did not reach the northern parts of Scandinavia.

The Lihult or Nøstvet culture spread first of all along the coasts of the peninsula. It had an especially rich area on the

[1] Anathon Bjørn, 'De ældste skiferredskaper fra Norges stenalder', *Tromsø Museums Årshefte*, vol. 1 (1927), no. 2. A slate spearhead of the same form was found in Denmark in the kitchen midden at Vaalse Vig; it is explained by Sophus Müller as an importation from Norway or Sweden: *Aarbøger for nordisk Oldkyndighed*, 1896, p. 313. This find is thus proof of a very widespread intercourse already at this early period.

[2] The Swedish finds have been brought together by Sune Lindqvist, *Nordens Benålder och en Teori om dess Stenåldersraser* (Rig, 1918).

[3] A. Brinkmann and H. Shetelig, *Ruskenesset, En stenalders jaktplass*, Norske Oldfund, iii (Kristiania, 1920).

west coast of Sweden and around Oslofjord. Then, starting from the west, the dwelling-sites extended up through central Sweden in the districts around the large lakes, Väner, Väter, Hjälmaren, and Mälaren, as far as the Dales. The Baltic coast, however, seems to have been more thinly settled. In Norway this culture extended along the southern and western coasts as far as the northern districts, where axes of trap now appear in the civilization of the flint-places. Thus we have here a North Scandinavian group, uniform in its main features, extending over the greater part of the peninsula, as well as a southern group which has its typical representation in the Danish kitchen middens. The latter group also extends over the neighbouring part of northern Germany. In Holstein and Pomerania antiquities are found in large numbers of precisely the same type as in Denmark, and in especially large numbers from Rügen. Finland, on the other hand, has hardly any connexion at all with Scandinavia in this period. The oldest settlements known in Finland constitute a group which has been given the name of Suomus-järvi culture, and it is restricted to the south-west of the country, but is further extended, without variation in type, along the south side of the Gulf of Finland, in present-day Esthonia. The group is characterized by small ground axes of volcanic rock; the most typical form, the Suomusjärvi axe, is comparatively flat, broad, and short, with an oval outline.[1] The geological levels go back to the same period as the kitchen middens in Denmark, but the forms of the culture have totally different connexions, eastwards with Russia and with the southern Baltic. It is clear that this early settlement in Finland has no contact with Scandinavia.

On the other side the kitchen-midden culture has, most definitely, very near parallels to the west. A complete parallel to the Norse culture is the civilization named after Campigny in France. Here foundations of small huts (*fonds de cabanes*) are found, fire-places and ashes from fires, abounding in worked flints, such as flakes of all kinds, scrapers, augers, and also, as leading forms, flake-axes (*tranchets*) and pick-axes (*pics*). In technical and formal particulars these implements correspond

---

[1] Aarne Europaeus, 'Fornfynden från Kyrkslätt och Esbo Socknar', *Finska Fornminnesföreningens Tidskrift*, xxxii, no. 1, pp. 149 ff., plates 1 and 11 (Helsingfors, 1922).

completely with the Norse forms; and this work appears as a
very widespread group extending from the south of Holland
southwards over Belgium and France as far as Dordogne. It is
true that this industry is absent from the regions between
Holland and Denmark, along the south coast of the North Sea,
but this is very easily accounted for by the circumstance that
the whole of this coast has sunk since the stone age, so that the
ancient dwelling-sites along the shore have now disappeared into
the sea. We thus have no opportunity of finding the connecting link which would provide geographical continuity between
the cultures of France and Denmark; but the striking correspondences in the flint work afford adequate grounds for assuming
that they are related. On the other hand, the French culture
presents a more complex picture. In the Campignian group
quantities of pottery are found even at a date so early, and some
of it is a very fine ware with geometrical decorations; there are
also bones of domestic animals, possible traces of corn cultivation, and simple ground axes of flint. All these features were
completely foreign to the primitive hunting people of the northern
kitchen middens.

On the basis of these relations a theory has been erected in
recent years that the kitchen-midden phase in northern Europe
is a weakened reflection, such as might be expected at the outer
edge of European civilization, of a much more advanced
neolithic culture in central Europe, especially in the regions
about the Danube.[1] From this centre, it is assumed, proceeded
impulses which produced certain cultural advances under less
favourable conditions in France, and from there made themselves felt among wholly primitive people in Scandinavian lands.
This conclusion is in itself not unplausible, but it conflicts irre-
concilably with the generally accepted chronology of the kitchen-
midden period. The oldest deposits at Brabrand are dated on
geological grounds at about 5000 B.C. and the oldest at Ertebølle
about 4000 B.C. Quite certainly no more advanced neolithic
civilization is to be found in central Europe at so early a date.[2]

[1] C. A. Nordman, 'Den yngre Stenåldern i Mellan-, Väst- och Nordeuropa',
De förhistoriska Tiderna i Europa, ii. 30 (Stockholm, 1927).

[2] The reckoning of these dates is, of course, beset with many complicated
problems. The dates adopted here are derived from Knud Jessen, 1928 (see
the note on p. 1). The latest contribution on the subject is Otto Rydbeck,

The view generally held up to the present time is therefore a different one. It is assumed that the Campignian culture in France and the kitchen middens in the north represent a definite early phase in the stone age of Europe, the first preliminary phase of the neolithic period, a phase which is also called proto-neolithic. Corresponding forms of flint are known more rarely from the south of England, but are to be found in abundance on the old raised coast-lines in Ireland, where Larne Lough in Antrim is the classic place for the group.[1]

A parallel—even if not completely parallel—flint culture is found in the Asturian group in Cantabria on the north coast of Spain. The whole of these groups can be summed up as a widely distributed West-European culture, which was undoubtedly connected with the kitchen-midden culture in the north. But it is likewise certain that similar forms are absent in the interior of the continent. The kitchen middens thus represent a distinctly coastal culture, and this character has been explained by the climatic conditions; during the Atlantic period with its mild and humid climate large areas of central Europe became covered with great forests, which made habitation, practically speaking, impossible. Then in the later stone age with a drier climate these continental regions again became accessible.

This explanation is, of course, an hypothesis, but it is the hypothesis which at the present time seems most probable. It is definitely accepted, however, that the kitchen middens and the Nøstvet-Lihult group parallel to them mark a definite period in Scandinavia between the bone age of Maglemose and the late stone-age civilization. The differences from the older period consist in a more advanced technique and more effective stone tools; as contrasted with the following periods, the culture of the kitchen middens still stands at the primitive stage of a hunting society, without domestic animals or the arts of agriculture.

Stenåldershavets nivåförändringar och Nordens äldsta bebyggelse (*The Changes of Level in the Stone Age Sea and the earliest Settling of Man in Scandinavia*, Summary in English), Kungl. Humanistiska Vetenskapssamfundet i Lund, Årsberättelse, 1927–8 (Lund, 1928). Professor Rydbeck here develops a theory that the kitchen middens are in great part later than is ordinarily assumed, practically contemporary with the height of neolithic civilization. His arguments are, moreover, quite different from Nordman's. But this is not the place to discuss the many interesting questions which arise in Rydbeck's treatise.

[1] R. A. S. Macalister, *The Archaeology of Ireland* (London, 1928), pp. 30 ff.

The three great groups presented in the preceding pages together comprise the first main division in the history of Scandinavian culture. It is the age of the hunting people. Throughout this long period, which according to geological chronology lasted at least some 4,000 years, the Norse population lived in primitive conditions, very like those of the aborigines in Australia or Tierra del Fuego. During these long ages the hunting people passed through varying geological periods; they saw the fir forests come in and later yield place to oak. Like all primitive people they lived in the most intimate association with surrounding nature, and they understood fully how to exploit all the available means of maintaining life. We know that they hunted the larger wild animals with bow and arrows, speared fish, fished with hooks, and caught birds. Shell-fish were gathered in large quantities to provide complete meals, just as hazel-nuts and other edible products were gathered from the plant world. The oldest known tame animals in the world are the dogs of Maglemose and Sværdborg; they were a very big sort of dog, though not unusually tall, crossed with tame wolf. In the kitchen middens this large type of dog becomes very common, and a new smaller variety also appears.[1] It is significant that dogs are much more numerous in this early period than they are in the later stone age in Denmark. We are able to form a living image of these oldest Norsemen in their daily life in the permanent dwelling-sites of the coast, or in their summer dwellings on the lakes, in their migrations or raiding expeditions. Through immemorially ancient experience they chose their sites with the most profound insight into natural conditions.

The classification of the oldest races is still an unsolved problem, since far too few skeletons and skulls are found sufficiently well preserved. At Maglemose the lower jaw-bone of a seven or eight years old child was found, at Sværdborg various parts of the skeleton of a man from sixteen to eighteen years old. Scholars are not in agreement about the classification of this people, which, moreover, is very difficult to determine from such young individuals.[2] These bones are probably remains of

---

[1] August Brinkmann, 'Canidenstudien, V. Die Hunde der dänischen und norwegischen Steinzeit', *Bergens Museums Årbok*, 1923–4, Naturvidenskabelig rekke no. 7.

[2] One suggestion is that the remains of the skeleton show strong palaeolithic reminiscences: see H. A. Nielsen, 'Fund i Sværdborg og Mullerup Moser av

persons who were buried in the dwelling-sites, which we can see sometimes happened in the kitchen middens. The dead were laid stretched out in a very shallow grave in the shell-heap itself, on which the survivors continued to live, and the grave was covered over with a new layer of refuse.[1] Such are the graves made in the dwelling-sites, the simplest form of burial, which we also know from the palaeolithic people of the ice age. Such a simple arrangement may give an impression of indifference about the dead, but that is not by any means necessarily the feeling which gave rise to this form of burial; on the contrary, this custom more probably had its origin in primitive sentiments of piety, in ideas about a connexion between living and dead members of a family, and there was some notion of securing a certain protection by keeping the dead so near the living.

The graves in the kitchen-midden dwelling-sites are surprisingly few in number, and it must be concluded that nothing like all the dead were actually buried. Burial was possibly reserved for the more distinguished persons, but it must, of course, be taken into account also that many were killed accidentally, in such fashion that burial would be out of the question. Such was the fortune of two men whose skeletons were found in banks of shell-fish at Stångenäs in the province of Bohuslän. They had both been drowned and their bodies had been deposited in banks of shell-fish belonging to the ancylus period, that is, to the Maglemose period.[2] The only one of these whose skull has been preserved shows a large cranium, markedly dolichocephalic; the bones of the skeleton are those of a tall and powerful man.

The simple graves in the dwelling-sites were naturally liable

Skeletdele av Mennesker fra den ældste Stenalder', *Aarb. f. nord. Oldk.*, 1921, p. 205 f. This theory was later opposed by John Arnborg, 'Underkäksfragment och lösa tänder av menniskor från Danmarks äldsta Stenålder', with a summary in German (Unterkieferfragmente und lose Zähne von Menschen aus der Maglemoseperiode in Dänemark), *Videnskabelige Meddelelser fra Dansk naturhistorisk Forening*, vol. lxxx.

[1] See Madsen, Müller, and others, *Affaldsdynger* (København, 1900), pp. 78, 100, 144; Erik Westerby, *Stenaldersbopladser ved Klampenborg* (København, 1927), pp. 27–9; A. W. Brøgger, *Vistefundet* (Stavanger, 1908), p. 26.

[2] Carl M. Fürst, *Stångenäskraniets renässans*, with a summary in German (*Das Wiederaufleben des Stångenäskraniums*), (Fornvännen, Stockholm, 1925), p. 274.

to be disturbed. There were dogs who gnawed bones round about the place and often dug into the refuse; and the people themselves on occasion levelled out the heaps to make the place more passable. Thus we have a likely explanation of the occurrence of scattered human bones, often in fragments, which are a constant ingredient in the deposits of refuse. This is a feature which is common to Scandinavian dwelling-sites of the whole stone age. Such human bones lie scattered and mingled with all manner of refuse from meals, and it is natural enough that they have raised the question as to whether the Scandinavians in the stone age were eaters of men. The idea at least should not be dismissed offhand; and the problem has, in fact, been discussed again and again. But up to the present no conclusive evidence of cannibalism in the stone age has been found. It should be noted especially that as yet no human bones have been certainly shown to be split for the marrow to be taken out, as was always done with animals' bones.[1] The simple form of burial is in any case sufficient to account for the remains of dismembered skeletons in the dwelling-sites. No importance was attached to preserving or guarding the graves; they were evidently forgotten quickly and were consequently readily disturbed. Under these conditions it is only to be expected that we should have very few skulls and skeletons preserved which could be used for anthropological classification of these oldest people of the Norse stone age.

From the kitchen-midden period three usable skulls are known in Denmark: one dolichocephalic cranium of a man from Fanerup in Jutland, one mesocephalic cranium of a woman from Holbæk in Zealand, and one brachycephalic man from Kassemose in Zealand. From Sweden none are known. From Norway we have a young boy who was buried in the cave at Viste near Stavanger, but he had a morbidly deformed skull (*scaphocephalus*) which is pathologically of very great historical

---

[1] Frequently mentioned human bones which have been split for the marrow date from the later stone age; they were found in the cave Stora Förvar on Stora Karlsö in Gotland: see Gustaf Retzius in the periodical *Ymer* (Stockholm, 1890), p. 287. Similarly Oscar Almgren believed that he found signs of cannibalism in dwelling-sites in Swedish Uppland: see *Uppländska Stenålders-boplatser* (Fornvännen, 1906), p. 113. It appears that these conclusions need further support. See H. C. Broholm, 'Holmegaard- og Sværdborgfundene', *Aarb. f. nord. Oldk.*, 1924, p. 141.

interest, but as a specimen of the population of the time is useless.[1] The highest authority on these problems has recently declared that even as early as the Maglemose period we must recognize a mixed population in Scandinavia, since we meet with divergent types, both long-skulled and short-skulled, among the few skeletons which are known from the Danish kitchen middens This is, in fact, the whole of the knowledge about their race which we possess.

There is, therefore, no good reason for going further into the various theories which have been advanced concerning the racial affinities of the oldest Scandinavian population, or for touching on the much-discussed problem of the ultimate ancestry of the Germanic peoples. We shall have occasion, how-ever, to return to these problems in later pages. Thus we come to the end of the first division of the history of Scandinavian culture, the age of the hunting people.

[1] Carl M. Fürst, 'Das Skelett von Viste auf Jäderen: ein Fall von Skapho-cephalie aus der älteren skandinavischen Steinzeit', *Videnskaps-Selskapets Skrifter*, I. Math. Naturv. Klasse (Kristiania, 1909), no. 1.

V

THE LATER STONE AGE. MEGALITHIC GRAVES.
THE BATTLE-AXE PEOPLE

THE true neolithic culture is distinguished from the older primitive stone age by a highly diversified complex of cultural phenomena: improvements and variations in implements and in the technique of production, the building of houses, developments in pottery and in decoration, and much else; but above all it is distinguished by the fundamental changes betokened by pastoral industry and the cultivation of corn. The free and uncertain existence of the hunting people was replaced by the forms of life which go with settled habitation. Man became dependent on his domestic animals and on the ground he cultivated; his subsistence and welfare could be made secure by systematic labour, and social relations upon an entirely new basis came into being. This is the beginning of the whole social development of later ages. This fundamental transformation of human life in almost all European peoples goes back to the stone age, to various periods in that age according to the degree in which cultural development was affected by geographical conditions. In the early neolithic period agricultural civilization advanced from the mouth of the Danube towards the central lands of Middle Europe; this culture was ultimately inspired by oriental influences. This is the culture of the band-pattern pottery (*Bandkeramik*), which, with its innumerable special groups, spread out over immense areas of tillable land in the interior of the continent. In the west along the Atlantic coast the megalithic civilizations appear, associated with sea-coasts, sea-voyaging, and trading connexions; these civilizations also originated ultimately from impulses from Mediterranean lands, from Egypt and Asia Minor. Between these two principal groups a third eventually appears, the culture brought by the battle-axe people, a mobile and varying culture which spread from central Europe over far-reaching areas.

It is an important side of our task to show how the Norse lands in various ways came into contact with the great European civilizations of the stone age, but we shall also see that the stone age of the Scandinavians was something much more than a mere reflex of foreign impulses. Denmark, with Skåne and the west of Sweden, was in fact one of the richest and most remarkable among the early provinces of culture in Europe. The climate and the natural conditions were favourable to the first development of agriculture; it was a constant and very mild climate, having a mean temperature about 2° C. warmer than now, while the damp Atlantic climate had been replaced by a drier continental one. In the Norwegian highlands the forest line then extended as much as to 200 metres higher than at the present time. These conditions give us the key to understanding the rich development of the stone and bronze civilizations in southern Scandinavia, where, moreover, the disposition of land and waterways afforded the best of facilities for the ancient modes of communication. In addition there was in Denmark and Skåne a wealth of natural flint, the best raw material for the industry of the stone age, and a special source of wealth also in the amber found on the west coast of Jutland. These are lands which to this day are among the first in wealth of important monuments and antiquities from this ancient flowering of neolithic civilization.

But this great progress was not common to all Scandinavian regions. In the more distant parts of Sweden, in Norway, and in Finland the more primitive form of life was still prevalent; only gradually and very slowly did the new civilization make its way among the northern hunting people, whose lives were otherwise wholly bound up with wild nature and the occupations of the older time. In these regions relics surviving from the palaeolithic bone age were still found, inherited Nøstvet forms, special types made of slate and quartz: the whole setting had an archaic character, yet step by step important new cultural elements were being adopted. The technical culture was influenced by the importation of flint implements, and domestic animals and the cultivation of corn were also introduced. In many places the conditions were further changed, apparently by the immigration of a new people. By the close of the neolithic period nearly the whole of Scandinavia had some part in the benefits of the new culture; but people of the more outlying districts never completely assimilated the civilized form of life. In the study of the Scandinavian stone age as a whole it is of special interest to observe the relation between the central cultural region in the south and the more primitive people on the outer borders. In this relation Scandinavia during the later stone age throws much light on the developments of civilization in general.[1]

The old and well-known system for reckoning the chronology of the later stone age in the north is based partly on the leading types of flint implements, and partly on the varying forms of monumental graves. The grinding of flint has always been recognized as an important criterion to distinguish the later stone age from the earlier. It is obviously an important technical advance, which was still, practically speaking, unknown among the implements of the Danish kitchen middens, whereas the art of grinding bone, horn, and volcanic rock had been known a long time before. The grinding of flint first appears in Scandinavia in a new type, the flint axe which has a pointed butt, a handsome, regularly shaped blade of flint with a pointed oval cross-section, and a convex edge-line. This type was first developed in western Europe on the basis of the pick-axe from the Campignian culture of the preceding age. Both the form and the technique of production were adopted in the north from foreign models. The type appears in comparatively small numbers in Denmark, but is more frequent in Skåne.

The second form of the series is the thin-butted flint axe, a fairly large and rather thin blade of flint which has a four-sided cross-section, slightly convex sides, and a wide but thin butt. Magnificent specimens of this form are found, upwards of half a metre long, admirably finished and of perfectly regular shape. A proportion of the thin-butted axes, and especially the handsomest specimens, were undoubtedly weapons; but they are also the type of the usual working axes of the time. They are found in extraordinarily large numbers. This type is a specially Scandinavian form, developed from the axe with pointed butt, possibly under influences from western Europe, where we meet with parallel, but not wholly identical, forms in France and the British Isles.

The latest of these types is the thick-butted flint axe, narrower and thicker than the preceding two, with a square cross-section, flat sides, and a straight edge-line. The butt is thick, and ends

[1] A. W. Brøgger, *Kulturgeschichte des norwegischen Altertums*, Institutet for sammenlignende Kulturforskning, Serie A, vi (Oslo, 1926).

in a flat square surface. This last feature hangs together with an altered method of hafting: the two older forms of axe-head were fastened into the haft, which had a hole bored right through it, so that the butt of the axe-head emerged free, whereas the thick-butted type was fitted into a socket in the haft which completely enclosed the thick end of the butt. This thick-butted axe is also found in extraordinarily large numbers, and it was pre-eminently a working tool. The thick-butted axes are a specially Scandinavian form. They appear, it is true, in the neighbouring parts of the continent through export from the north, but they are unknown in western Europe.

Next to the flint axes the flint daggers are the most important leading type among the implements current in the last phase of the stone age.

This series of forms gives a sufficiently detailed gauge of chronological order within the later Scandinavian stone age, and this chronology can be paralleled to a great extent in the three principal forms of megalithic graves, the dolmens, passage-graves, and stone cists.[1] This system of neolithic periods was at first too rigidly schematic in its association of flint axes with particular forms of graves, but later investigations have rendered it less purely theoretical. And its order is practically certain. The passage-graves came into use later than the dolmens, and the stone cists were the latest form, though it has been discovered that the older form was not abandoned until after the new one had come into use. Dolmens and passage-graves were built to some extent contemporaneously, but many dolmens existed before the oldest of the passage-graves. On the whole it seems clear that the form of the antiquities is a safer basis of chronology than the graves. Comparing them, we may say in broad outline that the flint axes with pointed butts are older than any of the megalithic graves in the north; the flint axes with thin butts begin to appear before the mega-lithic graves, and they occur in the older dolmens and the very earliest of the passage-graves; the axes with thick butts mark the true period of passage-graves, but they are also found in dolmens; the latest form of grave, the stone cist, belongs wholly to the time of the daggers.

[1] Oscar Montelius, *Les Temps préhistoriques en Suède et dans les autres pays scandinaves* (Paris, 1895), pp. 33–8, plates III–VI.

The dolmens, the oldest form of megalithic grave, are also the simplest, being constructed as a four-sided or polygonal room from heavy upright blocks of stone, with a single heavy block as a roof (Pl. 6). The chamber may reach a width and height of over 2 metres. Quite often the dolmen has an opening left to form an entrance on the south or east side; this entrance is either completely open or has a lower stone as a threshold. As a rule the dolmen was surrounded by a mound of earth, but the roof-block was always visible. When the simple dolmen is surrounded by a circular mound of earth, it is called a round dolmen; its outer edge is encircled with large boulders. The long dolmen is a long rectangular mound which enclosed several dolmen graves set in a row lengthwise in the mound. The long dolmens also are bordered with large stones. The second form of grave, the passage-grave, is a more elaborate structure, a fairly large chamber from which a covered passage led out into the open[1] (Pl. 6). The walls, both in the chamber and in the passage, are made of large blocks of stone, and the spaces between them are filled up with small stones. The roof consists of a number of heavy stones laid over the chamber and sometimes over the passage. The oldest passage-graves have round chambers; in the later examples the ground-plan is oblong, oval, or square, and the passage opens into the middle of a long side. A rarer form, restricted to Jutland, is the passage-grave with a smaller side-chamber connected with the larger one. The chamber is usually from 4 to 7 metres in length, and rarely more than 10 metres. The height is from 1 to 2 metres. In Sweden, however, graves of larger dimensions are found. The largest passage-grave in the north, at Karleby, near Falköping, has a chamber 16·65 metres long and a passage 12 metres long. The passage-graves were always surrounded by a mound of earth, but the roof-stones were usually visible. Double passage-graves also occur, in which one mound encloses two chambers, each with its own entrance. This form is peculiar to eastern Denmark.

In the latest form of passage-grave the passage is found opening into a short side, flush with the floor of the chamber, and this type supplies the transition to the stone cist, the latest

---

[1] C. A. Nordman, 'Jættestuer i Danmark', *Nordisk Fortidsminder*, ii (1918), p. 55; summary in French.

PLATE 6

a. Dolmen at Hjortegaarde, Denmark. After Hans Kjær

b. Passage-grave at Steenstrup, Denmark: the entrance as seen from the interior. After C. A. Nordman

PLATE 7

Flint dagger. After S. Müller

of the classic forms of graves in the Norse stone age. The stone
cist is a long chamber, always rectangular, constructed of raised
flat slabs of stone and covered with flat slabs. The length is
usually from 2·50 to 4 metres, but may in rare instances attain
to approximately 10 metres. In this type there is never a
passage into the grave, but there is sometimes a more or less
rudimentary opening as a reminiscence of its origin in a basic
type with special entrance. A group of stone cists in central
Sweden shows an interesting detail, the end-stone being pierced
in a round or oval opening, a vestige of the original entrance
into the grave-chamber. This form has striking parallels in
England and France.[1] The stone cists also were surrounded by
an artificial mound of earth, which did not always, however,
cover the whole of the grave-chamber.

The graves in all three of these forms were communal, intended
to be used for successive burials over a long period, and when
they are found undisturbed, excavation as a rule brings to light
remains of numerous skeletons. Already in one of the oldest
dolmens skeletons of six persons are found, and in the passage-
graves the number may rise to nearly a hundred. The last to be
buried have been found stretched out in a recumbent position,
or else sitting, supported by the wall. When the space in the
chamber became too crowded, the remains of older burials were
cleared to one side to make room for the new. Recent investigations have shown that the graves received new burials continually for a period, which might be of long or short duration.
On the Danish isles the passage-graves are often overfull, while
those in Jutland are far poorer; the megalithic culture there
came to an earlier end. Some Swedish graves have produced
a number of skeletons surpassing the yield of any others.

It can be seen that the burial was performed in accordance
with definite forms. The dead man or woman was provided
with an adequate equipment of implements, ornaments, and
pottery. On certain occasions fires were lighted inside the
grave, probably as part of the rites connected with the cult of
the dead.

The large stone graves undoubtedly mark the spread of
certain definite religious beliefs concerning death, probably also

[1] Montelius, *Les Temps préhistoriques en Suède*, pp. 43–4. Cf. Gabriel and
Adrien de Mortillet, *Musée préhistorique*, 2me éd. (Paris, 1903), plate lxi.

of definite social forms, and with these graves went also a certain common character in the whole material civilization, wherever they appear: in short, they mark out the sphere of megalithic culture in the stone age of Europe. As is well known, the dolmens had an extraordinarily wide distribution in the ancient world. This form of grave extended from the Mediterranean lands to the west of Europe, to France and England, and there can be little doubt that influences from these western regions introduced the dolmens into Scandinavia. Not long afterwards the later forms came, the passage-graves, and in the north they also go back to west-European connexions. The megalithic culture is very definitely linked to the Atlantic coasts, and it spread over great distances by way of the intercourse between Scandinavia, Britain, Brittany, and Spain, but on the other hand it does not touch the central regions of the continent. The connexions of Denmark and western Europe have been attested in many ways. Attention has been drawn to a few thick-butted flint axes found in England, and similarly pieces of Danish pottery have been discovered in East Anglia, of the type found in passage-graves, and are quoted as indubitable proof of intercourse. Stone-age ornaments of amber from Jutland are found both in western and southern Europe,[1] and amber ornaments of British type are found in Jutland. A detailed study of the graves has discovered indications in the dolmens of an origin in England, while the passage-graves possibly came from Brittany by way of Holland. The passage-graves with side-chambers, however, have very close British parallels. All this leaves no doubt that there were connexions, even though it is surprising that the stone-age people could make voyages straight across the North Sea.[2]

The megalithic culture of the north was undoubtedly introduced from the west of Europe, and in the north it remained in close contact with west-European countries. Apart from the monumental grave-structures, and the flint axes with the pointed and thin butts, which have already been mentioned, many other

---

[1] C. A. Nordman, 'Den yngre Stenåldern', &c., p. 113.

[2] In a recently published work Professor Rydbeck assumes that the Dogger Bank in the North Sea at this period still provided islands which could be used as stations on the way from England to Denmark. See *The Changes in the Level of the Stone Age Sea*, &c., p. 124. The geologists, however, decline to accept the possibility of Dogger Bank islands at so late a period.

evidences can be adduced: double-edged battle-axes, slender pointed arrows made from flint flakes, flat points of flint for arrows (leaf-shaped or provided with barbs and tang), arrow-polishers, ornamental plates, and various other forms which are all common to the megalithic groups in France, England, and Denmark. The relation is so unmistakable that it suggests an immigration of western European people into Denmark, and, if this supposition is right, the source would probably be the British Isles. The suggestion has been strongly supported by several scholars.[1] It has been argued that the amber in Jutland was a source of wealth which would tempt the megalithic people, and the land in itself might well invite colonization. We can hardly deny that the available evidence speaks strongly for this conclusion. On the other side, the Danish archaeologists have always been reserved in their treatment of the problem,[2] and recently they have tended more definitely in the direction of rejecting the theory of a megalithic invasion. And, indeed, no conclusive proof of the immigration can be produced.

The anthropological studies of skeletons from the megalithic graves have been used both for and against the theory of an immigration. All that we know about the races in actuality is that the megalithic people in the north show a mixture of different types, the mesocephali and brachycephali being most prevalent in Denmark and Skåne, the dolichocephali pre-ponderating farther north in Sweden. In details the picture is more complex: there are not merely two principal types, a long-skulled and a short-skulled, and mixed forms of these, but within both groups there are characteristic variations which may justly be called special types. In Denmark five groups are made out which must be accepted as established types; and four differ-ent types of skull can be distinguished during the stone age in Gotland. Peculiar jumps occur in the distribution of certain forms, as when a characteristic small local group in Denmark

---

[1] Knut Stjerna, 'Före Hällkisttiden', *Antikv. Tidskrift för Sverige*, vol. xix, no. 2 (Stockholm, 1911), pp. 61 and 91; Otto Rydbeck, *The Changes of the Level of the Stone Age Sea*, &c., p. 115.

[2] Sophus Müller, who first declared the question to be quite an open one, in *Vor Oldtid* (København, 1897), p. 188, later favoured a long and gradual immigration of a new people: see 'Sønderjyllands Stenalder', *Aarb. f. nord. Oldk.*, 1913, especially pp. 317–18. The latest Danish pronouncement, by J. Brøndsted, rejects the notion of a megalithic immigration: see *Det danske Folks Historie* (København, 1927), i. 133.

reappears in identical form in a find in Skåne. One thing at least is certain, that a very complicated mixing of races was already far advanced in the later stone age in Scandinavia; but we do not know when or where this mixing was accomplished. We do not know the racial character of the megalithic people's predecessors in the bone age and on the kitchen middens, and we are therefore unable to judge what new elements may have come in with the hypothetical later invasion. Comparison with British skeletons has not yet yielded any positive results.[1] The theory of an immigration must be based wholly on the archaeological factors already mentioned.

Before leaving the skeletons, however, we must draw attention to some observations concerning them, made in the anthropological studies of the megalithic graves, as they are of considerable interest in the history of culture. Danish researches give a very clear idea of the length of life among the people from the great stone graves, and, as might be expected, it is distinctly lower than at the present time. This brevity of life may still be observed among the more primitive peoples to-day. Of 294 individuals whose age can be ascertained only six were more than sixty years old, and the heaviest percentage of mortality falls as early as the age between twenty and thirty years. The average life of adults was about ten years shorter than it is in Denmark at the present time. Mortality among children cannot be directly studied, since so few skeletons are preserved. Of disease and injuries the skeletons give a considerable amount of information. Dental decay is found during the stone age in Denmark in 13–14 per cent. of the adults; from Sweden, too, both dental decay and dental abscesses are reported. Chronic arthritis is strikingly prevalent in Denmark, as it is in Sweden, and rickets also is very common. Some isolated cases are observed of abscess on the brain and in the ear. Broken bones occur, as is quite natural, and the fractured

---

[1] It is outside our scope to review the anthropological accounts of skeletons from megalithic graves in Scandinavia. The reader is referred to Gustaf Retzius, *Crania suecica antiqua* (Stockholm, 1899); Carl M. Fürst, *Zur Kraniologie der schwedischen Steinzeit*, Kungl. Svenska Vetenskapsakademiens Handlingar, Band 49, no. 1 (Uppsala, Stockholm, 1912); H. A. Nielsen, 'Bidrag til Danmarks forhistoriske Befolkning, særlig Stenaldersfolkets Anthropologi', *Aarb. f. nord. Oldk.*, 1916, and by the same, 'Yderligere Bidrag til Danmarks Stenaldersfolks Anthropologi', ibid., 1911.

bone has often been very badly set. Five cases of cranial lesion from the blows of weapons are especially interesting; only one of these men died from the wound, while the other four were healed, and three of them after surgical trepanation performed with great skill.[1] Apart from the last three cases, which are indeed a most remarkable feat, there is nothing in the patho-logical condition of the stone-age people which can be called surprising. It is easy to understand that rheumatism would be a sore affliction to the Norse people of the stone age, just as it has been in much later times, and injuries such as wounds from weapons and the fracture of bones are only what we might expect. There is a peculiar attraction in such studies. With such a large number of skeletons from a definitely limited period, it is as if we stood face to face with the stone-age people themselves.

The great stone graves mark the first unfolding of a higher culture in Scandinavia. Many features give evidence of im-pulses from the civilized peoples of western Europe, possibly even of an immigration of a new population into the North, but in many particulars Norse culture developed independently. We have already mentioned the flint axes, the thin-butted type, and, still more, the thick-butted type, as independent Norse forms. So also are the flint daggers, a group which is definitely characteristic of the Norse megalithic culture. The older daggers occur in passage-graves, but still in comparatively small numbers; it is in the stone cists, in the latest phase of the stone age, that the daggers first occur frequently and reach their full development. The later forms are distinguished by a special shape of handle (Pl. 7), while the earlier daggers were only simple blades without any handle. It is generally believed that the flint daggers were modelled on older daggers of metal which were in use in the south of Europe, and they undoubtedly mark a high point in the technical treatment of flint. The best of these daggers are produced with a technical mastery that has never been sur-passed. They are the consummation of centuries of experience and knowledge of flint work.[2]

---

[1] Søren Hansen, 'Om forhistorisk Trepanation i Danmark', *Aarb. f. nord. Oldk.*, 1889, p. 170 f.

[2] Sophus Müller, 'Flintdolkene i nordiske Stenalder', *Nordiske Fortids-minder*, i (København, 1890–1903).

The pottery of the megalithic culture is a subject of special interest. After the extremely rough and simple pots and bowls of the kitchen middens there follows in the transition period, contemporary with the axes with pointed butts, a somewhat better ware, pots with rounded bodies and ornamental lines under the rim, produced by the impression of a cord, or decorated with punctuations of pegs and with border patterns. In the dolmens several forms are found, but they are still simple and certainly developed on home ground, a large vase with a high wide neck, round-bodied beakers, and flasks with a projecting collar around the neck (the German *Kragenflaschen*, usually known as 'collared flasks' in England). The usual decoration consists of vertical stripes which cover the lower part of the pot, or of embossed ribs laid onto it. But the period of the passage-graves is the flowering time of the stone-age pottery in the north. By the side of the older forms new, more clearly defined forms were adopted from foreign models, bowls and pots with one or two handles, the wide 'fruit-bowls' (so called) on a tall stem. The decoration shows a rich variety of motives in various combinations, zigzag or crisscross lines, triangles, and rhombs (Pl. 8). Several styles can be distinguished in this pottery, one following another: 'the large style' with strong plastic effects in the ornament; 'the beautiful style', more elegant, with lighter lines which are often picked out with white material; and finally the period of decadence when design and production are retrograde.[1]

On the whole it is an excellent pottery that is known from the passage-graves. It is admirably finished; the pot has a dark shining surface, black or brownish. The ornament is produced sometimes by a cord wound round it, sometimes (and in an increasing degree) by means of stamps of wood or bone, or with the edge of a cockle shell. The whole production bears the impress of a fully developed school of work. This highly developed megalithic pottery belongs in type to the most interesting groups of the European stone age. That it was produced locally is not to be doubted; but in the sphere of ceramics, too, the megalithic culture of Denmark was in inti-

[1] Sophus Müller, *Stenalderens Kunst i Danmark* (København, 1918), and the same author, 'Fællesstilarter i Europas yngre Stenalder', *Aarb. f. nord. Oldk.*, 1923.

mate contact with similar civilizations in western Europe, where closely related pottery is found. This early flowering of the potter's art in the north was inspired by influences which can be traced ultimately to the Spanish peninsula and Mediterranean regions. The motives of this ceramic art are distributed over the same regions as the megalithic graves.

By the side of the pottery, flint implements, battle-axes, and maces of volcanic rock, the ornaments should also be named— especially ornaments of amber—as an important element in the finds from megalithic graves. Among the ornaments of bone are various forms of pins and perforated plates worn as pendants, together with beads. Amber was the most precious material available in northern Europe at that time, and the amber coast of Jutland was undoubtedly an important source of wealth. Export of amber from Denmark is attested by finds from Norway, England, Brittany, and Spain. Even from very early times in the later stone age collections of amber ornaments are found buried as treasures in Jutland, up to 4,000 ornaments in a single find; and ornaments of amber are a constant and prominent feature among the antiquities derived from the passage-graves. Characteristic forms are the beads shaped like double axes, or double mace-heads with a hole bored through them; these were clearly made on the model of the actual weapon. Otherwise the forms found are generally cubic or ring-shaped beads, oblong or flat pendants, and buttons with a passage bored through them from the under side in the form of a Λ. These last belong to the latest phase of the stone age, continue into the bronze age, and are common to Great Britain and Scandinavia, as is indeed well known.[1]

The megalithic culture in the north has its central domain in the Danish Isles, especially in Zealand, where nearly 3,500 megalithic graves still survive. A large part of Jutland also was thickly settled by the megalithic people, especially the part towards the north and east. In the south of Sweden, in Skåne, on the other hand, the megalithic culture is more slightly represented, but it dominates the western coast in the provinces of Halland and Bohuslän, and it has a new centre in the fertile

---

[1] Carl Neergaard, 'Ravsmykker fra Stenalderen', *Aarb. f. nord. Oldk.*, 1888, p. 281; C. A. Nordman, 'Studier öfver Gånggriftkulturen i Danmark', ibid., 1917, p. 255.

districts south of Lake Väner in the province of Västergötland.[1] From this point lines of megalithic graves radiate out into the central Swedish regions, and those of the latest form, the stone cists, stretch out to the nearest part of Norway, on both sides of Oslofjord. The spread of megalithic graves was without any doubt accompanied by the spread of a certain characteristic culture, certain forms of agriculture, society, religion, and beliefs concerning death; and there is every reason to believe that the advance of this culture on the Scandinavian peninsula was accompanied by a gradual colonization which emanated from the megalithic people in Denmark, from Jutland to the western coast of Sweden, from Zealand along the coasts of Skåne to Öland and Gotland.

The megalithic culture during its spread in Scandinavia was, of course, constantly imposing itself upon the primitive manner of life belonging to the preceding age, the life which we know from the kitchen middens; and the tradition from the old hunting life still survived beside the new civilization. There were still people who sought their sustenance in fishing, fowling, and hunting along the coasts; dwelling-sites are found there of essentially the same character as the kitchen middens of the older period, but readily distinguished from them by the presence of cultivated cereals, bones of domestic animals, and implements of megalithic type. This raises a problem which has recently been much discussed, as to whether the people who lived on these dwelling-sites were the same as those who built the megalithic graves, as may quite reasonably be held, or whether we can trace here the more profound difference of two distinct peoples. If the second of these alternatives is the right one, the dwelling-sites along the coast must represent the earlier native population which held fast to its old manner of life, while the immigrants, megalithic people from the west, took possession of the farming land.[2] This view is justified inasmuch as the hunting people of the kitchen middens were undoubtedly still present in the country when the megalithic culture made its way in; but we can hardly suppose that an antagonism,

---

[1] See the map of the Swedish megalithic graves in Oscar Montelius, *Kulturgeschichte Schwedens* (Leipzig, 1906), p. 60.

[2] This theory was recently worked out in full detail by Otto Rydbeck in 'The Changes of the Level of the Stone Age Sea', &c., *Bull. de la Soc. Royale des Lettres de Lund*, 1927–8.

PLATE 8

a

b

Megalithic pottery. After S. Müller

PLATE 9

Pottery from a single-grave in Skåne. After Folke-
Hansen

or even definite hostility, could be maintained for centuries between the tillers of the soil and the fishers in the same country. There must have been constant intercourse between the various groups of population, as is indeed attested by the much-blended race evident in the skeletons from the megalithic graves. The simpler, more primitive forms of life which we know from the dwelling-sites along the coasts thus have a place in the complete picture of megalithic civilization in Scandinavia.

But the megalithic civilization was still far from covering the whole of the Scandinavian area. The great stone graves prevail in almost all Denmark and in the limited area in Sweden defined above. Apart from these regions the Scandinavian people still lived in the more primitive state, which was in the main a continuation of the hunting life of older times. Even in these districts, however, the conditions were gradually changed by influences from the megalithic culture, by the introduction of domestic animals and corn cultivation, by the importation of flint articles and technical progress; yet there was always a profound difference between the superior civilization in the south of Scandinavia and the more primitive northern culture, commonly known as the Arctic stone-age culture: this will be described in the next chapter.

The megalithic culture is the first and most important infusion which produced higher cultural developments in the Scandinavian stone age. But the great influx from the west was not the only connexion between the north and the larger European culture groups. From the continental region to the south foreign groups made their way in and encroached upon the megalithic domain. The most important of these is the group represented by the 'single graves' in Jutland.[1] The form of burial in these graves is a complete contrast to the mass-burial in the megalithic monumental graves: each person is buried individually in his own grave, and is laid quite simply in the earth and covered by a low mound. The body lay on its side, with the knees bent; the bottom of the grave was covered with small stones, the sides walled with stones and then lined

---

[1] Sophus Müller, 'De jydske Enkeltgraver fra Stenalderen', *Aarb. f. nord. Oldk.*, 1898, p. 157.

with wood; and finally the grave was closed by wooden planks.
It was dug about a metre deep, and the mound raised above it
to a corresponding height. The articles in the grave are almost
invariable. In a man's grave will be found a battle-axe with
a hole for the haft, made of trap, or a thick-butted axe of ground
flint; also a flint chisel and a sharp flint blade, a flat stone
mace, an earthenware beaker, and two large disks of amber
which belonged to the clothing. In a woman's grave there are
always long neck-bands or strings of amber beads, and, more
rarely, an earthenware beaker. The articles are quite different
in form from those found in megalithic graves.

These single graves are prevalent in the western and central
parts of Jutland, and wherever the single graves have a home
there are no megalithic monuments. The two groups are
mutually exclusive, just as they are fundamentally different in
burial custom and in structure. There can therefore be no doubt
that they represent two different peoples, and it is likewise
clear that the single graves belong to a new invading people who
were pushing into Scandinavia from the south. Whereas the
northern megalithic culture had its source in western Europe,
it can be shown that the single-grave people, with their characteristic battle-axes and their own pottery, came from the south,
from central Europe. There are graves in Germany related to
these in every particular; the graves and the accompanying
forms are found in Hanover and eastward as far as Mecklenburg, and graves of similar formation are found in various
places in the south-west and centre of Germany, in Bavaria,
and in Switzerland. From these regions emigrations streamed
northwards, bringing the single-grave people through Holstein
and Slesvig into the south-west of Jutland.

The oldest of the single graves made their appearance in the
same period as the large dolmens and the oldest 'giants' chambers' (passage-graves); they evidently started from a district
in the south-west around Holstein, but spread out rapidly over
larger areas until they had driven the megalithic people from
the whole of the Jutish peninsula and even made conquests in
the Danish isles to the east. The chronological order can be
made out with certainty, because in many cases several successive burials are found in one and the same grave-mound. The
oldest grave lies sunk below the original surface; this is called

the 'lower grave'. A later grave may be placed somewhat higher, on a level with the original surface of the surrounding ground; this is called a 'basic grave'. Lastly, the most recent graves might be made in the same mound, which was gradually increased in size by the additions of the successive burials; these last are called 'upper graves'. The relics from the various stages in the mounds show distinctly different forms, which always appear in the same order, and therefore may be understood to mark the changes which took place in the course of the whole single-grave period. In the older graves the types are more sharply characterized, while the later graves are distinguished by slender, elegant types, in particular the well-made handsome battle-axes with a hole for the haft. The earthenware beakers from the older graves have a curvilinear outline with a rounded body and a wide neck which is decorated with cord impressions—in general a rough and unvaried pottery. In the later beakers the form is always cylindrical with a straight side, but the decoration becomes richer and more varied under the influence of the superior pottery of the megalithic graves.

It is extraordinarily interesting to follow the spread of the single-grave culture on Danish ground. The later forms of the single graves advance northward until they reach the most northerly part of Jutland, and in a number of places it can be seen clearly that the single-grave people have overcome the megalithic people.[1] In a number of passage-graves in Jutland a break in the continuity can be seen, since the deepest layer in the grave contains megalithic types, while a higher layer contains antiquities of the single-grave type. This, then, is an older grave which a new people has taken possession of. Similarly it is striking that all the passage-graves in Jutland are much less filled by burials than those on the Danish isles, and the latest forms of pottery in particular are absent from them. From this it is evident that burials ceased at an earlier period in the Jutish passage-graves, while the graves in the islands to the east continued in use for a long time. In the later part of the passage-grave period Jutland was completely subjected to the single graves, and they even appear as the beginning of an invasion in the islands. Only rarely in

[1] C. A. Nordman, 'Studier öfver Gånggriftkulturen i Danmark', *Aarb. f. nord. Oldk.*, 1917, p. 293 f.

prehistoric archaeology can one produce such indubitable proofs of an invasion of a foreign people and their expansion among an already settled population. The result here is due to the admirable researches carried out by the Danish archaeologists.

On the Scandinavian peninsula we find no specially remarkable influences from the civilization represented by the single graves in Jutland, but in their stead appear other currents which also emanated from the battle-axe people in central Europe. An important type is the faceted battle-axe which is assumed to have come into the north very early in the passage-grave period. The region of its occurrence is in Sweden and Norway: no examples are found west of the Sound. The type had its origin in a south-easterly direction, probably on Hungarian ground, where it existed side by side with the oldest axes of metal—just as, in general, all these handsome types of stone axes had their prototypes in copper. A faceted battle-axe of copper has been found in Skåne, and it must have been imported across the Baltic. It was by this route that the type came to Scandinavia; it is found very frequently in Sweden and appears also in the east of Norway.

Of still greater importance is the somewhat later form, the boat-shaped battle-axe, which appears in the later part of the passage-grave period. This form also must have been made on the model of early metal weapons in central Europe; a specimen made of copper is known which was found in eastern Russia and presumably came there by way of export from its original home.[1] From its place of origin in central Europe the type makes its way to north Germany, and from there across the Baltic to Bornholm and Skåne without touching the Danish area. In Sweden several hundred specimens of the boat-formed axe have been found; they appear there in single graves which are of essentially the same form as the single graves of Jutland, but are distinct in the types of antiquities which they contain. In addition to boat-shaped axes, flint axes and daggers are found in these graves, and also certain forms of earthenware vessels which are related to the corded ware in Germany (Pl. 9). In Sweden, too, three distinct stages can be distinguished in the history of the single graves; they are named after the localities

---

[1] Julius Ailio, *Die steinzeitlichen Wohnplatzfunde in Finland* (Helsingfors, 1909), i. 37, Fig. 30.

of characteristic finds, Sösdala, Hvellinge, and Augerum, the chronological succession following the order of the names.[1] In the south of Sweden whole cemeteries of such graves are known, as well as a number of isolated graves, quite sufficient as evidence of a foreign immigration from the continent during the later stone age.

A contemporary and parallel movement can be traced in Finland. There we come upon characteristic single graves, boat-shaped battle-axes, other axes of thick-necked type, and earthen vessels which are a variety of the central European corded ware. The whole group is closely related to the corresponding one in Sweden, and it has sometimes been assumed that the whole boat-axe culture in Finland is due to Swedish influence, and that these continental forms first found their way to Finland through Sweden. But certain local differences are found which point in another direction. The true Finnish boat-shaped axes are not identical with the Swedish, and similarly the pottery shows divergences. Pieces imported from Sweden occur and can be easily distinguished. The most probable hypothesis is that the single-grave people with their characteristic battle-axes and their special pottery came to Finland for the most part as a direct invasion from the south across the Baltic. Gotland and the Åland Islands must have played an important part as intermediate stations, but we must also reckon with connexions to the south-east, with the Baltic lands and the west of Russia, where the boat-axe culture is also evidenced. A certain contact with parallel groups in Sweden is therefore not excluded.[2]

The single-grave culture makes its way into Finland in the

---

[1] Gunnar Ekholm, *Finländska stenåldersfrågor ur svensk synpunkt* (Fornvännen, 1922), p. 148, and the same author in Max Ebert's *Reallexicon der Vorgeschichte*, vol. ix, plate 94; J.-E. Forssander, *Die schwedische Bootaxtkultur und ihre kontinentaleuropäischen Voraussetzungen* (Lund, 1933).

[2] The problems touched upon here have not yet been thoroughly worked out. Sweden is championed as the original home of the boat-shaped axes of Finland by O. Montelius in particular in 'När kommo svenskarne till Finland?', *Finsk Tidskrift*, 1898, p. 81, and recently also by Gunnar Ekholm in Ebert's *Reallexicon der Vorgeschichte*, ix. 50–1. Finnish archaeologists in recent times have advanced essentially the same view as is set forth above: Aarne Europaeus, 'Fornfynd från Kyrkslätt och Esbo Socknar', *Finska Fornminnesföreningens Tidskrift* (Helsingfors), xxxii. 152 ff.; C. A. Nordman, 'Den yngre stenåldern i Mellan-, Väst- och Nordeuropa', in Friis Johansen's *De forhistoriske Tider i Europa* (København, 1927), ii. 139–40.

earlier part of the passage-grave period.[1] It appears here in a country which is wholly untouched by megalithic influences. The primitive life of the hunting people was still prevalent as a continuation of the Suomusjärvi culture (p. 45), in association with related peoples in east Baltic lands and the north of Russia. We shall return to this relationship in a later chapter; here we shall merely state that the single graves and the boat-shaped axes mark the first stage of a higher development in Finnish culture. We must conclude that it was this invasion which first brought agriculture and domestic animals to Finland, since we can see that habitation there now assumes new forms, and is no longer as closely bound to the shore and the sea as it was earlier. At the same time the work in stone also appears in new forms; boat-shaped axes of beautiful design and admirable execution are the most prevalent work of native material, of a variety of diabase which is peculiar to a limited area in Sata-kunta in the south-west of Finland.[2] In technical production the boat-shaped axe in Finland represents an important advance on the primitive local culture.

The same result was produced also in Norway, which had had least contact with the battle-axe culture. The boat-shaped axe, as well as the faceted axe, spread from Sweden to Norway and is found in large numbers in the eastern part of the country, though it is more weakly represented in the west and north. From various indications it appears that the special pottery and the types of grave which accompanied the boat-shaped axe in Sweden and Finland must also have existed on Norwegian ground; but up to the present we have not found any certain and typical graves of this type in Norway. It is accordingly still uncertain how far the boat-axe culture in Norway is due to the immigration of a new people, and how far to importation and cultural borrowing, except that we must reckon in some degree with a settlement of foreign immigrants. But on the other hand it is certain that many of the battle-axes in Norway were made of native stone; many half-made specimens which have been found bear witness to native production, and we find some

---

[1] In Finland the geological period is indicated by the boat-axe culture never being found at a lower level than 21 metres above the sea.

[2] Aarne Laitakari, 'Die Schaftlochäxte der Steinzeit von geologischpetro-graphischem Standpunkt', *Finska Fornminnesföreningens Tidskrift* (Helsing-fors, 1930), xxxvii. 1.

types with specially Norwegian variations.[1] While Norway is poor in natural flint, the country has a rich variety of rocks which are very suitable for battle-axes.

The handsome battle-axes with a hole for the haft in their general technical production represent a very interesting side of the stone-age civilization in Scandinavia. Special methods of production were developed for work in volcanic rock, which was chosen with an eye to handsome appearance. It was often a red rock, reminiscent of copper, or heavy coal-black stone, or variegated porphyry. Stone which was difficult to work was not rejected if it seemed specially suitable. We even find artistic shaping of such difficult kinds of stone, we might say, an almost plastic treatment of the stone. Features of the type are a projecting socket around the hole for the haft, the convex knob at the butt, fine raised lines which meet at acute angles, all produced with perfect precision and given a high polish. These are products of a definitely artistic technique, of a delight in finished weapons which is very remarkable.

As has just been demonstrated, we see that the battle-axe civilization in the north falls into three divisions which all belong to the same primary group in neolithic European culture; the most important of the three divisions is the single-grave people in Jutland, and besides them are the bearers of the boat-shaped axe on the Scandinavian peninsula and in Finland, the last two being nearly related to each other. Much light seems to be shed by the discovery that these forms in Scandinavia had their origin in the south, from the battle-axe culture in central Europe, which in later neolithic times obtained a very wide distribution, and was then introduced into the north by immigration of new peoples: this is firmly established in Jutland and Finland, and highly probable in Sweden also.[2] We have no direct evidence as to which race these battle-axe people belonged to, since no sufficient number of skeletons has been preserved in their graves in the north. But by indirect inferences an hypothesis has been reached which has at least strong probability on its side. It has been observed that the battle-axe

---

[1] Shetelig, *Primitive Tider i Norge* (Bergen, 1922), p. 256.

[2] A contrary view is advanced by Nils Åberg, in most detail in his great work *Das nordische Kulturgebiet in Mitteleuropa während der jüngeren Steinzeit* (Uppsala, 1918). Compare Gunnar Ekholm's 'Nordischer Kreis' in Ebert's *Reallexicon der Vorgeschichte*, ix. 50–1.

culture in its expansion over large areas of Europe carried with it those forms which philological researchers declare to be characteristic of the earliest Indo-European culture, and it may be deduced from this that the spread of the battle-axe marks the expansion of the oldest Indo-European people. The immigration of the battle-axe people into the north must then be the starting-point of the Germanic-speaking people known in later times in Scandinavia.[1] But 'Germanic-speaking' is by no means the same thing as Indo-European or Germanic in race. Everywhere during their expansion the battle-axe people were blended with earlier local populations, and a new type of people arose as a result of this assimilation.

This was what happened in the north. It can be demonstrated with especial clarity in Denmark that the two groups who at first were sharply opposed, megalithic people against battle-axe people, were later assimilated and became a unity. No more 'giants' chambers' were built, and the dimensions of the stone cists diminished to modest proportions suited to individual burials in each cist. The single graves had won the victory over the megalithic graves. On the other hand the battle-axes definitely lost ground; they are hardly found in graves any longer and, generally speaking, they had passed out of use. The weapons of the time are now daggers, spears, and arrows, which are undoubtedly influenced in form by earlier weapons of metal, and they are produced with the perfect technical treatment of the flint that has already been spoken of. On the other hand the potter's art is decaying; only very simple pots without decoration are now to be seen, serving as an introduction to the rude pots which we know in the following centuries. This is the period of the dagger, the last phase of the stone age in Scandinavia, which in all outward appearances shows a wholly new picture of culture, a civilization which forms a natural transition to the bronze age.

[1] Sophus Müller, 'Sønderjyllands Stenalder', *Aarb. f. nord. Oldk.*, 1913, pp. 315 ff.; C. A. Nordman, 'Den yngre stenåldern i Mellan-, Väst- och Nordeuropa', in *De förhistoriska Tiderna i Europa*, ii. 160.

VI

NORTHERN SCANDINAVIA IN THE LATER STONE AGE. THE 'ARCTIC STONE AGE'

THE higher forms of neolithic civilization which we describe in the preceding chapter never came to hold sway over the northern part of the Scandinavian peninsula and Finland. Farther north the manner of life and the culture were still definitely in the more primitive state which had prevailed during the kitchen-midden period, here and there mixed with reminiscences of still older times. As we have already intimated, it was this primitive culture which was the basis of further local development in Norway, Sweden, and Finland, and produced the characteristic Norse culture which in its later phase goes under the name of the Arctic stone age.[1] The culture of this age everywhere resembles very closely the way of life which we know from the kitchen middens, and the remains which have survived are accordingly restricted for the most part to the deposits of refuse on the old dwelling-sites on the coasts of the North Sea and the Baltic. In Sweden this northern group has usually been classed as a culture of dwelling-sites in contrast with the agricultural civilization of the stone-grave and battle-axe peoples. The people of the dwelling-sites are still mostly hunters and fishers in neolithic times, in contrast with the tillers of the soil in southern Scandinavia.

Here in the north we come upon a wholly different sphere of life from that which we know farther south, a sphere in which the material equipment of tools and hunting weapons is characterized by a complete set of special forms for the most part produced in other material than flint, usually in trap and other varieties of volcanic rock or of quartzite or slate. There are also articles of bone—harpoons, fowling arrows with flint edges, bone points for throwing-spears, bone hooks of both earlier and later types. A conspicuous and attractive feature of the Arctic stone age in the north of Scandinavia is a distinctive naturalistic art

[1] A. W. Brøgger, 'Den arktiske stenalder i Norge', with a summary in German, *Videnskabs-Selskabets Skrifter*, ii, Hist.-filos. klasse (Kristiania, 1909), no. 1. In this work the organic unity of the whole of the North-European stone age in Scandinavia and Russia was first established.

which we find first and foremost in rock-carvings and rock-paintings in Norway and Sweden, but also in small engravings and sculptured images of animals.

In varying degree according to the different conditions influences from the megalithic culture and the battle-axe culture in the south of Scandinavia were brought to bear upon the north, as has already been described. But in spite of all local variations this neolithic culture has a common character over a large area of northern Europe, in Norway, Sweden, Finland, the Baltic region, and the north of Russia. From the geographical position of the group its culture merits the name of Arctic stone age, and it has its natural place as such in the history of European culture: in these regions the traditions of palaeolithic culture, the traditions of the bone age in the north and around the Baltic, are much better preserved than in western and central Europe. The weapons and implements of this culture are rich in survivals from the oldest times, and the methods of fishing and hunting, the way of life, and the means of subsistence undoubtedly preserve the same stamp of antiquity. Many traces of these primeval conditions have been preserved in the north even down to the present age.[1]

On the Scandinavian peninsula this primitive stone-age culture prevailed on the western and north-western coasts of Norway and, on the other side, on the Baltic coast of Sweden, while the west of Sweden and the east of Norway were more or less subject to the megalithic culture. It has already been related how the great stone graves advanced up the west coast of Sweden and from there spread out into the central Swedish regions. In the east of Norway we have only a few megalithic monuments, but the material civilization was just as strongly impressed by powerful impulses from the megalithic culture. Shortly after the Nøstvet period implements of megalithic type appear here, partly through direct importation of flint articles from the south, partly as local imitations of these flint articles. The leading types of axes succeed each other in the same order as in Denmark, proving that the east of Norway was constantly in close contact with the megalithic culture. The same relation is observed in Sweden in the border districts lying immediately

[1] A. W. Brøgger, *Kulturgeschichte des norwegischen Altertums*, Instituttet for sammenlignende Kulturforskning, Serie A, vi (Oslo, 1926).

north and east of the megalithic farm settlements. This is what we call sub-megalithic culture; it does not possess the huge grave-structures, and it clearly has not been introduced by immigration of megalithic people, but nevertheless on the material side these districts soon adopted much of the higher culture emanating from the south.

Along the western and eastern coasts, on the other hand, the Scandinavian tribes lived the life of a hunting people, and their whole round of life was centred upon much simpler needs.[1] The true working tools, the axes, are very small and inadequate. The old types which we have already mentioned in the account of the kitchen-midden period, the types of Limhamn, Nøstvet, and Sigersvoll, and similarly the rounded axes, were still used at a much later time in the northern stone age, as were late varieties of the flake-axe, produced in volcanic rock. There were also simple axes long-oval in shape, of various types. A new west-Norwegian local form is the Vespestad type, a short and comparatively thick axe with strongly convex sides, presumably produced under the influence of the thin-butted flint axe; its name is derived from a work-place on the island Bømlo on the coast between Bergen and Stavanger. Finally, we have the latest of the series, known in Norway as 'the West Norwegian type'; but it is in reality a widely distributed form found also in Sweden and Finland. It is ordinarily a rather large axe, well and regularly made, with a rectangular cross-section and smooth sides.[2]

Another interesting type is the 'Russo-Carelian' axe, a thick narrow axe with a triangular cross-section; it is not frequently found in Norway, but is more usual in Sweden and Finland and

[1] The best summary accounts of the forms, apart from the work of A. W. Brøgger already mentioned, are given by Helge Gjessing, *Rogalands Stenalder* (Stavanger, 1920); O. Montelius, *Minnen från vår Forntid*, i (Stockholm, 1917); Julius Ailio, *Die steinzeitlichen Wohnplatzfunde in Finland* (Helsingfors, 1909). See also Gunnar Ekholm, 'Nordischer Kreis' in Ebert's *Reallexikon der Vorgeschichte*, vol. ix.

[2] The whole character of the form precludes derivation of the 'west-Norwegian axe' from the thick-butted flint axes. It is clearly of independent origin, and the most probable explanation is no doubt that first suggested by Knut Stjerna, 'Före Hällkisttiden', *Antikv. Tidskrift för Sverige*, xix, no. 2, p. 82. It is shown in this article that the west-Norwegian axe must have developed from the Gullrum type, a diminutive chisel which may have originated as a stone form of a bone chisel which we know from the Maglemose civilization. See also Shetelig, *Primitive Tider i Norge*, p. 267.

the Russian area. In all these types it is the rule that the edge is asymmetrical, and is what we call a 'cross-edge', a feature which is typical of the more primitive implements among the hunting people and disappeared in the megalithic culture.

These axes are almost entirely made of close-grained volcanic rock, or sometimes of hard slate, that is, of materials that had been discovered as early as the Nøstvet period. Men had already learned at an early period to quarry stones from the solid mountain, just as flint was obtained from mines in Skåne, in Belgium, and in England; and in neolithic times an increasing specialization of the industry can be clearly perceived. Analyses have demonstrated that axes of identical material are distributed over large areas. This is known of the rare stone grorudite, which is found only in the immediate neighbourhood of Oslo, while axes made from it are found over the whole of south-eastern Norway. Similar results have been obtained from investigation of certain axes made of trap; the stones must have been quarried in one and the same place, and distributed from there over a wider area.[1] We have already mentioned (p. 43) the stone quarry on the island of Bømlo, where a number of work-places from the later stone age also were investigated. The island was an industrial centre for the production of trap axes. There was another such centre for green slate at Olonets near Lake Ladoga, from where the products were conveyed to Finland and Esthonia.

Beside the axes, which are the most important implements, a rarer, but interesting group of weapons may be mentioned, namely, maces of various forms. They are sometimes slender pointed weapons resembling choppers; sometimes they are shaped like a cross or a star (Pl. 10). They are in the main limited to the Scandinavian peninsula, and are often made of soapstone and decorated with patterns of incised lines. These forms probably had prototypes in older times in hartshorn, elkhorn, and similar materials.[2] We can indeed trace both in the shapes and in the geometrical decorations a legacy from the bone age to the Arctic stone age. The adaptation of the local

[1] W. C. Brøgger, 'Om bergartene i de skafthulløse økser av sten', in A. W. Brøgger's 'Studier over Norges Stenalder', *Videnskabs-Selskabets Skrifter*, i, Mat.-naturv. klasse, 1906, no. 2, p. 167.

[2] O. Montelius, *Minnen från vår forntid* (Stockholm, 1917), text pp. 16–17, nos. 339–48.

PLATE 10

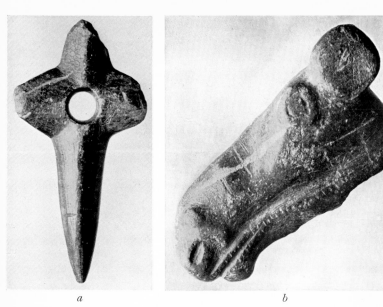

a　　　　　　　　　　　　　　*b*

a. Cross-shaped mace of soapstone. After Gjessing
b. Stone mace sculptured in the shape of an elk's head. After Ailio

c. Early comb pottery from Finland. After Aarne
Äyräpää

material, soapstone, is also significant: it is too soft for working tools, but is heavy and solid enough to be suitable for maces. By the side of the more artistically made maces there appears over the whole of the northern region a simple round club-stone which has either a hole bored through it for a handle or a groove around it by which it could be firmly tied to a handle. A late peculiar form appears in the maces shaped like animal heads, often designed with admirable art. Their home is on the Russian side in East Carelia, but they are found not infrequently in Finland and sporadically in Sweden (Pl. 10). They are an expression of that keen delight in plastic animal shapes which distinguishes the whole of the east-European stone age, and which we shall have occasion later to discuss more fully.

A characteristic tendency of the Arctic stone age is seen in the extended use of quartz, rock-crystal, and fine varieties of quartz-ite which can be split into sharp flakes almost in the same way as flint. The same forms, too, are produced in quartz as in flint, certain slender or blade-formed arrowheads and the like. It is clear that quartz was used as a substitute for flint in the districts where there was no flint. Finds of quartzite are met with in especially large numbers from the north of Sweden,[1] but they are frequent also in Norway and Finland.

But the group of forms which have always been regarded as most characteristic of the Arctic stone age are the articles of slate, including a rich variety of arrowheads, spearheads, knives, and daggers, of strikingly original form and distinctive in material and technique also. These articles of slate formed the basis of the first account[2] of the Arctic stone age, distinguishing it from the flint culture of southern Scandinavia, and they are still recognized as one of the most prominent features in the whole of this northern culture. The technical production of the slate articles was conditioned by the nature of the material, inasmuch as slate can be split into thin smooth plates and is soft in comparison with volcanic rock. Slate was seldom hewn like flint or the other hard stones; plates of slate were rubbed or ground to a tolerably even thickness and were then sawn

---

[1] Eskil Olsson, *Översikt av de fasta fornlämningarna i Ångermanland* (Forn-vännen, Stockholm, 1914), p. 56 f.

[2] Given by Oluf Rygh and Oscar Montelius at the International Archaeo-logical Congress at Stockholm in 1874.

into strips, broad or narrow, which formed the material for points of weapons or for knives. The article was finally completed by grinding. This is a method which is without doubt closely related to the work in bone and horn, and there is every likelihood that the technique applied to the softer slate was derived from the work in bone, which had old and strong traditions going back right to palaeolithic times. Other points of contact also can be indicated: heads of spears and arrows have the same shapes, in some degree at least, in slate as in bone, and there is exhibited in both a fondness for decorating these articles with geometrical patterns or other figures such as we know already from the bone articles of the Maglemose period.

We are, then, able to state that the 'slate culture', as it has been called, was developed upon the original foundation provided by the epipalaeolithic civilization in Scandinavia,[1] and it is only natural that the first slate articles should appear very early in the Norwegian stone age.[2] Typical pieces made of slate have been found on several occasions in indubitable association with dwelling-sites of the Nøstvet period, and from Denmark there is a broad spearhead or dagger of slate from the kitchen midden at Vaalse Vig on Falster.[3] This last is unique among Danish finds from so early a period, and must certainly be explained as an isolated piece imported from northern Scandinavia, where certain forms in slate must therefore have been developed as early as the kitchen-midden period in Denmark.[4]

The slate articles fall in the main into two principal groups, one of knives and daggers, the other of arrows and throwing weapons such as hunting spears, fish-spears, harpoons, and the

[1] A. W. Brøgger, 'Studier over Norges Stenalder', *Videnskabs-Selskabets Skrifter*, i, Mat.-naturv. klasse, 1906, no. 2, p. 68 f.

[2] Anathon Bjørn, 'De ældste skiferedskaper fra Norges stenalder', *Tromsø Museums Årshefte*, vol. 1 (Tromsø, 1928), no. 2.

[3] Sophus Müller, 'Nye Stenaldersformer', *Aarb. f. nord. Oldk.*, 1896, p. 314. The slate point from Vaalse Vig is decorated with characteristic geometrical designs.

[4] This theory refers only to conditions in Norway. In Sweden it is evident that articles of slate first appeared considerably later, during the period of the passage-graves, and, it is believed, only under the influence of megalithic flint types. See Axel Bagge, *Om skifferspetserna i svensk stenålder*, *Fornvännen* (Stockholm, 1923), p. 9, with a summary in German, p. 284, and Sune Lindqvist, 'Le problème des objets de schiste dans l'age de pierre en Suède', *Acta Archaeologica* VI, p. 99 (Köbenhavn, 1935). In Finland, however, it seems that conditions were parallel with those in Norway.

like. The various slate points for arrows and other hunting
weapons naturally do not exhibit any widely differing forms.
The points may be very narrow and slender, or they may have
an oval or triangular outline, with or without barbs; the forms
are all closely related to each other, and most of them are found
in identical shape both in slate and in bone.[1] The knives of slate,
on the other hand, exist in a wealth of different types and local
variations. We have strong, straight, two-edged knives, the
form of which usually bears clear witness of imitation from
megalithic daggers of flint; while others are wholly independent
types, such as the elegant, slightly curved shapes (e.g. banana-
shaped knives) and the strongly curved, one-edged type with a
short blade.

The different regions have their own definite special forms.
In Finland we find only simple, almost unvaried forms,
arrowheads without barbs and straight, rude blades for knives
and daggers. On the other side of the Baltic, Ångermanland in
the north of Sweden was a rich centre for the manufacture of
slate articles, especially for the large handsome daggers and
slender arrowheads which were exported from there to the
central Swedish districts. The slate industry in Norway had
its corresponding centre of distribution on the west coast, north
of Trondhjem, where extensive work-places have been found
with innumerable slate pieces, arrowheads, knives, and scrapers,
mostly in fragments, together with quantities of half-worked
material and refuse from the processes of production. The work
has a regular and workmanlike character. Thus we come upon
slate articles under the same conditions as have already been
described in connexion with implements of volcanic rock: the
manufacture was carried on in a few known places where the
best raw material was obtainable, and the finished articles were
distributed over the surrounding areas. The Scandinavian
articles of slate are found in greatest numbers in the north, but
they also have a southward distribution along the whole coast
of Norway as far as Oslofjord, and in Sweden as far south as
Gotland. Two slate points have been found in a passage-grave
in Bornholm.

[1] A typical selection of Norwegian forms has been collected by Shetelig,
'Les Pointes de flèches en schiste de Norvège', *Bulletin de la Société Préhistorique Française* (Paris, 1928), p. 256.

The pottery of a primitive culture is always an attractive study: here the art of the craftsman is unfolded with rich variations in a responsive plastic material; various styles are formed, characteristic of the different periods and of each district. We have already seen that the megalithic culture and the battle-axe culture can be distinguished by their individual ceramic art, and the primitive stone-age culture along the coasts of the Baltic also has its own distinctive pottery. In the eastern Swedish dwelling-sites we find an abundance of pottery which may have been derived from the rude pots of the kitchen-midden period, but it was later crossed by influences from the megalithic pottery of the passage-graves and stone cists. A series of different styles can be distinguished in the ornament. There is the Åloppe style, with vertical designs derived from passage-grave forms; the Säter style and the Körartorp style, more independent, with decorations of lines, grooves, and impressions of serrated stamps, and, lastly, the Tierp style, which has connexions with the stone cist pottery. These styles are named from characteristic dwelling-sites within each group, and they succeed each other in the order in which they are named.[1] On the Åland Islands, where the same culture is found as in the eastern Swedish dwelling-sites, the pottery assumes an independent and distinctive style, inspired, however, by the corded ware of the battle-axe culture. The various foreign influences thus provide a chronology for the local styles of pottery, which then become the best means of dating the dwelling-sites.

While the pottery of the Swedish dwelling-sites in its origin and development belongs wholly to the Scandinavian peninsula, we meet with a foreign group in Finland, the comb pottery, which has its widest distribution towards the east, in central and northern Russia, but advances its western outposts into the Baltic lands from Finland to East Prussia. The characteristic element in the decoration consists of lines of dots which are impressed by a comb; the designs are horizontal bands of lines and grooves. In central and northern Finland the comb pottery (Pl. 10) appears in precisely the same form as in the adjacent part of Russian Carelia, but in western Finland with local

---

[1] Gunnar Ekholm, 'Nordischer Kreis' in Ebert's *Reallexicon der Vorgeschichte*, vol. ix.

variations, of which three styles are distinguished. The oldest of these is the Urjala pottery with strong lines and grooves; the next is the Jäkärlä pottery with the punctuations of the comb wide apart; and the third is the Uskela pottery, ornamented almost exclusively with grooves. These styles succeed each other in the order named, and the series ends with the Kiukais pottery, produced in a mixed style which is crossed with corded ware elements from the battle-axe culture. It is generally believed that the first of these styles goes back to the beginning of the passage-grave period, and the fourth is certainly contemporary in part with the last phase of the stone age in southern Scandinavia.[1] The east-European textile pottery appears in Finland in the last phase of the stone age, but only as a purely subordinate element.

The pottery thus gives a striking illustration of the profound difference between the eastern and western sides of the Baltic during the later stone age. The Åland Islands belong wholly to Sweden, while Finland belongs to the Baltico-Russian area of culture. Inasmuch as the culture of the whole of this north European area is uniform in its more essential features, this uniformity must be due to a parallel development from the common basis, the older culture of the bone age, which has already been described. We must beware of underestimating the communications already established by this time over great distances. Especially illuminating in this respect is the occurrence of amber ornaments in the north of Scandinavia. Amber was an exceedingly precious material at this period, and these ornaments made on the amber coasts of Jutland and Prussia often give valuable information about trade-routes and the communications between the various inhabited areas during the stone age. In the south of Norway amber ornaments have been found near Stavanger in Jæren; they had been imported from Jutland. Amber from Prussia has been found in Finland and Sweden, and from Sweden it found its way farther overland to the north-west of Norway, where we have important finds of

---

[1] Aarne Europaeus, 'Fornfynd från Kyrkslätt och Esbo Socknar', *Finske Fornminnesföreningens Tidskrift*, xxxii, no. 1 (Helsingfors, 1922), p. 124 f.; id., 'Stenålderskeramik från kustboplatser i Finland', ibid. xxxvi, 1927, and 'Die relative Chronologie der steinzeitlichen Keramik in Finland', *Acta Archaeologica*, i (København, 1930).

hoards of Prussian amber ornaments.[1] In these we have an indubitable proof of communication between the neolithic peoples over the whole of the Scandinavian area, and this inference is confirmed by many other evidences. Ornaments of slate of Finnish type are found in Norway; Swedish articles of slate are found in Finland, and weapons of Carelian type, shaped like animals' heads, were imported into Sweden.[2] The culture of the hunting people was not a hindrance to distant communications; on the contrary, the population during this primitive stage was very mobile and wandered frequently from place to place.

Among these northern tribes with their uniform culture and way of life exchange was natural and freely reciprocated; but the relation with the civilized people in the south of Sweden was quite different. Many elements in this higher culture were, of course, not directly accessible to primitive hunting people. A manner of life which is dependent on agriculture and domestic animals, and still more on the new forms resulting from settlement and social organization, requires an adjustment which could not be effected in the north of Scandinavia otherwise than slowly and gradually. We can readily understand that the cultural borrowing most easily effected was the adoption of the purely material equipment of implements and weapons: the northern districts imported flint articles of megalithic type, which were, naturally, much superior to the primitive articles of rock and slate which the Arctic stone age produced.

When we look more closely into the introduction of flint articles from the south, we perceive that, as is natural, the importation began in a comparatively small way with the older types of axe (the type with pointed butt and the type with a wide butt); but later imported forms gain ground and enlarge their domain, until the latest types of flint axes and daggers are spread over the whole peninsula. Special mention must be made of one find which sheds much light on the trade in flint. Near Bjursele on the estuary of the River Byske in Väster-

---

[1] A. W. Brøgger, 'Et norsk ravfund fra stenalderen', *Bergens Museums Årbok*, 1911, no. 11.

[2] Aarne Europaeus, *Översikt av den skandinaviska importen til Finland under stenåldern* (Rig, Stockholm), vols. ii–iii, p. 107; Oscar Almgren, 'Ålgbilden från Alunda', *Upplands Fornminnesförenings Tidskrift*, xvii (Uppsala, 1911), p. 255.

botten, about midway between Umeå and Haparande, whole collections of flint axes and other stone objects have been discovered time after time during the last century, and all within a very limited extent of ground.[1] This locality was evidently a dwelling-site during the Arctic stone age, but it is likewise a place where whole stores of these excellent implements of foreign flint are found: in all about 175 flint axes are known from this place. In the stone age the site was on an arm of the sea which afforded harbourage, and the place was clearly a trading station for flint axes. In passing we may note the highly interesting fact that flint from Skåne was taken to the north of Sweden by sea.

We have given the flint axes the first place among the leading types which distinguish the later periods of the stone age, but there were also whole series of megalithic types, chisels, scrapers, arrowheads, blades of flint shaped like a half-moon, the megalithic axe with a hole for the haft, and not least in importance the daggers which are prevalent in the last phase of the Norse stone age. It is clear, too, that this importation of flint articles indicates an absorption of highly important cultural elements into the north of Scandinavia; the imported articles themselves provided an extensive supplement to the older body of native implements, and the new forms among them exercised a profound influence on the local industry. Certain types of trap axes were affected by the flint forms, and new axes were made of native rocks with the flint axes as models. The same is true of knives of slate; long arrowheads of slate with serrated edges are imitations of a known megalithic form, as are also the leaf-shaped or heart-shaped arrowheads of slate. The straight two-edged slate knives are often absolute copies of flint daggers. The new forms made their way in and mingled with the older native forms in a process of gradual assimilation, though the megalithic culture never actually became dominant in the northern area.[2]

---

[1] Gustaf Hallström, 'En importvara til Västerbotten för 4000 år sedan', *Västerbottens Läns Hembygdsförenings Årsbok*, 1924–5.

[2] Finland was, practically speaking, unaffected by importation of flint from southern Scandinavia; altogether ten finds of such flint are known, all from south-western Finland: see Ailio, *Die steinzeitlichen Wohnplatzfunde*, p. 68. But large quantities of Russian flint are found as the material for arrowheads and scrapers. This is only one of the indications that the Finnish stone age had its most important connexions towards the east.

These influences from the megalithic culture first made the people of northern Scandinavia acquainted with the subsistence provided by domestic animals and the cultivation of corn. But, of course, these influences operated with greatly varying force in the nearer and more distant tracts of the peninsula. In the south-east of Norway there was a continuous influx of mega-lithic forms from the beginning of the later stone age, and it grew in volume during the whole of that period. It would be possible to show in detail how the latest forms advanced farthest forward, as the settlements grew more extensive; it is the latest type, the thick-butted axe, which penetrates farthest up the dales. In the east of Norway we find, in the later stone age, a material culture which seems to be thoroughly permeated by influences from the megalithic civilization; the same impression is given by the Swedish districts which lay in closest contact with megalithic culture. Here we have the form of culture which is well named submegalithic; it is strongly affected by megalithic civilization, but does not become identical with it, and in particular lacks the great stone graves which were the most conspicuous expression of communal life and belief among the megalithic people.

The submegalithic culture has been brilliantly and fully illumined by the excavation of the village which had been built on logs in Dagsmosse near Alvastra in Östergötland.[1] This village had been a quite extensive structure built on a platform of tree-trunks. The site in a soft inaccessible bog must have been chosen for ease of defence. There were probably approaches from the shore leading to narrow bridges. On the platform there were rough fire-places of stone and traces of huts built of raised piles. The list of articles found there is quite ordinary: axes of trap of the thick-butted type, perforated double-edged axes, scrapers and other small objects of flint, a chisel of harts-horn, pins of bone, &c. The types of the axes found demon-strate clearly a connexion with the neighbouring megalithic district in Västergötland, and a bead of amber shaped like a megalithic double-edged axe undoubtedly came from the same direction. It is therefore not at all surprising that excavation also produced evidence of domestic animals and the cultivation

---

[1] O. Frödin, *En svensk pålbyggnad från stenåldern* (Fornvännen, Stock-holm, 1910), p. 29 f.

of corn. Among the remains of meals bones of wild animals were found, including, as usual, bones of the elk, hart, roe, and bear; but there were also bones of pigs, goats, sheep, dogs, and possibly of oxen. Of vegetable foods hazel-nuts were found in quantity, and there were also grains of barley and wild apples. The grains are six-lined barley, the identical variety cultivated by the pile-dwellers in central Europe and still known in modern times among the Lapps of northern Scandinavia. Of apples were found both the small (generally wild) variety and another larger sort, which was possibly a cultivated variety. All this points to megalithic influence, while the pottery, on the other hand, is the same as in the eastern Swedish dwelling-sites.

For typical representation of the Arctic stone age in East Sweden we must look to the dwelling-sites at Säter near Bråviken in Östergötland and at Åloppe and Mjölkbo in Uppland.[1] To the same group belong the dwelling-sites in Gotland, the most important being those at Hemmor, Gullrum, and Visby,[2] and also at Jätteböle in the Åland Islands.[3] Everywhere in these dwelling-sites we can trace the life of a hunting people, and the remains of meals consist almost entirely of bones of wild animals, birds, and fish. Those at Åloppe may be named in illustration: the greater part of the bones there were of seal, wild boar, and elk; in smaller numbers bear, fox, martin, and others, as well as the dog as the only domestic animal. Of birds there were white-tailed eagle, black grouse, swans, and ducks. There were also quantities of fish bones. It is a rare discovery to find, as at Åloppe, traces of small round huts; they were made of timber placed upright and only 3 or 4 metres in diameter, and yet they had a fire-place and a floor strewn with sand or covered with spruce-needles.[4] As a rule these frail dwellings have disappeared without leaving a trace; only deposits of refuse beside the former shore-lines mark the places where hunting people had their resort.

---

[1] Oscar Almgren, *Uppländska Stenåldersboplatser* (Fornvännen, Stockholm, 1906), p. 1 and p. 101.

[2] Nils Lithberg, *Gotlands Stenålder* (Stockholm, 1914), p. 60.

[3] Björn Cederhvarf, 'Neolitiska Lerfigurer från Åland', *Finska Fornminnesföreningens Tidskrift*, xxvi (Helsingfors, 1912).

[4] Sune Lindqvist, *En uppländsk gårdsanläggning från stenåldern* (Fornvännen, Stockholm, 1916), p. 164; summary in German, p. 250. Cf. Montelius, *Kulturgeschichte Schwedens* (Leipzig, 1906), p. 15.

In Norway conditions differed from those on the low-lying shores of the Baltic. The whole of the southern and western coasts of Norway are precipitous cliffs, where the stone-age people could find shelter in natural caves and under overhanging rocks.[1] It is characteristic of the oldest period, the time of flint-places, that no dwelling-sites in caves are known from then. It was first in the Nøstvet period that the age of cave-dwellers began in Norway, as has been mentioned in the account of the find at Viste (p. 34). We know of a few other cave-dwellings also from the same period, and during the later neolithic period it was apparently quite general for the people to make their dwellings in caves and under rocks: they are found in countless numbers along the whole coast of Norway. As a typical example of a hunting station Ruskenesset may be specified, a short distance south of Bergen.[2] Habitation there dates from the latest phase of the stone age, or perhaps more accurately from the transition to the bronze age, contemporary with the stone cists in the south of Scandinavia. The dating is fixed beyond all doubt by the flint daggers, by certain forms of ornament and bone pins, and most of all by pieces of bronze which were found in the refuse heap below the cave. There was an extensive deposit of refuse consisting of ashes and the remains of meals; but the people lived in the place for only a certain part of the year, spring and early summer, to hunt hart and seal. They had their permanent dwelling-site elsewhere. Hunting and fishing were not by any means the only occupations of this people; bones of domestic animals were found, and there were impressions of barley on the earthenware. These new means of subsistence were, of course, due to contact with the higher megalithic culture; but at the same time ancient types too were found, such as harpoons of various forms and simple hooks without barbs. Other hooks were of later, more developed form with barbs; and there also slate points were found, simple adzes of hard rock,

---

[1] A comprehensive summary of the cave-finds is given by Shetelig in *Primitive Tider i Norge*, pp. 183 ff. In Sweden cave-finds from the stone age are known only from Stora Karlsö in Gotland; see Bror Schnittger, *Grottan Stora Förvar*, i (Stockholm, 1913), Kungl. Vitterhets Historia och Antikvitets Akademien.

[2] August Brinkman and Haakon Shetelig, *Ruskenesset*, Norske Oldfund iii (Kristiania, 1920).

arrowheads of quartz and flint, firestones of flint, and many other articles.[1]

Here we have a vivid picture of a curiously mixed civilization, which was characteristic of the last phase of the stone age in western Norway. It is a culture which had gradually assimilated such important elements as the care of cattle and agriculture, and it had adopted tools and weapons which were in many respects more highly developed. Such complex articles as fire-kindling devices made of flint and pyrites belonging originally to the Danish megalithic culture are significant; they are also known from the dwelling on logs at Alvastra and from other Swedish dwelling-sites.[2] It is equally significant that the hunters on Ruskenesset knew of bronze, which also appears in contemporary megalithic graves. But by the side of these cultural loans we find the true forms of the Arctic area, and in the equipment for hunting and fishing forms are preserved which belong to the most ancient hunting culture.

This strongly conservative tendency of the primitive northern stone age moreover extends far beyond the stone age itself. On the coast of Finmark Lappish dwelling-sites have been excavated which date from the Viking age, but they have a culture which in its implements still makes bone the most important material, and they have a series of forms surviving from the stone age, harpoons of ancient form, hooks of the same sorts that we know from Ruskenesset.[3] Elements of the Norwegian stone age were thus present among the Lapps by the Arctic Ocean, surviving even into historical times, while other features of this find show contact with the Norse iron culture of the migration period (the fifth and sixth centuries A.D.) and with the later east-European iron culture. But even among the Norse population hunting and fishing were often carried on with the primitive methods

---

[1] This aspect of stone-age life in Norway is even better illustrated by a recent excavation described by Johs. Bøe, 'Boplassen i Skipshelleren', *Bergens Museums Skrifter*, no. 17 (Bergen, 1934).

[2] Georg F. L. Sarauw, 'Le Feu et son emploi dans le Nord de l'Europe aux temps préhistoriques et protohistoriques', *Annales du XXe Congrès archéo-logique et historique de Belgique* (Gand, 1907), tome i, p. 196; Shetelig, 'Pierres à feu néolithiques de la Norvège', *Bergens Museums Årbok*, 106, no. 9; Frödin (Fornvännen, 1910), p. 59, Fig. 55.

[3] O. Solberg, 'Eisenzeitfunde aus Ostfinmarken', *Videnskaps-Selskapets Skrifter*, ii, Hist.-filos. klasse, 1909, no. 7; id., 'Ein neuer eisenzeitlicher Fund aus Ostfinmarken', *Prähistorische Zeitschrift*, iii, 1911.

and implements of antiquity, right down to the most recent times;[1] there is an account from Rogaland in the eighteenth century of a barbarous method of securing sea-birds which may well have originated in the stone age.[2] In Skogsvåg quite near Bergen, whales were shot with bow and arrow only a generation ago,[3] and there are accounts from Møre of a most primitive form of seal-hunting, practised within memory of persons now living: the seal was chased towards land by throwing stones and clubbed on the shore. Interesting accounts of seal-hunting have also been collected in Gotland,[4] where the seal was caught in a drag-net and then clubbed. These are only a few scattered examples. Such old forms of hunting are usually dependent upon local conditions; but for precisely that reason they may also rest upon traditions of high antiquity. There is another practice too, which, though insignificant in itself, gives us a further glimpse of the tenacious survival of small devices that are useful in daily life: the neolithic hunters of Ruskenesset used to cover the coals of the fire with green bracken, so that the fire should not die out completely, and the same is still done to-day by the men who pass their lives in the great forests of Norway.

It is natural that the life of the people in these northern lands should take its character from the natural conditions, which have remained unchanged in many respects throughout the ages. The caves along the coast were inhabited by hunters and fishers from the stone age right down to historic times. In the mountain country of the Hardanger highlands hunters made the reindeer their quarry, and in the ancient dwelling-sites there we find arrowheads of slate, flint scrapers, iron arrowheads from Viking times, and also pieces belonging to much later times. The means of subsistence remained unchanged, because it was dependent on unchanging natural conditions. In this connexion the question has recently been raised as to whether the northern

[1] Shetelig, *Préhistoire de la Norvège* (Oslo, 1926), p. 39 f., Instituttet for Sammenlignende Kulturforskning, Serie A, v.

[2] The wings of young sea-gulls were cut at the root so that they could not fly, and they were killed in the autumn to be salted for the winter. This is related by Amtmann De Fine in 1745, and is cited here from A. W. Brøgger.

[3] J. Brunchorst, 'Hvalfangst med bue og pil', *Naturen* (Bergen, 1899), p. 138 f.

[4] Nils Lithberg, *Gotlands Stenålder* (Stockholm, 1914), p. 118 f.

Scandinavian stone age with the forms of its material culture persisted for any length of time after the superior stone-age civilization in Denmark, western Europe, and elsewhere had come to an end. We shall return to this question when considering problems concerning the bronze age in the north of Scandinavia and in Finland, but we may say here and now that the forms of the Arctic stone age are for the most part limited in time to a period which must be contemporary with the megalithic age. The influences from both the megalithic culture and the battle-axe culture which can be seen so clearly in the stone work and pottery of the north-Scandinavian stone age must obviously have been exerted when these cultures were in full vigour, that is, during the flowering of neolithic culture in the south of Scandinavia. This conclusion is supported by geological researches. For example, in Uppland along the coast of the Baltic the shore-line of kitchen-midden times now lies about 64 metres above the present level of the sea; the dwelling-sites of the later stone age at Åloppe lie on an old shore-line from 30 to 40 metres above the sea, while the finds of the bronze age give evidence of a continued and later elevation of the land.

In Finland closely corresponding conditions have been observed.[1] The latest of the stone-age dwelling-sites lie in large numbers on former shore-lines, for the most part about 40 metres above the present level of the sea, and they must be contemporary with the stone cists of the megalithic culture. In the stretch of land which lies below this line practically no stone-age finds occur; a few rough perforated axes are known, a certain number of rude adzes and arrowheads of quartzite. On the whole, the richly diversified body of stone articles and the pottery which distinguish the stone-age culture in Finland is never found at a lower level; there are now extensive districts without a single find from the stone age. But it is precisely in such districts that the great majority of the bronze-age graves occur, both along the Gulf of Finland and the Gulf of Bothnia, nearer the coast than any dwelling-station of the stone age. One receives an impression of a somewhat abrupt ending of the neolithic culture with its many-sided and experienced technique

---

[1] Aarne Europaeus, 'Stenålderskeramik från kustboplatser i Finland', *Finske Fornminnesföreningens Tidskrift*, xxxvi (Helsingfors, 1927), p. 77.

in the choice and treatment of stone, and its characteristic ceramic art.

In Norway, too, development has proceeded in a way which is essentially the same. What we have called the Arctic stone age is a culture which during a definite period is in contact with the megalithic and battle-axe cultures, and this stone age is succeeded during the bronze age by other forms of material civilization. As we shall see later, Norway, like Finland, and to some extent Sweden, has a very poor bronze age, and it is an age of which there is in many particulars very little evidence in the north of Scandinavia. Nevertheless we will continue to apply the term 'bronze age' from the time when the types and monuments of the new period appear within the domain of the Arctic stone age. In recent years a very lively discussion of this question has arisen in Scandinavian archaeological literature;[1] but the dispute has in fact been more concerned with the name than with the reality. No archaeologist has ever denied that materials such as stone, bone, horn, and wood were still used during the bronze age, as they have been used at all times since then. There are certain forms in stone which we know positively belong to the bronze age: late flint daggers which sometimes imitate the form of bronze daggers, battle-axes of porphyry, arrowheads of flint and quartzite, heavy simple working axes with a hole for the haft. But we know just as certainly that the corpus of articles as a whole which have been found on stone-age dwelling-sites belong to the neolithic period, that these forms are in fact older than the period which we designate the bronze age. This holds good of all the phenomena which have been described here in the account of the Scandinavian stone age.

It was a discovery of fundamental importance to archaeological research when Scandinavian archaeologists first worked out the classic system which distinguishes the phases of cultural history of ancient northern Europe. There may, of course, be ground for dispute as to what is the best choice of names; but the names 'stone age', 'bronze age', and 'iron age' give expression in the most pregnant form to the great steps of cultural progress in the ancient world, and the archaeologists themselves

---

[1] See p. 141, footnote.

have always been the first to insist on a correct understanding of them. Bronze was still used after iron was discovered, just as stone was still used in the bronze age. We now speak also of a bone age, because there was a time when bone was the principal material used, and flint had only a secondary part in the material culture. This conception of a bone age should surely not be confused by bone being also used for arrowheads in the late iron age. We have ventured to make these general comments in order that it may be clear that in this account we use the name 'stone age' of the oldest times when the use of metals was unknown, or, in the later stone age, copper and bronze were so rarely obtainable that they could have no importance in the material culture worthy of mention.

We have finally to notice a most essential feature which distinguishes the Arctic stone age from the following period which we call the bronze age. The stone-age people of northern Scandinavia did not know the monumental forms of graves, the barrows and cairns which are so richly represented in the bronze age, and in general they did not know any sort of careful construction and furnishing of graves. Consequently the graves of the stone age can seldom be found; they were so simple that as a rule they have disappeared in the earth without leaving a trace. The most frequent vestiges of burial are found in the refuse deposits on the dwelling-sites, where scattered human bones are very commonly found and they must come from graves that have been disturbed. These graves in the dwelling-sites have already been described in the account of the Danish kitchen middens, and they still appear during the whole of the stone age in the north of Scandinavia.

As examples of undisturbed graves in a dwelling-site of the last phase of the stone age, those at Ruskenesset near Bergen may be mentioned. There three old persons were buried on the northern edge of the dwelling-sites, and in the grave a small, simple dagger of flint was found which belonged to one of the skeletons. In the layer of refuse on the dwelling-place was also found the grave of a child and fragmentary remains of the skeleton of a child five or six years old, which lay undisturbed and without doubt had been buried there when the place was inhabited in the stone age. Another example, which has been exhaustively studied, is a find in a stone-age dwelling-site at

Visby in Gotland. In the illustration, Fig. 4, the layer of stone-age refuse is shown in black, and we see three graves within a small space. On the left we have a skeleton lying with the head to the north-east; around the hips a large number of pierced seal-teeth were found. To the right in the illustration were two skeletons which lay side by side close together, the heads turned to the north; one of them was a very young man who had also worn pierced seal-teeth on his belt, and the other was an older man who had with him a stone axe pierced with a hole for the haft.[1] This form of burial in the dwelling-site itself, the simplest form possible, was clearly very general.

But we have also evidences which indicate that at the same time simple burials were made in the ground outside the dwelling-site. I am referring now to a find from the south-west coast of Norway.[2] The grave was made on the south side of a great stone standing fast in the ground; the grave had a basic layer of fine, light-grey sand which had possibly been burnt, and on it was a layer of partly burnt stone. In this grave there lay close together a little axe of trap, three small flint axes, and a spoon-shaped flint scraper; in the earth around these articles were small fragments of burned wood and possibly some slight remnants of bone. The skeleton had practically disappeared, as it always did in Norway when the body lay in the earth unprotected. A series of other finds, though less completely understood, give indication that certain definite forms had been established in graves. It appears that the graves often lay near a great stone that was fast in the ground, or near a cliff, and also that there was sometimes a simple frame of stone placed around the grave, or else it was covered with a layer of stone or a small cairn, and lastly, that a fire was often lit in or beside the grave.[3]

It is quite possible that graves of this kind are primarily due to impulses from the battle-axe culture, where we have seen that the leading type was the single grave, often surrounded by a frame of stones or a heap of stones, and covered by a low

[1] O. V. Wennersten, *Boplats från Stenåldern i Visby* (Fornvännen, Stockholm, 1909), p. 198.

[2] Helge Gjessing, 'En Stenaldersgrav paa Gaarden Vestre Hauge, Vanse', *Oldtiden*, ix (Oslo, 1922), p. 107.

[3] Helge Gjessing, *Rogalands Stenalder* (Stavanger, 1920), p. 76; Shetelig, *Primitive Tider i Norge* (Bergen, 1922), p. 334.

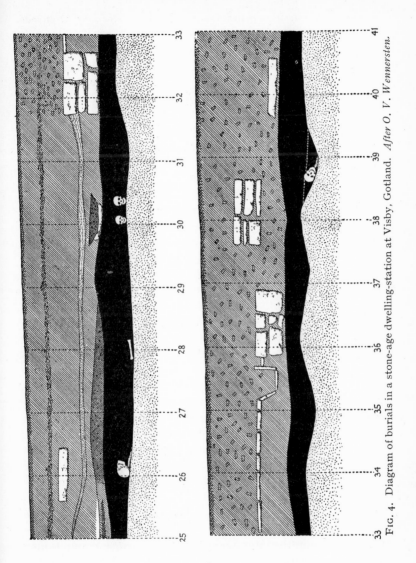

Fig. 4. Diagram of burials in a stone-age dwelling-station at Visby, Gotland. *After O. V. Wennersten.*

grave-mound. In the primitive stone age of Norway, then, we may establish contact at this point with the higher civilization which came in from the south, while no corresponding burial custom has yet been discovered in the Arctic civilization of Sweden or Finland. In Finland as a whole graves from the stone age are practically unknown.

From the nature of the graves it is evident that we can learn very little from skeletons of the dwelling-site culture in Scandinavia and Finland, and we have therefore no chance of identifying anthropologically the race to which this culture belonged. The question of race in the Arctic stone age is one of the most obscure problems in Scandinavian archaeology, but it is also one that has been especially attractive to popular interest. We cannot traverse here all the differing theories that have been advanced on purely theoretical bases; none of them actually arrive at any convincing conclusion. It must suffice to mention a few of the most weighty opinions. The conditions are least complicated in Finland, since only two cultural elements are encountered there, the battle-axe culture which represents an immigration from the south, and on the other side a dwelling-site culture which has its roots in the country itself as far back as habitation can be traced, and in its development stands in closest relation to the east-European stone age. It is now the unanimous opinion among Finnish archaeologists that this dwelling-site culture was the possession of the earliest Finno-Ugrian people, the race which constitutes the principal element of the present population of Finland.[1]

On the Scandinavian peninsula a corresponding dual origin of the population has long been an accepted hypothesis. Usually an original people of short-skulled type has been assumed as surviving from the kitchen-midden period, as well as a later immigration of megalithic people, who have been taken to be the originals of the long-skulled people which we know as the principal type in the later Norwegian and Swedish populations.[2] The latter race was also taken to be the ancestral type of the

[1] Aarne Europaeus, 'Finland: Steinzeit' in Ebert's *Reallexikon der Vorgeschichte*, iii. 331.

[2] O. Montelius, 'Über die Einwanderung unserer Vorfahren in den Norden', *Archiv für Anthropologie*, xvii. 151; Andr. M. Hansen, *Landnåm i Norge* (Kristiania, 1904); Carl M. Fürst, 'Zur Kraniologie der schwedischen Steinzeit', *Kgl. Svenska Vetenskaps-Akademiens Handlingar*, vol. xlix, no. 2, 1912.

Germans in the north. Later the theory was also produced that a third race appears in the Arctic stone age of the north, which may have come in from Finland to the eastern Swedish provinces, Jämtland and Ångermanland, and from there to the north of Norway.[1]

The first comprehensive treatment of the whole problem of the races in the north we owe to the distinguished German archaeologist Kossinna.[2] In his brilliant and clear manner of reasoning he has traced lines from the palaeolithic culture to the 'bone age' in the north and around the Baltic, and he believes also that this culture is directly continued in the kitchen middens, the Nøstvet culture, and the culture of the Scandinavian dwelling-sites in the later stone age. To the whole of this series he assigns an original population of short-skulled type, which he believes to be the stock of the Ugro-Finnish peoples. This stock spread out to the east, to Finland and the Baltic provinces, partly, perhaps, under pressure from a new people who invaded the north, a people which might reasonably enough be identified with the long-skulled neolithic type, the parent stock of the 'Indo-Germans'.

These theories illustrate clearly enough how easy it is to build up hypotheses about the races of the stone age without any confirmatory anthropological material. For on the anthropological side it is held that the few fragments of bones which are preserved from the Maglemose period in Denmark show a close correspondence with the race from Cro-Magnon, and therefore belong to a long-skulled type,[3] and this discovery has led to a complete reformation of the earlier theories. The long-skulled Germanic type is now to be regarded as the oldest, and the brachycephalic elements are said to have come in later with the megalithic culture and the battle-axe people.[4] This is

[1] A. W. Brøgger, *Den arktiske Stenalder i Norge* (Kristiania, 1909).

[2] Gustaf Kossinna, 'Der Ursprung der Urfinnen und Urindogermanen, und ihre Ausbreitung nach dem Osten', *Mannus-Bibliothek*, i, 1909.

[3] H. A. Nielsen, 'Fund i Sværdborg og Mullerup Moser af Skeletdele af Mennesker fra den ældste Stenalder', *Aarb. f. nord. Oldk.* (København, 1921), p. 205 f.

[4] O. Montelius, 'De mandelformiga Flintverktygens Ålder', *Antikv. Tidskrift för Sverige*, xx (Stockholm, 1919), no. 6; id., 'Paleolithic Implements', *The Antiquaries Journal*, i (London, 1921); Sune Lindqvist, *Nordens Benålder och en Teori om dess Stenåldersraser* (Rig, Stockholm, 1918), p. 65. The latest orientation in this problem is given by Gunnar Ekholm, *De arkeologisk-*

a theory which has been worked out with considerable force of logic, but its whole basis is unsound, in that the classification of the bones from Sværdborg is not certain. We have already mentioned (p. 48) that their classification is highly controversial.

The various theories are, and will be, weakly grounded as long as we have no usable skeletons of stone-age people in northern Scandinavia. The theories suffer little from this weakness, it is true, since they all start from the modern population of the Scandinavian peninsula, and from this try to reconstruct the anthropology of the stone age. It should be observed especially that the racial problem in the later stone age admits of being summed up in a single formula just as little as at the present day. Where we have available material, as in the megalithic graves in Denmark, this material presents a very complex picture. Accessions of new population were probably continual. Cultural impulses and trading connexions result in intercourse between individuals of different peoples; in the mixture of races in the stone age we have not only actual immigration to take account of, but also infiltration of separate individuals or of small groups, in addition to the slave trade which flourished everywhere in ancient times, and perhaps most important of all in this connexion, the rape and purchase of women. These are all factors which affect anthropological conditions very slowly, but they have been in operation through long ages, and they are strong enough to produce definite variations in the character of the whole population. It may be added here that we should be very cautious about using the anthropological conditions of the present day as a gauge of the races of Scandinavia in the stone age.

There is no doubt that the discussion about the races of the north has suffered from being constantly involved in the problem of the original home of the Germanic people. We do not actually know whether the later Germanic speech was at all periods proper to one particular race, and we have no right to transfer our conceptions of historic nations to the

etnologiska Problemen i Östersjöområdet (Ymer, 1923), p. 51; id., De Ostbaltiska Nationalitetsförhållandena i förhistorisk tid (Rig, Stockholm, 1925); A. M. Tallgren, De förhistoriska Nationalitetsförhållandene i Nordöstra Europa (Rig, Stockholm, 1923), p. 127.

distant and primitive time which we are considering here. We shall therefore not touch upon the many hypotheses concerning the original home of the Germans which have been advanced in recent years.[1] We shall not go farther than to say that our principal groups in the Norse stone age in all probability represent different peoples of more or less different character; there are the older forms of culture, belonging to the Maglemose people and the kitchen-midden people, the Nøstvet culture in Norway, the Suomusjärvi culture in Finland, with the accompanying dwelling-site culture of the Arctic stone age extending over the whole of northern Scandinavia; and sharply distinguished from these primitive hunting peoples are the already more civilized peoples whom we know from the megalithic graves and the battle-axe culture. We have to reckon with the certainty that all these elements enter into the formation of the later Scandinavian people, both in the Germanic North and in Ugrian Finland; but just as certainly, too, later times brought accessions of new racial stocks. A very mixed origin is common to all modern nations in Europe.

[1] Gustaf Kossinna, *Die deutsche Vorgeschichte, eine hervorragend nationale Wissenschaft* (Würzburg, 1915). The author has developed with great ability a theory that the original home of the Germans was in the north, from where successive migrations subsequently spread out over large areas of Europe. The same theory has been advanced by Nils Åberg in *Das nordische Kulturgebiet in Mitteleuropa während der jüngeren Steinzeit* (Uppsala, 1918), an elaborate presentation with a comprehensive survey of the whole archaeological material. We have already mentioned (p. 72) an opposite view suggested as a possibility by Sophus Müller in 1913 and later approved by good authorities like C. A. Nordman and O. Rydbeck, which was that the north was Germanized by the invasion of the battle-axe people. The reasoning resembles the chain of ideas which was passing about the same time in the mind of Sigmund Feist: see his *Kultur, Ausbreitung und Herkunft der Germanen* (Berlin, 1913), p. 480 f. Feist believes that the peculiar developments of Germanic speech are to be explained by a prehistoric Germanizing of the northern people who had originally spoken a different language. He thinks this Germanizing of the north was very probably connected with the great expansion of the Celts in the last millennium before Christ. This theory is one of the most attractive that has been produced. It must be observed, however, that Feist speaks of the older Scandinavian people as an unmixed ancient people; as we have seen, neolithic Scandinavia already exhibits an advanced blending of peoples.

VII

THE ART OF THE ARCTIC STONE AGE

ONE of the most distinctive elements of the north-Scandinavian stone age is its naturalistic art, which is wholly foreign to the megalithic and battle-axe cultures. It is an art almost exclusively devoted to the representation of animals, whether in carvings on a large scale in solid rock, as in coloured figures on sheer cliffs, or in smaller sizes, as in images and drawings on various articles of bone, wood, and stone. This art is nearly related in kind to that which flourished among the people of the ice age in western Europe, and parallels are known among many primitive peoples in later times and in various parts of the world. It is the art of the hunting peoples, and it belongs to a definite stage in human development, to certain definite conditions of life and natural surroundings. There is no productive soil for this art among peoples who live by grazing and tilling the earth, and it is therefore not found among the neolithic people, though they possessed a higher culture; but it is revealed in unusual richness within the region of the Arctic stone age in Norway and Sweden. This art of the Scandinavian stone age provides an excellent gauge of the culture of the northern hunting people.

Not many of such works of art are at present known to exist; in Norway twenty-three rock-carvings (*gravures sur roches*) and eight rock-paintings have so far been found; in Sweden three carvings and three paintings; in Finland two paintings. But new examples are continually being found,[1] and we are clearly only at the beginning of a comprehensive survey of these monuments. It is not easy to find these stone-age carvings, which very often lie in out-of-the-way isolated places far from roads and habitation; and they are not easy to recognize. We can say with confidence that the few which we now know are only a small proportion of those which have survived from the stone age in Scandinavia.

---

[1] Our present knowledge of these monuments is excellently summarized by Johs. Bøe, *Stenalderens naturalistiske kunst*, Nordisk Kultur, xxvii (Stockholm, 1931), and by A. W. Brøgger, *Die arktischen Felsenzeichnungen und Malereien in Norwegen*, (I.P.E.K., 1931). Both with bibliography.

The carvings are found on flat cliff-faces, usually rather steep or quite vertical, and for the most part they consist of animal figures drawn in outline with incised lines. The lines are now shallow and have a rounded cross-section, and must have been produced by chipping with a sharp stone, the process known as 'pecking' (*piquetage*), which was also used in the production of stone-age implements. Occasionally the lines have been ground into the surface. Only once has a carving been found which had clearly been cut in the cliff with a sharp implement, namely, the carving at Hell; but there the cliff is of rather soft clay slate. The paintings are laid on the cliff in red or reddish colour, and they are always depicted in mere outline, like the carvings. In one instance a trace of colouring has been found in the lines of a carving, and it is possible that many of the carvings were originally thrown into relief by means of colour.

The animals which are depicted in these carvings belong as a rule to the hart kind, namely, the hart itself, the elk, and the reindeer; other subjects are sea-birds with long necks, fish (halibut, whale), and bears. Sometimes the animals are represented in full natural size, or even larger; but many are smaller, and we often find carvings of comparatively small figures. The quality of the pictures also varies; the best show a lively appreciation of form, a direct and striking naturalism which could not be conceived more perfect, as long as technique is limited to the barest outlines; others again, especially where the figures are small, are stiff and formal, without any trace of lively observation. Here we have obviously to distinguish different groups of stone-age carvings.

As has often been noticed, the best of the stone-age pictures in Scandinavia are those which resemble most closely the naturalistic art of the ice age, both in a general way in their developed, yet primitive, naturalism, and in definite details.[1] The classic example of such large animal pictures is provided by the well-known carving by the stream Bøla near Trondhjemsfjord. The stream falls into Snåsen Lake through continuous rapids and cataracts, and among these in one place are three small foaming fosses tumbling over a mountain ledge 3 metres high. The side of the ledge is nearly vertical, and on it can be

---

[1] This relation has been strongly emphasized by Dr. G. Hallström, the best authority on the Scandinavian carvings.

seen from some distance away an image of a reindeer standing
in an exquisite natural setting. The rock is a micaceous schist
with a smooth even surface; this is eminently suitable for carving, but there is only the one figure to be found here, a bull
reindeer depicted in natural size, 1·80 metres long and 1·36
metres high at the hindquarters. The lines are strongly drawn,
about 2 cm. wide and about 1 cm. deep where they are least
corroded. The reindeer is represented in a natural horizontal
position, as if it were going down along the ledge. The back
part is covered by the foss during most of the year.

Less striking, but also a remarkable piece of naturalistic art,
is the carving at Hell in Stjørdalen. About 30 metres above the
sea there is a sheer cliff which bears life-size representations of
two full-grown reindeer. They stand one close behind the other,
the one in front a little lower, as if it were on its way down the
mountain-side. The position of the head in relation to the neck
is very characteristic. But the lines here are cut on a slaty
rock with a rather uneven surface, so that it would not be easy
to make the drawing as free and graceful as we see it in the
carving at Bøla. As far as possible the artist at Hell has followed
the strata of the slate and has adopted the natural rifts in the
face of the mountain as elements in his work of art. A little
lower on the side of the mountain two smaller animals are to be
seen, also very clearly and skilfully portrayed. In all the
animals of this group of carvings we encounter a feature of great
interest, a system of triangles which are cut within the animal
figure. There is no ground for supposing that this was intended
to represent harness, and it is therefore no proof that reindeer
were tamed in Norway in the stone age. They are conventional groups of lines placed within the figure: such patterns
are known also from French palaeolithic drawings, which
reproduce remarkably closely, sometimes, motives in the
carving at Hell—for example, in the figure of a horse in the
cave Les Combarelles, and in an ibex at La Mouthe.[1] Even
apart from the animal figures geometrical designs are found at
Hell, sometimes unintelligibly chaotic lines, but also clear and

---

[1] Capitan and Breuil, 'La Grotte des Combarelles', *Revue de l'École d'Anthropologie de Paris*, 1902, i, Supplément; id., 'Les Figures peintes à l'époque
paléolithique sur le parois de la grotte de Font-de-Gaume' (Dordogne), ibid.,
1902, vii.

ornamental patterns, in particular a series of narrow rhomboid lozenges filled with close lines (see Fig. 5).

FIG. 5.   Geometric pattern from rock-carving at Skjomen.
After Gutorm Gjessing.

Passing from Trondhjemsfjord up Stjørdal where the railway now runs, we come to the nearest rock-carving on the Swedish side of the boundary, near Landsverk in Jämtland. The carving is found on a headland on the north-western side of Ånn Lake; two animals are depicted, one following the other, quite close to the shore, as if they were moving along the water's edge. The beast in front is an elk, admirably drawn and true to life, in about natural size or a little smaller; it is 1·65 metres long. The beast behind must be a bear, though the similarity is not immediately striking, whereas the elk is excellently characterized.[1]

In the same group as these carvings should be mentioned a painting of an elk near Forberg in Lista, on the south-west coast of Norway. It is a cow elk of about natural size, 2·20

[1] Dr. Hallström states that he once showed a picture of the whole of these carvings to a Lapp, who identified the animals without hesitation as an elk and a bear. Is it conceivable that the bear is consciously caricatured? See Hallström, *Fornvännen*, 1907, p. 186.

metres long and 1·5 metres high, painted with reddish pigment on a slightly overhanging cliff about 13 metres high, rising straight up out of the sea. The mountain hangs over above, so that the painting is sheltered from rain; it is this same fortunate circumstance that has preserved the few other stone-age paintings known in Scandinavia, though there must have been many others which stood unprotected from the northern climate and have long since disappeared without leaving a trace. The elk at Forberg is not among the best of the stone-age pictures, but it is nevertheless executed on the whole with skill and confidence. But at the hump on the shoulders—so characteristic of the elk—the artist apparently made a mistake: it can be seen that this detail was first drawn a little too far forward, and was afterwards corrected by drawing the line farther back with greater emphasis. A similar revision of unfinished work can often be seen in the art of the ice age in western Europe. The foreland at Forberg is an isolated, deserted place even to-day, as it has been for thousands of years. There is no soil for any sort of agriculture in this district; at best, a little hunting and fishing can be carried on from time to time. It is not strange that this painting was only discovered a few years ago.

A carving which, unlike this one, has long been known and is one of the most famous, is the one in Bardal near the village of Stenkjær on Trondhjemsfjord. On a sloping surface of bare rock, close to the buildings of a farm, stands a group of large elks. Unfortunately they are much worn, and perhaps they had also not been completed; at any rate there are various figures drawn in a sketchy fashion over and inside one another, in a manner frequently found in palaeolithic art too. The outlines are also confused by large and numerous carvings from the bronze age which were later cut over the whole mountain-side. Yet in spite of all this these pictures of elks are among the best that are known from the stone age: we perceive an exquisite feeling for nature in every line. At the bottom of the slope, which is inclined at an angle of thirty degrees, a pair of long-necked sea-birds were later discovered, drawn as if they were floating on a surface of water at the foot of the rock. They, too, are clearly to be counted among stone-age carvings, and at the time when they were engraved the water probably reached right up to where the birds are swimming. The same kind of sea-birds were also carved on a steep cliff not far from Bardal, at Hammer in the Beitstad district.

We now pass on to the most northerly memorials of stone-age art at present known in Europe.[1] As we turn up from the south we first meet with an extensive group of carvings on the island of Åmøy in Meløy parish. The island is wild and desolate, with high peaks, sheer precipices, and chasms. It is significant that the rock-carvings were discovered by a party that had gone out to look for eagles' nests. The approach to the carvings is rendered difficult by bogs and rocky screes. Immediately beside the headland Klubba the carvings can be seen stretched out on a smooth sloping cliff to an extent of some 100 metres. At least twenty figures can be made out, reindeer and elk and a single whale. They are life-size and are drawn with great skill.

Three Norwegian miles north of the Arctic circle stands another very important group of carvings at Fykanvatn, in-land from the head of Glomfjord and north of the great glacier Svartis. Fykanvatn is a lake which has an outlet through sheer waterfalls with a drop of 89 metres down into the fjord. A difficult, little-used path climbs up to the lake, but people rarely come here, as the inner part of Glomfjord possesses only a few scattered farms; and the impression of wild nature is therefore all the stronger in this lonely mountain world. On the left of the foss, as one leaves Fykanvatn, and behind it are large areas where the granite rock lies bare and open to the light. This is where the carvings are found, twenty-four figures in all, and all in natural or larger than natural size, all moreover among the best of the stone-age representations of animals; some, indeed, are of quite extraordinary artistic merit (Fig. 6). They are well characterized, so that there is no difficulty in identifying the kinds of animals represented. The reindeer completely dominate the group, and among them is found the largest of all the figures, a great reindeer nearly 4 metres long. There is also a reindeer calf which is among the most exquisite and most sympathetic pictures of animals that are known in the whole

[1] A complete survey of the carvings of northern Norway is provided by Gutorm Gjessing, *Arktiske helleristninger i Nord-Norge*, Instituttet for Sam-menlignende Kulturforskning, Serie B, xxi (Oslo, 1932) and ibid. xxx (1936); with a summary in German.

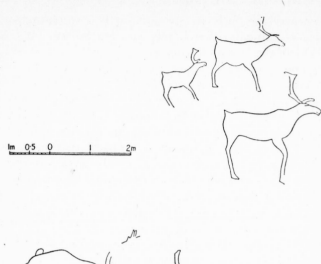

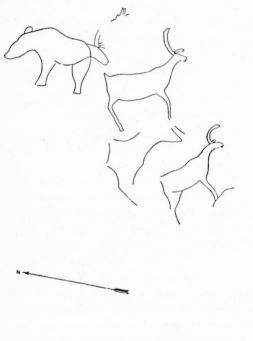

FIG. 6. Bear and reindeer from the rock-carving at Fykanvatn.
After Gutorm Gjessing.

range of primitive naturalistic art. Only one figure can be
certainly identified as an elk; but we also find here a rarity, a
representation of a bear, and, lastly, a large fish, almost 2
metres long; it is evidently a halibut. This last has a counterpart in the carving on Åmøy near Stavanger.

Just as remarkable as the pictures themselves is the technique
of the carving at Åmøy and Fykanvatn. The rock is granite,
with a smooth, worn, and even surface; on this the lines are not
hewn, but are ground into the stone, and they now appear as
white streaks from 1 to 2 cm. wide in the same plane as the
surrounding surface, or in some parts even a little raised, as the
grinding has protected them from decomposition. It is certain
enough that these carvings are genuine products of the stone
age. The same technique is shown in two other carvings farther
north, the reindeer by the Sag river in Sagfjord and the carvings
on Leiknes in Tysfjord. The carving near the Sag is a very fine
one: two reindeer of natural size, attractively drawn, both at
the same height, one following the other. They stand on a
steep cliff, directly above the river, so that it is difficult to get
a near view of them. These carvings, too, are set in magnificent
natural surroundings, with a splendid vista of snow-capped
mountains stretching away to the Swedish boundary. Stone-
age carvings can be traced still farther north, to Sletfjord in
Ofoten, to Leiknes in Tysfjord, and to Balsfjord. But we will
not enter into any further detailed description of the northern
carvings; it will suffice only to mention that on Leiknes traces
of red colouring can be seen in the lines ground into the
rock to form the figures, and it is possible that this combination of painting with carving once existed in others of the
pictures also.

Lastly is to be added a recently discovered rich and interesting set of carvings at Skjomen in Ofoten. Skjomen is a
narrow little fjord between high, steep mountains, and it is on
these that the carvings are seen, on a smooth mountain-cliff
below the farm Forselv. Here can be made out a whole series
of reindeer excellently portrayed, a whale, fish, and spaces filled
with geometrical patterns of rhomboid figures (Fig. 5), and
also new story-telling motives which have not hitherto been
found in Arctic carving. There are two boats, fishing-lines, and
even a fish biting on the line, and one of the reindeer has a fish

in its mouth. We shall return to this stylistic feature in connexion with certain of the carvings in Trondhjemsfjord.[1]

Now we turn back southwards to a smaller group of similar
carvings in the east of Norway.[2] Pictures such as those found
here had long been known in the northern part of the peninsula;
it came as a great surprise when a new set of carvings was
discovered at Ekeberg right in the city of Oslo. The group
includes six or seven animals, probably elks, though possibly
harts, all rather indistinct, and several visible only in the
brightest sunlight. Then there is the elk at Åskollen in Eiker,
near the city of Drammen, a carving which had been known
about 1860 and then was forgotten again; and, in 1930, a new
carving discovered in the garden of a suburban cottage in
Drammen, including extensive groups of elks, harts, whales,
fish, and one bird of exquisite design (Pl. 11).[3] At Gjeithus
in Modum is found a group of two elks which seem to be represented in the act of copulation, and near them a single figure of
an elk. The east Norwegian carvings are not to be ranked as high
artistically as the carvings of the north which have just been
reviewed; a quality has been lost, and something elusive, but
immediately striking, is lacking in the naturalistic conception
of the animal, as if the whole scale of the art had been reduced.
The elk on Åskollen is about natural size, well characterized
as an elk, but as a drawing it is unsuccessful. On Ekeberg and
Gjeithus the animals are small, less than half natural size, and
they also are well characterized. In the carving on Gjeithus
a new feature appears: inside the figures of the animals lines
are drawn which must presumably denote the inner organs of
the beasts. In this carving we also observe that each of the elks
has two ears, two front legs and two hind legs, while the reindeer at Bøla and elsewhere, like all the best stone-age representations, show a conventional profile with two legs and one
horn. Here, then, a more definite care appears in the drawing,
an effort to make everything distinct and clear, even details
which cannot be seen when the beast is alive. This is the first

---

[1] G. Gjessing, 'The Skjomen Carving', *Acta Archaeologica*, ii (København,
1931), p. 278.

[2] Eivind S. Engelstad, *Østnorske ristninger og malerier av den arktiske gruppe*,
Instituttet for Sammenlignende Kulturforskning, Serie B, xxvi (Oslo, 1934).

[3] E. S. Engelstad, 'Den nye arktiske helleristning i Drammen', *Universitets
Oldsaksamlings Årbok*, iv, 1930 (Oslo, 1932).

PLATE 11

a. Rock carving, Drammen. After Engelstad

b. Human figures in the rock-painting at Ovnen, Nissedal. After
Engelstad

step from the purely primitive, naturalistic art, the first stage
at which reasoning can be observed. But relationship with the
carvings already mentioned lies in no doubt, even though the
east-Norwegian carvings seem to be a somewhat later local
development, in which the drawing begins to lose the original
power which was the peculiar property of the naturalistic art
in its best form. Of the same character as these east-Norwegian
carvings are the elks at Evenhus near Trondhjemsfjord, a big
elk and a whale at Bogge in Romsdal, and a figure of an animal
at Vingen in Nordfjord. They are very impressive and well-
executed pictures, but they cannot be counted among the
greatest and finest examples of Norwegian stone-age art.

Finally, we have as the third group a number of carvings with
animal figures in wholly fixed conventional forms (Fig. 7). In
carvings of this group there is always a number of animal
figures close together and they are very small, drawn quite
without art, life, or anything to give them character, so that it
may often be difficult to see what sort of animal is intended.
Human figures also appear, mostly of men, but sometimes a
man and a woman together. Typical of this conventionalized
sort are the carvings at Bogge and Vingen,[1] the two last mentioned, though there is also a larger figure in each which is more
naturalistic in style. At Bogge especially one can see a deliberate
contrast of the two forms of art belonging to different periods,
and we may assume that the naturalistic pictures are older than
those which are strongly conventionalized. The carvings themselves unfortunately give no direct evidence of the chronological order.[2] The same schematic form is to be seen also in
the carving at Tennes in Balsfjord in the far north of Troms
county, and in the two Swedish carvings near Glösa in Jämtland
and at Nämnfors in Ångermanland, the latter presenting a rich
variety of pictures, of elks and other animals, birds, and fish
which must almost certainly be salmon; there are also human
figures, two among them in an erotic scene, and drawings of ships
of the same sort as in the well-known bronze-age rock-carvings.

[1] Johs. Bøe, 'Felszeichnungen im westlichen Norwegen', *Bergens Museums
Skrifter*, no. 15 (Bergen, 1932).
[2] The striking difference between the two styles was observed by the
first who studied these carvings: R. Ziegler, *Arkeologiske undersøgelser*, 1900,
Det kgl. Videnskabernes Selskabs Skrifter (Trondhjem, 1900). Cf. Hallström,
Fornvännen (Stockholm, 1909), p. 137.

Fig. 7. Red deer, part of rock-carving at Vingen. *After Bøe.*

At Nämnfors we thus no longer have stone-age art in its pure and original form. The animal forms of the naturalistic art meet and mingle with motives of bronze-age forms, motives of the two groups occurring side by side in the same carving. This is found also in the carvings at Sporanes in Telemark, at Skjomen, and at Evenhus, which has been mentioned above. The relation of the two styles must be assumed to be this: the stone-age art was still living when this northern region began to receive impulses from the bronze-age culture. The two forms of carving, so profoundly different in nature and origin, were able to meet and mingle at the transition between these two epochs of early Norwegian culture.[1]

It can be established in various ways that the naturalistic rock-carvings date from the stone age, and there is one monument in particular which affords decisive evidence, the rock-carvings at Bardal which have already been mentioned upon a preceding page. On an inclined surface of rock is found a group of large elks, two long-necked sea-birds, and rhomboid ornamental figures, the whole a very typical example of the primitive art of the stone age. But in the same place is found also a very extensive and typical rock-carving from the bronze age, a carving with numbers of figures which have become somewhat worn in the long passage of time, but in their origin go back to the latter end of the early bronze age. A large part of these carvings still exists with deep and clear lines, and it can be clearly seen that they cut across other weaker lines which formed the group of large elks mentioned earlier. Thus in this instance it is certain that the bronze-age carvings were made later, probably a very long time after the others.[2] All of the later carvings are cut as if the others did not exist; the elks

[1] A wholly different hypothesis has been put forward by Gunnar Ekholm, 'De skandinaviska hällristningarna och deres betydelse', *Ymer* (Stockholm, 1916), pp. 275 ff. and especially p. 305. Dr. Ekholm argues that the north-Scandinavian animal pictures were descended from the same origin as the bronze-age pictures, and that both groups developed as parallel phenomena. This theory does not carry conviction, since the two forms are essentially different and clearly belong to two widely separated stages of culture; generally speaking, there is nothing in the bronze-age art answering to the vivid naturalism of the northern portrayal of animals.

[2] We are here following Dr. Hallström's account. Th. Petersen (in 'Fra hvilken tid stammer de naturalistiske helleristninger?' *Naturen*, Bergen, 1922) comes to the conclusion that there is no great difference in age between the animal figures and the bronze-age carvings at Bardal.

must have been an ancient forgotten carving which was never noticed by the later carvers. The same relation is seen also at Åmøy near Stavanger: there a big fish is found drawn in outline, which must be reckoned among the carvings of the stone age; over this fish two ships are carved which belong to a very large rock-carving from the bronze age.

There is no longer any reason to doubt that the naturalistic animal pictures in Norway and Sweden belong essentially to the stone age and date from times earlier than the bronze age; but it would be just as important to find out how far back in time this stone-age art can be traced. Here the geological relation enlightens us in the same way as on the dwelling-sites. There are features which point to the carvings having originally been cut close to the shore or by the water-line, and when they are now found at a certain height above the sea, this height gives a geological date. In itself this position is obviously no proof that the carvings were not placed a long way from the sea in their own period; but we see that beside lakes and rivers, where the natural relation must have remained unchanged in the important features, the animals are found, more often than not, quite near the water. They are obviously drawn as if they were going to the water's edge, as if to drink, for example. We can reach the same conclusion indirectly when a group of carved figures stands at a constant height above the shore, even though there is no apparent reason why the carvings should not have been cut at the water's edge; the lowest points of the old carving must then represent the old shore-line. This is true of the extensive carvings at Vingen in Nordfjord, and they can be dated accordingly from the later stone age.

The last few years have brought us some vitally important contributions towards determining the age of the oldest carvings.[1] The most valuable of these is the carving by the river Sag which is found in a place now practically inaccessible, on a steep mountain-cliff, 48 or 49 metres above the sea. The only possible inference here is that this carving was executed from a boat at a time when the sea stood correspondingly higher than its present level. This gives us a date much farther back than the *tapes* subsidence, certainly as far back as the Magle-

[1] Gutorm Gjessing, *Arktiske helleristninger i Nord-Norge* (Oslo, 1932), pp. 44 and 71.

mose period or even anterior to that age. It is, moreover, a
striking fact that all the north-Norwegian carvings which are
executed by grinding the lines into the rock are at a higher
elevation than those which are cut in the cliff: they must therefore in all probability be the oldest. But the incised carvings
also extend up to the coast-line of the *tapes* subsidence, and
hence they date as far back as the period of the kitchen middens
and the Nøstvet culture. These indications are sufficient to
show that the carvings extend over a very long period of time,
from the bone age to the end of the stone age.

The only art comparable with the stone-age carvings of
Scandinavia, considered in all aspects as a primitive naturalistic
form of art, fully developed in its own kind, is the palaeolithic art of western Europe—and that only with the best of the
Scandinavian carvings. This is evident in the pictures as a
whole, their character and their quality, as it is evident in various
details which are common to the palaeolithic and the oldest
Scandinavian art. In groups of several figures it is seldom that
we can trace any intentional connexion between the individual
pictures. Yet there must be a connexion in some carvings in
which two reindeer or two elks are seen with one close behind
the other; and in the carving at Gjeithus it is thought that the
two elks are drawn in the act of copulation; both of these types
have their counterpart in palaeolithic art. But usually the
figures stand without any order or grouping. This is an art
which never conceives any scenes of actually dramatic content.
Hunting-scenes, for example, are never found in the stone-age
carvings, even though the artists must often have been on the
verge of this conception, since the pictures always represent
wild animals that were hunted. There is another link with
palaeolithic art in the geometrical designs which are found
combined with the pictures of animals. These are zigzag
motives, patterns of rhomboid lozenges, rows of triangles placed
side by side, and more irregular combinations of lines which
may at times be very difficult to distinguish. These patterns
can hardly be called ornamental; as a rule they are indistinct,
disorderly, and lack composition, as do these carvings in general.
One can almost believe that the geometrical motives are not
merely conventional, but are in some way connected with
the representation of the animals. The same is true of the

conventional groups of lines set into the animal figures, also found in French palaeolithic drawings, sometimes corresponding remarkably with certain of the Norwegian carvings.

It is very tempting to assume that the north-Scandinavian rock-carvings are a continuation of the palaeolithic art of western Europe: it seems impossible that art so similar both in general aspect and in details could be developed independently twice in the stone age of Europe.[1] But then an equally difficult problem appears, as to how such a relationship is to be explained. It is natural to look for connecting links with the early stone age of the north in the Maglemose civilization, which is a successor to the palaeolithic; but the difficulty is that here we find very few animal pictures. The classic specimen is an axe of hartshorn, found in the district around Ystad in Skåne, an axe which from its type undoubtedly belongs to the Maglemose group; it has been mentioned earlier (p. 27). On both sides of the axe fine drawings have been scratched, and we see two animals of the hart type, a pattern of rhomboid checks, and also a number of irregular strokes (p. 28); the whole composition is a complete link between palaeolithic art and the Scandinavian rock-carvings. Of similar significance is an oblong pendant of bone found near Stavanger, in Jæren, together with a harpoon with large barbs.[2] On this ornament is scratched a representation of an elk, clear and life-like, but not completely finished, just like the figures we know from the stone-age carvings. Moreover, we find in the Maglemose civilization a decided fondness for making patterns on bone articles, especially angles, zigzag lines, and lozenges, the same geometrical motives that we find in the carvings, and are likewise present in the French art of the reindeer period; but, except for the two pieces which have just been mentioned, actual drawings are not known in this civilization.[3] In the oldest Norse stone age we find a poverty of such art which is a notable contrast with

[1] This view is supported by A. W. Brøgger, 'Elg og ren på helleristninger i det nordlige Norge', *Naturen*, (Bergen, 1906); by G. Hallström, *Fornvännen*, (Stockholm, 1908), pp. 77 ff., and Th. Petersen, *Naturen*, 1922, p. 106. See also Shetelig, *Primitive tider i Norge* (Bergen, 1922), pp. 139 ff.
[2] Helge Gjessing, 'Fra Jæderens Stenalder', *Oldtiden*, iv (Kristiania, 1914), pp. 44–6.
[3] Sophus Müller, *Oldtidens Kunst i Danmark, Stenalderens Kunst i Danmark* (København, 1918), pp. 2–3.

the profusion of small pictures of animals in the palaeolithic civilization, and it is difficult to understand how this art could come into flower again without any previous preparation, in the Norwegian and Swedish rock-carvings of animals. But the possibility is not to be denied. The links now missing may have been drawings on more perishable material, pictures of animals scratched in the sand along the shore or cut in the turf or in the moss of softer ground.[1]

A point which is even more pertinent is that the chief home of the Scandinavian bone-age culture, Denmark and northern Germany, lacks the natural rocks required for such carvings. It must not be forgotten that, even though we lack definite material links, the Scandinavian stone-age drawings are based upon the same psychological motives as are the drawings of the ice age in western Europe. It was an art which had a magical or religious significance, not an art for the sake of art. This is sufficiently clear when it is observed that the carvings and paintings of the reindeer period are often found in dark parts of the caves and where they can only be reached with difficulty, so that they should not be accessible to all and sundry. Much the same attitude is evident when the Australian aborigines keep careful watch that no stranger shall come near their primitive rock-paintings, which are their meeting-places for religious ceremonies. It is remarkable also that useful wild animals take such a dominant position in stone-age art, and in this we trace a primitive form of magic; the pictures are to produce plenty of the kinds of animal portrayed. It is reasonably certain that palaeolithic art was for the most part connected with such conceptions, and the Scandinavian pictures, too, are found mainly in the neighbourhood of good hunting-

---

[1] Palaeolithic art has left us work even in these more perishable materials, as the sculpture in the cave Tuc d'Audubert, described by the Comte de Begouen, *L'Anthropologie*, xxiii, and the drawings of fish in soft clay in the cave of Niaux: Cartailhac and Breuil, *L'Anthropologie*, xix, 1909. Cf. Baldwin Brown, *The Art of the Cave Dweller* (London, 1928), pp. 113–15. A more modern example of this perishable art is the White Horse near Uffington, Berkshire, and the similar horse on Bratton Hill, Wiltshire. Lately Anathon Bjørn has proffered the theory that the origin of the Arctic rock-carvings should be ascribed to eastern influences transmitted through the Komsa culture of Finmark. This hypothesis must be admitted as a possibility, though not yet supported by decisive arguments. See Anathon Bjørn, 'Ny litteratur om naturalistiske helleristninger', *Naturen* (Bergen, 1933), pp. 57–9.

places, where the animals came down to drink, or else by the sea. We find the pictures precisely in the places where the ancient hunter wished the wild animals to come.

When we review the evidence for an actual continuation of the palaeolithic art to the late stone age in Scandinavia, we find it conceivable that the pictures in both groups are a spontaneous expression of the psychology of the hunting people, contingent upon similar conditions of life and similar means of subsistence. Survival, or fresh development—these are the two opposing interpretations of parallel phenomena, in this case, phenomena of stone-age art; such parallelism is found also in many other domains of prehistoric archaeology. The present writer is still convinced, however, that the rock-carvings of the Scandinavian stone age must be explained as evidence of a living tradition descended from the hunting people of the ice age, evidence of an inherited magical belief which was expressed in carving representations of animals on the mountain side in a naturalistic form imitating the original, and with subordinate motives of lines (in lozenges and angles) combined with the animal figures. Just as the cave at Ruskenesset shows us the palaeolithic forms of harpoons and bone points at the end of the stone age, palaeolithic art, too, has its descendant in Norwegian and Swedish animal pictures.

In a position different from that of the great naturalistic pictures of animals stands the small group of carvings already mentioned above, those comprising a large number of small animal figures of stiff conventional form. This type of animal picture is best represented in the carvings at Bogge in Romsdal, Vingen in Nordfjord, Tennes in Balsfjord, Glösa in Jämtland, and Nämnfors in Ångermanland. The majority of scholars have been unanimous in the opinion that this group must have been produced by a new foreign influence in the later stone age, that is, more precisely, by impulses from the lands east of the Baltic. The line of their advance can be traced back from the north-west of Norway across Jämtland to Olonets near Ladoga and farther on to the carvings in Siberia.[1] Throughout the whole series the pictures are found crowded very close together, including a large number of small animal pictures

---

[1] A. W. Brøgger, *Den arktiske Stenalder i Norge* (Christiania, 1909), pp. 105 ff., German résumé, p. 249.

of stiff conventional form, but together with them various other representations, notably human figures in a variety of situations, suggestions of hunting-scenes and battles and the like, motives which are wholly foreign to the great naturalistic pictures of Scandinavia. In this new group we meet with human figures in the Scandinavian examples also: a man and a woman together at Nämnfors and likewise at Vingen, conventionalized human figures in carvings at Flatruet in Herjedal, and painted on the mountain side at Rønningen in Landsmark, west of the town Skien, and at Ovnen in Nissedal (Pl. 11). Special mention must be made of a most remarkable painting which was discovered in the Solsem cave at Leka in Namdal (north of Trondhjem). The painting is in the inner dark part of the cave and reaches a length of 6 metres with fourteen figures on one wall; there is a smaller group on the opposite wall. The figures are painted on the rock with red colouring, and they all represent persons in a highly conventionalized form, the body drawn as a single stroke with a large round head at the upper end and projecting arms and legs. This painting may have a magical significance; it was perhaps a religious dance or some similar ceremony which was proper to the dark cave, just as in certain palaeolithic pictures. Excavation of the cave has made it certain that the painting dates from the later stone age, and it is of the greatest interest in the history of northern culture.

Now that these conventionalized pictures are explained by impulses from the Baltic lands, we will recall that we have other evidences that the Scandinavian peninsula was brought into relations with the eastern European stone culture. The most important of these evidences was the importation of Prussian amber ornaments, which has already been mentioned, and they include among other forms small sculptured images of men or animals. We will recall the animal figure from Linnesøy, north of Trondhjem, and a man's head in amber from Västergötland, both of which are Prussian images. This taste for making small plastic images is introduced into Scandinavia also. At the excavation of Solsem cave at Leka, just mentioned, a little bone figure of a bird was found, which from its type might well have been a piece imported from the Baltic; but zoologically the image is identified as a great auk (*Alca impennis*), and therefore it is in all probability Norwegian. A small human head of soapstone from Rørås is nearly related to similar pieces of amber from the Baltic region, but the Norwegian variety of stone affords evidence that this head is a Scandinavian product. We may also mention a very characteristic little image, a divided piece of gray slate, shaped with unmistakable stone-age technique and formed to represent two animal heads, an elk and a bear, conceived with great fidelity to nature (Pl. 12). The piece was found in a bog at Tømmervåg, on the island Tustra in Nordmøre, Norway.[1] In Sweden the classic example is supplied by two small images of elks which were found on the dwelling-site at Åloppe in Uppland; they are made of burned clay, are undoubtedly a local product, and show a lively naturalistic conception of the animal.[2]

It is not apparent that these small images have any practical purpose. They are made for their own sake, as an expression of the hunting people's interest in the forms of the animals, and they have a parallel in the small images of bone, horn, and such material, from the late palaeolithic period. We may also recall the little animal figure of amber from the Maglemose period in Denmark (Pl. 3). But in the neolithic period these small Scandinavian images of animals must have their closest connexions with the Baltic and the east-European stone-age culture. In East Prussia, Poland, and Russia we find a large number of these small images of men and animals, made of amber, dropstone, bone, and even flint, while such images have no home in the south of Scandinavia, nor in central and western Europe.

In the stone age in the east small images also begin to appear in applied art as a form of decoration worked on various articles. We have already mentioned earlier the remarkable group of stone weapons formed like beasts' heads, or adorned with a plastic animal head as an added decoration (Pl. 10). There are smiting weapons with a hole for the haft, sometimes pointed maces resembling choppers with a roughly executed

---

[1] Th. Petersen, 'Solsemhulen på Leka', *Oldtiden*, iv (Oslo, 1914), and id., 'Meddelelser fra stenalderen i det nordenfjeldske Norge', *Aarb. f. nord. Oldk.* (København, 1920), pp. 30–1. Elk and bear are also the constant motives in the Carelian animal heads in stone which will be described below; these two animals are also depicted together in the carving at Landsvärk in Jämtland.

[2] Oscar Almgren, 'Nordiska stenåldersskulpturer', *Fornvännen* (Stockholm, 1907), pp. 114 ff.

PLATE 12

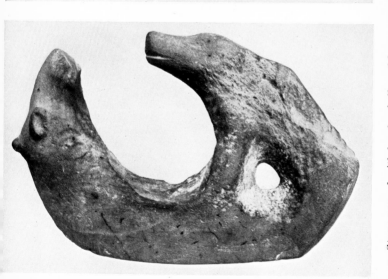

b. Wooden spoon from Puntala, Finland. After Ailio

a. Stone carved with heads of elk and bear. Tustra, Norway. After Th. Petersen

PLATE 13

Clay idols from Jätteböle, Åland. After Cederhvarf

animal head at the blunt end, sometimes having the whole club-stone shaped as a freely modelled animal's head.[1] It has been shown that these weapons belong to the last part of the Norse stone age, and it is highly probable that the form is inspired by the central European battle-axe, especially by the boat-shaped axe, which spread to the eastern Baltic region. In isolated cases the forms are undoubtedly influenced by the forms of the battle-axe. The modification is characteristic of the profound difference between the battle-axe culture, which was artistically poor but highly developed technically, on the one hand, and on the other hand the north-eastern hunting people who still preserved the original interest in naturalistic images of animals. The true home of the animal-head weapons is Olonets and Carelia. Half a score of pieces are found in Finland, three in Sweden; a number of the Finnish specimens are importations from the adjacent parts of Russia, but others are Finnish products. The type is characteristic of the 'comb-pottery' culture which we mentioned earlier.

The quality of the work in the animal images varies greatly; primitive, quite incompetent forms are found side by side with excellently finished specimens. Where the rendering is success-ful, it is almost always the elk or bear which supplies the model for the head. The finest piece known is an elk head of soapstone from a stone-age dwelling-site near the village of Palojoki in Hvittio hundred, Satakunta (Pl. 10). It is a true work of art, the most remarkable in the primitive art of northern Europe; no other piece of sculpture is known from the Scandinavian stone age which shows a treatment carried out in such detail and with such sympathy. The well-known Swedish elk head from Alunda in Uppland is more conventional, but it is also admirably characterized.[2] It has been questioned, and with some reason, whether these splendid pieces can have been weapons for daily use. The elk weapon from Alunda is not com-pletely pierced; on the under side a hole was made which was not carried all the way through the stone, giving an impression that the piece was intended to be carried at the end of a staff,

---

[1] J. R. Aspelin, *Antiquités du Nord Finno-Ougrien*, i (Helsingfors, 1877), Figs. 71–6.
[2] Oscar Almgren, 'Ett karelisk Stenvapen med Älghufvud funnet i Uppland', *Fornvännen* (Stockhoim, 1911), pp. 152 ff.

but not to be used. Other examples, on the other hand, were undoubtedly used as weapons. Some of these animal images have been regarded as insignia of honour for chiefs, others as votive objects, a kind of amulet which would bring luck to the hunter. The animal-head weapons are thus produced by the same conceptions that found expression in the naturalistic rock-carvings in Scandinavia. It is also conceivable that the stone animal heads took the place of actual animal heads as trophies of the chase; it is always the bear or the elk which is represented, the largest of the wild animals of the north. Possibly these beasts were the objects of a kind of cult, as we know the bear was in later times.

The Carelian and Finnish weapons adorned with animal heads are apparently connected on another side with bronze weapons of similar form, which are well known in the east-Russian bronze age.[1] But these must date from a later time than the Norse stone weapons, and the interesting correspondence in form must be due to a common basis, from which both were derived. The connexion between Finland and the stone age to the east is further confirmed by a charming little work of art which is among the rarest antiquities of the north-European stone age. It is a little wooden spoon, found in a bog at Puntala in Laukaa parish in Tavastland[2] (Pl. 12). This spoon is narrow and oblong, with a fully-shaped animal's head as a handle. The wood is remarkably well preserved, and affords an opportunity for the study of the stone-age technique in fine wood-carving. The outer side of the spoon is faceted with lengthwise, shallowly concave marks of cutting, while the hollow bowl of the spoon and the animal head are cut out with fine close strokes running obliquely in relation to the grain of the wood. This piece shows what excellent work could be produced with stone-age tools, in this instance even with tools of slate or other kinds of rock, not with flint. The blade of the spoon is not more than about 3 mm. thick, and the animal head is shaped with a sure and fine touch. The whole spoon is 20·5 cm. long. To judge from the kind of wood used, *Pinus cembra*, the spoon must have been

[1] J. R. Aspelin, *Antiquités du Nord Finno-Ougrien* (Helsingfors, 1877), p. 60, Figs. 240–2; A. M. Tallgren, 'Die Kupfer- und Bronzezeit in Nord- und Ost-russland', *Finska Fornminnesför. Tidskrift*, xxv (Helsingfors, 1911), 1, p. 142.

[2] Julius Ailio, 'Zwei Tierskulpturen', *Finska Fornminnesför. Tidskrift*, xxvi (Helsingfors, 1912), 257.

made in the country around the north of Ural, and was brought from there to Finland.[1] It was evidently a rare and precious article even in its own time. The bog where it was found is thought to show traces of a place of sacrifice, and the spoon itself was presumably intended for sacramental use.

Another unique little work of art is a comb of bone from a stone-age dwelling-site at Gullrum on the island of Gotland.[2] The comb was an ornament, very finely carved and decorated with an animal head and a human face. The head was at first taken to be that of a horse, but it is very sketchily formed, and should rather be regarded as an elk, especially as this animal is much favoured as a subject for carved images in the Norse stone age. The human face is likewise much conventionalized and it is without doubt of the same species as the similar images in amber from Prussia. As has already been mentioned, there is also an amber ornament in the form of a human face, found on Swedish ground, in Västergötland; here we trace once more the connexion between the native sculptured pieces and the precious imported ornaments of amber. It is most probable that the amber ornaments supplied the models for local production.

A similar decorative use of small plastic images is met with lastly in a group of daggers and knives of slate from the north of Sweden; there is also a single example from Norway, but this must be regarded as an imported piece. These daggers and knives are handsome little weapons, with the handle finished off in an animal head of extremely conventional form, sometimes so much simplified that its nature can only be understood from comparison with the better specimens.[3] It is quite impossible to say what animal these small heads represent; it has been guessed that they are dogs, but this does not seem very likely, when the art of the Arctic stone age is otherwise exclusively concerned with wild animals. We could more readily believe

---

[1] Dr. Ailio, loc. cit., argues that the spoon was made in Olonets, even though the wood was imported from Ural. Olonets was the central district for images of this kind, weapons adorned with animal heads, and rock-carvings.

[2] Hans Hansson, 'En stenåldersboplats på Gotland', *Svenska Fornminnesför. Tidskrift*, x (Stockholm, 1898), p. 12, Fig. 11; O. Montelius, *Minnen från vår Forntid*, i, Fig. 688.

[3] Oscar Almgren, *Fornvännen* (Stockholm, 1907), p. 116; A. W. Brøgger, *Den arktiske Stenalder i Norge*, pp. 62–3.

that it is the elk which has inspired these small heads on the slate knives, since that stately animal is otherwise known to be the favourite subject of Scandinavian stone-age art. In all probability the elk in such applications was given a significance beyond the purely decorative: the hunting-knife bearing an elk's head was a weapon which assured good hunting. This seems to be confirmed by a very interesting find from Gästrikland in Sweden, a plate of slate on which an elk is engraved; the piece has no practical use, but was intended to be suspended or carried by a cord.[1] It must be an amulet, and the image of the elk is the essential part of it. In this connexion should also be mentioned a knife of slate from Åfjord in Norway. On both sides of the blade this knife has drawings of fish strikingly identical in style with the north-Scandinavian rock-carvings of fish.[2] It is usually assumed that these pictures were cut on the knife with the magical purpose of obtaining good luck in fishing. This last example also explains the close psychological connexion between the stone-age rock-carvings and the small animal images on individual articles. Both forms take their origin in the same sphere of conceptions, conceptions highly characteristic of the hunting culture.

A different position is occupied by those small plastic images which are perhaps the most remarkable products of the stone-age art in Scandinavia: these are a group of small human images of clay from the dwelling-sites near Jätteböle on the Åland Islands, and a single specimen from Pihtipudas in the east of Finland.[3] At Jätteböle about 100 fragments were dug up, which belonged to at least 60 different figures. Among these images are a certain number of animal figures, especially images of the elk, similar to those mentioned above from Åloppe in Uppland. But most of them are human figures, some of which represent men, some women, in conventionalized and simplified outline, incised ornamental lines indicating the dress, decorated with fringes (Pl. 13). A detail of interest is that the images

[1] Hanna Rydh, 'En ristning på lös skiferplatta', *Fornvännen* (Stockholm, 1921), p. 61.

[2] Th. Petersen, 'Nye fund fra det Nordenfjeldske Norges Helleristningsområde', *Finska Fornminnesför. Tidskrift*, xxxvi (Helsingfors, 1927), p. 25; Shetelig, *Primitive Tider i Norge* (Bergen, 1922), p. 287.

[3] Björn Cederhvarf, 'Neolitiska Lerfigurer från Åland', *Finska Fornminnesför. Tidskrift*, xxvi (Helsingfors, 1912), plates III and IV.

have each a little hole on the top of the head, which must have been intended for the insertion of a feather or for some similar adornment. These clay images must have been idols, and they invite comparison with the similar small images from the lands around the Danube and from the north of the Balkan peninsula; they show a surprisingly close correspondence with the finds from Butmir in Bosnia.[1] Here we have evidence of far distant cultural connexions, of an influence which made its way to the Baltic lands across Silesia and Prussia. The human figures from Jätteböle thus have a different origin from the small animal images of the Scandinavian stone age described earlier. While these latter had an ancient tradition among the Scandinavian hunting people, the idols were brought into being by a new current of culture which must have brought in with it some new religious ideas. So far as we know up to the present, these later impulses did not touch the Scandinavian peninsula. In Scandinavia magical conceptions were connected with the wild animals, and the idea of magical powers in nature gained expression in images of the elk and the bear. The statuettes from the Åland Islands stand quite isolated, as a foreign element in the north-Scandinavian stone age.

[1] M. Hoernes, *Urgeschichte der bildenden Kunst in Europa* (Wien, 1898), Tafel II, V.

VIII

THE PHASES AND TYPES OF THE BRONZE AGE

THE archaeological system of distinguishing the prehistoric periods in Europe, the originally Scandinavian system with its three great periods—the ages of stone, bronze, and iron—is now so generally understood and accepted that any explanation of it would be superfluous. It has been established beyond all doubt that man in his first era of culture lived during an immensely long period in a pure stone age; and then copper, and after it bronze, was discovered, and they remained in use as the most important metals of the ancient world, until at last iron came to the fore and took the leading place.[1] All indications point to the conclusion that the means of extracting copper was discovered in Asia Minor very early in the third millennium before Christ, and from there knowledge of the process spread to the Caucasus, Egypt, and the Mediterranean lands. Copper was in use in Egypt under the earliest dynasties, and it is in evidence around the shores of the Mediterranean by about the middle of the third millennium. In the Iberian peninsula especially, in a setting which otherwise belongs to the megalithic stone age, copper very early became prominent in the cultural picture, while the local copper mines were being exploited. Copper was similarly prominent in central Europe in the districts where copper ore was easily accessible: the Alpine area and Hungary very early became important centres for the production of copper by mining and smelting. It is this period, when copper was used side by side with stone and the metal was thus an element in the culture of the stone age, which has been given the name 'aeneolithic period', or has even been called 'the copper age'. It is not altogether a period of metal: it is a stone age which also possesses some copper, and the conditions reflected in the twofold types of weapons and implements are precisely those of a period of transition. Sometimes it is the form of the stone article which is imitated in cast metal,

---

[1] See the British Museum *Guide to the Bronze Age* (by Reginald A. Smith), 1920, Introduction.

in particular in the flat axes of copper without haft-hole, which are shaped on the model of corresponding axes of flint; on the other hand the superiority of the metal as a material, as also the technique proper to the treatment of the metal, was the source of new forms which were more shapely and more complex, especially battle-axes having a hole for the haft and thin flat blades for daggers and halberts. These earliest types in metal were then imitated in stone, in somewhat heavier (and sometimes simplified) forms, as was necessitated by the more difficult nature of stone as a material; but the model is unmistakable for all that. Various handsome forms of battle-axe were produced in this way in the stone age in central Europe, and the flint daggers in the north were undoubtedly derived from dagger-blades of metal.

Within certain areas of central Europe this period could justly be called a copper age; in Hungary especially, around the middle part of the Danube basin, copper weapons held a conspicuous place. Farther north, in Germany, France, and England, copper was wholly subordinate to stone, and in Scandinavia the amount of metal is negligible during the later stone age in comparison with the enormous number of flint tools and weapons. The common types of copper articles were flat axes and small broad daggers of triangular shape; of these a number have been found in Denmark and Skåne, sufficient to show that copper was a known commodity of trade in southern Scandinavia during the greater part of the neolithic period.[1] Of special importance for the determination of chronology is a store which was found near Horsens in Jutland; it consists of four flat axes, a dagger-blade, and three spiral rings, and some lumps of copper, the whole collection being placed in an earthenware pot which can be dated from the dolmen period.[2] The find is parallel with the collections of amber ornaments which have several times been found in earthenware vessels of the same period.[3] Copper was at that time a precious material,

---

[1] Sophus Müller, *Urgeschichte Europas* (Strassburg, 1905), pp. 41 ff.; O. Montelius, *Minnen från vår Forntid*, Figs. 147–52, text pp. 10 and 14; Otto Rydbeck, 'Nyare förvärv från koppar- och bronsåldern', *Fornvännen* (Stockholm, 1926), p. 120.

[2] C. A. Nordman, 'Den yngre Stenåldern i Mellan-, Väst- och Nordeuropa', in *De Förhistoriska Tiderna i Europa*, ii (Stockholm, 1927), p. 115.

[3] See Hans Kjær, *Vor Oldtids Mindesmerker* (København, 1925), p. 125.

as amber was, while flint and stone formed the usual material for all practical needs. The European copper age is in Scandinavia a stone age with a few isolated copper articles; but it is a stone age which has taken colour from a more southerly civilization where metal had already attained to a position of importance. In the Scandinavian peninsula north of Skåne not a single copper piece of this kind has yet been found, nor in Finland either; in this most northerly region of Europe the copper age is marked only by a reflex of the early metal forms, appearing in the daggers of flint and the battle-axes of stone.

It can even be said that the copper age was not anywhere more than a slight variation of stone-age culture. The decisive advance came in reality with bronze, with the remarkable discovery of alloying copper with tin; metal now for the first time appeared as a new material in every way superior to the makeshifts of the older time. Bronze has great merits which copper had not: it is easier to melt, gives a more complete cast, is stronger and tougher in use. The exploitation and treatment of this metal formed a basis for the development of new cultural forms which spread with the metal itself from the Near East and Egypt to the Mediterranean lands, and from there to the more northerly parts of Europe. Throughout the whole bronze age in the ancient world we find a common character in technical details as well as in style and taste.

The chief centre of development in the early bronze age on European soil was the Cretan domain on the islands and coasts of the Aegean Sea, but for the lands in the north Italy was of much greater importance as a primary source. The Italian bronze age had its origin in influences from Greek bronze culture, and for a long time flint and stone were used side by side with bronze. The most important types in metal were flat axes and daggers with broad triangular blades, both derived from forms which had previously been known in copper, but they were gradually improved, until by this time the daggers often had the handle cast in metal and the axes had flanged edges to support and steady the haft. A weapon of new form is the halbert which has a pointed blade like a dagger; it appears first in Spain, but is also known from Italy, being several times depicted, for example, in the peculiar rock-carvings of the Ligurian Alps. These different forms also find their way into central and western Europe. The broad Italian daggers are found in Switzerland, in France, and in Germany right up to the Baltic. Flanged flat axes of a form especially common in Italy are found in Switzerland and eastward into Hungary and also farther to the north. Halberts are found in Hungary and over the whole of northern Germany.[1] These forms are unknown in Greece, and some of them are rarely found in Spain; hence it can be established beyond doubt that the bronze age in central Europe was first brought into being by influences from Italy, and that a large proportion of these northern bronzes were directly imported Italian products. But at the same time it can also be shown that even at this early stage a beginning had been made in casting bronze locally north of the Alps as well. There is evidence to prove this of the halberts in northern Germany; in the south these weapons always consisted of a blade of bronze fastened into a haft of wood, but in northern Germany the haft as well was made wholly or partly of bronze. These large and complex works are striking evidence of the knowledge of bronze-casting in northern Europe at this early period.

This period, which farther south may justly be called the beginning of the bronze age, must still be regarded as a stone age in Scandinavia. In the stone cists and the single graves articles of stone predominate, with daggers of flint as the leading type. Flat Italian axes, pointed halberts[2] (and, once, a dagger with a bronze handle) appear in Denmark and Skåne as scattered isolated finds in comparatively small numbers, in the same way as copper had earlier been manifested. The early bronzes are never found in graves, and we may infer from this that bronze had not yet gained any considerable currency in daily life. The period which represents the first phase of the bronze age in southern and central Europe is in Scandinavia the final phase of a highly developed stone age. This conclusion is in no way invalidated by the circumstance that scattered pieces in metal, regarded as rare treasures, made their way in, and penetrated even as far as the more distant part of the Scandinavian peninsula. From the cave on Ruskenesset near Bergen, as we

---

[1] O. Montelius, *Chronologie der ältesten Bronzezeit in Nord-Deutschland und Skandinavien* (Braunschweig, 1900).

[2] Sophus Müller stated in 1909 that twelve pointed halberts from Denmark were then known. Cf. Montelius, *Minnen*, Figs. 835–6.

have already mentioned, two quite small pieces of bronze are preserved, which can be proved to have been buried at the same time as the stone-age articles at the hunting-station: the period is determined by the flint daggers, bone needles, and other similar articles, all in forms which are characteristic of the stone-cist period. This is the earliest manifestation of the age of metals that we can trace within the domain of the Arctic stone age.

But soon afterwards we meet with sure signs in southern Scandinavia that the use and treatment of bronze had been incorporated as an organic element into Norse civilization. The beginning of the bronze age may be reckoned from the time when bronze first appears in graves. In Holstein and Slesvig, as in the rest of Denmark and in Skåne, the first phase of the bronze age is marked by graves which are supplied with a dagger-blade of bronze, a direct continuation of the burial custom of the end of the stone age, when the constant burial equipment was a flint dagger (p. 72). The known graves of this kind are not numerous, and they may be best understood as a sign of the transition between the two periods. A bronze dagger belonging to this group was found in Denmark together with flint daggers in a grave cist of the stone age; but another was found together with the oldest Norse fibula of bronze. Most of these daggers are of Italian origin or from central Europe, and were imported as foreign wares into Scandinavia; the same is true of two swords from Italy which were found in Danish bogs. From the bog-finds come also a group of flat axes, most of them large and having a wide expanded edge, some of them resembling British forms and undoubtedly imported. The bronze culture of both the south and the west contributed elements to this first age of metal in Scandinavia. Yet in the same period we come upon the first local Scandinavian bronzes too, weapons made on foreign models: they can be distinguished by the less competent shaping and a plainer finish. The oldest purely Norse bronze types appear as heavy axes with a hole for the haft, often handsomely decorated and undoubtedly of native manufacture.

Thanks to the admirable researches of the Danish archaeologists we are now able to elucidate step by step the beginning and development of the bronze age in Scandinavia.[1] We are

---

[1] Sophus Müller, 'Bronzealderens Begyndelse og ældre Udvikling i Danmark', *Aarb. f. nord. Oldk.* (København, 1909).

able to point out the first metal pieces which found their way into Scandinavian lands, first the pure copper, then bronzes with a very slight alloy of tin, and finally the classical proportion of one part of tin to nine parts of copper which is maintained more or less consistently through the whole period. We can follow the increasing knowledge of technical treatment of the metal and the increasing production of native bronzes; at the first stage the imported pieces are greatly superior in numbers, but later, during all the succeeding phases of the Scandinavian bronze age, the imported work is completely subordinate to the bronze produced in Scandinavia. It can be shown that the style of the Scandinavian bronze culture, both in form and in decoration, began as a fumbling imitation of foreign models, but gradually attained to the confidence and elegance which even in the earlier half of the bronze age gave Scandinavian work a rank among the finest in Europe.

After an initial introductory stage comes the first flourishing of the bronze culture in Scandinavia, and it continues through the following thousand years in varying forms, always in response to the advance of civilization among the southern peoples, but at the same time retaining the peculiar character which was proper to development on home ground. This is an age of bronze in the truest sense, for it is the bronze work which determines for us the character of the age; and if we judge from this work alone, we must give the Scandinavian bronze culture a very high place in European civilization of that age. This early and highly remarkable development of bronze culture in the north is to be explained partly by the antecedent conditions in the stone age. Already in the stone age the south of Scandinavia had been a link in the greater European circle of civilization, and civilization had long been advancing its frontier there against the purely primitive form of life; the megalithic culture and the battle-axe culture during a long age had been founding a base for the further advance during the bronze age. It must also be remembered that the bronze age belongs essentially to the time of the most favourable climate which the north of Europe enjoyed after the ice age, the subboreale period (p. 10), which was both warmer and drier than the climate of the present day. It was a period which afforded specially favourable conditions of life in the south of Scandinavia.

On the other hand it is easy to overvalue the Scandinavian bronze age when one studies the beautiful and admirable bronzes which have been preserved from that time. The finished technique and the similarly mature art exhibited in the treatment of the bronze give only a very limited view of the life of the time as a whole; the houses of the same period were mere huts, primitive enough, and no true art of building was known. There was a vast difference between the civilized people of the eastern Mediterranean and bronze-age society in northern Europe.

The south of Scandinavia possesses an extraordinary wealth of antiquities from the bronze age, and they have been closely studied for a considerable length of time, and arranged according to types and according to the ornament, so as to exhibit the successive styles in each phase. The whole bronze age was first divided into two principal periods, an early and a late, and within these periods shorter phases can be distinguished. The basis of the chronology was partly the imported southern bronzes whose period in their own home was known more or less definitely; when these are found together with Scandinavian bronzes, they give a preliminary working indication of date. As a check on their evidence, certain late Norse bronzes have been found in south Germany, France, and Switzerland, where their age can be fixed in relation to the central European bronze age.[1] But just as important is the close study of the Norse bronzes themselves, since their chronological order can be determined from the interrelation of the forms. By these methods the relative chronology has been worked out in reliable detail for the whole of the Scandinavian bronze age,[2] in a form

[1] O. Montelius, 'La Chronologie préhistorique en France et en d'autres pays celtiques', L'Anthropologie, 1901, p. 620, and id., 'Der Handel in der Vorzeit', Prähistorische Zeitschrift (Berlin, 1910), p. 265; Joseph Déchelette, Manuel d'archéologie, ii (Paris, 1910), pp. 395–6.

[2] O. Montelius, Les Temps préhistoriques en Suède et dans les autres pays scandinaves (Paris, 1895), p. 63; id., Minnen från vår Forntid, i (Stockholm, 1917). Montelius divides the Scandinavian bronze age into six phases and assigns each of them a date in round figures, according to the following scheme:

1st phase from the beginning of the 18th century to the middle of the 16th century before Christ.

2nd phase, from the middle of the 16th century to the end of the 14th before Christ.

3rd phase, from the beginning of the 13th century to the end of the 12th before Christ.

which has met with universal approval. There is distinct disagreement, however, about the absolute dating when it is to be
expressed in relation to historical chronology; yet even then
it is possible to establish certain general correspondences
beyond all doubt. The early bronze age roughly speaking fills
the last of the second millennium before Christ, and then the
late bronze age follows for about 500 years. The beginning of
the period obviously offers the most difficult problems; the later
portion can be determined more certainly by its connexion with
the Hallstatt period in central Europe. For our present purpose
the rough dates just given will suffice to give an idea of the
position of the Scandinavian bronze age in the general history
of European culture.

We will now give an account of the principal features seen in
the course of the bronze age in Scandinavia, adopting as our
chronological basis the six phases distinguished by Montelius.
The first phase at the beginning shows marked dependence
upon foreign imports and foreign models, as has already been

4th phase, from the beginning of the 11th century to the middle of the 10th
before Christ.
5th phase, from the middle of the 10th century to the middle of the 8th
before Christ.
6th phase, from the middle of the 8th century to the end of the 7th before
Christ.

Sophus Müller, *Oldtidens Kunst i Danmark, II, Bronzealderens Kunst* (København, 1921); id., 'Bronzealderens Begyndelse', &c., *Aarb. f. nord. Oldk.*, 1909.
Sophus Müller first divides the bronze age into two main divisions, the early
and late bronze age, and then into nine shorter phases, each of which is characterized by its own definite forms and its own special style. No fixed dates are
given as limits of the periods, except that the bronze age in the north had its
beginning about the middle of the second millennium B.C. and lasted about
800 years all told. In the absolute dating there is thus a discrepancy between
the estimates of the two distinguished investigators amounting to several
hundred years. The discrepancy rests in the main upon different computations
of the first phase, and this disagreement in turn is connected with different
theories about the late stone age, in particular, about the passage-grave period.
See Montelius, 'Die mykenischen Kuppelgräber und die nordischen Gang-
gräber', *Fornvännen* (Stockholm, 1909), p. 334. The dating of the end of the
bronze age on the other hand depends upon the time when the iron age is
reckoned to begin. We shall return to this question later. Among recent
contributions to the discussion of bronze-age chronology special reference may
be made to Nils Åberg, *Bronzezeitliche und früheisenzeitliche Chronologie I–III*,
Kungl. Vitterhets Historie och Antikvitets Akademien (Stockholm, 1930–2),
and H. C. Broholm, 'Studier over den yngre Bronzealder i Danmark med
særlig Henblik paa Gravfundene', *Aarb. f. nord. Oldk.* (København, 1933).
Both these authors agree with Sophus Müller's conclusions.

mentioned, yet even thus early we also come upon the first stage
of an independent development, in that the heavy cast axes
of simple form (but richly decorated) are, practically speaking,
peculiar to the north, as are spearheads with the same decoration. The decoration consists of straight lines, rows of triangles,
borders of small semicircles such as are well known on imported
pieces, swords from central Europe and flat axes from England.
It is this foreign style which is adopted in the earliest Norse
bronzes.

The second phase is marked by the first great flowering of
the casting art in Scandinavia. The flat axes with flanges are
replaced partly by the elegant ornamented palstaves, partly by
socketed celts, the former being weapons, the latter working
tools. The axes used as weapons were handsomely made, with
a long convex edge (Pl. 14); the spearheads have slender
graceful forms. Besides the imported swords, the Italian type
with flanged grip and the south German type with grip all of
bronze, the well-known Scandinavian form is now predominant,
with richly decorated handle of bronze and leaf-shaped blade
(Pl. 14). It is an independent Scandinavian type, originating
in a modification of the earlier imported swords of the first
phase; the shape is highly elegant, the handle always richly
ornamented, sometimes with gold or amber, and the blade with
a central rib edged with fine lines. The women's ornaments
are just as striking—round plates for the belt (Pl. 16), broad
collars, and the older forms of the Norse fibula. There was
further a miscellaneous equipment of minor requisites, knives,
belt-clasps, buttons, combs, razors, tweezers, awls, small chisels,
&c. Bronze was used freely and with full mastery in every kind
of application. Of gold, finger-rings are found, arm-rings and
diadems, and this precious metal was by no means rare: from
Denmark several hundred ornaments are known.[1] This early
gold in Scandinavia appears in forms which have parallels to
the south-east, in the last reaches towards the Austrian Alps
and Hungary: it was mainly from these regions that Scandinavia during the bronze age imported its gold. But in three

---

[1] Sophus Müller, *Ordning af Danmarks Oldsaker* (*Système préhistorique du
Danemark*), i (København, 1888–95), p. 58, nos. 4–9; O. Montelius, 'Bronzezeitliche Goldarbeiten in Schweden gefunden, *Fornvännen* (Stockholm, 1916),
p. 239.

PLATE 14

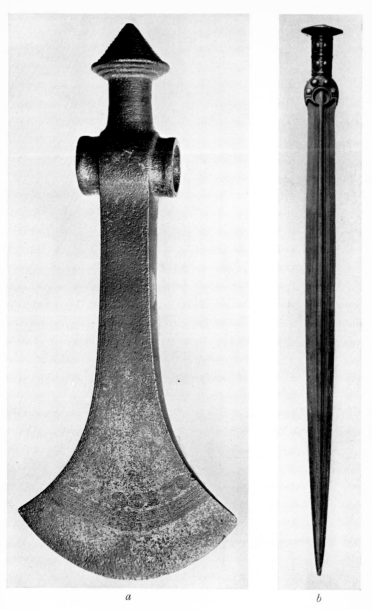

a
b

a. Bronze battle-axe. After Madsen
b. Bronze sword with decorated handle. After Madsen

PLATE 15

Pendant vase of bronze. After S. Müller

places also the familiar lunulae of Ireland have been found on Danish soil.[1]

Special interest attaches to the decoration which appears on the Scandinavian bronzes in this phase. We still find the simpler geometrical motives, combinations of lines, small borders of triangles, or groups of circles; but the form of decoration already predominant is the closely rolled spiral drawn in fine lines. It is usual for the surface to be divided into zones, each of which is filled by a connected group of spirals, and quite complex patterns are also found, such as double figures of connected spirals, or borders in which the spirals are enclosed in pairs by a continuation of their own line. Examples are also found in which the wider surfaces are entirely covered by a unified and connected system of spirals. The motive is always the same, lines rolled up into a spiral and then running on to the next spiral, but many variations are used. The execution is wonderfully perfect: the lines were punched in the bronze with a small chisel, and yet it is difficult to distinguish the marks of the separate strokes. This style of decoration is applied above all to the women's larger ornaments, the belt-plates and collars, and likewise to the battle-axes, which afforded a suitably wide surface for ornamentation; but the spiral was used elsewhere too, wherever it was possible, on sword-handles, belt-clasps, buttons, &c.

The spiral style in the Scandinavian bronze age provides some very interesting problems. It is well known that this form of decoration had its original home around the east of the Mediterranean. It is a motive for which special predilection was shown during the bronze age in Egypt, and in the Mycenaean civilization likewise we find spirals used freely and in great variety, in architecture, on grave-stones, on metal, and on other materials. But this style did not find its way into the west. In Italy the spirals are known, but they are of little importance, and in the bronze culture of western Europe, in Spain, France, and the British Isles, they hardly occur at all.[2] In the south-east

[1] Sophus Müller, op. cit., p. 63, no. 164; George Coffey, 'The Distribution of Gold Lunulae in Ireland and North-western Europe', *Proc. Royal Irish Academy*, vol. xxvii, 1909.

[2] Spirals on some few stone monuments in Ireland are explained by G. Coffey as due to influence from Scandinavia: George Coffey, *New Grange and other incised Tumuli in Ireland* (Dublin, 1912), p. 62.

of Europe on the other hand the spiral style was adopted from
its connexion with the Mycenaean culture. We meet with spiral
decorations in Hungary and south Germany, though not with
anything like the same frequency as in the north. Thus we are
confronted by the peculiar circumstance that the spiral ornament has its richest development at the two opposite ex-
tremities, in Mycene and Denmark, and in remarkably similar
form in these two regions. The Scandinavian decorative artists
knew precisely the same combinations of spirals as are characteristic of the Greek bronze age. And yet there is no trace of
any direct connexion. It is true that amber from Denmark has
been found in graves at Mycene, but no articles from the
Mycenaean area are ever found on Scandinavian ground, while
we have already stated that Italian bronzes do occur. Impulses
from Mycenaean art must have come to the north through
intermediate links, and hence almost certainly across Hungary,
Austria, and southern Germany, the areas from which Scandinavia derived its gold, and undoubtedly also most of its necessary
supplies of bronze as raw material. It was this cultural connexion more than any other that gave the Scandinavian bronze
age its dignified classical character. As we shall see later, not
only the decorative art, but also many other elements of higher
culture found their way at this time to the people of the northern
bronze age. This relation is obviously of the greatest importance too for the determination of Scandinavian chronology;
it would be difficult to understand how the spiral style in the
north could belong to any time much later than the flourishing
of the Mycenaean culture in Greece.

The spirals in the north belong specifically to a clearly defined
period, which in the main coincides with what we have designated the second phase of the bronze age. They can still be found
in the third phase, as on the women's bronze collars and on some
of the fibulas, but the style is retrograde and soon disappears
entirely. Decorative art then assumes new forms, characterized
by ornaments which are more boldly cast, often emphasized by
the inlaying of a dark mass of resin, which has an effect similar to
enamel. The types of the articles vary upon the basis of the forms
in the period immediately preceding, and they are still characterized by a graceful and charming elegance, though there is a
growing tendency towards stronger profile. Among the changes

of this phase it may be noted that the palstaves disappear and from this moment are wholly superseded by socketed celts; the women's bronze collars also pass out of use at the beginning of the third phase. By way of compensation several new ornaments appear, a slender neck-ring, and a little box to be carried in the belt. Of the imported articles special mention must be made of thinly chased vessels and bowls of bronze, among them an Etruscan wine-carriage, consisting of a vessel shaped like a cauldron fastened on a little wheeled waggon, from Skollerup in Denmark, and remains of a similar one from Ystad in Skåne.

The transition to the fourth phase, which initiates the later division of the Scandinavian bronze age, passes without any marked changes in any direction. The types of the preceding phase are continued, but variations of form and ornament arise gradually, for taste evidently changes, and changes steadily in the direction of more extreme and exaggerated forms. The belt-plates become steeply arched; the armlet grows as wide as a sleevelet, the neck-ring becomes thicker and is worn tripled, the parts being joined by a nail—the whole a heavy and pretentious ornament; the earlier square sword pommel is extended on each side and becomes a cross-piece. In all the forms we perceive this taste for the striking and the grotesque which is the outstanding characteristic of the late bronze age. At this time too the cast ornamentation and the resin inlaying, which resembles enamel work, disappear from the decoration and the bronze is ornamented only with fine chiselled dots and lines arranged in bands or in rows of arcs, stars, or meanders (Pl. 15). These are the elements of late bronze-age style which form the basis of the rich development in the following phase, and it can be shown that this movement in Norse style still remains intimately connected with contemporary art in central Europe and the south. In Hungary and westwards in France we find the same patterns of close fine lines in rings, semi-circles, and arcs edged with dotted lines. The meander, which is an innovation in the Scandinavian world of special interest, was ultimately borrowed from Italy.

Like the spiral style of the early bronze age, this new style of arcs and meanders is no local phenomenon, but a wave in the common European stream of tradition, and it came to the north from those countries where Scandinavia procured its bronze and its gold. The new decorative style was communicated in the contacts of peoples and their trading connexions, as is abundantly attested by the imported metal articles found in Scandinavia from this time. There are round shields (Pl. 16), and large urns of thinly chased bronze, curved daggers, bronze bits and other fittings for horse-gear, and flanged celts from western Europe. This period is also richer in gold than the early period of the bronze age, partly in the form of arm-rings, but above all in beakers and vases of hammered gold. These golden

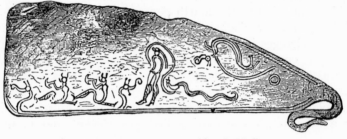

FIG. 8.   Bronze razor.   *After S. Müller.*

vessels form one of the most remarkable groups of antiquities from the bronze age of northern Europe. It is assumed that they were imported into Scandinavia from southern or central Germany, where about twenty specimens of the kind are known; a single one has been found in France, compared with thirty pieces in Denmark and two in Sweden. There is some evidence that these vessels of gold were used for sacramental purposes, and most of them are found in circumstances which point to their having been offerings.

With the importation of foreign works of art, Scandinavian art now for the first time became interested in representing living figures. Birds' heads and horses' heads may have occurred earlier as terminal ornaments, but they now became usual, and complete figures of birds as well, which were common on the foreign bronzes. Horned ox-heads and representations of horses, men, and ships are also found. The small bronze razors supply a ground specially favoured by this infant pictorial art (Fig. 8), but figures of living creatures are also found as motives in the ornament of numerous other objects, in Denmark even in the local art of pottery. These artistic

PLATE 16

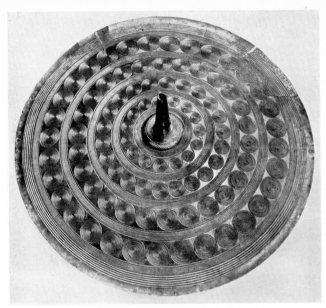

Plate for woman's belt, with spiral decoration. After Brøndsted

Shield of hammered bronze. After Montelius

PLATE 17

Statuette of a female deity. After Hans
Kjær

motives and forms register distinctly the intimate interplay between the Norse bronze age and the whole of contemporary European culture; the Norse developments in taste and forms proceed on the same lines and keep the same pace as developments in central Europe and Italy.

This is the foundation upon which the style of the late bronze age reaches the height of its development in Scandinavia. The magnificent forms of the fifth phase—pendent vessels, belt ornaments, neck-rings, spearheads—are covered with a wealth of patterns of interwoven bands, meanders, arcs, and stars; these patterns are varied with free running spirals, half-moons or graceful double curves, and bands often ending in small animal heads, bird heads, or even human figures (Fig. 9). There is a capricious freedom and fantasy in this art of line-decoration which is astonishing in a period so ancient and in a barbarous land: it is a bronze-age *style flamboyant* which forms the consummation and the end of a great epoch. The close connexion with central Europe is still unmistakable, and certain almost identical motives appear in Scandinavia, France, and Switzerland, such as a peculiar combination of semicircles used as a border on the socket of spearheads.[1] But here there is no question of a direct borrowing of a fixed style. In the application of motives and in the treatment of details the Scandinavian style is markedly independent, and the best work stands if anything higher than the corresponding work in the south. It is the common style of the period, which has been stamped in each region with minor individual variations upon the common basis, a common style which had been produced by the interplay of reciprocal influences meeting and mingling in the contacts of peoples and incidental personal relationships.

Contact with the central European style during the immediately preceding phase is reflected also in the taste for figures of various kinds, human figures, ships, fish, and others, which were engraved on the bronze articles; but now there are likewise small plastic images in bronze. These are sometimes human figures or heads, used as terminal ornaments on small implements, on a knife or a pin, and sometimes they are complete figurines. Several examples of a small kneeling figure of a woman have been found (Pl. 17), presented naked or in a garment of fringes

[1] Sophus Müller, *Oldtidens Kunst i Danmark, Bronzealderen*, p. 41.

FIG. 9. Late bronze-age ornament, from pendent vases. *After Montelius.*

and adorned with a neck-ring or with ear-rings;[1] from a slightly later time there is a group of bronzes which show a woman standing nude with her arms akimbo and with one or more neck-rings.[2] These small figures are a very interesting pheno-menon, even though they bear no special distinction as art. Most of them are undoubtedly Norse work; the characteristic dress, the fringed kirtle, is known from a Danish grave. But the taste for these images, as also the ideas possibly associated with them, must have been inspired by intercourse with the peoples to the south, with the early Hallstatt culture and through it with northern Italy, where similar small images occur; there they are usually taken to represent a female divinity of fertility. It is far from certain, however, that people in Scandinavia understood and adopted this religious significance along with the images; it is quite conceivable that they were adopted as a purely decorative form.

This phase marks the last high peak of forms and technique in the Norse bronze age. The types are carried to their highest development, especially ornaments, belt-plates with a steeply arched top, and twisted neck-rings (torcs) terminating (at the ends which join to close the ring) in broad ornamented plates and spirals. The fibula consists of two round convex plates fastened together by a short bar, the so-called spectacle-fibula, a typically exaggerated development of the slender safety-pin of the early bronze age. In this late period the spectacle-fibula may assume almost monstrous proportions. Conspicuous also is the fondness for cast chains of bronze, heavy and often several times doubled, with loose-hanging bronze plates at-tached, as also for large ornamental pins, the top of which is wound into spiral form. In many particulars we find the taste of the Hallstatt culture continued in the Scandinavian bronzes. Imported articles are also very common, especially the charac-teristic Hallstatt swords, heavy torcs, razors, tweezers, hammered shields, vases, and beakers of bronze. But the greater number of the antiquities found in the north show themselves unmis-takably to be of Scandinavian workmanship, both by their individual forms and by the technical treatment.

[1] See Hans Kjær in *Bergens Museums Årbok*, 1926, Hist.-ant. rekke no. 1, p. 39.
[2] T. J. Arne, 'Einige in Schweden gefundene Bronzestatuetten in barbar-ischer Arbeit', *Fornvännen* (Stockholm, 1909), p. 336.

The late bronze age in Scandinavia carried the casting of bronze to a perfection which cannot be surpassed. Hammered and chased metal-work, which was already highly developed in the south, was an unknown art in the north all through the bronze age. This concentration in the north upon the casting of bronze explains in part the complete mastery of the art attained there. The method followed varied according to the nature of the article to be made. Some articles were cast in permanent moulds of stone or metal; some were cast in moulds of clay or sand, and for the more difficult objects the more complex method à cire perdue was employed. After the casting the bronze was trimmed and decorated. This work can be illustrated from finds of half-finished or rejected pieces, from finds of stores of bronzes intended to be recast, and finally in Denmark some very interesting details have come to light in an investigation of the refuse from a bronze-casting work-place.[1] Through the many hundreds of years this industry was developed in the late bronze age to an astonishing pitch. The pendent vases cast in thin bronze and with a complex profile are indeed work which it would now be very difficult to reproduce. Still more impressive as feats of casting are the great trumpets, the lurer, which are among the most remarkable antiquities in Europe (Pl. 18).

These great horns first appear towards the end of the early bronze age, and it is in the following phase that they reach their full development to the well-known type of long slender trumpets of peculiar curved form, with the curve running upward and outward, and a broad plate of bronze around the mouth. It is a signalling horn with a comparatively limited range, only the natural notes of a single octave.[2] These horns are always found in pairs; they must clearly have been used in pairs, or with four or six in a set, as also appears in the rock-carvings of the bronze age. In consideration of their graceful lines, of the difficult double swung curve, and even of their

[1] Carl Neergaard, 'Haag-Fundet. En Affaldsdynge fra en Metalstøbers Hytte, fra den yngre Broncealder', Aarb. f. nord. Oldk., 1908, p. 278. Similar places excavated in Halland in Sweden are described by Georg Sarauw, Götaälvsområdets Fornminnen (Göteborg, 1923), p. 261 f.

[2] K. Kroman, 'Nogle Bemærkninger om Bronzelurene i Nationalmuseet i København', Aarb. f. nord. Oldk., 1902, p. 79. Hubert Schmidt, 'Die Luren von Daberkow', Prähistorische Zeitschrift, vii (Leipzig, 1915), p. 85.

PLATE 18

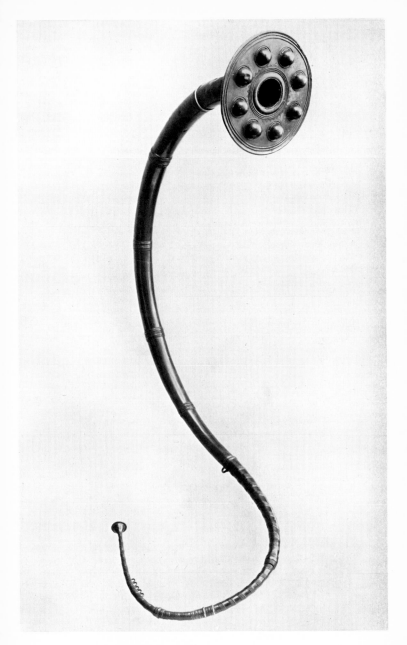

Bronze trumpet, Denmark. After Madsen

musical properties, we must regard these great horns as the most astonishing masterpieces of ancient bronze casting.

With this phase the true bronze-age culture comes to an end, since the sixth and last phase which we reckon to this age is in reality a period of transition, when the old forms were retrograde and giving way before new influences. Certain old types of ornaments were still in use, such as neck-rings, armlets, and pins, and these in even more colossal proportions than ever before. But others of the old forms have completely disappeared, and new features are in evidence. It is especially significant that we know very few weapons of bronze from this phase, but on the other hand iron begins to appear, armlets of iron from Zealand, a bit from Gotland, a sword from Östergötland. The small working axes, the socketed celts, are still made of bronze, but it is evident that we are standing near to the close of the bronze age.

Even during this preliminary review of the bronze age in Scandinavia, the reader may have been surprised that the northern people of that age were able to provide themselves with such a constant and abundant supply of bronze. Every piece of metal must have been transported a long way; part of the supply came from the British Isles, but by far the greater amount from central Europe to the south-east, and it is obvious that in such conditions bronze must have been costly. There was also gold, which was by no means rare in Denmark in some phases of the bronze age. But the bronze was so generally accessible that, as we have seen, a distinctive native art of casting was developed with its own peculiar forms and an independent style of decoration. It has been conclusively established that the amber from the west coast of Jutland was the source of wealth which made possible the importation of this bronze and gold to Denmark.

We have already touched upon the part which this precious stuff played in the stone age, when amber from Prussia was carried to central and eastern Europe, to the Baltic lands and finally to Norway, while the amber from Jutland in this earlier time found its way over great distances to the British Isles and from there farther on to France and the Iberian peninsula. In the Mediterranean lands amber first appears in the bronze age. In Italy we come upon amber in graves and in the pile-dwellings during the transition from the stone age to the bronze age, and again in the late bronze age and in the Villanova period. During the whole of this time amber was highly prized and much used; it was evidently credited also with magical prophylactic properties. In Greece amber beads are found in large numbers in the shaft-graves at Mycene, as also in the Mycenaean domed tombs. The demand in southern Europe gave amber an enhanced value which made it a prime factor in the development of the Danish bronze age. The principal route northwards for this trade passed down the Elbe and from its mouth by sea along the west coast of Slesvig and Jutland, where the amber was found. Here by the North Sea lay Denmark's richest and most populous settlements, especially in the early bronze age; the harbours can be traced here from which the routes branch out in various directions inland. The greater proportion of the gold rings and gold wire of the bronze age, when they were a current medium of exchange, is found in these districts of west Jutland, the centre of the amber trade.

It is in this region first and foremost that the Norse bronze age assumes its proper character and its cultural wealth, and from this starting-point the bronze culture spread, in varying strength, into the other Scandinavian areas. The Danish isles have a complete representation of all the bronze phases, and in the late bronze age they became the richest of the Danish lands. The point of gravity moves from west to east in a manner which must be connected with the general conditions of European trade. Communications with southern Europe no longer went mainly by way of the Elbe, but rather by the south coast of the Baltic, perhaps, as has usually been assumed, because the amber from Prussia began to play a more important part in foreign markets.

The central domain of the Scandinavian bronze age is preeminently Denmark, but it includes Skåne too, and in some degree the island of Gotland. From here the culture of the time, its bronzes and its style, were transmitted to the northern area on the Scandinavian peninsula, but in varying intensity according to local conditions. As we have already mentioned, these regions of Scandinavia had in part been occupied in the preceding age by the 'submegalithic' culture, and in part formed the domain of the Arctic stone age; and we have seen that the people of these regions received a considerable amount of flint from the south of Scandinavia, from Skåne and Denmark. It is very natural that bronze should follow the routes which had already been established by the flint trade; and early pieces even from the first phase of the bronze age are found distributed northwards as far as the district around Trondhjem and the north of Sweden. But it should not cause surprise that the bronzes here in the north are comparatively rare, so rare that some writers in recent times have even concluded that in the greater part of the Scandinavian peninsula it is not justifiable to call this period a bronze age at all.[1] We need not be troubled by these doubts; Norway, Sweden, and Finland have also their bronze age, analogous to the corresponding age elsewhere in northern Europe, and it is characterized not only by bronzes, but, even more, by the form of burial, by social and religious conditions which we shall describe in detail in the next chapter. We shall then see also that in the northern area the forms belonging to this culture diverge from those of the Danish area. It should be mentioned here, however, that the east and middle of Sweden, with its centre in the lands around Mälaren, afford evidence of a lively intercourse during the late bronze age with Finland, Russia, and the east of Germany; in these Swedish territories there are bronze types which show independent development in several particulars, and influences from here can be traced on the one side into eastern Europe, on the other side into the north-west of Norway.[2] Bronze-age remains in Finland are of precisely the same character as in the east of

[1] Lauritz Weibull, 'Det arkeologiske Treperiodesystemet. Dess uppkomst och dess giltighet', *Historisk Tidskrift för Skåneland*, v (Lund, 1923); Curt Weibull, *Sveriges Bebyggelse. Bronsålderens Karaktär* (Lund, 1923); A. W. Brøgger, *Kulturgeschichte des norwegischen Altertums* (Oslo, 1926), p. 125 f. Brøgger's account gives, perhaps, a too primitive picture of conditions in Norway during the bronze age, and concludes thus: 'Auch ist es durchaus ein Misverständnis, wenn man in diesem Zusammenhange von einer Abschaffung der Bronzezeit redet. Die lässt sich nicht abschaffen, wohl aber muss man sie so ansehen wie sie wirklich gewesen ist.' Cf. Montelius, *Les Temps préhistoriques en Suède* (Paris, 1895), p. 97: 'Le bronze étant toujours assez précieux, on continua pendant l'âge dit du bronze à fabriquer des haches de guerre, des pointes de flèche et de lance en pierre.' This is true indeed of all countries, Egypt or Italy or England, that flint and other stone continued to be used during the bronze age.

[2] A. M. Tallgren, 'Die Bronzecelte vom sog. Anánino-typus. Berührungen zwischen den Bronzekulturen Skandinaviens und des Wolga-Kamalandes', *Finnisch-Ugrische Forschungen*, vol. xii (Helsingfors, 1912), p. 76.

Sweden. It would indeed be possible to speak of a Scando-Baltic bronze age whose special character is decided by lines lying more to the east than those which touch Denmark and Norway.

In this review of the phases of the bronze age and its various styles we have dealt exclusively with the bronzes, since these provide the basis of the division into phases and give the culture of the age its special character. The bronzes were precious articles, to a great extent articles of luxury which are found in graves of the distinguished, among religious offerings, or in stores of carefully hoarded treasures, and this in itself implies that in the life of the Northern people of that age there were elements incompletely represented in the civilization which the bronzes alone seem to attest. Thanks to the admirably conducted Danish excavations we now know the dwelling-sites of the time also, and the whole inventory of daily usage.[1] These dwelling-sites are marked by open, extensive deposits or by heaps of refuse gathered into specially made pits; the contents are the refuse of everyday life. Bronzes are very rare here, occasional pins or buttons, a little knife or an awl, all small articles which could easily be lost; and the inhabitants must have taken care to prevent the costly metal from being covered with refuse. Yet there is evidence of bronze casting in the dwelling-sites, melting-pots, and casting moulds. The principal articles of these finds are potsherds, which are found in extraordinary quantity and give quite a new conception of the pottery of the Danish bronze age. There is clay ware in all sizes, sometimes heavy pots of various—often highly elegant—forms, but without decoration. On the whole the impression is very different from that given by the clay ware of the stone age; moreover, the pottery of the bronze age is marked by a response to the general European orientation of taste, and it bears witness to a highly cultivated workmanship. The quantity of this clay ware excludes all notion of importation; it is a local product which in its own way is as important in characterizing the period as the bronzes are.

The refuse also contains a great amount of chipped flint; in one single dwelling-site, near Bulbjerg, it was possible to collect

[1] Sophus Müller, 'Bopladsfund fra Bronzealderen', *Aarb. f. nord. Oldk.*, 1919, p. 35.

over 7,000 pieces of flint refuse from chipping, and there were also found all manner of scrapers, knives, augers, hammer-stones, &c. It is quite unmistakable that flint was indispensable as material for all kinds of daily working equipment, which was produced by the same technique and in the same forms as in the stone age. This applies equally to axes of hartshorn and daggers and pins of bone. In the sphere of workaday life the ancient traditions were fully alive all through the bronze age. Even a battle-axe of variegated stone has been found in a dwelling-site of the late bronze age. This relation of stone and bronze, which in itself is very natural, is essential to complete the picture of bronze-age culture. The dwelling-sites provide a deeper cross-section of the life of the period, while the graves and the finds of bronze, as we shall see in the next chapter, illustrate the wealth and elegance which might be achieved among the higher classes of society.

Before we leave the dwelling-sites, it remains only to add a word about the manner of life and the means of subsistence. The bones among the refuse, which are obviously the remains of meals, include bones of wild animals, birds, and fish, especially bones of the hart, occasionally of the roe, as well as of swans and geese. But most of them are of domestic animals, sheep and goats, and especially prominent, bones of oxen, more rarely those of horses. These are the same domestic animals as were kept in the late stone age. The cultivated plants were, as we know from other sources, barley and wheat as in the stone age, and in the bronze age oats and millet also. Flax too was cultivated. With the bronze age there also comes a great advance in tillage: the hoe is superseded by the plough. In a bog in Uppland, Sweden, part of a primitive plough made of wood has been found, and by means of a geological determination has been dated in the early bronze age; and in Denmark also a primitive wooden plough has been found, in a bog near Hobro. A man ploughing with oxen as draught animals is depicted in a well-known Swedish rock-carving at Aspeberg in Bohuslän.

IX

BRONZE-AGE GRAVES. FINDS OF RELIGIOUS OFFERINGS

AS we have seen in the preceding chapter, the coming of bronze wrought revolutionary changes in the material culture of Scandinavia, in its technique, forms, and art of decoration, producing a new cultural era, profoundly different from the conditions of the stone age. This radical transformation is also evident when we turn to the forms of graves and the burial customs in the bronze age. The changes are introduced without any sudden break in tradition; we have already mentioned that the beginning of the period is fixed by the occurrence of the first few bronzes in the graves, which are still laid out in the manner of the stone age—individual burials in stone cists of comparatively modest dimensions, with a dagger of flint or bronze as the only grave furniture. But soon a change appears in response to an impulse which characterized the early bronze age over a great part of Europe. This is primarily a desire to raise more imposing grave-mounds as monuments. The great barrows of the heroic age, which extend from the Bosporus into central Europe and to the British Isles, came to be regarded as a necessity in Scandinavian lands, too, for every grave of importance. There are in Denmark some very impressive monuments of the kind,[1] 3 or 4 metres high or even higher, usually made entirely of turf built up layer upon layer (evidently at considerable expense of useful grassland), or else of earth and sand, as is especially common in Jutland. Denmark still possesses a wealth of these beautiful old memorials of antiquity, clustered in fairly large numbers in places where the settlements were thickest, or set out in long rows in the countryside beside the old travelling routes. At the centre of the mound there are often stone structures or stone heaps of various forms, more rarely a visible ring of stones around the base of the mound. Occasionally a circular fence of stones is

---

[1] See the classic account by Sophus Müller, *Vor Oldtid* (København, 1897), p. 295. Detailed descriptions in the article by L. Zinck, 'Broncefolkets Gravhøie', *Aarb. f. nord. Oldk.*, 1871, and Georg F. L. Sarauw, 'Lyngheden i Oldtiden', ibid., 1898.

PLATE 19

Grave mounds in the island of Karmoy, Norway

found inside the margin of the mound, hidden under its slope, an arrangement which is of special interest in the history of this type of grave. This feature is known in grave-mounds in Denmark and Norway and in sepulchral cairns in Sweden, and something very similar is found in Germany and Great Britain. This distribution demonstrates that the grave-forms of the Norse bronze age were evolved in contact with western and central Europe.[1] The imposing grave-mounds of Scandinavia are not produced by local development: they are the product of a common European movement which touched Norse lands and others as well. They are among the new ideas of the bronze age.

Grave-mounds of turf, earth, or sand are the types which prevail in Denmark and Skåne; they occur more rarely in Norway and Sweden, where they also appear in the typical form,[2] especially in the Swedish province of Halland and in certain districts in the south and west of Norway (Pl. 19). But on the Scandinavian peninsula the sepulchral monument usually assumes a somewhat different form, a cairn of bare stones without any intermixture or covering of earth or sand; as a rule it was set up on a hill or mountain by the sea, often on a headland or on a ridge with a steep slope down to the shore. But they are also found in inland districts. These cairns, known as *åsrøiser*, 'hill-cairns', or *munkerøiser*, 'monks' cairns', are the forms characteristic of the bronze age on the Scandinavian peninsula, and they are similarly prevalent during the same period in Finland. They are found in Denmark along the coasts, wherever there is a good supply of stone available on the shore, and on the island of Bornholm.

The graves themselves are set in the centre of the mound, either dug down into the ground below it, or, more usually, built on the original surface under it. The bronze age inherits from the stone age the grave cist of stone, built as an oblong right-angled chamber just long enough to accommodate a man, or, more usually, a little longer, wide and deep enough to

---

[1] Harold St. George Gray, *Report on the Excavation at Wick Barrow, Taunton Castle*, 1908.

[2] H.R.H. Crown Prince Gustaf Adolf and Oscar Almgren, *Kung Björns Hög*, Monografier utgifna af kungl. Vitterhets Historie och Antikvitets Akademien, no. 1 (Stockholm, 1905), with a summary in German. Shetelig, 'Norske Kulturforhold i Bronsealderen', *Årsberetning, Foreningen til norske Fortidsminnesmerkers Bevaring* (Kristiania, 1907), p. 7 f.

afford plenty of room for a single body. The sides are sometimes made of boulders set on end, or of slabs, or sometimes the
cist is walled with small stones; a covering stone is laid
horizontally above. The whole cist is carefully and strongly
built; in Norway traces have been found of cists having been
covered with birch bark. The stone cist is the usual form of the
bronze-age grave in Norway and Sweden, but it is less frequent
in Denmark, where the grave more often appears as an open
structure of stone, a frame, or a bed of stones; and usually
remains of wood can be traced in it, indicating that the grave
originally had a cover or a cist of planks. Of similar type is the
other well-known form of Norse bronze-age grave, the 'oak cist',
a coffin made from a thick trunk of oak, split and hollowed out,
in many examples specially protected by a casing made of a
still larger hollowed oak trunk fitted around the first one.

This careful structure of the graves is, with the variations
mentioned, common to all the Scandinavian lands, and accordingly must give expression to common conceptions concerning
death and the cult of the dead. A remarkable monument in
Skåne gives us a glimpse of the religious ceremonies at burials
and offerings: this is the grave at Kivik, which dates from the
transition between the second and third phases of the bronze
age. Each of the two long sides in the grave-chamber consisted
of four upright slabs, the inner sides of which bear incised
pictures; there is a procession of people in long garments,
evidently an offering scene, a man driving a wagon, a horse
fight(?), sun symbols, a group consisting of two large axes
(undoubtedly divine symbols also) one on each side of an altar,
and still more of the kind. We can hardly hope to interpret
these pictures in detail, but they give some idea of the various
religious ceremonies associated with the grave. In other Swedish
graves there are engraved pictures of ships, foot-prints and
other symbolic tokens.[1] In some Norwegian grave-cists the side
stones bear sun symbols or pictures of ships and decorative
symbols of the same kind as in the grave at Kivik.[2]

The religious ideas reflected in the bronze-age graves are

---

[1] O. Montelius, 'Et märkligt fynd från Södermanland', *Svenske Fornminnesför. Tidskrift*, x (Stockholm, 1897–1900), p. 189.

[2] E. de Lange, 'Ornerte heller i norske broncealdersgraver', *Bergens Museums
Årbok*, 1912, no. 4.

uniform throughout the whole of Scandinavia, but in the richer
or poorer furnishing of the graves there are very striking differences between the various districts. In the north, in Norway,
Sweden, and Finland, we often find that these massively constructed graves with their huge mounds or cairns entirely lack
sepulchral furniture. Although a great work may have been
devoted to the dead in the form of an impressive grave monument, the builders were yet unable or unwilling to offer him
any of the precious bronzes to furnish his tomb. It is the exception to find graves in this northern area containing the personal
equipment of weapons and ornaments. But it is quite otherwise
in the south of Scandinavia, especially in Denmark, the classical
land of bronze culture. In Denmark the dead were buried
arrayed in costume and accompanied by the most precious of
their personal possessions. In the men's graves are found sword
and dagger, palstave, spearhead, bronze buttons for the belt,
tweezers and razors, and not infrequently also an arm-ring of
gold. The women are laid in the grave with their broad collar
of bronze, belt-plate, fibulas, broad spiral rings for the arms,
and in some cases with fringes of bronze which were trimmings
of their dress. Often the women, too, bore a dagger, but never
a sword or other weapon.

The complete picture of this personal equipment is obtained
from the oak coffins mentioned earlier (Pl. 20). In favourable
conditions, when the coffin itself is well preserved, the tannen
in the oak preserves many objects of perishable material which
would otherwise have disappeared without leaving a trace.[1]
We are then able to study minutiae of the burial which we
never see in other graves; in many of the oak coffins the dead
lie upon an outspread cowskin and are covered by a long woven
cloth of wool. We also find antiquities in them which are not
known from any other finds. There is the palstave with its
original haft of wood, the sword in its wooden scabbard, daggers
with handles of horn. We find skins and textile fabrics, combs
of horn, pails of birch bark, boxes made of thin wooden boards,
and cups, beakers, and bowls carved in wood. Larger wooden
bowls with handles are regularly decorated with patterns of
stars on the bottom and bands around the sides; the markings

---

[1] Vilhelm Boye, *Trouvailles de cercueils en chêne de l'âge du bronze en Danemark* (Copenhague, 1896).

are brought into relief by darker colouring, and they are bordered with closely set rows of small tacks of tin. A rarity unique in the north of Europe is a complete little folding stool of wood with a seat of otterskin, a piece of furniture which appears in exactly the same form in Egypt, and is also known in the ancient culture of Crete. From Holstein and Sweden come some metal mountings which belonged to similar stools.[1] A form like this illustrates better than anything else the strong influence from southern culture which made itself felt in Scandinavia during the early bronze age.

But the most interesting contents of the oak coffins are the bronze-age costumes which they have preserved (Pl. 21).[2] The men have a kirtle reaching to the knee, fastened with straps over the shoulders and girded at the waist by a belt; over this is a somewhat longer cloak, thrown loosely over the shoulders and fastened at the neck with a fibula; the feet and ankles were covered by shoes of cloth or leather, and on the head a cap with a round crown was worn. Trousers were evidently not used, since this garment is never found in the graves. A woman's costume from Egtved near Kolding consists of a close-fitting short jacket with sleeves reaching to the elbow, and additional to this only a light short skirt extending from the hips to a little below the knees; it is a peculiar garment, made entirely of woollen fringes, and one that must have required some skill to make. With it was worn a narrow belt with belt-plates of bronze (Pl. 22, 23). The same light skirt of fringes is found on several figurines in Denmark. A woman in an oak coffin at Borum Eshøi near Aarhus had a fine hair net round the back of her head, fastened to a cord which passed around her forehead, while the other grave, at Egtved, showed the hair tied with a cord.

The costumes from the oak coffins also provide full information concerning the materials and the weaving of the bronze age. The material was black wool, always mixed in greater or lesser degree with hart's hair. The fabric is comparatively

---

[1] Fr. Knorr, *Klappstühle aus Gräbern der Bronzezeit*; O. Montelius, *Minnen från vår Forntid*, Fig. 990; Bror Schnittger, 'Våra Kulturförbindelser med östra Medelhavet under den äldre Bronsåldern', *Ord och Bild*, xxviii (Stockholm, 1919), p. 67.

[2] H. C. Broholm et Margrethe Hald, *Les costumes de l'âge danois du bronze*, Nordiske Fortidsminder (Antiquités scandinaves) II (København, 1911–35), p. 331.

PLATE 20

Interior of an oak coffin with the body uncovered, showing a young
woman with dress and ornaments. After Thomsen

PLATE 21

Man's costume from an oak coffin: kirtle, cloak, and cap. After Broholm and Hald

coarse, but it is of regular two-shafted weave; it is a thick and warm material. But other kinds are known, too, some of them fine fabrics of difficult weave. The men's caps are made shaggy on the outside, having threads hanging loose and ending in a little knot. The hair nets, the women's belts, a shawl with fringes are choice and skilfully made things which bear witness to a highly developed domestic art among the women. From Västergötland in Sweden a splendid mantle of the bronze age is known, of complex four-shaft weave; from analysis of the weaving it has been shown that several weavers worked at the same time on this valuable piece. Later, after a duel, it was presented as an offering at a spring.[1] In Norway, too, in Østfold and near Stavanger, some remains of bronze-age woollen costumes have been found.[2]

The Danish oak coffins give a wonderfully intimate picture of the bronze-age people, just as they lived and moved. The men are clean-shaven, as could also be inferred from the large number of razors in the graves. The women wore the hair cut short over the forehead and long at the sides. In a birch-bark pail desiccated remains of cranberry wine were found, mixed with myrtle and honey. The woman in the Egtved grave was blonde, of medium height, slender-waisted; she was little more than twenty years old. A little sprig of yarrow blossom was found in her coffin, showing that she had died in the summer-time. By her left side, wrapped in a cloth, lay the burned bones of a child seven or eight years old.

This is one of the earlier examples in Scandinavia of the new form of burial, cremation. Already early in the second phase of the bronze age we find cremation practised now and then in Denmark, and this custom gradually gains the upper hand. Towards the end of the early bronze age burial without cremation was, practically speaking, at an end, and during the whole of the late bronze age cremation was the sole prevailing custom. From the very nature of this custom important changes were

[1] L. von Post, Emilie von Walterstorff, and S. Lindqvist, *Bronsålders-manteln från Gerumsberget i Västergötland*, kungl. Vitterhets, Historie och Antikvitets Akademien, Monografiserien no. 15 (Stockholm, 1924–5), with a German translation.

[2] Ingvald Undset, *Norske Oldsager i fremmede Museer* (Kristiania, 1878), p. 80; Gabriel Gustafson, *Norges Oldtid. Gammel norsk kultur i tekst og billeder*, published by the Norsk Folkmuseum (Kristiania, 1906), p. 45.

brought about in the form and furnishing of the grave. There was, however, some reluctance to give up the customary form, the great stone grave as long as a man's body, even though now only small charred pieces of bone left after the burning were buried. At first the long grave-cists were built just as before, or else the urn was placed in an oak coffin, and the usual equipment of weapons and ornaments was still provided. Then after this came a change and shift to the new forms which were the natural results of burning the body; in the late bronze age the grave is a very small chamber which only just allows room for the urn, usually a simple earthenware pot containing the charred bones, or else the urn is set unprotected in the earth. At the same time the sepulchral furniture disappears; there is no longer any demand for large costly bronzes as offerings in the grave, and neither men nor women now receive any other equipment than some unimportant trifle, a pair of tweezers, a pin, a razor, or some such article.

The urns, too, are of the simplest kind, plain earthenware pots without decoration, of the same sort as we find in the fragments of broken earthenware on the dwelling-sites. The same jars as were used for food and cooking in daily life were finally made into burial urns. An exception is formed by the rare earthenware urns modelled as little round huts with an obvious door; they are in the same category as the 'house-urns' in Germany and Italy. The symbolic idea is clear enough: the urn represents the dwelling of the dead. Urns of this type occur in Denmark and Skåne, in Gotland and in Sweden proper, but their number is hardly noticeable among the other urns of the bronze age; the conceptions expressed in the house-urns evidently did not play any important part in Scandinavia. Still rarer are graves in which a precious vessel of bronze was used as an urn, though examples of this use are known.[1] More frequently the simplest of all grave structures is found, either with traces of a wooden urn, or the charred bones laid between stones, without any trace of a burial urn.

This simplification of the graves prevails over the imposing monuments, too. Large mounds are no longer raised, but the simple small graves proper to the late bronze age were made by

---

[1] Chr. Blinkenberg, 'Etruskisk Kjedelvogn fundet ved Skallerup', *Aarb. f. nord. Oldk.* (København, 1895), p. 360. In this article an Etruscan bronze vessel is described, found used as an urn in an oak cist of the third phase.

PLATE 22

Woman's costume from an oak coffin: jacket, skirt, and belt. After Thomsen

PLATE 23

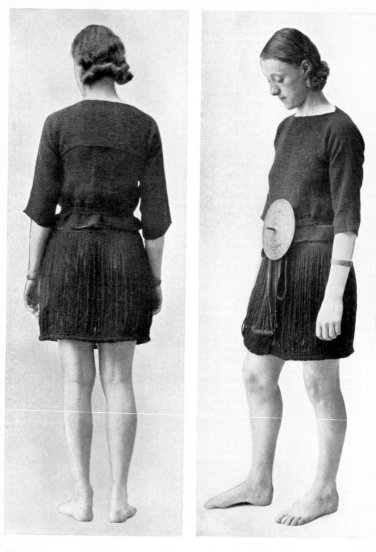

Bronze-age woman's costume in Denmark, restored. After Broholm and Hald

preference in the older mounds, which the ancient conceptions of death and the cult of the dead had invested with a venerable sanctity. The huge grave-mounds of the bronze age originally raised over great graves of stone or over oak cists ordinarily contain one or more of the small graves with burned bones from the late bronze age—testimony of the strong continuity of ideas about the dead throughout the whole bronze age, in spite of the changing burial customs. When there was no opportunity of finding a place for the urn in an older mound, the grave was covered with an insignificant little mound or cairn, or else a simple urn-grave was made below the level surface of the ground.[1] In the later examples of these graves we find the first implements of iron; this is indeed the burial custom proper to the early iron age. The form of burial (urn-graves below a level surface), together with the transition from bronze to iron, was brought in, as we can plainly see, by influences from the great urn-field groups in the east of central Europe.

There is one new and remarkable form of grave monument which deserves special mention, that which is known from its 'ship-formed' enclosure of stones (Pl. 24). This consists of raised stones set in rows so as to form a long enclosure with pointed ends, in the contour of a ship; and sometimes the end stones are higher than the others in imitation of the stems of a ship. There can be no doubt that monuments of this form actually were intended to be symbolic representations of ships. These ship-formed structures are well known both in Norway and Sweden, and it has long since been demonstrated that they enclose graves from various phases of the iron age; they have usually been associated with the ship-graves and boat-graves from the last phase of the heathen period in Norway. In recent years, however, a group of similar ship-formed enclosures has been excavated and found to contain graves from the late bronze age and the earliest phase of the iron age.[2] In these graves burial without cremation again occurs, a local phenomenon which appears in Gotland in the transition between the bronze age and the iron age.

[1] For examples see Bror Schnittger, *Flatmarksgraver från den yngre Bronsål-dern*, &c. (Rig, Stockholm, 1919), p. 104.
[2] Bror Schnittger, 'Gottländska skäppssättningar från bronsålderns slut och järnålderns början', *Aarb. f. nord. Oldk.* (København, 1920), p. 43.

There can hardly be any doubt that the ship-formed monuments are connected with the idea that man after death has to
make a journey across the sea. This conception is well known
from the Egyptian bronze age and was also widespread among the
classical peoples of ancient times. It is of the greatest interest to
trace this same belief in the grave-forms of the Scandinavian
bronze age. There is of course a natural reason for the island of
Gotland being the place where this idea first received concrete
expression in the grave-monument, but the rock-carvings, which
we shall discuss a little further on, also show that related ideas
were widespread among the Scandinavian people at this time.

In the later centuries of the early bronze age (during
the second and third phases) cremation became universal in
the Scandinavian lands, as far as our knowledge extends of the
graves in the Scandinavian peninsula in this period, and the
consequent alteration of the grave, both in form and furnishing,
was carried out uniformly everywhere. This profound and
radical transformation of the burial customs must have been
produced by a strong current of new ideas concerning death,
new conceptions of man's circumstances after death, as well as
by fear of peril to the living from the dead and his grave. We
cannot embark upon a general history of cremation here; we
will only emphasize the extraordinary interest which is attached
to the custom in this period of Scandinavia's earliest culture.
Cremation was unknown in the Scandinavian stone age, as also
in the first phase of the bronze age, and it was thus comparatively late when this manner of burial made its way to the north
of Europe. It took some time still, quite two centuries from the
first appearance, before cremation became the sole prevailing
burial custom. But the surprising thing is that the displace-
ment of the older burial custom should be so complete. We
have no right to compare this change with a change in religion;
and we can find no indication that this new burial custom had
any connexion with the worship of the gods in the Norse bronze
age. Yet cremation undoubtedly represents a profound change
in the conceptions about death, the grave, and the dead.[1] It
was in the period immediately preceding 1000 B.C. that the
change was carried through in Scandinavia.

[1] Concerning the idea in cremation, see Erwin Rohde, *Psyche* (Leipzig, 1894),
and Sophus Müller, *Nordische Altertumskunde*, i (Strassburg, 1897), p. 360 f.

PLATE 24

Ship-formed enclosure of stones around grave. After Ekholm

PLATE 25

The sun-image from Trundholm, Zealand. After Sophus Müller

The principal source of our information about the general nature of the bronze-age religion is in the finds of offerings or votive objects, that is, hoards of valuable articles which are buried in the earth or sunk in lakes or streams as offerings to supernatural powers. Offerings of this kind are known in Scandinavia from all prehistoric periods, varying in form and importance in the different ages. In the late stone age the most valuable articles of the time, the large weapons and implements of flint, were those deposited as gifts to the gods: the large flint axes, of the thin-butted or thick-butted types, flint daggers, flint saw-blades. In one group of finds only certain definite kinds of objects have been collected: nothing else than flint axes, as a rule two or three of them, but sometimes more, and flint daggers in number up to thirty, or a similar number of saw-blades of half-moon shape. Many finds contain other weapons, superior battle-axes or spearheads of fine workman-ship, and working-tools such as chisels of flint or bone and scrapers of flint, which appear with frequency in Norway. In some hoards it can be seen that the pieces had been placed in a certain order, or had been packed together with great care. It is a striking fact that the finds consist partly of the most superior and valuable pieces and partly of plain implements of rude workmanship, or, as the extreme antithesis, of collections of unworked and unformed pieces of flint. A similar difference can be observed in the condition of the objects; usually they are new and unused articles, but not a few are worn and damaged pieces.[1] We may recall in this connexion the finds of amber articles buried in bog or meadowland, especially the notable finds in Jutland mentioned earlier. The deposit may be of large or small content, sometimes several hundred pieces in all, occa-sionally several thousand, placed together in a vessel of earthen-ware or wood. A modest parallel to these Jutish finds is provided by the amber ornaments of the stone age in Norway, where they are always found in bogs and several times in hoards.

Very similar conditions are encountered in the bronze age.

[1] Sophus Müller, op. cit., p. 422; Otto Rydbeck, *Slutna mark- och mossfynd från stenåldern*, Lunds Universitets Historiska Museum (Lund, 1918); Helge Gjessing, 'Votiv- og depotfund fra stenalderen', *Oldtiden*, vii (Kristiania, 1918), p. 21; Shetelig, *Primitive Tider i Norge* (Bergen, 1922), p. 314.

Here we may mention the handsome heavy axes of bronze which are occasionally found in peat-bogs or in work involving excavation; also finds of swords sometimes from the early bronze age, sometimes from the late bronze age, from two to four pieces in each find; and the thick bronze torcs, which are regularly found in pairs. Especially characteristic are the trumpets, the greatest works in bronze from the Scandinavian bronze age. They are nearly always found in pairs, once six together, and always buried in bogs. It may be added that many of the largest and most valuable articles from the bronze age are found separately in very similar conditions, deposited near or under a great stone, in a bog or in the earth. The largest and handsomest bronze swords known come from bogs, as also the largest bronze axes, massive and certainly too heavy for actual use. To this list should be added articles of gold: two or three massive armlets of gold, from two to eight spiral rings for the finger or the arm of double gold wire. One group of finds consists entirely of golden vessels hammered thin, which we have mentioned above as articles imported from central Europe; in several examples in Denmark, however, a handle has been added, terminating in a horse's head. But quite insignificant articles may be found in the same conditions, such as a small saw-blade of bronze, a very rough working-tool; usually several articles of the same kind were deposited together.

We also know of valuable bronzes from the Scandinavian bronze age which were buried as hidden treasures, intended to be taken up again at some later opportunity. These are often costly and beautiful things;[1] but such deposits have evidently a different character: the articles are more miscellaneous and more fortuitously brought together than in the group which has been described above. The finds of that group, of peculiarly regular composition, demand some special interpretation. It is clear that the similar hoards of the stone age and bronze age must have been brought into being by the same motive, by some custom which has had a continuous tradition during this immense period of time. The explanation of the hoards from both these ages which is now generally accepted is that they were religious offerings. Custom decided that certain

[1] C. Neergaard, 'Dépots d'objets de l'âge de bronze', *Nordiske Fortidsminder* (Antiquités scandinaves), i (København, 1890–1903), p. 112.

kinds of articles should be preferred as offerings; a vow to a god sometimes determined the nature and the quantity of the gift, and the less valuable unfinished materials or raw flakes of flint may possibly represent a substitute for a corresponding number of objects promised in the vow. These are forms of offerings *ex voto* which are known in other ancient religions too.

A special type of offering, of considerable interest, is seen in the bronzes deposited in springs and wells, known from certain finds in Denmark, the most important from Budsene on the island of Møen.[1] The well was a hollowed tree-trunk which reached down to a water-bearing stratum below the earth and clay. In this trunk there were various bones of animals and a hoard from the late bronze age consisting of two hanging-vessels, a belt ornament, and three spiral arm-rings, all apparently deposited there together on the same occasion. In another find on the island of Fyn a bronze sword was discovered, a spearhead and a chisel of bronze, in an ancient well made of a hollowed oak bole; these, too, are from the late bronze age. From the early bronze age there are three bronze swords, found in a prehistoric spring in Roskilde. One is reminded of the offerings in curative springs in Switzerland, France, and Italy, especially when it is found that the water in the well at Budsene contains a high percentage of mineral salts (natron or magnesia), and that the spring in Roskilde contained a large amount of iron. We are reminded in particular of a find at St. Moritz in Engadine, where two handsome bronze swords and other bronzes were found at the lower end of a hollowed tree-trunk which formed the well-shaft to the spring. It therefore seems reasonable to regard the finds in Denmark also as evidence that the springs were worshipped as sources of healing, because of their curative properties.

We know other articles, too, from the Scandinavian bronze age which are undoubtedly votive articles, that is, objects made to be offered and not for any practical use; and certain others can only have had a religious purpose. The typical find of the former category is the well-known one from Nors in Denmark, a hundred small boats of gold which lay one inside another in an earthenware vessel, covered with a flat stone and

---

[1] C. A. Nordman, 'Offerbrunnen från Budsene', *Aarb. f. nord. Oldk.* (København, 1920), p. 63.

buried in a gravel-bank. These boats are made of thin sheets of gold laid on a slight framework of bronze, some of them decorated with concentric circles. They are obviously very frail, and could not have had any practical use. In the same category must be reckoned two pairs of large handsome axes,[1] decorated in part with gold; they are cast with only a thin covering of bronze over a core of clay. These axes are so weak that they would be worthless for any real use, and they may well have been votive pieces, though one may think also of religious symbols, perhaps the axe-symbols of the sun-god. In the grave at Kivik in Skåne, mentioned above, two axes were engraved symmetrically on each side of an acute cone, and in the rock-carvings men are depicted carrying axes of the same shape. It is certain at least that these interesting pieces had some connexion with religion. They belong to the early bronze age, to the transition between the second and third phases.

A parallel case is the sun-image or sun-altar from Balkåkra in Skåne, a horizontal circular disk of bronze engraved with five concentric nimbuses and riveted onto the end of a broad cylindrical band of bronze which is pierced in round holes; projecting from the other end of the cylinder are ten circular rings, each enclosing a cross. The whole is very definitely characterized as a sacred object, whether it be regarded as a symbolic image or as a votive gift.[2] This piece, too, was found buried in a peat-bog, as was also the best known of the bronze-age images in Scandinavia, the sun-image from Trundholm Mose in the north of Zealand (Pl. 25).[3] The sun-disk stands on a six-wheeled carriage of bronze, to which a bronze horse is attached. The sun is represented by a round, slightly convex disk, of which the two sides were cast separately and then fitted

---

[1] One pair was found at Brøndsted in Jutland, another pair at Skogtorp near Eskilstuna in Sweden.

[2] It is dated by Montelius from the first phase of the bronze age. G. Ekholm later called attention to a very similar piece found at Ödenburg in Hungary, and he concluded from this that the sun from Balkåkra had been imported into Skåne from the south, and also that it is not as early as Montelius thought. See O. Montelius, *Die Chronologie der ältesten Bronzezeit* (Braunschweig, 1900), p. 75, and G. Ekholm's article 'Balkåkra' in Ebert's *Reallexikon der Vorgeschichte*, i (Berlin, 1924), p. 334, plate 73.

[3] Sophus Müller, 'La Représentation solaire de Trundholm', *Nordiske Fortidsminder* (Antiquités scandinaves), i (København, 1890–1903), p. 322, plate xxxvii.

together. Both sides are richly decorated with spirals and circles in the best style of the early bronze age, and one side is also inlaid with gold. The sun-disk had been attached to the horse by a band which was passed through a little loop at the front edge of the disk. It is clear that the sun was conceived as drawn across the heavens by his steed, and the wheels are added so that the whole image could be moved and represent the passage of the sun. Beyond all doubt we have in this disk an image of a god, as well as a choice and precious piece of work which was offered to the god himself by being buried in the peat-bog.

It is doubtful whether this image was actually revered as sacred to the sun, or whether, as has also been suggested, since the disk is only a quarter of a metre in diameter, it is a small copy of an image on a larger scale which was used in sun worship; in this case the disk would only be intended to be an offering. This sun from Trundholm affords extraordinarily important evidence of the religion of the bronze age in Scandinavia, of a definite ritual in sun worship, in which the sun-disk is drawn forward by the horse as a symbol of the god. Related sun-images from the bronze age are found in Ireland.[1] This same combination of sun-disk and horse is also found several times in the Scandinavian rock-carvings, which are the most important and the most extensive documents for the study of the religion of the bronze age in the north of Europe.

[1] Reginald A. Smith, 'Sun-Discs of the Bronze Age in the British Museum', *Proceedings of the S. A. L.*, 2nd Series, xx, 1903.

X

THE ROCK-CARVINGS OF THE BRONZE AGE

THE rock-carvings of the bronze age in Scandinavia consist of large or small groups of drawings engraved, quite without art, on smooth sheer mountain cliffs. On the Scandinavian peninsula there is ready access almost everywhere to cliffs worn smooth by glaciers during the ice age, and eminently suitable for pictures of this kind. In Denmark similar carvings are found on large boulders, especially in the north of Zealand. These pictures are found in great numbers over the whole of Scandinavia, though north of Trøndelag the number is inconsiderable; while in Finland no such carvings have yet been discovered. They are especially numerous in Østfold in Norway and the adjacent Bohuslän in Sweden; but they are also found more widely scattered in all districts, within the limits just mentioned. In these carvings there is very often a large number of figures grouped together on a single surface, and such groups invariably convey a strong impression of accumulation, through new figures being added from time to time during a long period. There is never any question of artistic grouping of the figures; and indeed the rock-carvings of the bronze age have in general very little connexion with art. The pictures are conventionalized to the uttermost degree, the representation is simplified and made as schematic as the natural form of the object will permit; the whole intention was that everything should be recognizable and readily intelligible as a simple idea. In the carvings of the bronze age it is the conception, the general notion alone that is of importance, and in this they are a complete antithesis to the naturalistic pictures of Arctic stone-age art. Thus we find in the sphere of the bronze-age carvings a psychological element of the greatest interest, an element which emphasizes the contrast between the primitive hunting people and the settled and more highly organized agricultural people of the bronze age.

In spite of their schematic forms these carvings have an extraordinarily rich and varied content. The most frequent representation is a ship of highly conventionalized and peculiar form, in which the line of the keel projects as a rough beak under the stem at each end; it is often provided with an ornament such as a spiral or an animal's head (Pl. 26). Often the ship's ribs are represented, and above the bulwarks a row of upright strokes appear which evidently denote the crew; more rarely one or more of the men on board may be represented in larger proportions than the others, and they are then always armed, and sometimes engaged in battle. Oars and rudder are very rarely to be seen, and no sail is ever shown; but the ships now and then bear symbolic images, the round sun-disk, a wheel, a tree, an animal figure, or two large axes. Human figures by themselves appear in some numbers; they are mostly armed men, sometimes in battle-scenes (Pl. 27), and trumpet-blowers. We see whole processions (Pl. 28), or two men holding a disk, one on each side, or a single man carrying a wheel. Very often we find symbolic representation of marriage, a man and a woman together. There are figures in active movement, as in a dance; there are ploughmen, archers, horsemen, wagons with two or four wheels drawn by horses or oxen. Of animals there are many, so conventionally represented that they can be recognized only with difficulty; the hart can be distinguished, and so can horses and oxen. Birds and snakes are rare. There are also pictures of trees. The figures are drawn in various sizes. The human figures usually do not exceed half a metre in height, while the largest known is a man 2·30 metres tall. The ships are normally from $\frac{1}{2}$ metre to $1\frac{1}{2}$ metres in length, the longest known being more than 4 metres.

To all these and other pictures which can be directly understood must be added a second group of pictures and figures which apparently have a conventional symbolic meaning. They are representations of weapons, such as axes or swords; the sole of the foot, either engraved in outline or cut out complete in the rock, sometimes representing a naked foot and sometimes the sole of some form of foot-gear; single circles or several concentric circles, one within another; wheels with four or more spokes, and lastly, the most frequent of all the tokens, the cup-shaped hollows which always accompany the pictures in these rock-carvings.[1] We come upon these cup-shaped hollows already in

---

[1] Full description and bibliography are given by Oscar Almgren in the article 'Felsenzeichnung' in Ebert's *Reallexikon der Vorgeschichte*, iii (Berlin, 1925), p. 212.

the late stone age, when they often appear in megalithic graves, not only on the roof-stone, but here and there on the wall-stones inside the grave, where they could not have been added at a later date. Once we even meet with circles and footsoles in a stone-age grave, and once also with wheel-symbols. These figures are thus the oldest of the elements found in the rock-carvings of the bronze age. What is more, these symbols have a clearly established international distribution in the ancient world, and it is around them that the whole system of engraved carvings grew up. The first of the bronze-age motives to appear is the axe, depicted with a haft and standing by itself, as in the carving at Simris in Skåne. The axe is engraved in the same fashion on megalithic graves in Britain, on stone graves in the department of Marne, and is painted on the stone sides of a stone-age grave-cist at Mernburg in Saxony. Next come the first rude pictures of ships, of which we have examples in the grave at Kivik; they are also known in megalithic graves in Britain and Ireland. Thus the earliest carvings belonged to the culture of an immense area, and corresponding phenomena were produced in various quarters of Europe, in Spain and Portugal and in the Alps around the boundary between France and Italy. The symbolism of these rock-carvings represents a sphere of thought which was made accessible to many nations of the northern world during the transition between the stone and bronze ages; its ultimate origin is to be found in the Orient. In this relationship lies the first key to the nature of the thought, and to the interpretation of its symbolic expression.

We have also certain fixed points in the chronological sequence of the Scandinavian rock-carvings. The axes at Simris in Skåne can be assigned from their type to the first phase of the bronze age, and a group of swords depicted in carvings of Östergötland can be placed by the same criterion in the second phase; and again, we have shields and trumpets of the late bronze age. When the carvings are found in stone grave-cists like those mentioned above (p. 146), their age can be determined from the character or the contents of the grave, as in the Kivik grave from the end of the second phase, or in the grave from the same period at Andeslingen near Bremen, where the roof-slab has three human figures engraved on it. Or it may happen that the rock-carving contains spiral ornaments in the style of the

PLATE 26

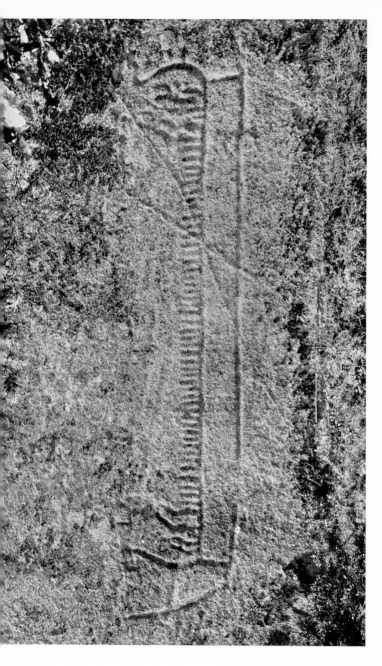

Rock-carving of a ship. Bjornstad, Skjeberg, Norway

PLATE 27

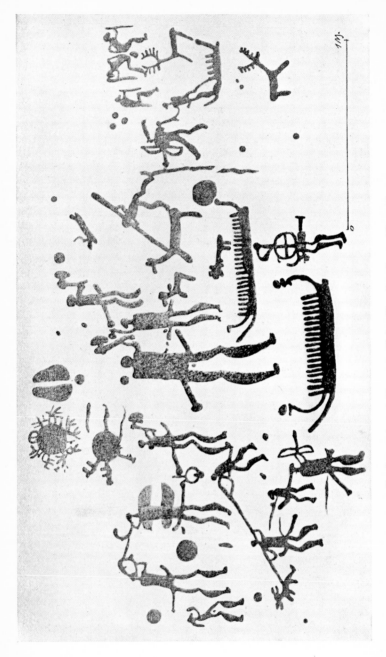

Rock-carving at Fossum, Bohuslän, Sweden. After Almgren

early bronze age, or the meanders of the late bronze age, and these will similarly determine the age of the carving; or, conversely, pictures of the type found in rock-carvings may be used as decorations on metal articles of which the date is known. A good example is the bronze mount of a blowing-horn found near Wismar, on which we have ships and wheel-figures, together with fine spiral decoration; the work can be assigned to the third phase of the bronze age. Similarly razors from the fourth and fifth phases are very often decorated with ships which have exact parallels in rock-carvings. There are also razors bearing pictures of men, serpents, and other subjects represented just as in the rock-carvings.

These comparisons have made it possible to group a large proportion of the rock-carvings according to their relative chronology. It can be shown that the pictures of ships under-went a gradual development from the first crudely simplified examples to the elegant and detailed pictures of the later period.[1] In general it may be said that rock-carvings begin to appear in the first two phases of the bronze age, but the rich and varied development belongs mainly to the later period of the bronze age. It can be shown, moreover, that the historical incidence of the carvings does not coincide exactly with the period of time which we call the bronze age; this is natural, since there is obviously no essential connexion between these pictures and the use of bronze or iron in practical life. We have examples of figures from the rock-carvings reproduced on earthenware vessels from the earliest phase of the iron age.[2] In this connexion we may also draw attention to the well-known rock-carving at Tegneby in Bohuslän, where a fight is depicted between mounted warriors, armed with spear and shield.[3] The shields have the right-angled oblong shape which we know was current in the early iron age,[4] while the shields of the bronze age, as far as is known, were round or oval.[5] It is, moreover, to be doubted

[1] Gunnar Ekholm, 'De skandinaviska Hällristningarna och deras Betydelse', *Ymer* (Stockholm, 1916), p. 292, Fig. 15.

[2] C. A. Nordman, 'Ormar och Hällristningar', *Oldtiden*, vii (Kristiania, 1918), pp. 200–1.

[3] Georg Sarauw, *Götaälvsområdets Fornminnen* (Göteborg, 1923), p. 286.

[4] *Nationalmuseets Bog om sjældne Fund* (København, 1925), p. 23, Fig. 12.

[5] A good selection of bronze-age shields may be seen in E. C. R. Armstrong's 'Prehistoric Leather Shield', &c., *Proceedings of the Royal Irish Academy*, 1909, p. 259 and plate xiv.

whether riding or fighting on horseback was practised in the bronze age; we have representations from that age of men standing in two-wheeled chariots with a double team of horses, and this seems a clear indication that war-chariots were then usual.

Equestrian figures are also found in the rock-carvings in the district around Trondhjem,[1] and other features there show that these characteristic compositions were executed sometime after the end of the bronze age. In the carving at Bjørngård in Stjørdal there appears a special type of ship with both stems terminating in a cleft formation which resembles two horns; and there is likewise a clearly drawn rudder on this vessel.[2] A nearly related type of ship is that which is depicted in the fragments of a rock-carving from Kårstad in Nordfjord, now in the Bergen Museum, accompanied by a runic inscription which points to the period round about A.D. 200.[3] Then there is also a Danish earthenware vase from the Roman iron age, ornamented with impressed wheel-figures and footprints.[4] In this vase we have indubitable evidence that the symbolism of the bronze age and the figures associated with it were still preserved many hundreds of years after the beginning of the iron age. Similar continuity is evident also in the ship-formed rows of stones mentioned above.

We have now set forth in brief outline the archaeological history of the rock-carvings in Scandinavia. There are groups of pictures and signs which have their origin in the late stone age and leave their last traces in the full-blown iron age, in the first centuries after the beginning of the Christian era: the history of the rock-carvings embraces a period of practically two thousand years. But it is also certain that the greater number of these carvings date from the bronze age; that was the age of their main growth and development, when they attained to the complete fullness of their varied content.

[1] K. Rygh, 'Arkeologiske Undersøkelser, 1910', *Det kgl. norske Videnskabers Selskabs Skrifter* (Trondhjem, 1910), no. 6, p. 32.

[2] Th. Petersen, 'Nye fund fra det nordenfjeldske Norges helleristnings-område', *Finska Fornminnesför. Tidskrift*, xxxvi (Helsingfors, 1927), p. 37. Petersen is inclined to date this rock-carving in the first phase of the iron age.

[3] Magnus Olsen and Haakon Shetelig, 'Kårstadristningen', *Bergens Museums Årbok*, 1929, Hist.-ant. rekke no. 1.

[4] Sophus Müller, *Ordning av Danmarks Oldsager* (*Système préhistorique du Danemark*), II. Jernalderen (København, 1888–95), Fig. 143.

The rock-carvings are difficult to interpret with any certainty; they have long been regarded as one of the most obscure riddles of Norse archaeology, though many different solutions have been advanced, such as the purely artistic view that the pictures were intended as art for its own sake, or the historical explanation that we have in these carvings a kind of pictorial chronicle of outstanding events. Most scholars, however, are now agreed that the pictures have a religious significance, and are connected with the bronze-age worship of the gods and cult of the dead. These two sides of religious life were very intimately connected, and they were both undoubtedly powerful factors in the evolution of the rock-carvings. The sacred symbols on graves, particularly the series of pictures in the grave-cist from Kivik, demonstrate clearly enough that such carvings had a connexion with the care for the dead; the presence of these signs would place the grave under divine protection and secure help for the dead in the future life. It must also be admitted as a possibility that the similar carvings on rocks, though never found in proximity with graves, may in some part have been devoted to the burial cult; but it can scarcely be assumed of all the carvings. No regular relationship can be proved between rock-carvings and graves; on the contrary, the local distribution of the carvings seems almost always to be wholly independent of graves, and their content is so greatly varied that very little of it could be naturally explained as belonging to the cult of the dead. It is not practicable to attempt any distinction in detail, because the grave-cult and religion proper made use to a great extent of the same symbols, above all the sun-figure; in all probability the greater number of the rock-carvings were made as shrines dedicated to public worship of the gods, especially to worship of the sun as the source of fruitfulness.

In this view the rock-carvings mostly become intelligible as religious monuments, even though there may be much that remains uncertain in the detailed interpretation of individual carvings.[1] The sacred figures give clear indication of the general nature of the bronze-age religion. The incised cup-shaped

---

[1] The problems and possibilities of interpretation have been brilliantly studied by Oscar Almgren in *Hällristningar och Kultbruk*, Kungl. Vitterhets Historie och Antikvitets Akademiens Handlingar, Del 35, (Stockholm, 1926–7), with a summary in French.

hollows have been regarded as sacrificial cups intended to receive libations or offerings of food; in Sweden the country folk in several localities continued to make offerings in these *älvkvarnar* ('elf-stones') during the whole of the modern era.[1] But the offerings do not preclude these cups from also being symbols of the higher power which received the offering. We pass over the interpretation of these cup-hollows as stars and stellar combinations and the various fantastic speculations suggested by these notions. It is much more plausible to suppose that these round hollows in the stone or cliff are sacred symbols of fire. The basis of this supposition is the striking similarity between the symbols in the carvings and the marks on a piece of wood which had actually been used for the production of fire by boring.[2] In this primitive method of generating fire sparks spring out of the hollow which is being bored: it is the well-spring of fire. But it has been observed on the other hand that the hollows in the carvings bear a remarkable similarity to certain symbols in India; in India there are cups encircled by a ring, from which a groove runs out to one side. This is the simplest form of the *lingam-yoni* symbol, the symbol of Mahadeva representing nature's fertility. These two interpretations are related, however, since the Rigveda compares the action of boring with fertilization.[3] In these cup-shaped hollows, the most venerable of the symbols in the Scandinavian rock-carvings, according to this interpretation, representation of fire and of fertility are united, and the offerings were associated with these significations.

Here too we have to consider the footprints, also among the most ancient signs in the rock-carvings. It is to be observed that the footprints often appear in company with other symbols or by the side of figures which can be taken to denote gods or manifestations of gods. Again we turn to India for enlightenment; there the combination of footprints and sun-symbols is often found, and current belief usually connects them with the wanderings of Buddha: hence in relation to these signs Buddha

[1] N. E. Hammarstedt, *Schwedische Opfersteine, Beiträge zur Religionswissenschaft*, herausgegeben von der Religionswissenschaftlichen Gesellschaft in Stockholm, ii. 1, 1914.

[2] Sophus Müller, 'Skaalformede Fordybninger. Hellige Tegn for Ilden', *Arab. f. nord. Oldk.* (Kjöbenhavn, 1917), p. 88.

[3] Oscar Almgren, loc. cit., p. 219 f.

PLATE 28

a. Rock-carving of man, sun-disk, and spear, at Bjørngaard, Stjørdal, Norway. After Th. Petersen

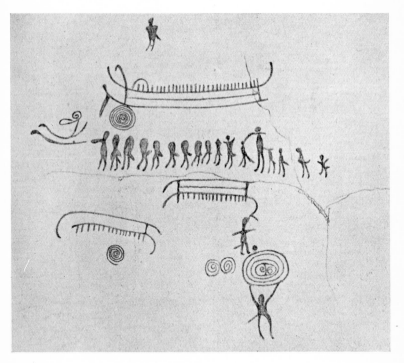

b. Section of a rock-carving showing a procession, man with sun-disk, ships, &c. After Nordén

must have replaced an older sun-god. There is in general an extraordinarily widespread manifestation in religion and folklore of the belief that engraved footprints, or natural marks which happen to resemble footprints, are due to gods or saints. The purpose of this symbol must originally have been to invoke the presence and favour of the god—the sun-god—in the place which was consecrated to his worship. But the footprints are also commonly associated with the belief that the god will confer magical fertility upon the earth.

The simple rings or the concentric circles, the wheels with four or more spokes in varying numbers, these are without any doubt sun-symbols, and they are the most numerous of the tokens in the rock-carvings. As has already been mentioned, we also have evidence of the sun worship of the age in sun-figures of bronze; but whole scenes of sun worship are often presented in the rock-carvings. We have the sun with a steed yoked to him, the same combination as in the image from Trundholm; again, we have the sun-figure set on a chariot with wheels; we see men carrying the sun-symbol on long poles, or else it is held up by a man on either side; finally, and very frequently, the sun-symbol is set in a ship. With the progressive analysis of the rock-carvings it has become quite clear that sun worship held a central position in the Scandinavian religion of the bronze age, and it is equally beyond doubt that these pictures, or at least the greater number of them, represent ritual ceremonies at the worship of the god. We have not only the holy symbols which hallowed the place, we also have pictures of the sacred objects which were carried about when the people were gathered for religious celebrations.

This theory provides the key to further interpretation of whole hosts of figures in the carvings. There are firstly the ships, the most frequently recurring motive in the whole body of carvings. It is to be observed that the ships are often provided with sacred symbols or are associated with other religious representations or tokens; and the representations of ships in graves will also be recalled. There can be no question of actual ships being represented, still less of warships and battles at sea; no single example of a battle between ships is found in any of the carvings. These circumstances, where so many details point to religious forms, induce us almost involuntarily to recall the ship of the sun which voyages across the heavens, known in many religions, and we recall that ships or images of ships have played a part in religious ceremonies in many places. We have a very definite intimation of this symbolism when we find in the rock-carvings men carrying a ship, or a ship with horses harnessed to it. But at the same time we are reminded of a feature in the belief concerning death, the ship which carries the dead over the sea. These two conceptions have been sharply opposed to each other in recent years in archaeological discussions in Scandinavia, but it is highly probable that both ideas were current among the people of the bronze age, though we are as yet unable to explain the meaning of each individual picture. We may even suspect that the two conceptions were identified, as they were in Egypt, where the dead were taken into the ship of the sun.

It would carry us too far afield to enter into detailed discussion of all the motives of the rock-carvings. It need only be said that nearly all of those which are represented more or less intelligibly can be readily explained as scenes from religious ritual. The regular disposition of a whole row of persons in a rank falls quite naturally under this head (Pl. 28); battle-scenes may represent a ceremonial weapon dance, or the symbolical combat which is often connected with religious festivals among the more primitive peoples; ploughmen, who indeed appear very often, may represent the ceremonial ploughing of a consecrated field to hallow the earth in the spring; the wagons may, in some degree at least, be the symbolical wagons which the sun-figure drove; a man and a woman together in conjugal embrace may be carrying out the symbolical process which secures fertility. We have trumpet-blowers in groups of two, four, or six, spearmen, and men carrying huge axes; there are leaping figures of men who seem to be racing with each other, figures in such active movement that we must suppose that they are dancing or performing acrobatic feats; and we see worshippers with uplifted hands.

All these can be best explained as features of religious celebrations, held for the purpose of invoking the higher powers which dispense fertility and fortune, and this conception alone is able to supply an inner connexion between so many miscellaneous pictures. The rock-carvings vary greatly in extent, as has already been mentioned. There may be a single picture by itself, or only some few figures arranged as a group, while others are very extensive, with a highly varied content, and cover large surfaces. We have seen that these large carvings have been produced by successive additions; they have grown gradually, and, as can also be seen, in a certain regular order. It may be guessed that each addition was made after a festival of special significance, that, in other words, the pictures and groups of pictures represent ritual ceremonies which were held actually on that very occasion. The rock-carvings then have not merely a generally symbolical and religious content; they represent a concrete actuality of bronze-age life, and certainly that side of life which made the strongest impression upon the men of that time, the feasts where many were gathered together at the great festivals of the year. But the purpose of the rock-carvings was clearly not to preserve the memory of a festival for later times. According to all that we know of ritual in the early religion of antiquity, the pictures held a deeper magical purpose; ritual ceremonies, correctly and scrupulously carried out, could in themselves induce or almost compel divine action according to the will of man, and in the same way the pictures of these same ceremonies would produce an enduring effect.

It is an obvious corollary that the place where the carvings were cut was also the place where the worship of the gods was held. Here we must mention some very important observations made in Östergötland, Sweden.[1] In a series of examples in that province immense remains of fire, ashes, and stones scorched and brittle from the heat have been found, in undoubted connexion with rock-carvings. A layer of ashes of this kind, 23 metres long and 60 cm. thick, lies among the mountain peaks which bear the splendid carvings of Himmelstadlund. The fires were lit in this place at festivals, and the ceremonies of the festivals are perpetuated in the carvings. A description of another example, of a somewhat different kind, has been published; it is in Fordal in Hegra, near Trondhjem, and it seems readily intelligible, as it consists of a very simple group of carvings. In two places here we see a single sun-image, and placed close around it a large number of horses. An interpretation which carries conviction

---

[1] Arthur Norden, *Felsbilder der Provinz Ostgotland in Auswahl* (Darmstadt, 1923) (Werke der Urgermanen); id., *Östergötlands Bronsålder* (Linköping, 1925).

is that the horse here was a sacrificial victim at the festival of
the sun, and the origin of the carved figures was that each sacrificial animal offered was represented by a new picture near the
sun-image.[1] In this instance, moreover, it is obvious that the
carving stands beside the place of sacrifice where the worship
of the gods was performed.

There still remains a problem to be mentioned, one that has
always been in the foreground whenever the interpretation of
the rock-carvings has been under discussion—and is, moreover,
of very great importance for the reconstruction of the bronze-
age religion—namely, whether, among all these religious pictures, there are any representations of gods in human form.
It may be said at once that this problem has not been solved.
It is remarkable that we often see individual human figures
in the rock-carvings which are exaggerated beyond normal
and natural size and more carefully executed than the multitude of other human figures. The fact should, moreover, be
emphasized that these large figures are depicted as a rule with
definite attributes: they have horned heads, or they carry an
axe, a hammer, or a spear, or they are accompanied by certain
symbols (Pl. 28). Pictures of this kind were indeed interpreted
some time since as personal gods.[2] It is not a valid assumption that the representation of divinities by symbols (the
sun-token, the wheel with four spokes, footprints, &c.) would
preclude the representation of these gods in human form;
from almost all religions there is evidence that personal gods
can very easily exist side by side with symbolic tokens which
represent the divine powers. More weight, however, must be
allowed to another objection which is based upon the general
spirit and content of the rock-carvings. It may seem difficult
to find a place for the gods themselves among these pictures
representing almost exclusively ceremonies performed by human
beings in the worship of the gods, and it would accordingly
seem more credible that the enlarged figures among the men
represent the persons who had the leading part, either the chief
or the priest (who might often be the same man). But this
explanation in reality comes very near to the other. It is a

---

[1] Th. Petersen in *Finska Fornminnesföreningens Tidskrift*, xxxvi (Helsingfors, 1927), pp. 35 ff.

[2] J. J. A. Worsaae, *The Industrial Arts of Denmark*, London, 1882.

widespread fiction in primitive religions that the god himself is present at his own festival, and he is then represented by a man who bears his attributes and performs in the ritual the functions which are imputed to the deity. The enlarged figure in the carvings would then be portrayed in this fashion because he represents the god, and as a further consequence of this custom the gods have at times been conceived of as existing in human form. We may recall here the Egyptian images in which gods and pharaohs are portrayed many times larger than the ordinary mortals.

Such comparison of rock-carvings with Egyptian and Cretan figures has in a general way been most fruitful in advancing the interpretation of the rock-carvings, since many of the same motives are found in both. There is a certain amount of common ground both in the conceptions and in their expression, proving once again that the Norse bronze age belongs to the same period and the same cultural sphere as the bronze-age people around the Mediterranean. From the Mediterranean emanated not merely discoveries in the advancement of material civilization, as, for example, in the technique, forms, or decoration of bronze work, but also spiritual impulses which left a deep impression in even the most northerly part of Europe.

The most northerly of the bronze-age carvings known in Scandinavia are found on the west coast of Norway north of Trondhjemsfjord, at Tjøtta in Helgeland, near the sixty-sixth degree of latitude. It contains ships and horses, double spirals, footprints, rings and hollowed cups, a combination of pictures and symbols which belongs exclusively to the bronze age. In the agricultural settlements of Trondhjem, where bronze-age grave-monuments appear in considerable numbers, a number of rock-carvings are found of the same content as those in the south of Scandinavia. But in these northern latitudes it also happens that the bronze-age pictures meet with Arctic stone-age art such as we have described earlier. We have already mentioned the carving at Bardal, near Stenkjær, not far from Trondhjems-fjord, where large ships, spirals, footprints, and schematized men and animals are cut without regard over older carvings, representing a group of large elks, on the same cliff-face. Here the chronology is beyond doubt; the bronze-age carvings were executed later than the naturalistic pictures. The same order is apparent in other carvings where the pictures were not made directly upon each other. The carving at Hammer in the same district as the last has a group of naturalistic sea-birds highest on the rock, while lower down we find ships and small schematized animals. It can probably be concluded that the carving was extended gradually, as such carvings often were, and that the naturalistic pictures here are of older, the bronze-age symbols of later origin. At Evenhus in Frosta, also in the Trondhjem district, we find similarly that ships and sun-figures are mingled with naturalistic pictures of whales. There are ships of a peculiarly primitive form, which shows that they must come from a very early period, although they clearly represent the same ideas as do the ships in other bronze-age carvings. The best authority on the northern rock-carvings has come to the conclusion that these figures extend continuously over a period from the late stone age into the bronze age.[1] The carvings at Nämnfors in Ångermanland, Sweden, also include figures of both kinds, naturalistic pictures of animals, especially of elks, and side by side with them a number of bronze-age motives, ships, circumscribed crosses, footsoles, men, hollow cups, and others.[2]

These carvings reflect in an extraordinarily interesting way a transition between two ages and two profoundly different civilizations. As has been argued on a preceding page, we must believe that the naturalistic pictures of animals were an expression of a primitive magic among the hunting people of the stone age. There is nothing symbolic in them; they are only concrete realistic pictures of the wild animals which were hunted and were the objects of all hunters' desires. It is quite possible, as has been suggested earlier, that wild animals such as the elk and the bear were looked upon with a certain superstitious regard, as bearers of hidden powers of nature, simply because hunting was then the essential basis of man's existence. But these animals could be brought into the hunter's power through pictures representing them. The animal pictures of the stone age were perhaps the most significant feature in the whole of this primitive 'Arctic' civilization. And now the bronze-age symbols appear in this quarter, a manifest proof of a new spiritual

[1] Th. Petersen, *Finska Fornminnesföreningens Tidskrift*, xxxvi. 27–32.
[2] G. Hallström in *Fornvännen* (Stockholm, 1907), p. 162 f.

current. What now appears is more than a new religion; it is, generally speaking, the first time we find traces of any definitely religious conceptions in the northern part of the Scandinavian peninsula. It is of special significance that the bronze-age carvings in several examples form a continuation and conclusion of the animal pictures of the early stone age. The symbols of the new era were added on the same rock that had already been consecrated by carvings of elk, reindeer, and whales, a clear proof of continuity in population and customs, in spite of the religious innovations.

In recent years there has been much lively discussion of the extent to which the true bronze-age culture made its way into the Scandinavian peninsula.[1] It is true—as has been stressed specially in this connexion—that the number of bronze-age bronzes known from the peninsula, apart from the south of Sweden, is surprisingly small. Even a cursory survey of the various Scandinavian museums will give a strong impression of Denmark's enormous wealth in bronze-age antiquities, as compared with more modest collections in Norway and Sweden. There can be no doubt that this difference reflects real conditions of culture in that period. It is evident from this that the more northerly people had not the means of obtaining such abundant supplies of bronze as the south Scandinavians. Consequently the graves here in the north are much more poorly furnished with bronzes, and there are far fewer valuable articles of bronze deposited as stores or offerings. Bronze was costly, and its price imposed limits on the ready distribution of the metal. But it may also have caused greater niggardliness in providing offerings and grave furniture, and it is therefore possible that bronze was not as scarce in practical use as would appear from our sources.

Interesting problems associated with the bronze age on the Scandinavian peninsula—to what extent the metal was replaced by other material, stone, bone, &c., and whether it is in general correct to use the term 'bronze age' of this period in the northern part of Scandinavia—these we do not intend to pursue in detail here. We now have to consider once more the

[1] See especially Brøgger, *Kulturgeschichte des norwegischen Altertums*, Instituttet for samenlignende Kulturforskning (Oslo, 1926), p. 114 f., and Anathon Bjørn, 'Tidlig metalkultur i Østnorge', *Oldtiden*, xi (Oslo, 1926).

distribution of the rock-carvings, which are extraordinarily important documents for this study. Even the most northerly carvings, at Trondhjemsfjord and on the coast to the north, comprise the same elements that we know in the south of Scandinavia. These are hollowed cups, circumscribed crosses, circles, footprints, ships, horses, and men ; more sporadically we also meet with spears, axes, trumpets, and other figures, or the sun-figure represented with a man on each side, and these figures appear very early, already in the second and third phases of the bronze age. These most northerly carvings are simpler and more primitive ; among them we miss the complex dramatic compositions, ceremonial processions, dances, weddings, and battle-scenes, which are so prominent in Bohuslän and Götaland. But the northern Norwegian carvings bear witness sufficiently clear to the worship of the same gods; identical religious conceptions are expressed by common symbols over the whole area of the Scandinavian bronze age. The grave-cists of the early bronze age and the subsequent spread of cremation give evidence in the same sense. The Scandinavian peninsula, even as far north as the district north of Trondhjem, was penetrated by religious impulses of sun worship and the cult of the dead, impulses which are characteristic of the bronze-age culture, and whose origin must be sought ultimately among the civilizations around the east of the Mediterranean.

But in the most northerly region of Norway and Sweden we find no traces of bronze-age civilization. The most northerly find from the bronze age in Norway is about 68° N. We must conclude that on the coasts of the Arctic and in the forests and highlands the forms of stone-age culture still persisted during the thousand years which in the lands farther south embrace the whole history of the bronze age. The complete picture of Scandinavian culture during this period must include all shades in the transition between the two extreme points, on the one side the attractive richness of early bronze culture in Denmark, and on the opposite side the last of the Arctic stone age in Finmark.

XI

THE EARLY IRON AGE

LIKE so many other important elements of ancient culture, the production and use of iron originated in the lands east of the Mediterranean and from there spread gradually to all the peoples of the ancient world. Thanks to a fortunate find, it has been established that iron was produced and used for weapons in Cappadocia, then part of the Hittite empire, before the middle of the thirteenth century before Christ; and in the course of the same century the new metal was introduced into Egypt and the Greek world, and a little later into Italy too. From the Mediterranean iron was brought into central Europe and there came into constantly increasing use during the tenth and ninth centuries before Christ. The transition between bronze and iron took place in this region during the Hallstatt period (so named from Hallstatt in Austria), and it was accomplished without any break in the continuous development. The forms of late bronze-age weapons and sometimes of ornaments were now produced unchanged in iron. The heavy, very characteristic iron swords from Hallstatt have precisely the same forms as contemporary and earlier bronze swords. As would be expected, it was from this area that iron made its way into general use in the north of Europe. But obviously one must not suppose that iron at a single stroke replaced bronze for all purposes. In the earliest iron age iron held in some degree the position of an exceptional metal, used primarily for weapons, for swords and spears. The simple working axes, the socketed celts, were very commonly of bronze in the earlier Hallstatt period everywhere in western and central Europe, just as in the early iron age in Italy. This was the period of transition when bronze and iron were used side by side.

Iron was known in Scandinavia to some extent long before the end of the bronze age. Already from the third phase an iron piece is found in a grave in Bornholm, and from the fourth phase, according to Montelius from about 1000 B.C., iron has been discovered in a few Danish graves. A bronze knife from this period has been found together with an iron pin, and on

another knife belonging to the same time the blade is ornamented with inlay of gold and iron; thus we see that iron was
still a rarity. During the last centuries of the bronze age iron
appears in knives, rings, a horse's bit, a miniature sword from
an urn-grave, and in other articles. From Östergötland there
is an iron sword of Hallstatt type which must be contemporary
with the late Scandinavian bronze age. It is evident that iron
was now becoming known in increasing quantity, though bronze
was still predominant in the north[1] in the periods which constitute the first iron age in central Europe. The transition to
conditions of the new age gradually becomes apparent as
weapons and larger implements of bronze become rarer; the
last of the bronze age is represented almost entirely in ornaments, pins, and neck-rings of various forms.

The group of remains which first gives a fairly complete
picture of the earliest iron phase in the north is found in the
Jutish *tuegraver* or 'mound-graves' (the German *Flachhügel-
gräber*). There are large burial-places, often with hundreds of
graves, and even up to two thousand, which lie close together,
each grave covered with a very low mound, a *tue*. In a small
grave in the ground under the mound there is a fairly large urn
containing the burned bones from cremation, carefully cleaned,
as was also the custom in the bronze age. A characteristic
feature is that the urns usually have the lugs knocked off; this
may have been done as a symbolical dedication of the grave-
urn, to signify that it should never again be lifted from its place.
Additional earthenware vases are rarely found beside the urn,
and the furniture was poor; only about one grave in three
contained any grave-goods. These were mostly small articles,
characteristic pins of iron with a bend in the stem near the head,
bronze rings for the belt, adorned with chased bronze plating.
This is a new inventory, different from that of the bronze age;
the burial custom too was different, in that the grave-goods
were burned with the dead on the pyre. But at the same time
late Scandinavian swords of bronze occur sporadically and bear
witness to the continuity between the two periods.

It is clear that the earliest phase of the iron age, as it appears in the mound-graves of Jutland, was a Norse Hallstatt

---

[1] The early finds of iron in Scandinavia are collected by Montelius in 'När
började man allmänt anvanda järn?' *Fornvännen* (Stockholm, 1913), p. 73 f.

culture very closely related to contemporary civilization in the immediately adjacent districts to the south and in others still farther to the south. In these parts of Germany the transition from the bronze age to the iron age is represented by the culture which takes its name from the great burial-places with urns lying under a flat surface of ground, known as 'urn-fields' (*Urnenfriedhöfe*). This culture descends from the late bronze age, and had already at that time given a characteristic stamp to a well-defined area with its centre in Saxony, Lausitz, Silesia, and the neighbouring districts. The form of the grave is very simple: the ashes from the pyre are collected in a large urn which is set under the level surface, and close around it stands a number of earthenware vessels, bowls, beakers, and the like. The furniture is otherwise restricted to small objects of metal, especially ornamental pins of bronze and iron, small knives, and such articles. This eastern wing of the Hallstatt culture is represented in immense numbers of remains in Germany, and it is on the whole very uniform over widely extended areas.[1] It stretches down the Vistula to the Baltic and down the Elbe to the North Sea. In this culture we find iron in practical use already in the eighth century before Christ. And it was this culture which made its way across Holstein into Jutland and there inaugurated the earliest iron age, represented in the mound-graves.

It is in connexion with the same cultural forms that iron is first seen in ordinary use in other districts of the north too, on the islands of Bornholm and Gotland, and on the Scandinavian peninsula. The grave-forms vary widely: there are mound-graves like those of Jutland, for example, in Oslofjord and near Stavanger, burial-places presenting a flat surface of ground, sometimes also cairns like those of the bronze age, and finally there are early iron-age graves made secondarily in older grave-mounds. An important innovation in the form of the grave is now encountered in Bornholm and Gotland, where it became customary to bury all the remains of the pyre, not merely the burned bones, as was usual to the old custom; the grave then

---

[1] C. Schuchardt, *Die Urnenfriedhöfe in Niedersachsen* (Hannover, 1911); Gustav Schwantes, 'Die Gräber der ältesten Eisenzeit im östlichen Hannover', *Prähist. Zeitschrift*, i (Berlin, 1909); Friedrich Knorr, *Friedhöfe der älteren Eisenzeit in Schleswig-Holstein*, i (Kiel, 1910).

appears as a hollow in the ground, filled with brands and ashes mixed with small white pieces of burned bone. These graves, which now appear for the first time, are called *brandplætter* in Denmark and in Sweden *brandgroper*; they are also known in the same period in the east German area, around the Oder and the Vistula. It is still uncertain where this new form of burial first arose; it came to play a considerable part in the subsequent phases of the iron age, and it is the constant characteristic of eastern parts of north Germany and Scandinavia, while Jutland and western Norway held to the custom of washing the bones after cremation, as had been done in the bronze age. In Gotland at this time some cases appear of the dead being buried without burning, an isolated and puzzling occurrence.

Only a poor picture can be formed of this period in Scandinavia, since the graves never contain large and valuable articles, and it was no longer the custom to deposit costly offerings in fields and bogs, a custom which provided most important sources of our knowledge of the bronze age. What we do know for certain, however, is that the later portion of the Hallstatt period coincides with the first phase of Scandinavia's iron age. We no longer find weapons and implements of bronze; on the other hand, we constantly come upon iron pins decorated with a knob or plate of bronze, and flat brooches of bronze with pins of iron; in other words, iron is the metal for use, while bronze is reserved for ornament. The really remarkable thing is that it took such a long time for iron to make its way into general practical use in the north, several centuries later than in central Europe, even though Denmark obtained its bronze from there. In explanation of this archaeologists have pointed to the conservative power which conspicuous excellence in the art of treating bronze would wield, while work in iron was a new and unknown art; the familiar metal would therefore be preferred. This must certainly have had some share in retarding the introduction of iron; but another factor should also be taken into account, namely, that iron in the earlier Hallstatt period was used primarily for weapons, and it can readily be imagined that the peoples already using iron would not be specially eager to share their superior metal with others.

But most important of all was the new discovery, the method of extracting iron, which had reached central Europe already in the Hallstatt period. There is detailed proof in France that the richest provinces of Hallstatt culture coincide with the thickest occurrence of prehistoric iron mines and traces of ancient working of iron. Similarly, over the whole of northern Germany there are countless traces of prehistoric smelting of iron, and from there the discovery was taken into Scandinavian lands. With this discovery went the great advantage which iron possessed: there was an unlimited supply of it in nature, compared with the needs of the ancient world, and it could be produced anywhere, whereas bronze could be produced only within limited areas. In most regions, therefore, the bronze of ancient times was a comparatively expensive material. This has been proved long since, and is generally known, but it must once more be emphasized, since the transition from bronze to iron has obviously greatest importance in outlying districts where bronze was obtainable only with difficulty. The people were no longer restricted to a metal which could only be obtained by importation from other lands; with iron the art of producing the metal on home soil spread from people to people over the whole of Europe. It was in this ease of production, before every other advantage, that the immense superiority of iron lay.

The source of the prehistoric production of iron in the north of Europe was always bog-ore: that is, iron compounds which are formed in the soil and are concentrated in still bog-pools by the action of water; the iron compounds are then precipitated in solid form as small lumps of ore found under the peat. Bog-iron has been used in Norway and Sweden continuously up to recent times, almost up to the present day, and we are very well informed concerning the processes by which this industry produced iron for the local needs of the district. Iron-smelting was a recognized farm industry which was to be carried on at certain times of the year in primitive forms handed down by tradition. The ore was burned in a funnel-shaped hollow (called in Danish a *hærdgrube*, in Norwegian *blæstre*) which was dug in the ground and lined with clay, forming a deep receptacle. Bellows were fixed on opposite sides of the pit, inclined so as to blow down into it. For the burning good dry wood was needed, best if mixed with a little charcoal. The metal was released gradually as it melted in the heat, and in this way the iron was extracted; but the process was quite incomplete, and much of the iron remained in the slag. Moreover, the iron which was produced in these pits was very impure and had to be hammered in the smithy until the slag came out.

The iron extracted in this way was a soft forge-iron of somewhat uneven quality, since the process of production was so primitive. But it was iron all the same and a highly useful metal. A moderate demand could be satisfied by such local production. Since the treatment of iron ore still took such simple forms as this in Norway in historic times, we are justified in assuming corresponding conditions in the prehistoric iron age. Moreover, there are innumerable evidences everywhere in Scandinavia of this working of iron ore, in the form of slag-heaps and smelting-pits, from very ancient times.[1]

The question which interests us here is, how early the production of iron was known in Scandinavia. It can be traced with certainty in the Roman period, the first centuries of the Christian era; in Sweden it is even established that smiths understood how to steel weapons and tools in the period round about A.D. 300.[2] From the earlier phases of the iron age no decisive evidence of native production of iron in the north has yet been found, and we are limited to the rather vague view that the Scandinavians were probably able to find out how to extract iron from the earth at a very early period. The conditions were very different from those governing bronze work, since the raw material, bog-ore, could be found almost everywhere, and the method of treatment was easy to learn. When iron was first introduced, one must believe that the art of producing the metal was not far away. In Bornholm, it should be observed, iron was worked on the spot in such large quantities that local production of the metal itself seems of necessity to be implied.[3] From the same period a fragment of the clay lining of a smelting-pit has been found in Østfold in Norway in a barrow. In Etne

---

[1] Niels Nielsen, 'Jernudvindingen i Nørrejylland i Oldtid og Middelalder', *Aarb. f. nord. Oldk.*, 1922, p. 1. Complete bibliographical list, p. 127, and detailed exposition of the technical processes, p. 78 f. A. W. Brøgger, *Kulturgeschichte des norwegischen Altertums*, p. 151 f.

[2] T. J. Arne, 'Vår älsta produktion av stål', *Tidskriftet Rig* (Stockholm, 1922), pp. 130–1.

[3] E. Vedel, *Efterskrift til Bornholms Oldtidsminder og Oldsager* (København, 1897), p. 51; with a summary in French.

in the Bergen diocese extensive traces of iron production are found in close connexion with graves, in conditions which make it probable that these finds are of the same period, the earliest phase of the iron age.[1] But the question is still much disputed. On the other side it is argued that we have no right to assume production of iron in Scandinavia before the period when it is clearly evidenced, and we should assume that the early Norse age worked on imported metal, just as in the bronze age. The present writer favours the view that production of iron was in all probability achieved already in the first centuries after iron was introduced.[2]

It cannot be denied that the first phase of the northern iron age makes a very poor impression. The furnishing in the graves seldom amounts to more than small accessories of the dress, iron pins, small knives and the like, and the urns are seldom other than simple rough pots of clay. Only a uniformly limited and meagre selection of the articles of the time can be obtained from the graves. Finds of offerings in bogs still occur from the early iron age, but the offerings are now far inferior in value to those of the bronze age. In the earliest phase bronze rings resembling crowns are still found as an inheritance from the preceding age, but later the offerings, with few exceptions, amount to nothing more than food supplies in plain pots set down in the bogs. Gold is not found, and silver had not yet appeared in northern Europe. It was a poor age, in Scandinavia as well as in Finland and the Baltic provinces. Moreover it is not only the poverty which is noticeable: the lowering of the level of culture is equally striking. The elegant, beautifully formed types of the bronze age with their highly developed ornament are replaced by rougher and coarser types in the early iron age.

[1] Anathon Bjørn, 'Fra vor ældste jernalder', Bergens Museums Årbok, 1926, Hist.-ant. rekke no. 3, pp. 38–9.
[2] A. W. Brøgger in his Kulturgeschichte des norwegischen Altertums, p. 152, restricts himself to consideration of the quantities of iron surviving from the various periods, and he comes to the conclusion that the first production of any real importance began in the migration period, in the fourth and fifth centuries A.D. J. Brønsted in Det danske Folks Historie, i (København, 1927), p. 217, assumes that it was the small supply of metal which made the earliest iron age in Denmark so poor; ignorance or incomplete knowledge of the art of extracting iron might account for the failure to provide a complete substitute for bronze; at the same time the amber trade of Denmark had waned, so that bronze could not be imported in the same quantity as before.

Montelius was the first to offer an explanation of this remarkable poverty of the early iron age in Scandinavia, when he showed that there had been an important shift in the amber trade carried on between the north and the Mediterranean. We have already remarked that the basis of Denmark's wealth in the bronze age was the amber trade of Jutland, and it appears that this trade now passed over to the Prussian amber coast, which has had almost a monopoly in Europe ever since in the production of amber. This change was obviously of great importance, but it does not really explain the extreme antithesis between the poverty of the north and the richness of central Europe.

Later other investigators—in the first rank of them Sophus Müller—brought the Norse iron age into clearer relation with the whole historical situation in Europe. It was precisely in this epoch that the Celtic peoples enjoyed their periods of greatest power and wealth, especially during the last of the Hallstatt period and the beginning of La Tène, when they launched forth forces that set half of Europe in turmoil. The historical events are sufficiently known—the Celtic migrations and their irruptions into Italy, the Balkan peninsula and even as far as Asia Minor. It is obvious that the Celtic expansion must have disturbed the ancient trade-routes passing from the north to the south across the mainland of Europe; the result was the isolation of northern Germany and Scandinavia. The connexion with the south, especially with Italy, which had been so important during the bronze age, was broken in the first phase of the iron age. There is no trace in the north of contact with Etruscan culture or with the flowering of classical civilization in Greece during these centuries when the lands in the south passed through the most remarkable epoch in the whole of their history. A single exception is the splendid bronze vase ornamented with palmettes found on the island Møen in Denmark, which it is certain was imported from a Celtic country in central Europe, during the first phase of La Tène. It has counterparts in finds from southern Germany. Scandinavian cultural connexions in the early iron age reached thus far and no farther, that is, as far as the Celtic districts north of the Alps. The general historical situation thus gives a wholly satisfactory explanation of Scandinavia's isolation and retrogression in the period when the Celts were at the height of their power.

But now other considerations appear which require special explanation. Not only does the earliest iron age in Scandinavia give an impression of a strikingly poor civilization, but its representation in remains is strangely meagre.[1] It is properly only in Jutland, on the islands of Bornholm and Gotland, and in certain districts of Norway that graves and other memorials of this period are encountered in any considerable numbers; elsewhere they are mysteriously rare, and moreover they grow rapidly fewer as we proceed northwards. This condition is most clearly marked in Norway. On both sides of Oslofjord, in the provinces of Vestfold and Østfold, we have important burial-places and many other finds from the early iron age; the finds in the interior north of Oslo are more scattered. The other centre of early iron-age culture in Norway is the southern part of the west coast, around Stavanger in the province of Jæren, the fertile coastal plain which had been the richest part of the country in the bronze age. In general we can say that the traces we know from the first phase of the iron age in Norway lie south of 60° N., and a corresponding limit is attested in Sweden, whereas the most northerly find from the bronze age on the Scandinavian peninsula almost attains to 68° of latitude.

The question at once arises: why do the finds of the early iron age recede behind a limit so much farther south than that of the bronze age? After being presented from this point of view the whole question was brought under discussion on the physical side, especially in the now famous hypothesis advanced by Professor R. Sernander of Uppsala.[2] By comparison of plant-palaeontological and archaeological researches Sernander believes that he can show that the equable mild climate which prevailed during the stone and bronze ages was brought to

---

[1] In Finland, practically speaking, there are no finds from the iron age before the second century A.D. The only exception is a find of three bronze neck-rings, from the bog of Kiukais, of the Scandinavian type belonging to the first phase of the iron age: see Aarne Europaeus in *Finska Fornminnesföreningens Tidskrift*, xxxii. 192. Possibly a bronze pin from a grave in Österkalmar, Åland, should be included; see A. Hackman in *Prähistorische Zeitschrift*, vi. 149, Fig. 47.

[2] R. Sernander, 'Die schwedischen Torfmoore als Zeugen postglazialer Klimaschwankungen', in *Die Veränderungen des Klimas seit dem Maximum der letzten Eiszeit*, Eine Sammlung von Berichten herausg. von dem Executivcomitee des 11 Internationalen Geologenkongresses (Stockholm, 1910). See also *Compte Rendu du XI*e *Congrès Géologique International*, p. 404 f.

an end by a very sudden and extensive lowering of the temperature round about the time when the iron age begins. This is in geological terminology the transition from the subboreale period with its comparatively dry and warm climate to the moist and cold climate known as the subatlantic period (see p. 10). It is the last of the more important changes in climate in Scandinavia after the ice age. It is self-evident that such a change in climatic conditions must produce corresponding changes in plant and animal life, and in this way cause extreme disturbance in the conditions of human life. All peoples have, it is true, a wonderful capacity for adapting themselves to changing conditions; but adaptation requires time, and the change of climate at the beginning of the iron age is assumed to have taken place in such a short time that in Norway and Sweden it must have produced an acute crisis, affecting the very means of the population's existence. The whole transition from warm to colder climate may have been completed in the course of two generations. The customary methods of pasturage and agriculture became impossible under the new and unfavourable natural conditions, and the result must have been destitution and famine over the whole of Scandinavia;[1] especially in the northern regions of the peninsula the population was placed in such a desperate plight that they migrated for the most part to the south.

The theory presented in this form can hardly be given direct proof, but it must be allowed a high degree of probability. It is sufficiently certain that a deterioration of climate actually did set in at this time, and Sernander's combination gives a plausible and natural explanation of several puzzling conditions in the early iron age in Scandinavia. His theory is supported also by later studies in central Europe, especially in the high-lying region of the Alps, where a small change in temperature and moisture will be as readily perceptible as great changes in much more northerly latitudes. In the Alps, too, the later part of the Hallstatt period is marked by adverse climatic conditions which

[1] According to Professor Hasund the most difficult problem under the new conditions was to provide for domestic animals over the winter. In the mild climate of the bronze age it was not necessary to house the animals during the winter, or to gather winter fodder in any large quantity, while the subatlantic climate made both of these an urgent necessity. See S. Hasund, 'Eit klimaskifte for 2000 aar sidan', *Meldinger fra Norges Landbrukshøiskole*, 1926.

produce considerable changes of settlement and culture.[1] This stage may be taken to be contemporary with the Upper Turbarian epoch in Scotland;[2] but, as far as I am aware, there have been no special researches to ascertain whether the climatic lowering there had any influence on cultural conditions. The explanation is perhaps that the Hallstatt period was hardly represented in Scotland, which, however, had a rich bronze age and a correspondingly rich late Celtic period.[3]

The first centuries of the Scandinavian iron age, until about the beginning of Christian chronology, are now usually called the Celtic period of the northern iron age. During the whole of this period the Celtic peoples were the rulers of central Europe and protagonists of the great civilizations which had there come into flower. The Hallstatt culture, with its point of gravity eastwards in Austria and having a close relationship with Italy, was spread through the whole of central Europe and into Belgium and England, as was its successor, the La Tène culture, which had its chief seat in the Rhineland, but also made its way eastward as far as the Black Sea. In the whole of this period, during more than half a millennium from the time when iron was introduced until the beginning of the Christian era, Scandinavian civilization received the impress of impulses from the Celtic peoples of central Europe. This Celtic iron age in the north is now usually divided into three phases.[4] The first of these, from 500 to 300 B.C., is marked, as we have seen, by the same culture as the German urn-fields belonging to the late Hallstatt period in central Europe; this phase in the north is in the main contemporary with the first phase of La Tène culture among the Celtic peoples. Among the most characteristic antiquities of this phase are the pins for fastening the dress. These are very large iron pins, with a peculiar bend near the head, and the head rolled into a spiral, or adorned with a plate or a sphere. Other accessories to the dress are rings with

[1] Helmut Gams and Rolf Nordhagen, *Postglaziale Klimaänderungen und Erdkrustenbewegungen in Mitteleuropa* (Münich, 1923), Landkundliche Forschungen, Heft 25.

[2] James Geikie, *The Antiquity of Man in Europe* (Edinburgh, 1914), pp. 278–81.

[3] Robert Munro, *Prehistoric Scotland* (Edinburgh, 1899).

[4] Oscar Montelius, 'Den nordiska Jernålderns Kronologi, I', *Svenske Fornminnesför. Tidskrift*, ix (Stockholm, 1896), p. 155.

a loop, evidently belonging to the belt, belt-hooks, flat brooches
of bronze often with perforated work, and large neck-rings of
bronze of varying form.

It was in the second phase of the La Tène period that the new
Celtic culture first began to establish itself among the Germanic
nations in Germany, and through them also in Scandinavia.
The change appears at the same time as the first advance of the
Germanic peoples to the west and south. A lively contact with
Celtic culture is now evidenced throughout the whole of Germany by imported articles and local imitation of the new forms.
Bronze pails from Capua and Celtic metal cauldrons find their
way into Scandinavia, the Celtic fibula replaces the pins of the
Hallstatt period, and we find large neck-rings of bronze and belt-
hooks of late La Tène form. On the basis of these types the
later Celtic iron age in Scandinavia can be divided into two
phases corresponding to La Tène II and III among the Celts,
with the division between them set accordingly at about 100
B.C. Gradually the graves become more richly furnished, frequently with weapons, and now and then with a bronze vessel
as burial-urn (Pl. 30a). An example of chariot burial is also
known, from the island of Fyen, carefully carried out in accordance with the Germanic custom of cremation. The war-chariot
was burned on the pyre, as well as classical bronzes, gold rings,
weapons, and other articles, and the whole buried in a large
Gaulish vessel of La Tène type.[1]

It is above all on the islands of Gotland and Bornholm[2] that
remains from this period have come to light in quantity. Cremation was universal; the equipment of the dead was burned with
the body on the pyre, and all the remains from the pyre, the
burned bones, brands, ashes and objects of metal were placed
together in the grave. To this period belong the greater number
of the classic burial-places of Bornholm, where the *brand-
plætter* form large connected cemeteries. The graves lie crowded
close together under a level surface, being mere hollows in the
subsoil filled with brands and ashes, without visible sign above

---

[1] F. Sehested, *Fortidsminder og Oldsager fra Egnen om Bornholm* (København, 1878), p. 307, plates XXVII–XXIX; summary in French.

[2] Oscar Almgren and Birger Nerman, *Die ältere Eisenzeit Gotlands*, Im
Auftrage der Kungl. Vitterhets Historie och Antikvitets Akademien dargestellt
(Stockholm, 1923); E. Vedel, *Bornholms Oldtidsminder og Oldsager* (Køben-
havn, 1887).

PLATE 29

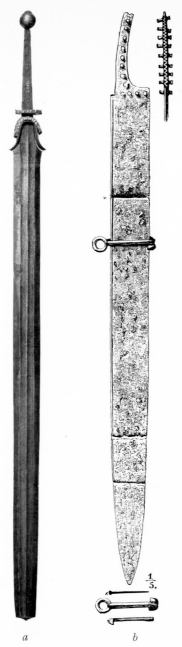

a   *b*

La Tène sword with two-edged blade. After Sophus Müller

Germanic sword, of the La Tène period, with one-edged blade. After Montelius

PLATE 30

b. Wooden shield from Hjortspring. After Rosenberg

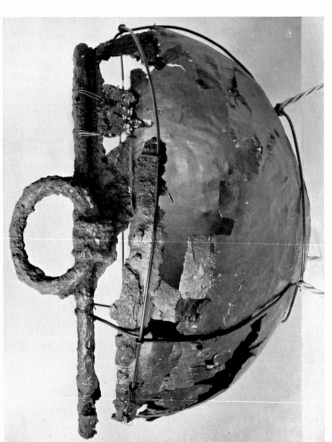

a. Vessel of bronze and iron. Sande, Norway. After Brøgger

ground. In Gotland the ground is as a rule a smooth level stretch of chalky rock, and the remains of the pyre lie in each grave as a deposit on the rock, covered by a low mound or cairn, known as a *brandflak*. Both types of grave have a wide distribution on the Scandinavian peninsula. In the western parts of Scandinavia we still come upon unmodified urn-graves of the older custom, in which the bones are placed clean and white in the urn. As a mixture of the two main forms there are graves in which the bones are mingled with brands and other remains of the pyre, but are collected in an urn. In the outer form of the grave several variations are found: we have the burial-places with a flat surface, or graves under low mounds, cairns, or rings of stones; or graves may be set close to the foot of a large conspicuous stone which happens to be conveniently situated.[1] In this period the custom appears for the first time of bending or rolling weapons together after the burning, before they are laid in the grave, a custom which was very generally followed in Norway and Sweden during all the subsequent periods of the heathen iron age, but always restricted to graves with cremation.

The Scandinavian antiquities from the La Tène period show considerable independence in the adaptation of new and foreign forms. Of weapons we find swords of iron, spearheads and iron bosses which protected the hand-grip of the shield. The swords are sometimes of the well-known Celtic form with two-edged blade, but the scabbard may have the independent form of a local Danish type (Pl. 29*a*); sometimes we find the characteristic Germanic weapon, a shorter one-edged weapon with a broad blade, undoubtedly an old Hallstatt type in a new form (Pl. 29*b*). From Gotland comes a group of special forms of ornaments and other gear which bears witness to a highly developed local art both in iron and bronze work. The art of enamelling also was known in Scandinavia, as is shown by a series of finds from Sweden and Denmark.[2]

[1] Shetelig, 'Den førromerske jernalder i Norge', *Oldtiden*, iii (Stavanger, 1913), p. 129 f.

[2] Ture Arne, 'Svenska emaljerade föremål från den förromerska jernålderen', in the *Skrift till Oscar Montelius* presented by his pupils (Stockholm, 1903), p. 121. Sophus Müller, *Ordning af Danmarks Oldsager* (*Système préhistorique du Danemark*, résumé en français), II. Jernalderen (København, 1888–95), Fig. 27. In Norway only a single enamelled ornament is known from

The most remarkable objects preserved in the north from the
La Tène period do not come from graves at all, but had been
deposited as offerings in bogs; such offerings were also of much
importance, as we have seen, in the stone age and bronze age.
The first to be mentioned is the find at Hjortspring on the island
of Als in Slesvig, a find which is perhaps somewhat older than
the full prevalence of La Tène culture.[1] In a very small bog,
barely 50 metres in length, a large number of weapons were
deposited, ringed mail-coats, wooden shields (Pl. 30*b*) and
spears, a few swords, and also small round bowls and other
articles of wood, skeletons of a horse and a dog, bones of
oxen, sheep, and pigs, all laid in—or close around—a boat,
which has an internal length of 10 metres. The boat is made of
maple, very light and slight, composed of a flat bottom plank
and two planks on each side; all the planks are thin, but over
half a metre wide, the whole being fastened together with thongs
and lashing, without any metal nails. The constructive details
will be described more fully in the ensuing chapter on Seafaring.
It need only be remarked here that the vessel shows in all
respects a remarkably primitive structure, and is comparable
with the ships depicted in rock-carvings and on knives of the
late bronze age. The deposit in the bog must in this instance
be interpreted as a thank-offering for victory after a battle; it
will be apt to refer here to what Orosius relates of the Cimbri
and Teutones after the Roman defeat at Orange in 105 B.C.:
clothing, mail-coats, and horse-gear were cut asunder and thrown
on the ground, gold and silver thrown in the river; the horses
were drowned, and the captives hanged on trees. 'All booty
was destroyed in accordance with a new and unaccustomed
vow' (v. 16). Caesar's account of the Gauls corresponds closely:
after a victory they brought all the spoils to a holy place as an
offering to the god of victory. Among many tribes, he says,
one sees heaped up mounds of such things in the holy places
(vi. 17).[2] The find at Hjortspring shows that this custom of

the La Tène period, a fragment of a bronze neck-ring, probably an imported
foreign piece: see Undset, *Das erste Auftreten des Eisens in Nordeuropa* (Hamburg, 1882), Fig. 67.

[1] *Nationalmuseets Bog om sjeldne Fund fra de seneste Aar* (København,
1925), p. 17, and G. Rosenberg in Ebert's *Reallexicon*, index word 'Hjortspring'.

[2] Sophus Müller, *Nordische Altertumskunde* (Strassburg, 1898), ii. 145.

making offerings was somewhat older than Caesar's time, and that it had already been adopted in Denmark at this period, where it was still alive in the period of the great migrations (see pp. 204–7).

Offerings of victory of this kind are not known in any corresponding form in the older periods; it is a new religious custom appearing for the first time in the early iron age. But it was otherwise with offerings of splendid costly articles of a sacral character, which have already been mentioned in the bronze age. To this category belong the two well-known wagons from Dejbjærg near the town of Ringkøbing in the county of Hardsyssel on the west coast of Jutland.[1] Both wagons were taken to pieces and scattered in the bog, but by good fortune the one which was the better preserved has been put together again (Fig. 10). It is a light four-wheeled wagon of ash with a low frame and upright corner-posts, and a loose seat for the driver. The felloe of the wheel is a single piece of wood bent round on itself and covered with an iron tyre. Both the wagon-pole and the frame are richly adorned with chased open-work mountings of bronze, on which we meet with the typical forms of the La Tène style, human faces, triskeles, open-work heart-patterns. The forms are unmistakably influenced by Celtic style, but the details show an independent treatment which attests a local product. Danish production of metal-work must have been considerable, when large and excellent pieces such as these wagons could be produced at home.

It must be regarded as practically certain that the wagons from Dejbjærg were intended for use in religious ceremonies; they were sacred objects of a kind somewhat like the Trundholm sun-image, and they were deposited where they were found in the bog as an offering to the gods. Similarly treated were a pair of very large and costly metal vessels of richly artistic production. The more famous one is a silver vessel from Gundestrup in Jutland, and it is quite the most beautiful piece of its kind known anywhere.[2] This vessel measures about 70 cm. in diameter; it has a round spherical bottom and a vertical side

[1] Henry Petersen, *Vognfundene i Dejbjærg Prestegaardsmose* (København, 1888).

[2] Sophus Müller, 'Det store Sølvkar fra Gundestrup i Jylland' (Le grand vase de Gundestrup en Jutland), *Nordiske Fortidsminder*, i (København, 1890–3), p. 35, plates VI–XIV, French text p. 62.

FIG. 10. The Wagon of Dejbjærg. *After S. Müller.*

which is formed by a double row of square plates with pictures embossed on them both inside and outside (Pl. 31). On the bottom on the inside is fixed a round plate with a representation of a bull; each of the outer plates bears a large human bust undoubtedly intended to represent a god, while the inner plates present a variety of scenes, the advance of warriors on horseback and on foot (Pl. 31b), human sacrifice, bull-fights, fabulous beings and foreign animals such as elephants, and other representations. The interpretation of the separate pictures—which, moreover, is difficult and uncertain—lies outside our scope here. The Gundestrup vessel was a Celtic product and was imported into Denmark. In the style of the pictures we find traits which point to contact with the Scythian art of southern Russia, and the silver cauldron may therefore be ascribed with most probability to the Celts on the Danube or by the Black Sea. A silver plate of nearly related style has been found in Holland.[1]

Another magnificent Celtic piece from the La Tène period is a huge bronze vessel, now fragmentary, found in a bog near Rynkeby on the island of Fyen.[2] The vessel was so big that the surviving piece was at first thought to be the frame of a light war-chariot, or the figure-head of a ship. This vessel too has a convex bottom and sides made of double plates. On the outside it is adorned with a large human face and two representations of bulls. An inner plate has two wild boars engraved on it, facing each other, one on each side of a ring with an embossed triskele. This vessel also was without doubt a sacrificial vessel of Celtic origin. We may recall Strabo's account of the prophetesses among the Cimbri, grey with age and in white clothing, who strode up to the captives in the encampment with sword in hand, placed a garland on them and led them to a bronze vessel which would hold some twenty amphorae; one of them then mounted a step, and, leaning over the vessel, cut the throat of the captive, who had been lifted up over the edge of the vessel. Strabo knew also that the Cimbri sent Augustus their holiest vessel as a gift, when they asked for peace and reconciliation. The Gundestrup vessel, which bears a picture of a sacrificial scene

---

[1] M. Rostovtzeff, *Iranians and Greeks in South Russia* (Oxford, 1922), Plate XXVII, 3.

[2] C. Engelhardt, 'Jernalderens Gravskikke i Jylland', *Aarb. f. nord. Oldk.*, 1881, p. 98 f.

answering in every particular to that which Strabo describes, was found in the ancient home of the Cimbri, Himmerland in Jutland.

It is in this period that documentary history sheds its first glimmer of illumination upon Scandinavian lands. The Greek explorer Pytheas of Massilia had visited northern Europe some time about 330 B.C., that is, in the first phase of the Celtic iron age. Of his work unfortunately only small fragments are preserved in the citations of later writers. We perceive, however, that he knew of the amber coast of Jutland, where he mentions the bay Mentonomon, the islands Albalos and Raunonia, and, among the peoples, the Ingaevones and Teutones.[1] He also reached the land of Thule, six days' sail north of the Orkneys, and, according to the astronomical detail which he gives, he must have visited the coast of Norway from Møre to Helgeland, south and north of Trondhjemsfjord.[2] Pytheas's observations have been shown by modern criticism to be remarkably reliable. He also gives the information about the northern peoples that they followed agriculture and that the corn was threshed in a building because of the damp northern climate, not under the open sky as in the south; also that these people made a fermented drink from corn and honey. Unfortunately it is not quite clear whether this information applies to the people of Thule or to those of the British Isles.

The Teutones whom Pytheas mentions were the inhabitants of the district of Thy, west of Limfjord in northern Jutland, and, the Cimbri were their neighbours to the east in Himmerland on the other side of the fjord. The names of these two tribes have been preserved in history for all time by their migration to the south and their battles with the Romans in the period 114–102 B.C. This was the first time that Scandinavian peoples appeared on the stage of history, an appearance which was to make a terrible impression both at that time and later. It was in connexion with these tribes too that the name 'Germans' made its way into written records for the first time, in Poseidonios.

The incursion of the Cimbri and Teutones has become well

---

[1] H. P. Steensby, 'Pytheas fra Massilia og Jyllands Vestkyst', *Geografisk Tidskrift*, xxiv (København, 1917–18), p. 12 f.

[2] Fridtjof Nansen, *In Northern Mists* (London, 1909), i. 43 f.

PLATE 31

a

b

a. Silver vessel from Gundestrup and *b*, detail of a panel from the vessel.
After Sophus Müller

known because it is a thread in the fabric of Roman history, but in reality it was no unique occurrence at that time. Archaeological sources give evidence that the Germans at this very period were making a powerful thrust forward against the Celts in southern Germany, and from the period immediately following we hear of Caesar's war with Ariovistus on the Rhine, where we also meet with a tribal name from Jutland, the Harudes, whose original home was the present county of Hardsyssel. This movement of tribes, the first migrations from the north that we know of, had also an extraordinary importance in the development of Scandinavian civilization. By this movement is explained the complete prevalence of the La Tène culture in Germany and Scandinavia; the Norse peoples could now acquire it on the Celts' own ground. The movement resulted further in the first contact, through the Celts, with the classical culture of the Greeks and Romans.

It is also from this period, from the time towards the beginning of the Christian era, that we get the first historical statement about the nationality of the Scandinavian people. They are reckoned as Germans, a comprehensive term common to a large group of northern peoples who were not Celts. The name *Germani* itself is of unknown origin and meaning, perhaps originally Celtic, and in any case clearly a name which these peoples did not use of themselves. It is thus obvious that the Scandinavians at the end of the La Tène period spoke a Germanic language, though contemporary writers, such as Sallust and Cicero, still have rather confused ideas of the difference between Germans and Celts. It was really Caesar in his account of his Gallic wars who gave the Germans their proper introduction to history.

XII

THE ROMAN PERIOD

THE designation 'Roman Period', which has been given to the Scandinavian iron age in the first four centuries of the Christian era, is fully warranted, since the whole cultural development of northern Europe was subject during that time to the dominating influence of Roman culture. While the Celtic peoples on the continent were being absorbed by Roman conquest, and the boundaries of the empire were pushed forward to the Rhine and the Danube, at the same time the ancient material and technical culture of the Mediterranean was subjecting new regions, until it came into direct contact, without any intermediary, with the Germans in Germany. Military expeditions made the Romans known throughout all Germania, and the fleet of Augustus sailed round Jutland into the Baltic; but of much greater importance was the trade and intercourse which brought Roman wares to the north and spread many elements of Roman civilization far beyond the limits of the provinces. A specially important intermediary between the German and Roman worlds during the first empire was Bohemia, where the kingdom of the Marcomanni had been founded by Maroboduus. While the German warriors on the Rhine frontier were continually disturbing the peaceful relations, Maroboduus chose alliance with Rome, and his kingdom became the first centre of Germanic culture under Roman influence. Here superior manufactured goods were imported, some from Italy, some from the northern provinces; here Roman merchants and craftsmen took up their dwelling, and independent Germanic work was produced with its traditional forms improved by Italian technique and taste. As has been fully established, communications from here passed along the Elbe to Jutland and along the Vistula to the Baltic and Sweden.[1] By these routes Roman manufactured goods were dispatched to the north, and also much of the new Germanic work produced in the kingdom of the Marcomanni.

[1] Sophus Müller, 'La trouvaille de Juellinge', *Nordiske Fortidsminder*, ii, part 1 (København, 1911), Oscar Almgren, 'Zur Bedeutung des Markomann-reichs für die Entwickelung der germanischen Industrie in der frühen Kaiser-zeit', *Mannus*, v (Würzburg, 1913).

Yet of at least equal importance was the trade by sea from Gaul, from the mouth of the Rhine to the Frisian Islands, across Holstein to the Scandinavian peninsula. The importance of this trade-route is shown by finds of coins, mainly *denarii* of the republican era, which Tacitus states that the Germans preferred to the later Roman silver coinage after Nero's reform of the mint. Fully 450 republican *denarii* have been found, according to a census of 1907, in the comparatively limited area from the Elbe to Holland, while such coins are not found in upper Germany, apart from a smaller group of early *denarii* in Posen.[1] Moreover, it has been shown that the Old Norse system of weights, right down to Viking times, was based on the republican *denarius* weight with the division of the ounce into seven; and the Old Norwegian weight-name *ertog* is descended linguistically from *denarius argenteus*.[2] This relation illustrates the importance to Norway of the connexion with the Frisian coast and through it with the Roman trade from the mouth of the Rhine. It can also be shown that precious Roman bronze vases and glasses were brought to Norway and Sweden by this route.

Somewhat later the trade-route overland to the Rhine frontier seems to have reached its full development, and the Rhineland became the most important Germanic contact with Roman culture. There was continual fighting in this area, but peaceful buying and selling also went on, and in the garrison towns there were German mercenary troops and allies completely under the influence of Roman town life. Within the frontier district itself Roman influence made a profound impression on Germanic culture, on armour and the forms of weapons, ornaments and metal-work. The Rhineland was the home of numerous special Germanic forms which arose in contact with classical industry.

According to the picture which we are able to draw with the help of archaeological sources, there is one district in particular among the Scandinavian lands at this time distinguished by a

[1] On the finds of *denarii* as a whole see Oscar Almgren, 'Några anmärkingar om denarskatterna från germanskt område', *Oldtiden*, vii (Kristiania, 1918), p. 209 f., and T. J. Arne, 'Tenetid och romersk jernålder i Ryssland, med särskild hänsyn til de romerska denarfyndene', ibid., p. 207 f.; A. W. Brøgger, 'Ertog og Øre', *Videnskapsselskapets Skrifter*, ii, Hist.-Filos. Klasse, 1921, no. 3, p. 17 f.

[2] Carl J. S. Marstrander, 'Spredte bidrag til vægtens og vægtterminologiens historie hos germanerne', *Videnskapsselskapets Skrifter*, ii, Hist.-Filos. Klasse, 1924, no. 9 (Kristiania, 1924), pp. 16–18.

resplendent richness, namely, Zealand and the other Danish isles.
This was evidently the meeting-place of the North Sea trade
and the Baltic trade, and likewise of the land-routes to the south,
and an astonishing wealth was accumulated there. We find
graves in great numbers with the most luxurious furnishing, laid
under a flat surface and without cremation. In these graves the
complete Roman service for a banquet was often set out for the
dead: wine-ladle with strainer, bronze bowl for mixing wine,
jars of bronze and beakers of glass or silver, and in addition the
native pair of drinking horns. A service of this kind, which was
found in a grave at Hoby on the island of Laaland, included two
silver beakers with beautiful representions in relief of scenes
from the *Iliad*, examples of the best Italian work in the time of
Augustus; these beakers stood on a plaque of bronze. There
were also in this find large cups, a wine-ladle, a splendidly
decorated wine-flagon, and a bronze bowl with a relief representation of Aphrodite. All these pieces go together as a wine-set
such as a distinguished Roman would have, and on the bottom
of the beakers (Pl. 32) we actually find the owner's name,
Silius, who was most probably that Silius who was legate of
Upper Germany in the years A.D. 14–21. Here we may appositely
recall that costly drinking vessels were the customary form of
diplomatic gift which the Romans gave Germanic chiefs or
oriental kings, just as the Senate earlier had decreed neck-rings
of gold as gifts of honour to Gaulish chiefs. In any case the
Hoby grave gives a living picture of personal connexions between Danes and Romans in the early years of the empire.[1]

In this district we see that men and women were buried with
equally rich outlay, always with magnificent provision of food
vessels and drinking vessels as for a festive banquet; bones of
domestic animals show that meat was set in the grave for food,
and in the wine-vessels traces are found of a fermented drink
made from malt and berry-juice.[2] The women wear their
ornaments, splendid fibulas, large hairpins with heads of gold
filigree, pendants and gold beads (Pl. 33); in a box are deposited
the small toilet articles, scissors, comb, and knife. The men on
the other hand never have weapons with them in the grave, a

---

[1] K. Friis Johansen, 'La Trouvaille de Hoby', *Nordiske Fortidsminder*, ii,
part 3 (København, 1923).
[2] Sophus Müller, *La Trouvaille de Juellinge*, p. 54.

PLATE 32

Silver cups from Hoby, Denmark. After Friis Johansen

PLATE 33

A woman's grave at Juellinge, Denmark. After Sophus Müller

feature which indicates that in this district they had at last given up the barbarous custom of going about armed in their daily life. If these Danish lands had had a written history in the Roman period, we should undoubtedly have heard of a powerful kingdom there, whose position in the north was as important as that of the Marcomanni in the south.

It is clear that the Danish isles were in the early days of the Empire a distributing centre of Roman culture to all the Scandinavian lands, but the impulses reached the various districts in somewhat different forms. In Jutland the dead were buried unburned and were supplied with a rich set of admirable earthenware vessels ornamented with meanders, a complete outfit of jugs, jars, bowls and cups, a few ornaments and the like, and now and then weapons. The grave-forms are marked by Roman influence, but in general imported Roman articles are not found. In Norway and Sweden the new cultural elements appear more sporadically, but in typical forms, producing a richer furnishing of graves, with Roman wine-ladles, glass beakers, and large vessels of bronze. At the same time we also meet with the new Germanic forms of ornaments and other metal products.[1] The waves of new culture in the Roman period were beginning to break up the firmly established way of life which we know in Scandinavia in the Celtic iron age preceding, and their effects were felt all the way to the coasts of the Northern Ocean, and also left traces along the Baltic coasts right into Finland.

The graves which have just been under consideration show a complete break with the belief and rites of the older time in Scandinavia. For about a thousand years cremation had been universally prevalent in northern Europe, and the furniture of the grave had been of the poorest imaginable. In the late La Tène period we have seen that examples of richer and more costly grave-goods began to appear, but the burial customs were otherwise unchanged. The first contact with Roman culture introduced a completely different form, burial without burning, and wholly new ideas about the furnishing of the grave. The

---

[1] Jan Petersen, 'Gravpladsen fra Store-Dal i Skjeberg', *Norske Oldfund*, i (Kristiania, 1916), pp. 38, 41, plates XII–XIV; G. Gustafson, *Et norsk gravfund fra den ældre keisertid*, Opuscula Montelio dicata (Stockholm, 1913), p. 265. Also Gunnar Ekholm, 'Zur Geschichte des römisch-germanischen Handels,' *Acta Archaeologica*, vi (København, 1935), p. 49.

conceptions which lie at the root of the grave-offering are given
clear expression when the woman at Juellinge is found with a
wine-ladle in her hand, while a large wine-jar stands close by her
head; or in Jutish graves where we find roast meat with a carving knife before the dead person's face, and close by a considerable number of drinking vessels, and at the feet a large round
earthenware jar with an accompanying cup. The arrangements
here are made for the dead in genuine Roman style, and in the
same manner as the survivors would end the funeral, with a
ceremonial feast.

But foreign burial forms were not established uniformly over
all parts of Scandinavia. Cremation was still practised practically everywhere by the side of the new custom. We find poor
urn-burials and *brandplætter* as before; but often the graves with
cremation have the richer furnishing of the later custom. The
urns may be costly bronze vases (Pl. 34), or a whole set of
food and drinking vessels may be laid in and around the urn.
Graves with cremation and provided with weapons are especially
frequent in the east of Norway and in Bornholm.[1] The true
idea of cremation, as it was manifested in the graves of the older
period, was now seriously disturbed and blurred by contact with
foreign conceptions. In Danish lands, however, it was the rule,
as before, that the burial-places lay under a flat surface, with
no visible memorial; on the Scandinavian peninsula imposing
grave-mounds or cairns again began to be raised, or the graves
were marked by an upright memorial stone. From this time
onward, throughout the ensuing periods of the heathen age,
Scandinavian burial forms are always a very complex blending.

When we draw the picture of Scandinavian culture in this
period, the most striking feature is obviously the presence
of imported articles, which are often handsome and superior
products of Roman factories. The largest group of imported
articles consists of vases, wine-ladles, jars, pails, and cauldrons
of bronze, which usually have the stamp of the factory on them,
and occasionally Latin inscriptions also.[2] Beakers of silver are a
rarity, and similarly cups and beakers of glass do not become

---

[1] E. Vedel, *Bornholms Oldtidsminder og Oldsager* (København, 1886), French
résumé p. 227; Sigurd Grieg, 'Hadelands eldste Bosetningshistorie', *Skrifter
utg. av Det Norske Videnskaps-Akademi*, 1925, ii, no. 2, p. 46 (Oslo, 1926).

[2] Gunnar Ekholm, 'Om romarnas handel på Nordeuropa', *Fornvännen*,
1934, p. 349 f. (Stockholm), summary in German.

frequent until the late Roman period, in the third century A.D. This applies also to glass beads, which were an important article of Roman industry, especially the larger beads with patterns made in mosaics of many colours.

It is a peculiar and striking fact that the older part of the period has the finest Roman goods. In graves of the first and second centuries we constantly find admirable articles, which have come from Italy, while products of the smaller provincial workshops predominate in the later finds. The glass becomes coarser, the bronzes no longer have quite the same well-made forms, nor the old solid quality. The cause of the change is that the direct connexions with Italy through the medium of the Marcomanni were broken off towards the end of the second century, and the Norse market was then supplied by the new industry which grew up in Gaul under Roman rule.

Finally, weapons were imported, and this had a more lasting significance than any other importation, since Roman influence in this sphere determined the native Scandinavian develop-ments in the making of weapons. The one-edged Germanic sword of the La Tène period was still in use in the older Roman period; but at the same time we also meet with the whole complement of weapons developed among the Germanic peoples on the Roman frontiers: broad, two-edged swords on the model of the Roman *gladius*, and others with long narrow blades; lances with leaf-shaped iron heads and throwing-spears with barbs; shield-bosses of iron and bronze in well-defined charac-teristic forms. We find in the Scandinavian Peninsula, especially in Norwegian graves, all the types of weapons known from the Marcomannic graves in Bohemia, from numerous other Germanic burial-places in Germany, and above all from the great Danish bog-finds which will be described below.[1] A few of the swords are proved beyond all doubt to be imported, since they bear a Roman stamp on the blade; a *gladius* from Stabu in Norway has a Victory inlaid in bronze at the upper end of the blade and the letters SF, evidently belonging to a factory in a Roman frontier province, even though the picture is rather barbarous and ill conceived. It may be safely assumed that we have more imported weapons than can now be recognized, as the stamp

---

[1] Martin Jahn, 'Die Bewaffnung der Germanen in der älteren Eisenzeit' *Mannus-Bibliothek*, no. 16 (Würzburg, 1916).

could easily be obscured by rust when the weapon lay in the earth. But in all probability the greater number of the weapons were made in Scandinavian lands, and they exhibit admirable workmanship.

We are thus brought to consideration of native work in general, and we see at once that Roman influence extended far beyond the importation of finished products. All the ordinary daily tools, large or small, were made in imitation of the Roman technique, which in this sphere was the standard. The highly cultivated Roman handcraft had first been taken up by the Marcomanni and other border nations, and it afterwards assumed an equally vital importance in northern Europe. By way of example may be mentioned the straight, strong knives of iron with a thick rounded back; scissors of iron, an implement which now came into use among the northern barbarians for the first time; small, thick axes hammered into facets. These forms have a genuine Roman effect, and they are, moreover, distinguished by a peculiarly neat workmanlike treatment; importance is given to the fine balance, the simplicity, and solidity, which are so characteristic of the Roman spirit. Decoration of fine lines and dots is added, though used with great restraint, and once we find ornamentation of silver inlaid in the iron.

We also have evidence that other metals were worked with the same skill, bronze, silver, and gold, though the articles of these materials are always of small dimensions, ornaments and the like. The most important of the ornaments of the period are brooches in the form of fibulas, a necessary adjunct to women's dress, but also ornamental and always made with taste and care. We find among the brooches from both the early and late phases of the Roman period various forms which are peculiar to Scandinavia, or even to more limited districts of Scandinavia, a proof that these small metal objects were of native workmanship.[1] There are ornaments cast in bronze or silver, and the bronze is usually adorned with a beaded silver thread, with embossed silver plate or filigree of gold or silver. There are some exquisite small pieces of goldsmithry, such as gold trinkets and beads, and large hairpins with the head of

[1] Oscar Almgren, 'Studien über Nordeuropäische Fibelformen', *Mannus-Bibliothek*, no. 32 (Leipzig, 1923).

PLATE 34

Roman bronze vase *in situ* as the urn in a cremation burial. After S. Grieg

gold filigree (Pl. 35a); these make it probable that other well-made articles of gold are native. The acquisition of the filigree technique and its tasteful application afford an excellent illustration of the whole Roman influence in northern Europe.

And now many more ancient traditions of southern handcraft and technique were introduced, to the benefit of the northern peoples. To the scissors mentioned above we may add the distaff for spinning (an invention which in the south goes back to the copper age, but in the north is first evidenced in the Roman period) and other small practical devices, such as latchets for the belt and spurs for riding. At the same time there came impulses which inspired a new flowering of Norse pottery under the influence of classical form and taste. We now find in Scandinavia the large round-bellied vessels which had been general at all times in Mediterranean lands, beakers upon a pedestal, bowls, jars, and cups with handles, flagons with spouts, and still others, a whole series of forms which had been unknown earlier in the north. In decoration of pottery, too, we trace a classical current, though various details attest local production. The potware is of especial excellence in Jutland, as we know it from the finds of graves. A complete table set here comprised a large jar, large and small jug, several bowls and flagons with handles, a pair of beakers on pedestals, and a cup. It is well-formed, strong ware, often with a shiny black surface, and tastefully decorated with lines in geometrical patterns, among which meanders are the most conspicuous. There are reminiscences of the German 'meander-urns' of the La Tène period, which, moreover, had in their turn been inspired by Greek models; but there was also a new element introduced from Roman example, as can be seen from certain forms of handle and rim on the jugs. The Jutish pottery was highly esteemed, and a certain amount of it was exported to Norway. The other Scandinavian lands also had a rich ceramic production in this period, as we know from the urn-fields, graves, and ancient sites of houses in various districts. Beside the Jutish products the elegant Gutnish vases with pedestal deserve special mention, and still more the pottery from Bornholm, where it was the custom in the *brand-plætter* to provide each grave with a complete set of table vessels, a large container with several lugs, a flagon or a bottle, a jar with a handle, and cups, a whole series of varying individual forms.

We reckon with Montelius that the Roman period of the iron age in Scandinavia includes the first four hundred years of the Christian era, and within it we distinguish an older phase, up to about A.D. 200, and a later phase lasting till about A.D. 400.[1] The transition from the early to the late phase is marked by a group of new types among the articles then in use. We may mention in particular new types of brooch, especially that known as the 'fibula with returned foot' (mit umgeschlagenem Fuss), a form produced among the southern Germans on the model of late La Tène forms, which were still in current use at that time in southern Russia. On this basis a number of new types of fibula was evolved; some of these were large and handsome, and spread among all the Germanic peoples, and from the Germans again to the Roman provinces. At the same time certain new forms of artistic work appear, as in the taste for embellishing ornaments, sword-scabbards, and other objects with embossed silver plate and filigree of gold and silver, combined with inset coloured stones and pieces of glass (Pl. 35b). At this time, too, runic inscriptions become widespread, as will be described in the following chapter. A whole complex of features characterizes the later phase of the period.

An interesting feature of the transition between the two phases is seen in the finds of Roman denarii in the north. It has already been mentioned that the earlier Roman denarii from the time of the republic and the first emperors are found almost exclusively in the north-west of Germany, mainly in the Frisian coastland from Holland to the Elbe. Very few denarii of this era are found in Scandinavia, and these few were probably brought to the north together with the later silver coins from the period around A.D. 200.[2] The later denarii, on the other

---

[1] Here and in the following discussion the system of dividing and sub-dividing the iron age is that of O. Montelius, *Les Temps préhistoriques en Suède et dans les autres Pays scandinaves* (Paris, 1895), pls. XIII–XX; but it must also be borne in mind that Sophus Müller has given the phases somewhat different chronological limits, and to some extent different names: see his *Ordning af Danmarks Oldsager* (*Système préhistorique du Danemark*) (Kjöbenhavn, 1888–95), p. 73. The divergences are not really very important, since these authorities are in substantial agreement about the classification of the individual forms and the general course of development. Sophus Müller distinguishes early and late stages within the first two centuries.

[2] The earlier Roman gold coins, *aurei*, are extraordinarily rare in northern Europe. One *aureus* of Tiberius and one of Vespasian can be adduced from Denmark, one of Titus from Gotland, one of Trajan from Öland; from the rest

hand, those minted for Trajan and the succeeding emperors, are found in Scandinavia in considerable numbers; in all about 7,000 such coins are known, of which over 5,000 come from the island of Gotland alone. Otherwise they were found evenly distributed over the Danish isles, Bornholm and Skåne, rarely in the other parts of Sweden, and still more rarely in Norway. As a rule, a large or small number of *denarii* are buried together in the ground as a hoard, the size of which varies from a mere few to several hundred; the largest hoard of *denarii* in the north consists of 1,500 coins, from Sindarfve in Hemse on Gotland.[1]

From comparison of the finds it can be seen that the importation of Roman coins into Scandinavia was limited to a very short period. The age of each hoard of silver as a whole can obviously be limited by the latest coins which it contains, and it can be made out from these limits that the influx of *denarii* began in the reign of Marcus Aurelius (A.D. 161–80), continues under Commodus (180–92), and ceases under Septimius Severus (193–211). It is possible to classify these Scandinavian finds according to the age of the coins, and it follows therefore that the hoards were not mixed after they came to the north. Thus the coins were not in circulation as a means of payment in daily trade. Nevertheless the *denarii* are, as a rule, very much worn, and this has been explained by their transportation overland. The coins must have lain in bags carried on horses during the long journey to the Baltic. Hoards of *denarii* of precisely the same character also occur south of the Baltic in the east of Germany, in east Prussia, Silesia, and Poland, in Galicia, and still farther distant in south-west Russia.[2] It is obvious that the *denarii* were brought into Scandinavia by the eastern route from the Roman frontier along the Danube and the Black Sea,

of Sweden one of Claudius, one of Nero, and one of Vespasian. Roman copper coins are just as rare in Scandinavia, though they appear in moderate numbers around the Oder and in east Prussia. In passing, we must mention the oldest coin known in Scandinavia, a barbarous Celtic copper coin found in Gotland; a similar specimen has been found in La Tène itself: see Ture Arne, 'Et keltiskt Mynt funnet i svensk jord', *Fornvännen* (Stockholm, 1906), p. 49.

[1] P. Hauberg, 'Skandinaviens Fund af romersk Guld- og Sølvmynt før Aar 550', *Aarb. f. nord. Oldk.* (Kjöbenhavn, 1894); Almgren and Nerman, *Die ältere Eisenzeit Gotlands* (Stockholm, 1923), p. 57 f.

[2] In Russia in 1916 at least fifty-four hoards of *denarii* had been found, containing eleven thousand coins in all; in Poland at least seventeen hoards containing over ten thousand coins. See T. Arne in *Oldtiden*, vii. 208.

and equally evident that an exportation of Roman coins so definitely limited in time and place must have a connexion with definite historical conditions. Towards the end of the second century the wars with the Marcomanni began which ended in the downfall of their kingdom, and about the same time the Goths began their expansion to the south; Almgren has concluded with great probability that the export of *denarii* in the last quarter of the second century was carried on through the Goths in the course of their peaceful relations with the Romans, and that it was broken off when Septimius Severus closed the frontier in Dacia. Under Caracalla the first war with the Goths is recorded (A.D. 214). Shortly after this the Goths pushed forward to the Black Sea, where they founded a kingdom of some note which was consolidated after the conquest of Olbia in A.D. 236. From this time onwards the Goths were the most powerful Germanic nation in the south, and it was from them that the most important influences were transmitted to the Germanic peoples farther north and to Scandinavia. The Goths themselves were conscious that their nation was of Norse origin; they had come in ships across the Baltic at a period anterior to Christian chronology, and names such as Gotland and Götaland indicate where we have to look for their earliest home—according to the latest investigation probably in Götaland.[1] During their expansion southwards the Goths still kept up a constant connexion with the north, which can be traced, for example, in the hoards of *denarii* just described. In the same way a taste for the new artistic work produced among the Goths was communicated to the north, seen in decorations of thinly plated gold or silver bearing embossed patterns, filigree work, and inset coloured pieces of glass. The oldest runic writing followed the same route, from Poland and Brandenburg to Gotland, the Danish isles, and the east of Norway, as will be described in more detail in the following chapter. Together with all this there also went a rich export of Roman manufactured goods, vases of silver and bronze, costly glasses, silver spoons, smaller silver articles decorated with niello-work, and lastly occasional examples of Roman pottery by the side of

[1] Birger Nerman, *Die Herkunft und die frühesten Auswanderungen der Germanen*, Kungl. Vitterhets Historie och Antikvitets Akademiens Handlingar (Stockholm, 1924), III F., i. 5, p. 53 f.

native earthenware. It was a new cultural wave that characterized the later phase of the Roman period, distinct from the cultural influences of the first phase.

The new impulses which set in with the third century gained their earliest and strongest dominance on Scandinavian soil in the Danish isles. Here burials were continued as in earlier times, without cremation and without visible monument on the grave, but with luxuriously rich grave-goods of costly vases, glass beakers, ornaments, glass pieces for the game of tables, and similar things; but weapons are still absent from the graves. Here the well-known but rare glasses bearing pictures in several colours are found, silver beakers of barbarous make with pictured bands of impressed silver, handsome brooches in the shape of a swastika.[1] All circumstances go to show that the new cultural elements were established in Denmark by a peaceful development, without any disturbance of cultural continuity, and the old connexions with the Rhine frontier and Gaul were still maintained. In Sweden we find comparatively faint traces of contact with the new Gothic culture,[2] which is, however, excellently represented in Norway, both on the west coast and in the eastern districts.[3] In Norway we also come upon imported products together with Germanic work in the form of embossed silver plate. Throughout the whole group we find the same richly furnished graves, bearing a well-defined common character. It is a definite and striking current of culture which is introduced in the course of the third century and continues undiminished during the greater part of the following century, and its coming demonstrates beyond all doubt that the Germans in Germany and Scandinavia maintained a constant and intimate connexion with the Goths in the south of Russia.

The current of culture was obviously set from the south to the north: from the southern lands which were nearest neighbours to the home of classical culture impulses went forth to the most distant barbarians, in this phase from the Goths, just as earlier from the Marcomanni. The direction of the movement is so clear that some have even thought that it was carried out

[1] Henry Petersen, 'Polyandre de l'ancien âge de fer à Nordrup en Sélande', *Nordiske Fortidsminder*, i. 15, pls. I–III.

[2] B. Salin, 'Et jernåldersfynd från Uppland', *Kungl. Vitterhets Historie och Antikvitets Akademiens Månadsblad* (Stockholm, 1896), p. 28 f.

[3] H. Shetelig, *Vestlandske Graver fra Jernalderen* (Bergen, 1912), p. 53 f.

by a migration of people from the south-east to the north-west, and that the graves of the kind just described must be taken as evidence of a northerly movement of Germans who had been settled for a period of some length on the north shore of the Black Sea.[1] By this theory it must be supposed that small groups of Germanic peoples in the south made their way north again just as history later records that the Heruli did. On the Danish isles, as we have seen, cultural conditions throughout the whole of this period show an unbroken continuity which practically precludes the idea of an invasion by a foreign people. In Norway, on the other hand, we have rich graves from this period which stand out as definitely foreign in the midst of the otherwise local manner of life, and they might well be explained by the invasion of strangers from the south.

Cultural conditions alone obviously do not necessarily require such an interpretation, but it is in no way improbable, when considered in the background of contemporary historical events. It was the period of tribal migration, and we have reason to believe that the still prehistoric peoples had also been touched by this powerful movement; and it is reasonable enough to look for traces of the migrations in the archaeological sources. In this connexion must be mentioned a group of archaeological finds which afford evidence of acts of war in the frontier districts precisely in these centuries, and we may believe that these events were brought about by movements among the Germanic peoples of the kind just indicated. The finds alluded to are the great finds in the Danish bogs from the third to fifth centuries. They are offerings deposited in bogs in the same way as the offering at Hjortspring in Slesvig described above (p. 186), which must be assigned to the Celtic period of the Scandinavian iron age; that find is a proof that the custom itself of bringing spoils as offerings of victory after battle is distinctly older than the Roman period and the migrations. Caesar mentions offerings among the Gauls similar to those which are so strikingly exemplified in the bog-finds of Slesvig and Fyen. There are the finds of Nydam and Thorsbjærg in Slesvig, of Vimose and Kragehul in Fyen, as well as some others of lesser size at Tranebær and Hedelisker in Jutland, Rynkeby in Fyen,

---

[1] Bernhard Salin, *Die altgermanische Thierornamentik* (Stockholm, 1904); see especially p. 353.

PLATE 35

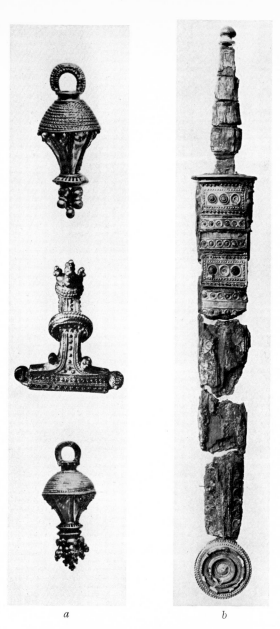

a   *b*

a. Gold filigree trinkets from Norway
b. Sword in scabbard with embossed silver decoration
from Avaldsnes, Norway. After Shetelig

PLATE 36

Golden horns from Gallehus, Slesvig. After G. Stephens

and several others; but they are all of similar content.[1] Weapons predominate, helmets and mail-coats, multitudes of swords, lances, shields, bows and arrows; also fragments of clothing, working-tools, riding-gear, occasional wagon wheels, gold used as currency, ornaments, and Roman coins, and much else of miscellaneous description; lastly, skeletons and skulls of horses sacrificed with all the rest; from Nydam also several vessels, a ship of oak 23 metres long, and pieces of a boat of fir.

Many of the weapons bear marks of hard fighting: the spear-points are bent, swords are broken, lance-shafts and bows are cut through. Many things, it is evident, were intentionally destroyed after the battle, as when several shield-bosses are smashed against each other, a large bronze vessel is cut through crosswise and then crushed together, a ringed mail-coat is divided into two pieces. It is an offering of victory, booty after the fight, destroyed, in part deliberately, by the victors.

The Danish bog-finds thus answer exactly to Caesar's words about the offerings of the Gauls of booty from the fields of battle: 'Among many tribes one sees things of this kind in heaps in the holy places.' The contents of the bog-finds had been deposited in the same way, weapons of all kinds and other things such as a defeated army leaves behind gathered in a heap in comparatively dry and firm ground in the bog, where the increase of the peat gradually rose up around it and at last covered it all. The question as to whether each of these finds was deposited as a whole on a single occasion, as is commonly assumed, cannot be discussed here, but there are certain features which may point to repeated offerings having been made in the same place. It is certain that the greater number of the articles from Thorsbjærg in Slesvig and Vimose in Fyen must be dated from the third century, those in the Nydam find from the fourth century; and they all show many affiliations with the cultural currents from the south-east which have just been mentioned. There are roman silver coins of the same group as in the later hoards of *denarii*, gold-work adorned with filigree or embossed and plated with silver, and, equally significant, a series of the

[1] The four great finds were all excavated by Professor C. Engelhardt, Thorsbjærg 1858–60, Vimose 1859–65, Nydam 1859–63, Kragehul in 1860 and later again in 1876–7. See C. Engelhardt, *Denmark in the Early Iron Age* (London, 1866); Sophus Müller, *Nordische Altertumskunde*, ii (Strassburg, 1898), p. 122 f.

oldest Germanic runic inscriptions cut on various objects, on a plane from Vimose, on a shield-boss and chape from Thorsbjærg. These are precisely the elements which, as we have seen, provide evidence of connexions between the north and the southeast, ultimately with the Goths in southern Russia.

The great bog-finds also show a close relationship with classical civilization. The chapes from Thorsbjærg are Roman in style, as are the sword-straps from Vimose; the bogs seem to teem with Roman weapons, swords with stamped blades, scabbards with classical decorations, shield-bosses, bronze knobs for the sword-belt. Barbarous weapons are not wanting, such as the one-edged swords of the ancient Norse type; but, as a whole, we must perceive that the armoury is more than half Roman, except that the costly protective armour, helmets and mail, is exceptional, as these pieces always are among the barbarians. Moreover, we have a distinct impression that this equipment was worn by men who had travelled in districts where they had full opportunity to imitate Roman arms, as in the frontier districts of the empire. And yet the bog-finds declare clearly that they fought on Norse ground, in Slesvig, on Fyen, and in battles of no small size. The bog-finds thus give support to the theory of an invasion of Scandinavia by a Germanic people from the south during the later phase of the Roman period. Moreover, these finds are in themselves of extraordinary importance, since they show how strongly and directly impulses of Roman culture could be carried across the continent into Scandinavian lands. In Norwegian and Swedish graves lie warriors who bore the same Roman weapons as we know from the bog-finds, and it is in connexion with these graves that most of the oldest runic inscriptions occur in Scandinavia. The great wave of culture from the south is clearly marked in the third and fourth centuries, and it reached within the same period even the most northerly district in Europe.

In Norway and Sweden no finds have been made of the same kind as the great Danish bog-finds; only a single find in Norway can be mentioned as in any way comparable, namely, the boats from Kvalsund in Møre, near the town of Ålesund, which were excavated in 1920.[1] In a peat-bog at Kvalsund pieces of a boat

---

[1] H. Shetelig and Fr. Johannessen, 'Kvalsundfundet og andre norske myrfund av fartøier', *Bergens Museums Skrifter*, ii. 2 (Bergen, 1929).

and of a larger vessel were buried; both of them had been deliberately broken up before they were deposited in the bog. The breaking of these vessels was carried out thoroughly: not a rib was whole, the keel and the prow were shattered, the oars snapped, clothing torn up, and no two timbers left fastened together as they had been in the vessel. Only the rudder of the ship and two of the oars were whole: otherwise every single piece had been broken. Together with all these fragments was deposited a number of long stakes, shaped in the roughest way from young trees which were lopped and pointed and stuck into the peat; there was also a great quantity of branches and twigs. All the circumstances show conclusively that this was an offering of boats made by depositing them in the bog, and many details are strikingly reminiscent of the arrangements in the great bog-finds of Denmark. We may therefore regard the Kvalsund find as an offering of the same kind, though here we miss the weapons and other objects conspicuous in the Danish finds. The boats from Kvalsund, moreover, clearly belong to a somewhat later time than the finds of weapons in Denmark.

This review of the antiquities, graves, and bog-finds of the Roman period is sufficient to show that Scandinavia in these first centuries of the Christian era possessed a far more varied civilization, more developed in many directions, than in the Celtic iron age preceding. From this comparison with the older period we see clearly that it was a new age which had emerged with a complex—one might venture to say, an almost modern —civilization. In so far as the antiquities have survived, they give an impression of a richer age, an age of growth and pro-gress. This new richness is given tangible expression in the increasing profusion of gold in the later phase of the Roman period. Already in the earlier phase we observe a taste for gold ornaments in the form of small filigree articles and plain finger-rings. In the later phase gold articles become larger and more numerous, finger-rings with broad plates, heavy rings for the arms and neck. The typical form of the time is the 'snake's head ring', a ring made in a spiral with the free ends shaped into animal heads. Other larger rings are completely closed and widened in front like a plate. In general, there are among the gold articles of this time several of the finest and most characteristic forms to be found among Scandinavian antiquities; they are always heavy and massive, and often very valuable.[1]

To this time belong the largest objects of gold ever found on Scandinavian ground, the two famous golden horns from Gallehus in Slesvig (Pl. 36). The first was found in 1639, the other a century later, in 1734, and both were lost in 1802 in a theft from the museum in Copenhagen. The first is said to have been 2 feet 9 inches long, and the other 1 foot 9 inches. Both were all of fine gold, and both consisted of an inner smooth horn which was covered by an outer shell in several pieces. The outer covering on both horns was adorned with numerous figures and symbols, partly in relief and partly in embossed lines, arranged as frieze-bands running around each section of the horn. There were human figures and animals in various scenes, serpents and anthropomorphous shapes with serpent tails, other indeterminate figures, and stars and ornaments. A runic inscription on one of the horns gave the name of the maker of this work of art.[2] No complete interpretation of the pictures on these horns has yet had the fortune to produce general conviction, though several attempts have been made. It is tempting to believe that these representations are of figures from the Scandinavian mythology of the period, just as Celtic gods have been recognized on the silver vessel from Gundestrup; but no certain conclusion will ever be possible, since we have no literary sources in the north contemporary with the golden horns. We have, however, a right to conclude that these golden horns were sacred articles, in the same category as those we have mentioned from the early iron age and the bronze age, and further, that they had been deposited in the places where they were found, dedicated as offerings to a god.

Though gold becomes more plentiful, yet, as we have seen, Roman gold coins are rare in Scandinavia until the middle of the fourth century. Then conditions begin to alter: during the reigns of Constantine the Great and his sons no small number

---

[1] A list of the Swedish finds of gold from the third and fourth centuries is found in Montelius, *Kulturgeschichte Schwedens* (Leipzig, 1906), p. 180 f. For Denmark see Sophus Müller, *Ordning af Danmarks Oldsager* (*Système préhistorique du Danemark*), ii (København, 1888–95), p. 88, Fig. 234 f.

[2] George Stephens, *The Old Northern Runic Monuments of Scandinavia and England* (London and København, 1866–7), i. 320; Sophus Müller, *Nordische Altertumskunde*, ii. 151.

of Roman gold coins, *aurei* and *solidi*, were brought to the north;
the largest hoard is of forty-seven gold coins from Brang-
strup on Fyen, the latest among them being coins of Constantine II (337–61). The importation into Scandinavia is confined
to a short period, about 350–75, and from the same time
we also have a series of the larger imperial medallions of
double, or more than double, the weight of a *solidus*, and
barbarous imitations of the medallions; but these too are of
a fine gold.[1] The demand for copies arose from the common
custom among the Germans of wearing medallions as insignia
of honour; they were mounted and supplied with a loop for
this purpose, and indeed had been struck specially as *sportulae*
or friendly gifts to allies.

It can be made out that the gold coins from the fourth century were for the most part exported across the Rhine frontier.
A major portion of them were minted in Gaul, and they are
mostly found in the west of Germany; in Scandinavia most have
been found on the island of Fyen, many also in Norway, while
they are very rare on Gotland, which had earlier received the
chief share of the *denarii* from the eastern route. Clearly an
importation of coins so definitely limited in time must have a
cause in contemporary historical events. Scholars have pointed
to the situation on the Rhine under Valentinian I (A.D. 364–75),
where there were wars with the Alamanni and the Franks until
the conclusion of peace with the Alamanni in 374. It is not
unlikely that Norsemen also took part in these operations and
in them acquired both medals and wealth.

We already stand well within the movement which history
calls the great Germanic migration. In the cultural history of
Scandinavia, however, we call the whole of this phase until the
close of the fourth century the Roman period, while influence
from Roman culture was still the leading factor in the development of northern Europe. But here, too, we stand at a critical
point. Towards the end of the fourth century began the great
convulsions which led to the downfall of the Western Roman
Empire, and so placed Scandinavian civilization on more
independent lines. But before we close this chapter it remains

---

[1] The Scandinavian finds of gold coins and medallions have been brought
together complete by A. W. Brøgger in 'Ertog og Øre, Den gamle norske vægt'.
Videnskapsselskapets Skrifter, ii (1921), no. 3, p. 47 f.

to say yet a word about conditions in Finland during the Roman period of the iron age.

The early iron age in Finland is even more sparsely evidenced than in the Scandinavian peninsula, and we can only suggest that a poor bronze culture of eastern character still continued there for several hundred years contemporary with the La Tène period. The Roman period was inaugurated in Finland in the first century after Christ with forms just as poor as in the preceding period. An early Roman wine-ladle, undoubtedly imported from Sweden, stands quite isolated;[1] it was found remarkably far north, by the Kyrö river in Österbotten, on the spot where there is the shortest distance between the Finnish and Swedish coasts. With the second century conditions begin to be more clearly evidenced, and Finland is then under the influence of the culture farther south in the Baltic, in Esthonia, and Lithuania. There are brooches of Baltic type, Baltic pins and ring-ornaments, and it is these that characterize Finnish culture in the earlier phase of the Roman period. The same connexion is maintained unbroken in the following two centuries. The later Baltic variations of the brooches with returned foot are introduced in this later phase, characteristic chains and rings, and ornaments decorated with enamel. The last are a specially interesting group. The art of enamelling in the east Baltic area is believed to have been derived from Germanic example, and the Germanic art in turn goes back to classical work. The Baltic enamel is found in East Prussia, over a great extent of Russia, more rarely in Finland; two examples of it have also been found in Sweden. It is a definitely eastern feature which had its origin in the culture stream flowing from the south-east in the third century, under classical influence.

The strong influences from Esthonia and the Baltic lands to the south, which stamp Finnish civilization during the Roman period, undoubtedly accompanied an invasion of Finno-Ugrian population from that direction; and archaeological sources show how this invasion gradually gained ground from the coast up into the interior of the country. But during the third and fourth centuries there is at the same time an increasing Scandinavian influence transmitted by way of the Swedish province of Norr-

[1] Alfred Hackman, *Die ältere Eisenzeit in Finland*, I. Atlas (Helsingfors, 1905), Plate 1, Fig. 1.

land. In the beginning it was only a matter of actually imported articles—weapons and costly articles such as brooches with embossed silver plate, neck-rings, and finger-rings of gold. Then the Swedish forms were imitated in local work and in cheaper material. In the following period, especially in the sixth century and later, we shall see that these Scandinavian influences grow steadily and become the determining element in Finnish development during the period of migration.

XIII

RUNES

THE ancient Germanic letters, the runes, are among the
most interesting cultural phenomena which come to light
in Scandinavia during the Roman period. Runes appear among
the Germanic peoples about the same time in the north as in
the south, roughly A.D. 200; that is, at a time when the barbarians were receiving a multitude of strong impulses from
classical culture: it is important to remember that this was the
situation when the art of writing first appeared among the
Germans. It is therefore quite certain that the runes were not
formed spontaneously, without any earlier prototype; but it is
also characteristic of the Germans that they did not immediately
adopt either of the existing alphabets which they would meet
with in Roman use, Latin and Greek: on the contrary, they
formed a set of letters which is independent in many particulars,
in form, in sound-value, in the names given to the individual
runes, and in the fixed position of the letters in the series. The
study of runes and their origins accordingly involves a number
of problems which are always tempting to investigators, but
are as yet a long way from any certain solution. Runes have
preserved their old attraction of mystery even to this day.

To the popular consciousness runes have always been something more than an ordinary form of writing. Even in recent
times popular belief has endued runes with mysterious magical
attributes; the runic art was a form of wizardry which conferred
powers of protection or injury, and this conception appears still
more clearly in the older sources. In the Edda poems,[1] which
still present an almost wholly heathen way of thought, there is
valuable information about runes. A myth about the origin of

[1] The most elaborate and complete edition of the Edda poems is that of
Sijmons and Gering, *Die Lieder der Edda* (Halle, 1906–31), including a complete
glossary and a full commentary. A sound text which follows the manuscript
more closely is given in Bugge, *Norræn Fornkvæði* (Christiania, 1867), together
with valuable textual notes. Translations: H. A. Bellows, *The Poetic Edda*
(New York, 1923: in a rough imitation of the original metre); Vigfusson and
Powell, *Corpus Poeticum Boreale* (Oxford, 1883), vol. i (prose; based on a somewhat mangled text).

runes is inserted in *Hávamál*, where Othin himself relates it (*Hávamál*, stanza 140):

nam ek upp rúnar,	I caught up the runes,
œpandi nam:	crying aloud I took them:
fell ek aptr þaðan.	down I fell from there.

The runes come from the highest of the gods:

Rúnar munt þú finna	Runes shalt thou find
ok ráðna stafi,	and letters bearing meaning,
mjǫk stóra stafi,	letters most mighty,
er fáði fimbulþulr	which the Great Counsellor coloured
ok gørðu ginnregin	and most holy gods devised
ok reist hroptr rǫgna.	and the spokesman of the gods had carved.

In *Sigrdrifumál* the valkyrie gives a complete set of instructions for the use of all kinds of runes which fulfil wishes and protect against evil, beginning with runes for victory:

Sigrúnar skaltu kunna,	Runes of victory shalt thou know,
ef þú vilt sigr hafa,	if thou wilt have the victory,
ok rísta á hialti hiǫrs,	and cut them on thy sword-hilt,
sumar á véttrimum,	some on the hilt-rings,
sumar á valbǫstum,	some on the plates of the handle,
ok nefna tysvar Tý.	and twice name the name of Týr.

So also there were runes for women in labour, runes against poison in drink, against distress at sea, runes to heal wounds, and runes that produce eloquence and wisdom. Many traces are preserved also of rites belonging specially to the employment of runes; for example, the runes were coloured red with blood, and when the letters which had been cut were shaved off, the chips could be used in various ways with far-reaching magical power. The valkyrie Sigrdrifa tells how runes originally got their magical virtue in this way:

Allar váru af skafnar	All [sc. the runes] were shaved off
þær er váru á ristnar	that had been cut,
ok hverfðar við inn helga miǫð	and mixed with the holy mead [sc. of inspiration]
ok sendar á víða vega.	and sent upon far ways.

The saga of Egill Skalla-Grímsson[1] shows us the old runic art

---

[1] *Egils saga Skalla-Grímssonar*, edited by Finnur Jónsson (Halle, 1924), or by Sigurður Nordal (Reykjavík, 1933); translated by E. R. Eddison, *Egil's Saga* (Cambridge, 1930).

still undiminished in power at the beginning of the historical period; the saga even implies that Egill's runes were the real cause of Eirik Bloodaxe's loss of his kingdom in Norway (A.D. 947). Runic monuments bear witness to the same traditions in older times. The most important monument of the kind is the Eggjum stone from about the seventh century, bearing a long inscription in which the language and the poetic style are nearly related to the Edda poems. This inscription consists of two stanzas of definitely magical purport, intended to protect the grave and secure vengeance for the man slain.[1] This example provides the key to the general nature of runic documents in early times: the purpose of the runes was not to make statements of fact; their significance was contained in themselves. For this reason the old inscriptions have only a poor and meagre content, according to our ideas. We are most anxious for information about the life of the time, but all we find are names of individual persons and brief formulized phrases. It was not the sense of what was written that held the primary significance: the runes themselves were to have an effect, if correctly used and arranged in certain numerical combinations.[2] The gold ring from Petroassa in Roumania is hallowed by a runic inscription, of which only one word can be interpreted with certainty: *hailag*, 'holy'. Runes on a spearhead give the weapon power, and they are cut on small implements to secure fortune and efficiency in their use. Runes on a trinket make it an amulet which protects its owner.

From all that we know about the magical use of runes, it was comparatively rarely that the runic art was employed in a way that would leave traces lasting into future ages; the runes had their use as an aid to sorcery to obtain immediate results on particular occasions, cut in perishable material, often obliterated again as part of the same magical rite. In the *Edda* (in *Sigrdrifumál*) part of the precaution against treachery was to mark

[1] Magnus Olsen, *Eggjumstenens Indskrifter med de ældre Runer* (Christiania, 1919: offprint from *Norges Indskrifter med de ældre Runer*, iii). Magnus Olsen's latest pronouncement on the date of this inscription is given in 'Runekammen fra Setre', *Bergens Museums Årbok*, 1933, Hist.-Ant. rekke no. 2, p. 69. Different views are advanced by Lis Jacobsen, *Eggjum-Stenen* (København, 1931).

[2] This connexion with numerical combinations has been thoroughly studied by Sigurd Agrell, *Runornas Talmystik och dess antika Förebild*, Publications of the New Society of Letters at Lund, vol. vi (Lund, 1927); summary in English.

runes on the back of the hand and scratch *Nauð* (the rune for
N) on the nail, so that in this instance the runes were written
on the actual person. The runes were generally not intended
to be read by others. A certain number of Norwegian runic
stones, among them the Eggjum stone mentioned above, were
buried in a grave mound with the notion that they would never
again be brought to light; the hidden runes would fulfil their
magical purpose. This circumstance is given special emphasis
in order to make it clear that the surviving records do not give
any reliable indication of the actual extent and use of runes in
the oldest times.

The original form of the runic letters was common to all
Germanic areas, and the Anglo-Saxon and later Scandinavian
runic alphabets were derived later from this common basis.
The Anglo-Saxon runic alphabet is peculiar in that several vowel-
tokens have assumed different values from those of the oldest
runic use, and also because the original series of twenty-four
runes is extended by several new runes added at the end of the
series. The later Scandinavian series which arose about the
beginning of the Viking age was simplified and reduced on a
consistent plan to sixteen runes; but its forms show marked
local variations. For our present purpose, which is primarily
concerned with the origin of runic writing, our attention must
be concentrated upon the early, common Germanic runes. The
twenty-four original runes were arranged in a fixed series, quite
different in its order from the Latin and Greek alphabets, and
indeed completely unlike any other known alphabet. The full
series is divided into three groups of eight runes each, known in
Old Norse as *ættir* (literally 'families'). The original order of
the runic series is preserved in inscriptions of the sixth century,
and it has remained practically unchanged ever since.[1] Each
rune, moreover, had its own individual name which contained
the sound represented by the rune, and, with one exception, the

[1] The most important of these documents containing the runic series are:
a stone slab from a grave at Kylfver in Stånga on the island of Gotland, most
probably from the fifth century; a gold bracteate ornament found at Vadstena
in Östergötland, Sweden (sixth century); a large silver brooch from Charnay,
dep. Saône-et-Loire, in the old Burgundian kingdom; a small one-edged sword
found in the Thames (often called 'the Thames knife'), now in the British
Museum, and probably from about A.D. 700. All of these contain runic series
set out in order, and the Vadstena bracteate also shows the division into three
ættir.

names are words of ordinary intelligible meaning in the old Germanic language.[1] It is the combination of these different features that gives the runic alphabet its peculiar character.

We reproduce from Von Friesen[2] the runic series in its three *ættir* in his normalized form:

ᚠᚢᚦᚨᚱᚲᚷᚹ : ᚺᚾᛁᛃᛇᛈᛉᛊ : ᛏᛒᛖᛗᛚᛝ
f u tha r k g w : h n i j ē p z s : t b e m l ng

ᛞ ᛟ
d o

Following are the names of the runes in Gothic form, as they have been reconstructed by Von Friesen:[3]

1 f faíhu, *n.*, cattle, property.
2 u urus, *m.*, urox.
3 þ (= th) þauris, *m.*, giant, troll.
4 a ansus, *m.* a god (ON. *áss*, pl. *æsir*).
5 r raida, *f.* chariot.
6 k kusma, *m.* abscess.
7 g giba, *f.* gift.
8 w winja, *f.* pasture, or wunja, *f.* joy.
9 h hagl, *n.* hail-stone.
10 n nauþs, *f.* need.
11 i eis, *n.* ice.
12 j jer, *n.* year.
13 ē aíhs, *m.* yew (*taxus*), bow.[4]

---

[1] The names of the runes are known from three Anglo-Saxon manuscripts of the tenth and twelfth centuries (all probably from Kent); Stephens's description of these manuscripts in his *Old Northern Runic Monuments*, i. 100 f. is inaccurate: see C. L. Wrenn, *Late Old English Rune-Names*, Medium Aevum (Oxford, 1932), i. 24; K. Sisam, *Cynewulf and his Poetry*, Proceedings of the British Academy, 1932, p. 16, where fuller descriptions are given. A manuscript from Salzburg from about 900 contains among other matters a Gothic alphabet, and to each letter is added a name which is in reality the Gothic name of a rune. The later Scandinavian names for the runes are known from a West Norwegian poem from about 1300 and from several later Icelandic manuscripts. See Sophus Bugge, *Norges Indskrifter med de ældre Runer*, Introductory volume (Christiania, 1905–13), pp. 40–1.

[2] Otto von Friesen, *Runorna i Sverige* (Uppsala, 1928).

[3] Otto von Friesen, 'Runer', *Nordisk Kultur*, vi (Stockholm, 1933), p. 62.

[4] Among the several necessarily uncertain details of the reconstruction the value of this rune is perhaps the most doubtful. It is of rare occurrence, and its values vary: in Old Norse it usually seems to stand for *e* or *i*, in Old English sometimes for *i*, twice for *h*, and one manuscript names it *hægel*, thus equating it with *h*. With the value *e* the rune would be abnormal in the series, since the sound represented does not appear in the name of the rune. There is something

14 p paiþra, *f.* ?
15 z algs, *m.* elk.[1]
16 s sauil, *n.* sun.
17 t Teiws, *m.* the god known in ON. as Týr and in OE. as Tiw.
18 b baírkan, *f.* birch, or baírkan, *n.* birch rod.
19 e egeis, *m.* horse.
20 m manna, *m.* man.
21 l lagus, *m.* water.
22 ng Iggws, *m.* name of a legendary hero, called Yngvi in Old Norse and Ing in Old English.
23 d dags, *m.* day.
24 o oþal, *n.* patrimony, inherited land.

The names are perhaps the most characteristic feature of these old letters. They are not the neutral, merely practical names of letters such as are used with the Greek and Latin alphabets; they are names of virtue which give each rune a living individuality of its own, and they are of essential importance in the magical use of runes. In runic lore the symbols were regarded as individual entities with special powers residing in the name of each. The Germanic runes in this respect are undoubtedly related to the Celtic ogam; the ogam system of twenty letters divided into four groups is quite different from the runes in details, but the principle is the same, as also the use of the letters primarily for magical purposes.[2]

These various properties are inseparably attached to the very nature of runes, and we must conclude accordingly that runes are not simply an adaptation of a foreign alphabet for the purpose of expressing Germanic speech. From the very first runes had a deeper meaning and also a much more limited use than ordinary writing. It was primarily the magical power of writing which caught the imagination of the barbarians, and it was this conception that determined the character of the alphabet formed according to their own views and purposes. The runes are therefore highly significant of the Germanic cultural position as compared with that of the classical peoples.

to be said for Brate's suggestion that the original value was the sound represented in Gothic as *hv* (resembling *wh* in the Scottish pronunciation of *which*).—*Translator's note.*

[1] In Scandinavian inscriptions the value of this rune is assumed to be R, a sound intermediate between *z* and the ordinary point-trill *r*.—*Translator's note.*

[2] R. A. S. Macalister, *The Archaeology of Ireland* (London, 1928), p. 214 f.

The question as to when and where the runic alphabet was first formed presents great difficulties, since it can only be answered by combining a variety of studies which normally cannot all be mastered by any one investigator, such as the purely epigraphic derivation from older alphabets, the language of the inscriptions, the archaeological evidence, and historical events and conditions of the time when the Germans were brought into contact with peoples who could write. All this is of importance. Moreover, it must be realized that the oldest distribution of runes, as it is known from the surviving records, does not necessarily indicate the place where runic writing originated, and that possibly the runic alphabet as a whole cannot be derived from the existing older alphabets. It is natural in an archaeological treatment to discuss first the age of the runes, so far as it can be ascertained from the surviving inscriptions.

The early runic records known outside Scandinavia are very few.[1] There are two spearheads of nearly related type, both bearing runes and other symbols inlaid with silver in the iron; one was found at Kovel in Volhynia, Poland, the other at Dahmsdorf in Brandenburg,[2] and both are to be dated in the earlier phase of the Roman period. The inscription is very short; obviously there is a single name inscribed on each spear, but it is uncertain whether it is the name of the owner or of the spear itself. There is a somewhat longer inscription on the famous gold ring from Petroassa in Roumania, which was brought to light in a great hoard of gold articles in 1837. Here too the interpretation is disputed, and unhappily the original is now definitely lost. But the first word, *gutani*, gives a definite indication of the nationality of the inscription, and the end, *hailag*, shows clearly enough that the ring was a sacred object. The whole hoard must have belonged to a Gothic fane, and the nature of the constituent articles shows that they were treasures

[1] The most recent study of these is the elaborate treatment by Carl J. S. Marstrander, 'De gotiske runeminnesmerker', *Norsk Tidsskrift for Sprogvidenskap*, iii (Oslo, 1929). A survey of all the older runic inscriptions found outside the north is found in L. F. A. Wimmer, *Die Runenschrift* (Berlin, 1887), p. 56 f., and in Von Friesen, 'Runer', *Nordisk Kultur*, vi (Stockholm, 1933), pp. 4 and 68.

[2] The latter was formerly known from its supposed place of finding, Münchenchenberg, but it was really found near Dahmsdorf, as has recently been shown by Professor Götze, *Die vor- und frühgeschichtlichen Denkmäler des Kreises Lebus* (Berlin, 1920: here cited from Marstrander, op. cit.).

which the Goths had acquired on the north coast of the Black Sea.[1]

Rather doubtful, however, as a runic document is the fourth inscription, from a *castellier* at Maria-Saalerberg in Carinthia. There are six letters cut on a bone awl, which are regarded by Marstrander as runes, but others read them as North Etruscan letters. The linguistic form does not settle the question, as the inscription consists entirely of consonants. Hence we will not venture here to reckon the awl from Maria-Saalerberg among the certainly runic documents.

The three oldest runic inscriptions outside Scandinavia are thus distributed along a definite easterly line, Roumania, Poland, Brandenburg, and this line gives an immediate indication, if not of the runes' earliest home, at least of the first spreading of runic writing. This impression is strengthened when we turn to the early runic finds in Scandinavia. The oldest inscriptions in Norse lands are on a spearhead from Mos in Gotland, a spearhead from Stabu in Toten, a small human figure in bronze from Frøihov in Ringerike (the last two from Norway); and the inscriptions on a sword-scabbard, a belt-buckle, a comb, and a plane in the Vimose find; and on a shield-boss and a scabbard in the bog-find of Thorsbjærg. All these inscriptions date from the third century. The spear from Mos is probably from the first half of that century;[2] the spear from Stabu has been assigned to about A.D. 200.[3] The Vimose find, according to Montelius, was deposited a little before or at the middle of the third century, and the Thorsbjærg find about fifty years later.[4] From the same time there is an inscription on a handsome silver brooch, found at Himlingøje in Zealand (Fig. 11).

[1] This view, which I advanced in *Archaeologia*, lxxvi. 111, receives fresh support from Marstrander, op. cit., p. 41. The hoard from Petroassa has met with a very unhappy fate. Of the twenty-two articles which were found, flagons, jars, cups, and ornaments, all of gold, ten disappeared before the hoard reached the National Museum in Bukarest, and later the collection suffered lamentable loss by theft in 1875 and fire in 1883. After the recent great war nothing of the hoard could be found at all.

[2] Birger Nerman, *Rig* (Stockholm, 1918), p. 50 f.; Almgren and Nerman, *Die ältere Eisenzeit Gotlands* (Stockholm, 1923), pp. 117–18.

[3] Shetelig, 'Tidsbestemmelser av ældre norske runeindskrifter' in Sophus Bugge and Magnus Olsen, *Norges Indskrifter med de ældre Runer*, iii (Christiania, 1914), pp. 12–13.

[4] Oscar Montelius, 'Den nordiske Jernålderns Kronologi', *Svenska Forn-minnesför. Tidskrift*, ix (Stockholm, 1896), p. 268.

In surveying these archaeological documents we have first to give some account of the graves at Stabu and Frøihov. Both of these were graves of cremated bodies, with rich furnishing of weapons burned with the body on the pyre; the Frøihov grave contained a Roman bronze cauldron, used as the burial

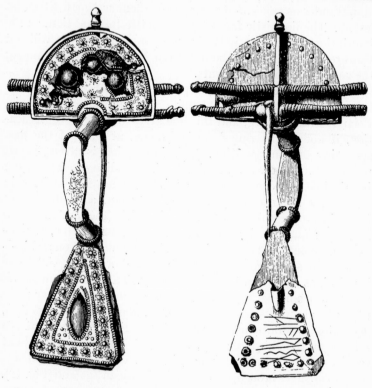

FIG. 11. Silver brooch found at Himlingøje, Zealand. *After Stephens.*

urn. It may be said of both that they belong to a type which was most conspicuous among the Marcomanni in Bohemia, and from there made its way into Norway in the earlier phase of the Roman period.[1] The obvious suggestion is that these oldest runic inscriptions of Norway, and the articles bearing them, the bronze statuette from Frøihov, and the spear from Stabu, were imported. Consideration of this relation some time ago led me to the conclusion that the kingdom of the Marcomanni

[1] Shetelig, *Préhistoire de la Norvège*, pp. 154–5.

in Bohemia was the distributing centre from which runic inscriptions first came to Scandinavia. This idea now seems to receive some support from the recently discovered Norwegian rock-carving with a runic inscription at Kårstad in Nordfjord (Pl. 37).[1] In this carving, together with pictures of ships and a large swastika, appear three words in runes, *ek, aljamarki*R, and *baiji*R (the penultimate rune uncertain); the second of these clearly means 'foreigner' and the last 'Bavarian', which in the usage of that time can only mean 'man from Bohemia'. On archaeological grounds it is likely that the rock-carving is older than the fourth century after Christ, and the runes therefore belong to the early group of inscriptions which are under discussion; the Kårstad runes are actually the oldest runic inscription on stone that we know of. It is highly significant that the inscription contains two such designations (here used as a man's name, or cognomen) as 'foreigner' and 'Bavarian'. Probably these names were given to a returned emigrant who had been a long time in a foreign land, and in that case the name of the particular country is indicated, namely, Bohemia. Such men were the first to bring runic inscriptions to the west of Norway, and this inscription forms a very important piece of evidence, if we have interpreted it rightly.

On the other hand, it cannot be denied that the earliest appearance of runes in Scandinavia is in many instances associated with cultural forms which we know to have emanated from the Goths in southern Russia. This is beyond all doubt true of the bog-finds of Vimose and Thorsbjærg, described in the last chapter (p. 204 f.), and also of the brooch from Himlingøie, which has the characteristic decoration of embossed silver plate and inset pieces of glass; on the back it bears the inscription *hariso*. Linguistically this may well be regarded as a Gothic form, and the ornament itself is probably Gothic work. Similarly the inscription on the belt-buckle from Vimose is said to be clearly in the Gothic language.[2] This relationship has very

---

[1] Magnus Olsen and Haakon Shetelig, 'Kårstadristningen, runer og helleristninger', *Bergens Museums Årbok*, 1929, Hist-ant. rekke, no. 1.

[2] Carl J. S. Marstrander, 'De gotiske runemindesmerker', *Tidsskrift for Norsk Sprogvidenskap*, iii. 84. The other early inscriptions which he regards as Gothic are the spears from Kovel and Dahmsdorf, the gold ring from Petroassa, and the spear from Mos in Gotland; of somewhat later inscriptions two monuments in Gotland, the stone from Kylfver, and the brooch from Ethelhem.

naturally caused investigators to look for the original home of
the runes in the Gothic kingdom in southern Russia. The
archaeological arguments are of obvious force, and the theory
is further strengthened by certain symbols on the runic spearheads (with the exception of the Stabu spear) by the side of the
inscriptions: these are magical symbols well known by the
Black Sea, e.g. in Olbia, which the Goths conquered in 236.
These weapons were almost certainly of Gothic manufacture
and imported into the north. From all evidences there can be
no doubt that a certain number of Gothic articles bearing runic
inscriptions found their way into Scandinavia. But this does
not necessarily imply that runes were wholly unknown in
Scandinavia before the introduction of these Gothic articles.

The archaeological evidences carry us to this point, that the
runes were known among the Goths in southern Russia in the
third century, and from there they spread northward; but
there are also indications which point to the kingdom of the
Marcomanni as a distributing centre at a somewhat earlier time.
This then is the point at which the epigraphic studies of the forms
of the runes are to be applied. The problem of the epigraphic
derivation of runes has been the principal subject of runologists'
attention, and it has proved exceedingly difficult to solve.
Strictly speaking, it lies outside the scope of the archaeologist,
and we shall accordingly be content with referring to the most
important of the theories which have been advanced in recent
years. The first really scientific treatment of the problem was
the work of the Danish scholar Ludvig Wimmer,[1] who came to
the conclusion that the whole of the runic alphabet was derived

---

[1] L. F. A. Wimmer, *Die Runenschrift* (Berlin, 1887). This work first provided
a solid foundation for runic studies, and it is still a standard work on the subject. The next contribution of importance was Sophus Bugge's paper on the
origin of runes read at the philological congress in Oslo in 1898, later expanded
and published in *Norges Indskrifter med de ældre Runer*, Inledning: *Runeskriftens Oprindelse og ældste Historie* (Christiania, 1905–13). Otto von Friesen's
book, *Om Runeskriftens Härkomst* (Uppsala, 1904), had already appeared; here
the archaeological arguments were very effectively used. A purely epigraphic
study: Holger Pedersen, 'Runernes Oprindelse', *Aarb. f. nord. Oldk.* (Kjøbenhavn, 1923), p. 37 f. Also Carl J. S. Marstrander, 'Om Runene og Runenavnenes
Oprindelse', *Tidsskrift for Norsk Sprogvidenskap*, i (Oslo, 1928), with a full
summary in French, p. 180 f. Finally, the most recent contribution (and a very
important one) is that of Magnus Hammerström, *Om Runeskriftens Härkomst*,
Studier i Nordisk Filologi, edited by Hugo Pipping, vol. xx, no. 1 (Helsingfors,
1929).

PLATE 37

Rock-carving at Kårstad. After Magnus Olsen

from Latin letters, but with a certain modification due to Celtic
elements, which Wimmer believed to come from the Gauls in
northern Italy. He dismisses the possibility of the runes having
taken form in contact with the Gauls on the Rhine, and the
argument is that the easterly Gothic inscriptions are among the
oldest, while the West Germanic inscriptions are distinctly later.
From the historical and archaeological point of view Wimmer's
hypothesis is clear enough, but it is, undeniably, inadequate as
an epigraphic explanation of the descent and development of
the runes. For a number of the runes the derivation from the
Latin prototypes adduced is extremely forced. Other investigators, notably Sophus Bugge and Otto von Friesen, have
therefore attempted to explain all details of the alphabet by a
combination of letters which were borrowed partly from Latin
and partly from Greek; and they found among the Goths by
the Danube and in southern Russia a manner of life in which the
barbarians might very naturally come into contact with both
languages and both alphabets.[1] Professor Von Friesen laid
special stress on the derivation of the runes from the Greek
alphabet,[2] and he looked for their prototypes not in the monumental forms of the letters but in the cursive script in use
among the people. He argued that this was the form of writing
which the barbarians would most readily become acquainted
with as mercenary soldiers and workmen in the Roman frontier
towns and garrisons, where the day's passing *graffiti* were always
to be seen on the street corners and in the barracks. By the
Danube the language of the people was Greek, but Latin was
the language of administration and the army; any one who lived
by the Danube frontier would be more or less familiar with both.
All this is true; and von Friesen goes one step farther: he
believes that the Goths by the Black Sea adopted the script in
practical use in administration and correspondence, and that
runic letters were then formed upon the basis of the Greek, and

[1] Bugge came to the conclusion that the runes were formed in the province
of Pontus after the expedition of the Goths into Asia Minor in A.D. 267. He
then explains certain peculiarities of the runes through contact with the Celts
(the Galatians) in Asia Minor, and the names of the runes he believed to have
been formed from similar names belonging to the Armenian alphabet. It may
now be regarded as certain, however, that the runes are older than the time
which Bugge assumed in this theory.

[2] Otto von Friesen, *Runorna i Sverige*, 3rd ed. (Uppsala, 1928); and recently
the same author, 'Runer', *Nordisk Kultur*, vi. 1 f.

in part of the Latin, cursive script, with such modifications as were necessary to express a Germanic language. It is also quite clear that Bishop Wulfila was acquainted with the runes when he devised his Gothic alphabet about A.D. 350.

This is a well-knit and very logical theory which has found widespread acceptance; but it has also met with objections. It is perhaps a secondary point, but it seems very doubtful whether runes were devised as a normal form of writing for practical use; it is more likely that the magical properties which are inseparable from runes during the whole of their later history were associated with them right from their earliest origin, and that the whole system of rune-magic is as old as the runes themselves. With this possibility in mind Sigurd Agrell compared the use of runes with the alphabetical magic of the Greeks and Romans under the empire.[1] His conclusion is that the runic series was devised entirely for mystical and magical use. According to his theory the runic series of twenty-four letters was formed by German soldiers in Roman service at the end of the second century A.D. The order of the runes and their names are derived from the alphabetical magic associated with the cult of Mithra, which was extraordinarily widespread in the Roman army at that time, in the reign of the Emperor Commodus. The names of the runes, he believes, were translated into Germanic from names occurring in Mithra's mysteries, and from its place in the series each rune has a numerical value of magical significance. As we cannot enter into any investigation of this interesting and difficult question here, we refer the reader to Agrell's book. We will only add that from the historical point of view it is very likely that the runic letters would be formed by German soldiers in the Roman army, in garrisons or on active service, where they would come into close contact with writing and likewise with mysteries, magic, and superstition among the other soldiers. It is a very serious objection, however, that Agrell breaks the traditional order of the runic series by transferring ᚠ *faihu* from the first to the last place.

Agrell's work does not touch the epigraphic problem, but this had again been submitted to critical treatment by Holger Pedersen, who returned to Wimmer's theory that the runic

---

[1] Sigurd Agrell, *Runornas Talmystik och dess antika Förebild* (Lund, 1927); summary in English, p. 209.

series was formed entirely on the model of the Latin alphabet during the early empire, though with certain traces of Celtic influence. The latest investigation of the origin of runes, by Carl J. S. Marstrander, goes even farther in the same direction: Marstrander also finds the ultimate archetypes of the runes in the Latin alphabet, and thinks that they were communicated through Celts, and also that they show clear reminiscences of North Etruscan letters, which were still used in Alpine lands in the earliest times after the beginning of Christian chronology. The conclusion to be drawn from these premisses is that the runes must have been devised very early under the Empire by Germanic people who were in contact with Roman culture and at the same time with a Celtic people in the Austrian Alps. This conclusion points directly to the Marcomanni, who very early became allies of the Romans, with the condition that they were to supply auxiliary troops to the Romans: thus we get an explanation which is, historically, fully plausible, of how Germanic runic writing came to be in existence already in the first centuries of the Christian era. According to Marstrander, certain peculiarities of the runes show that they were originally formed to express the sounds of a West Germanic language, which would naturally be that of the Quadi and the Marcomanni.

Thus we are brought to the same result as has already been reached from a basis of archaeological arguments. From the archaeological point of view it is obviously a difficulty that we do not know of any certainly runic inscriptions from the country of the Marcomanni, since the inscription from Maria-Saalerberg is not above suspicion; neither are the supposed runes on the stone found at Prex near Asch in Bohemia. On this stone there are only two letters ᚷᚨ, which might well be the runes for G and A, but they might also be letters from other alphabets. But the lack of runic finds in Bohemia is not conclusive evidence, since runes from their nature may have been used for a long time without being cut in any enduring material; from the whole of the South German area only the three scattered Gothic inscriptions (Petroassa, Kovel, and Dahmsdorf) are known, but these presuppose an extensive distribution of the runes, quite different from that indicated by a general impression of the runic documents, which are nearly all

Scandinavian. The evidences are and will remain very incomplete, but, on the whole, with due consideration of the historical situation, it seems most likely that the runes were first formed among the Marcomanni in the first or second century A.D. and were transmitted by them to the Goths; we should in all probability assume a continuous communication of runes to the north, first from the Marcomanni and then from the Goths.

This hypothesis is in complete accord with the general cultural conditions of the early Roman period, when the Germans in many quarters were receiving impulses from the classical peoples. But the riddle of the runes has not yet been finally read, and its real difficulty lies in the epigraphic problems, since there is no other alphabet which alone will account for all the peculiarities of the runic letters. In spite of all the researches no one has yet provided any complete explanation. We must also mention as a possibility that the runic forms may have been evolving during a long period before the oldest inscription which we know. This would be quite in accordance with the primary character of the runes as a mysterious and magical form of writing. It is even conceivable that the runes in their earliest origins go back to the late La Tène period, when the Germans pushed forward in central Europe and came into intimate contact with Celtic culture.

We must again recall that the late La Tène period marks a great emergence of new cultural forms among the Germans. In the immediately preceding centuries Germanic culture had been remarkably conservative. The form of burial was always cremation in urn-fields, following ancient custom; dress and ornaments followed the same old traditions. The Germanic peoples lived quiescent in their own localities until nearly the second century before Christ. But towards the end of this period it can be shown that the northern frontier of the Celts was receding, and the change comes at the same time as the first great advance which history knows of Germanic peoples pressing southwards. A lively contact with Celtic culture[1] is then evidenced among the Germans by imported articles and native imitation of Celtic forms; the costume is modified, as may be seen from the use of fibulas, which now becomes general, and from the belt-hooks

[1] For a survey of the Celtic La Tène culture see *De Forhistoriske Tider i Europa*, ii (Kjøbenhavn, 1927), pp. 302–16.

of pure Celtic form; in pottery new forms were adopted, fine shiny vases, all black, often decorated with meanders, all under strong influence of the Celtic ceramic art. The graves too become more richly furnished. Everything shows that Germanic culture was undergoing a powerful and rapid transformation, produced by conquest of regions of Celtic culture. It was a period of transitional change; and its processes were continued without interruption in acquisition of elements of classical Roman culture, after the Germanic peoples were no longer confronted with Celts, but with frontiers of Roman provinces.

Marstrander has urged strongly that the names of the runes, with their mythological content, are nearly related to the corresponding names of the ogam letters, which he believes to go back to the ancient Gaulish religion. In ancient Gaulish then we would have the common source of peculiarities found both in Irish and Germanic letters. This theory seems to imply that the runes originated from very early contact of the Germans with the alphabet and religion of the Gauls, in the Celtic rather than the Roman period of the iron age in central Europe. In view of the great difference in form between ogam and runes, it should perhaps be pointed out that the curious system of the ogam, in which each letter is denoted by the number of its position within its group, is essentially a system of secret or cipher writing; this secret form must have been based upon an older alphabet with individual letters, in the same way that twig-runes are based on the normal runic series.[1] This alphabet which the secret form eventually superseded would be the original Celtic alphabet which may have been the actual prototype of the runic alphabet. As this theory has been worked out by Magnus Hammerström,[2] it seems at present to provide the most probable solution of the runic problem.[3] This theory

---

[1] Thus, for example, the twig-rune ⚛ represented the first rune of the third group, that is, Týr = T.

[2] *Om Runskriftens Härkomst*, Studier i Nordisk Filologi, xx (Helsingfors, 1929).

[3] A passage in the *Germania* of Tacitus (cap. 10) has sometimes been taken as proof that runes were used in sortilege by the Germans already in the first century A.D. The process of sortilege described by Tacitus is essentially the same as to *fella blótspán* in Old Norse, and in Norse sortilege rune-marked chips were sometimes used. See Chapter XXIII below, p. 426, and also p. 213 above. The chips for sortilege were taken, according to Tacitus, from a 'nut-bearing tree', and the traditional word for a rune-inscribed chip in the

obviously does not affect the conclusion already reached, that the earliest diffusion of runes to the north was through the agency of the Marcomanni and Goths in the second and third centuries after Christ.

In the Gothic translation of the Bible Wulfila used *runa* to render the Greek μυστήριον, 'mystery, secret', and indeed runes are to this day the great mystery of Germanic archaeology. We conclude this survey of modern runic studies without reaching any definite conclusion; the origin of the runes is still an open question.

The spread and later history of the runes exhibit some very interesting phenomena. Among the southern Germanic peoples, where the runes were undoubtedly formed, only the very few early inscriptions already mentioned are known, while Scandinavian lands have preserved a far greater number even of the oldest runic documents, as will be described in the next chapter. We may surmise that the southern Germans gave up the use of runes very early, since Christianity made them familiar with writing in other forms; but this influence did not reach Scandinavia, and the runic art found its principal home there during long ages. The runes were carried to England by the Anglo-Saxons, and in the sixth century they were adopted by the West Germanic people in the Rhineland. But from the forms of the letters it is clear that the runic writing of the West Germans (other than the Anglo-Saxons) is based upon the preceding epigraphic development in the north, and consequently they must have been reintroduced into the south through Scandinavian influence. Another indication of this origin is that these West Germanic inscriptions are to a great extent cut on ornaments of Norse type. The West Germanic runes, however, were a very transient phenomenon; they soon disappeared again, while the Anglo-Saxon runes in England were still used for a long period, and the Scandinavian runic art

Germanic languages is seen in OE. *bōc*, which means etymologically 'beech'; cf. OE. *bēce* and *bōctrēow*, 'beech'. These indications cannot be taken as conclusive, however, and there is really no certainty that the *notae* of Tacitus were runes; before the age of runes other kinds of marks may have been used in religious magic. Yet the possibility that the marks were runes must be admitted; Wimmer and other investigators dismissed the possibility too readily, because it did not harmonize with the chronology of their own theories.— *Translator's note.*

was still in full flower in the Christian Middle Ages. In some districts in Scandinavia knowledge of runes never really died out. Popular tradition of magical runes is there confronted with the first learned literature on runes.

XIV

THE MIGRATION PERIOD. GOLD HOARDS AND GRAVES. RUNES AND MEMORIAL MONUMENTS. HILL FORTS

SCANDINAVIAN culture during the later Roman period, which has been described in the last two chapters, derived its character primarily from great cultural waves from the south-east, emanating ultimately from the Goths by the Black Sea, and reaching the north in the third and fourth centuries. This flow of new culture from the south-east, which held a profound significance for all the East Germanic and Scandinavian peoples, came to an end after the middle of the fourth century. At that time there were clearly several dominating factors producing momentous changes among the barbarous northern peoples, both in relation to each other and to the cultured lands of the south. The most important, perhaps, was the abandonment of eastern Germany by its Germanic population in the fourth and fifth centuries; this region remained sparsely populated for a long time, as is proved by archaeological evidences, supported by the express statement of Procopius that the Heruli passed through desolate regions when making their way to the north about A.D. 512. The scattered remnants of the Germanic population which still remained in the east were too weak to maintain the old cultural connexions, and trade through central Europe again had to take the western route along the Rhine and Elbe. It was in this period too that the first great outburst of Germanic migrations came; these were directly connected with the invasion of the Huns.

Shortly after the middle of the fourth century the Goths in the south of Russia were overwhelmed by the Huns; multitudes of Goths had to flee westward to save themselves, and in the spring of 376 the West Goths obtained permission to cross the Danube and find an asylum on Roman soil. In form this was arranged as a voluntary alliance with the Roman emperor; in reality it was the signal for a great invasion of all the western provinces: Italy was occupied first by the West Goths, later by the Heruli, East Goths, and Langobards; Gaul was divided between the Franks, Burgundians, Alamanni, and West Goths. The West Goths of southern Gaul then conquered Spain; while the Vandals crossed into Africa and the Anglo-Saxons to England. The fifth century was a period of rapid change. It began with Alaric's sack of Rome, and before its end all of the western Roman provinces were in the hands of Germanic peoples. The most tangible traces now remaining of these historical changes and of the new political conditions are the finds of gold hoards. The plunder of rich provinces, of Italy itself, and the imperial subsidies created a veritable age of gold for the northern barbarians from about the middle of the fifth century to about the middle of the sixth. We know, for example, that the Goths in Pannonia in A.D. 459 were granted three hundred pounds of gold each year, and it is significant that the greater number of gold coins found in Germanic soil were minted for the Emperors Theodosius, Leo, and Zeno, precisely those who, according to the record of history, paid out subsidies to the Goths on the Danube; the last emperor whose coins are represented in any large number is Anastasius, 491–518. The very latest whose coins are found is Justinian I (527–65), and with these Germanic acquisition of Byzantine gold comes to an end.

Such events and conditions brought a golden stream of Roman coins into the Germanic world. Great hoards of gold were amassed among tribes and by kings, as among the Vandals in Africa, and the Goths at Ravenna; and from the Goths coins and gold were carried northward to related nations, from the Danube lands to the Baltic, and the way is marked by finds of coins in Germany, especially around the lower course of the Vistula. This Roman gold which begins to be exported in the fifth century has a different character from the Roman coins which came to Scandinavia in the preceding century. The time of the great gold medallions is past; now only the current gold coins, *solidi*, are acceptable, which for a long time had always been minted in uniform weight and with a uniform content of gold. In Scandinavia the finds of such coins are mostly concentrated in Gotland, Öland, and Bornholm; on these islands alone nearly 400 *solidi* have been found, while the total from the whole of Scandinavia is about 500. In Denmark the gold coins are found mostly on the islands of Zealand and Fyen, the areas which were marked by such conspicuous wealth in the preceding centuries; and on the Swedish mainland most *solidi* have been found in the province of Uppland. In Norway, and in Finland as well, these gold coins are very rarely found.[1]

But the gold coins represent only an inconsiderable part of the Roman gold which has come to light in Scandinavian lands. From the same source without doubt were derived the hoards of gold in the form of ingots, plain bars bent into spirals or rings or worked into heavy massive ornaments. Cast or hammered ingots are rare. Most of the gold is in the form of 'ring-money', simple spiral rings whose only purpose is to give the gold suitable form as a precious metal. Pieces cut from bars and rings are also found in large numbers, varying according to the amounts required. Yet gold was also worked artistically in Scandinavia in considerable quantity. The heavy double neck-rings with stamped ornament are a specifically Norse type; specially Norse too are similarly ornamented arm-rings, and without doubt finger-rings of certain forms, pendants and beads of gold. A more elaborate form of work was employed on gold mountings and ornaments on the hilts and scabbards of swords, sometimes mosaic of coloured stones, sometimes filigree ornament in relief on a basis of stamped and perforated gold. This ornamental form is pure Scandinavian, and its artistic handwork reaches a remarkably high level.[2] To this group belong the most beautiful gold pieces preserved from ancient times in Scandinavia, three heavy collars of gold from Sweden, one found in Öland (Pl. 38), and the other two from Västergötland. These collars are each composed of several hollow rings, three, five, and seven respectively, and they are richly adorned with figures in filigree; among the figures is a number of small human forms, warriors in mail carrying shields. Of related work is a fragment

---

[1] The most recent list of the coins and hoards of gold in Denmark is the work of Carl Neergaard, 'Guldfundene fra den efterromerske Jærnalder', *Aarb. f. nord. Oldk.* (Kjøbenhavn, 1915), p. 193. A complete list for Norway is supplied by Johs. Bøe, 'Norske Guldfund fra Folkevandringstiden', *Bergens Museums Årbok*, 1920–1, Hist.-ant. rekke no. 2. The finds of gold in Sweden were collected up to the time of publication by O. Montelius in *Kulturgeschichte Schwedens* (Leipzig, 1906), p. 218 f., and more recently by Olov Robert Janse, *Le travail de l'or en Suède à l'époque mérovingienne* (Orléans, 1922). In this book Dr. Janse gives a complete catalogue of all the *solidi* found in Scandinavia up to 1920. See also Alfred Hackman, *Die ältere Eisenzeit in Finland*, i. 288.

[2] Sune Lindqvist, *Vendelkulturens Ålder och Ursprung*, Kgl. Vitterhets Historie och Antikvitets Akademiens Handlingar, Del 36, i (Stockholm, 1926), p. 55 f.; splendidly illustrated.

PLATE 38

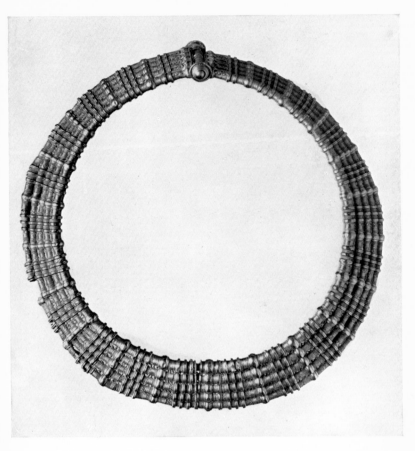

Gold collar from Torslunda, Öland. After Stenberger

of a very heavy Swedish gold ring found in Halland; it is so big that it is thought to have been a belt.

An especially distinctive group among the articles worked in gold is formed by the characteristic Scandinavian ornaments that pass under the name of gold bracteates. They are pendants resembling coins, made from a thin gold plate stamped on one side only, framed in a thicker rim and provided with a cord to wear around the neck. The oldest bracteates are quite unmistakably imitated from the larger Roman mintage, the gold medallions already mentioned, but they show a simplified technique. The image can be clearly recognized as the effigy of the emperor on coins from the time of Constantine, or else there is an equestrian figure or several standing figures, due no doubt to an arbitrary preference for the reverse-image on coins. Often too we see corrupt reminiscences of legends from coins, misunderstood Latin letters mingled with occasional runes. But soon a new composition, purely Norse in character, is developed; a large human head is placed directly over a four-footed animal, sometimes a horse, sometimes a horned animal which may be a goat, and the group is accompanied by constant attributes, such as a bird, swastika, or triskele, as well as runic inscriptions of varying length which undoubtedly have a magical significance.[1]

In this process of modification the bracteates became something other and much more than a barbarous perversion of Roman mintage; the coins provided the original model, but the figures of the bracteates now became, just as definitely, an expression of Norse ideas and Norse mentality. Both the design and the technique seen in the effigies passed beyond the clumsiness evident in the imitations of classical images, and assumed a confident and constant style, which may be called barbaric, but has yet a beauty of its own. The bracteates were not ornaments alone; they were also amulets, hallowed by sacred symbols and magical runes. It is quite possible that the bracteates inherited this property from the Roman medallions, which we have seen were worn by German and Norse chiefs in the fourth century. Worship of the emperor was doubtless the form of

---

[1] On the bracteates in general see Olov Robert Janse, *Le travail de l'or en Suède*, 1922, p. 70, where references to the earlier literature on the subject may be found. Gutorm Gjessing, 'De norske gullbrakteatene', *Universitets Oldsaksamlings Skrifter*, ii (Oslo, 1929), p. 127.

Roman religion which the Germans first became acquainted with in the camps or garrisons on the frontiers; the emperor's image on the coins might easily be endowed with magical protective powers, which were then transferred to purely Scandinavian ornaments. Yet on the bracteates the fundamental meaning of the image is completely altered: now it is in every detail an expression of Norse conceptions.[1] It is only in the later forms of gold bracteates, it seems, that their magical properties disappear; the representation of figures ceases and gives place to purely ornamental animal motives. The evolution of the bracteates was accomplished mainly in the course of the fifth century, and the later forms were still in use in the first half of the following century. The bracteates undoubtedly originated in Scandinavia, where we can follow their development right from their beginning at the close of the fourth century, and they appear in much larger numbers in Scandinavia than in any other area. Among the northern Germans the bracteates were probably due to Scandinavian influence, and partly to direct importation. Gold bracteates, almost exclusively late forms, are found in England, in Friesland, and along the Rhine, but in very small numbers.[2]

The smaller ornaments of gold, bracteates, finger-rings, beads, are sometimes found in graves, especially in Norway, but the greater part of the gold from the migration period in Scandinavia is found in hoards buried in the earth. A single hoard may consist of only one or two pieces, but more usually of many, up to a very considerable quantity of gold articles. The largest hoard known in Denmark consisted of fifty-two articles, among them three large neck-rings, four arm-rings, seven gold bracteates, bars, ingots, &c., with a total weight of over 4 kilograms of gold.[3] The hoard from Sköfde in Västergötland had a total

---

[1] Bernhard Salin attempted to show that two of the principal types of bracteates represent the gods Othin and Thor: see the *Festskrift 'Till Oscar Montelius af Lärjungar'* (Stockholm, 1903), p. 136. O. Janse (op. cit., p. 136) holds the view that the bracteates have no mythological significance, but that they represent the Hunnish king Attila and episodes from the legends attached to him.

[2] G. Baldwin Brown, *The Arts in Early England*, iv (London, 1915), p. 451; Friedrich Holter, *Das Gräberfeld bei Obermöllern aus der Zeit der alten Thüringen* (Halle, 1925), Taf. XXIV.

[3] F. Sehested, *Fortidsminder og Oldsager fra Egnen om Broholm* (Kjøbenhavn, 1878), French text p. 310, plates XLI–XLIV.

weight of a little more than 7 kilograms, but the largest in Scandinavia is the hoard from Tureholm in Södermanland, also in Sweden, containing more than twelve kilograms of gold, in this instance entirely in money-rings and ingots.[1] Such great treasures are of course exceptional, but they illustrate what wealth of gold may be found. The tremendous value of the hoarded treasures accorded with the conditions of the time; the amount of gold acquired was quite out of proportion to the economic needs of Scandinavia. Accordingly a certain unwillingness to set gold in circulation prevailed; it was to be hoarded and watched over, surrounded with a mystical reverence, as we know from the *Nibelungenlied* and the epic *Beowulf*.[2] The coins which were brought to the north in the fourth century were not mingled with the coins of later acquisition, because the earlier hoards already rested safe in their deposit in the earth. This practice of burying hoards was one expression of the new conception of gold as the basis of all material values. The gold was always weighed to decide its value, and rings were made in definite units of weight.[3] The Old Norse weight-name *eyrir* (modern *øre*) is itself derived from Latin *aureus*. In the oldest Norwegian laws the gold ring, *baugr*, is still the constant unit in wergelds, and it was the chief's gift to the warrior whom he wished to retain in his service. In this way the gold of the migration period provided a new basis for standards of value and for an economic system which remained firmly established far into the historic period.

There has been considerable discussion about the motives for depositing gold hoards in the earth. The simplest explanation, that it was a precaution to preserve the treasure in a safe place where it could be recovered later, has not found much favour, since the gold generally was not taken up again. On the face of it, it seems reasonable to assume that the hoards were sometimes deposited as offerings, and that in other instances the

[1] Ture Arne, 'Le trésor d'or découvert à Sköfde', *Fornvännen* (Stockholm, 1906), p. 92; O. Montelius, *Kulturgeschichte Schwedens*, p. 220. Only about a tenth part of the treasure has been preserved. It was discovered in 1774.

[2] Knut Stjerna, *Essays on Questions connected with the Old English Poem of Beowulf*, published for the Viking Club (London, 1912), p. 136 ('The Dragon's Hoard in *Beowulf*').

[3] A. W. Brøgger in *Ertog og Øre* (1921), p. 24 f., demonstrates that a number of gold rings were made to contain a definite number of *eyrir*-units, varying in the main between six and thirty-six of such units.

gold belonged to a temple. In the preceding pages we have several times mentioned similar offerings from earlier periods. But another motive should also be mentioned. According to Snorri Othin promised that every man should bring to Valhall the wealth which he had with him on the pyre, and also that he should enjoy all that he himself had buried in the earth;[1] obviously the hiding-place was a secret, and the intention was that the treasure should never be recovered by living men. The gold was dedicated to the future life, *galdre bewunden*, 'surrounded with incantations', as it is said in *Beowulf*. In all probability the hoards of gold provide the explanation of the extreme poverty of contemporary graves in most Scandinavian lands. The hoard of gold took the place of furniture in the grave.

In most of Scandinavia the graves of the fifth and sixth centuries are little known. In Denmark examples of graves with cremation are known in Jutland, as in the burial place at Donbæk near Fridrikshavn, while in Zealand burials without cremation are found; but both types of grave are inconspicuous, without any trace of grave-goods. When such graves are turned up now, they are often indistinct, or they are not noticed at all. Again it must be emphasized that the gold hoards on the Danish isles are concentrated in the same district that possessed so many rich graves in the preceding Roman period, and it seems evident here that the gold hoards have replaced the luxurious furniture of the graves. In Sweden also graves of these centuries are rare, apart from Bohuslän on the west coast and certain northern districts, Helsingland and Medelpad, where we find examples of the richer Norwegian grave-forms, which will be described a little farther on; moreover, scarcely any other period of antiquity has left so few distinct graves in the whole of Sweden as these two centuries, when the gold hoards are larger and more

---

[1] 'Ynglinga saga' (chapter 8) in *Heimskringla*; trans. Magnusson and Morris, *Saga Library*, iii. 20. In the Old English poem *The Seafarer* (lines 100–3) there is apparently a direct reference to the old belief in the efficacy of burying hoards of gold. A Christian poet is commenting on the futility of heathen rites, and he says it is useless to bury treasure with the dead; also 'gold will be unable to help the soul that is full of sin in the face of God's wrath, when he has hidden it while still living in this world'. This is one of many references in Old English poetry to peculiarly Scandinavian practices, apparently based on traditions descended from the migration age; thus the literary indications agree with the archaeological evidence of a close connexion between Scandinavia and the Anglo-Saxon peoples in that age.—*Translator's note*.

numerous than in any other period, and Swedish art left such splendid memorials as the great golden collars. Even on the island of Gotland, which can show such an astonishing number of rich graves in both the preceding and following periods, very few are found that can be assigned to the period A.D. 450–550.

This decided simplification of the graves and their furniture which prevailed over large areas of Scandinavia is all the more peculiar because the other Germanic peoples held to the custom of giving their dead rich and costly grave-furnishings of ornaments and weapons, a certain number of tools, pots, glass beakers, &c. The same provision is well known from the German *Reihengräber*, from burial places in France and northern Italy, and among the Anglo-Saxons in England; everywhere Germanic graves are marked by an abundance of antiquities which presents a striking antithesis to the contemporary graves in Denmark and Sweden. Quite a different course was taken by the developments in Norway, which received a comparatively small share of the golden treasures of the migrations; Norway, instead of burying hoards, held fast to the richer form of burial as a tradition from the Roman period. The two principal forms of burial, cremation and inhumation, occur side by side over the whole country, and new generations were buried in the old-established burial places according to the old custom. In cremation the grave-goods were burned with the body on the pyre, and the grave was constructed with or without cinerary urn, which was often a foreign vessel of bronze. The furniture is generally quite modest, but occasionally we find in the cinerary graves remains of costly ornaments, of burned glass beakers, and globules of melted gold. In some instances it can be seen that a boat has been burned on the pyre; these are the earliest boat-graves known in Scandinavia.[1]

Greater interest, however, attaches to the graves without cremation, which in Norway display a remarkable wealth in the fifth and sixth centuries. In construction and furniture these graves are very nearly related to the rich graves without cremation in the late Roman period: these have already been described in a preceding chapter. We still have the same large grave-cists made of stone or wood, covered by a barrow which is often

[1] Shetelig, 'Tidlige Båtgraver', *Oldtiden*, iv, Avhandlinger tilegnet dr. Sophus Müller (Kristiania, 1918), p. 73.

of most imposing dimensions. The cist is lined with birch bark; skins and cloths are laid on the floor. The dead was laid out in full costume and also wrapped in woollen shrouds, and finally a cloth was spread over the whole. In some instances it could be seen that the cist was filled finally with bracken and leaves before the grave was closed with stone slabs.[1] By way of furnishing we now find in the first place all that was accessory to the costume: clasps with gilt knobs, richly made belts, brooches, pins, gold bracteates, rings, and beads. On the belt smaller articles were worn, knives, tweezers, keys, and tinder-box. The men always have their weapons, in most cases the full equipment, sword with belt, two spears, arrows, and the shield laid at the feet, while the women are provided with implements for spinning, weaving, and dressing hides. Common to all the graves is a rich equipment of vessels for food and drink, mostly cups, flagons, and jugs of earthenware, goblets and bowls of wood, pails with mountings of metal; but also the more costly cauldrons and basins of bronze and beakers of glass. As a rule these vessels are placed by the feet of the dead, or, when the furnishing is very rich, divided into portions at each end of the cist; the glass beakers are always set close to the head.

These graves are characterized in every particular by the same ideas as we encountered during the Roman period in Scandi-navia, and these ideas are also found expressed in the same period in the burial customs of the new Germanic nations in western Europe. The community of burial custom must with-out doubt have its origin in Norwegian connexions with western Europe; but in certain details we also trace survivals from the older Norwegian custom. There is first of all the orientation of the grave. In the greater number of graves in Norway the body is laid with its head to the north, north-east, or east, and this Nor-wegian custom determined very largely the disposition of the graves; while among the southern Germans custom required the head to be turned to the south. It is a specially Norwegian feature also that very high and large grave-mounds were still raised. Farther south the German graves lie under a flat sur-face, while in Norway no burial of any importance was conceiv-able without a huge barrow thrown up over the grave as a

[1] Shetelig, 'Die norwegischen Skelettgräber der Völkerwanderungszeit', *Prähistorische Zeitschrift*, iv (1912), p. 351 f.

monument. In Norway barrows had never passed wholly out of use, as they had in Denmark and Germany. Another feature which may also be mentioned as specifically Norwegian is the great stone-built cist, which can seldom be paralleled in other countries; but in the same period we also have Norwegian examples of wooden coffins, which agree with the western Germanic form of burial. Thus in essential points there are elements of a specially Norwegian character, even though the group as a whole is very nearly related to the West Germanic graves in England and France.

Apart from the hoards of gold it is, practically speaking, from the Norwegian graves alone that we derive our knowledge of Scandinavian antiquities of the fifth and sixth centuries. The importation of foreign manufactures was still considerable, but the nature of the goods bespeaks clearly the altered conditions of a new age. During the wars and disturbances in the fourth century and the deluge of invasion which followed, the economic life of western Europe was crushed to the ground, and Roman industry and handcrafts in the provinces suffered like everything else. The care for good quality faded, forms and decoration were barbarized. Yet the Roman traditions did not wholly disappear. Industrial products preserved the regular and standard form of the factory, which was quite foreign to Germanic handcraft. In the workshops of Gaul glass and bronze articles were still produced which are found spread over the whole of the Germanic world, and they bear witness to a very uniform and extensive production.[1] The quality is indeed considerably rougher than before, but it was none the less a true tradition of Roman work which survived the tempest of the migration period and provided the basis for a new development.

These products of half-barbarous manufacture from western Europe were now imported into Scandinavia. There were glass articles, probably from the Rhineland, tall drinking cups, goblets, and drinking horns of clear greenish glass decorated in the same colour with patterns of threads laid on the surface. Similar glasses are found in central Europe, France, and England, and they appear in the north wherever the graves of this

---

[1] See G. Baldwin Brown, *The Arts in Early England*, iv. 466 and 480; also Anton Kisa, *Das Glas im Altertume* (Leipzig, 1908), i. 199.

time have the richer furnishing, occasionally in Bornholm and Jutland, and an especially large number in Norway. It is remarkable that the glasses found in Scandinavia are almost invariably of thicker, more solid quality than those found in lands farther south; we can only assume that a specially strong quality was still manufactured for export to distant markets. In addition to the glasses there was a certain kind of bronze cauldron which was exported in large numbers, a form with triangular lugs and a sharp angle between the bottom and sides, which is also well known in England. They are found very generally in Norwegian graves, both in those with cremation and those without it. A rarer type is the low shallow bowl of bronze with turned-out edges ornamented with a close row of bosses beaten up from the back, a distinctive and regularly made article which probably came, like the others, from the workshops of northern Gaul. These foreign goods undoubtedly came to Scandinavia through the North Sea trade with the lands around the mouth of the Rhine, which we have seen was well established at a much earlier time.

In native work too, in metal and in pottery, the fifth century introduces a new cultural period in Scandinavia. The influence of Roman civilization is no longer the leading factor in the development; even though we find many significant reminiscences of classical culture still perceptible, yet these two centuries, the fifth and the sixth, derive their character primarily from independent Scandinavian development, during continuous contact with the new Germanic kingdoms in western Europe. But the influence of these Germanic nations was not as overwhelming as the great waves of classical culture in the first centuries of the Christian era. There was no longer such a great difference in the level of culture as there had been in the Roman period; the other Germanic peoples were in much the same position as the Scandinavians, and in some degree we can even speak of reciprocal influence. We have mentioned earlier that runic writing was transmitted from Scandinavia to the West Germans in this period (p. 228); this is true also of the gold bracteates which are mentioned above, and also of certain types of large silver brooches.

The decorative art well illustrates the distinctive character of this new development in Scandinavia. At the same time as the gold bracteates were being evolved as a specially Norse group, as has already been described, we also find a new Norse style in the decoration of other objects, especially the larger brooches of silver, which were the most distinctive ornaments of the period. We will reserve the full description of this decorative art for a later chapter, and will only mention here that the fifth and sixth centuries also provide the first phase of Scandinavian animal ornament, the style which we call the migration style, following Sophus Müller; it reached its earliest flower in the sixth century. Important also are the new native types of ornaments, a group of various forms, all of which originated in the late Roman period.[1] The large silver brooches with square head-plate were at first made of plain silver with stamped and engraved decoration (Pl. 39a), a more solid production replacing the older technique of laying thin impressed silver plates on a basis of bronze; later this type became still more solidly cast with ornaments in relief, and thick showy gilding, sometimes with inlaid gold plates and filigree and sockets for garnets.[2] The largest and most magnificent of them are quite gigantic ornaments, barbarous in taste, but bearing eloquent witness to the high quality of Scandinavian handcraft in the sixth century (Pl. 39b). Gold filigree was still cultivated, and other admirable pieces of work are preserved, such as medallions with inset stones, and, in particular, mounts for scabbards, and the large collars and other articles already described in connexion with the gold hoards.

By the side of the rarer pieces of precious metal are found simpler ornaments cast in bronze. The most important are those known as cruciform long brooches, very handsome ornaments of simple strong form in solid metal, with only a very restrained use of engraved ornamentation, and in one instance inlay of silver (Pl. 39c). The cruciform brooches belong to the period from the fourth to the sixth century. They are especially fre-

---

[1] Bernhard Salin, *Die altgermanische Thierornamentik* (Stockholm, 1904), p. 41 f.

[2] The mould of a cast-silver brooch found recently in the foundation of a house at Stavanger shows, according to Dr. Jan Petersen, that it was first cast as a flat sheet and then hammered into the desired shape, and finally the ornaments were engraved in the silver. See Jan Petersen, 'Eine Giessform aus der Zeit der Völkerwanderung', *Bergens Museums Årbok*, 1931, Hist.-ant. rekke no. 6.

R

quent in Norway; otherwise they are evenly represented in Scandinavia and England.[1] In addition to the one large ornament, a silver brooch or a long cruciform brooch, the women at this time wore as a rule several pairs of quite small bronze fibulas, which were, however, practical necessities for the costume rather than ornaments proper. Of other small ornaments which are characteristic of the time the clasps for the sleeves should be noted, fastened with ornamental knobs of gilt silver; also the belt with clasps, buckles, and buckle-plates, often richly produced.

A very interesting feature of native industry at this time is the pottery. The forms are pleasing, some being new variations of older types belonging to the Roman period, others completely new. In Norway at the end of the fourth century a series of such new forms appeared, pots shaped like small pails, and clearly formed on the model of pails or buckets of wood. The type is exclusively Norwegian, and was accorded special favour in the industry for some two centuries. Small technical discoveries were made in production, such as the addition of asbestos or mica to the mass of clay, so that the vessel could be made very light and thin, and special forms were developed in decoration, interlacing of broad bands and patterns of stamped figures (Pl. 40). It can be seen that this pottery was not a domestic industry but the production of an organized craft. The Norwegian art of pottery perhaps had its richest and most original production at this time.

The West Norwegian graves are our chief source for forming a full and balanced picture of Scandinavian culture in the migration period. But we have also to note a characteristic and interesting feature common to the whole Germanic North at this period, namely the extensive use of runes. In the preceding chapter we have set forth what we know of the origin of runes and their earliest diffusion; here we have to add that the older common Germanic runes have nowhere left so many monuments as in Scandinavian lands in the fifth and sixth centuries. The gold bracteates very often bear runes, in the beginning undoubtedly produced in imitation of inscriptions on Roman coins, the original models of the bracteates; we have examples

[1] Shetelig, 'The Cruciform Brooches of Norway', *Bergens Museums Årbok*, 1906, no. 8.

PLATE 39

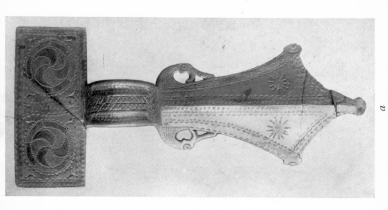

a. Silver brooch of the early 5th century, from Vestfold, Norway. *b*. Silver brooch, heavily gilt, 6th century, from Sunnfjord, Norway. *c*. Cruciform long brooch, 6th century, from Hardanger, Norway

of bracteates in which the inscription is mainly in corrupted Roman letters, mixed with occasional runes; such, for example, is a bracteate from Mauland near Stavanger. But just as the effigy on Roman coins was given new meaning by the Norse mentality, the Roman letters were soon transformed into actual runic inscriptions. A few bracteates bear the whole runic alphabet, which in itself had magical significance. Other bracteates have inscriptions sufficiently full to give intelligible sense, as, for example, a Swedish bracteate from Tjurkö in the province of Blekinge, on which we read: 'Hjald made runes on the Roman treasure (i.e. on the gold) for Kunimund.' But from most of the inscriptions on bracteates it is hard to extract sense; they probably contain certain formulae, magical words and abbreviations, of which we have no key to unlock the meaning. The bracteates provide typical examples of the use of runes for magical protection. We also know of amulets of bone, in which the objects themselves have no other purpose than to bear a runic inscription; such are the two well-known amulets from Lindholm in Skåne and Ødemotland near Stavanger, both of serpentine shape and covered with long rows of runes.

Inscriptions on other miscellaneous objects must be regarded from the same point of view. The most conspicuous example is a large brooch of silver gilt from Fonnås in Østerdal, a magnificent specimen of the goldsmith's art in the migration period (Pl. 48). This ornament is richly decorated on the front, but the back is smooth shining silver, on which a long inscription is lightly scratched, difficult to read in parts and not certainly interpreted. Short inscriptions are known on small implements for dressing skins, on sinkers (for fishing), and whetstones.

The most important group of runes from the migration period in Scandinavia are memorial inscriptions in stone. There are inscriptions on detached memorial stones (*bautasteinar*), either as independent monuments or set up on a grave-mound; inscriptions on a stone hidden in the mound or on the stones which form the cist of the grave; and finally some few on the solid rock of a mountain-side. Of the inscriptions of this kind about ten are known in Sweden and thirty in Norway,[1] but none

---

[1] A list of the Norwegian inscriptions will be found in Magnus Olsen, *Norges Indskrifter med de ældre Runer*, iii (Christiania, 1914–24), p. 334, with a map, p. 332. Von Friesen gives an up-to-date index of all the runic inscriptions of

from so early a time in Denmark. The oldest inscribed stone stands to this day on the grave-mound where it was obviously set originally, at Einang in Valders, in a burial place of the fourth century; the inscription is DAGAR ÞAR RUNO FAIHIDO, that is, '[I], Dag, wrote these runes'. It may seem odd that the inscription contains only the name of the 'rune-master' who inscribed the runes, and not the name of the person commemorated by the stone, but in reality this arrangement arises naturally from the very nature of runes. It was not intended that the inscription should give information; it was written as an effective means of protecting the monument and the grave. The name of the rune-master possessed magical power, because he was master of the occult art.

A number of inscriptions contain nothing more than a single name in the nominative case, the shortest possible formula, while others are fuller. Among the oldest is the Tune stone from Østfold in Norway, from the beginning of the fifth century, on which we read: EK WIWAR AFTER WODURIDE WITADAHALAIBAN WORAHTO R[UNOR], that is, 'I, WiwaR, made these runes in memory of Wodurid, my comrade in arms'. On the other side of the same stone there is another inscription, unfortunately obscure and difficult to make out, which Sophus Bugge has translated thus: 'Three daughters raised this stone in memory of Wodurid. Those who were next of kin divided the inheritance.' This is exceptionally full information. Another group may be made of inscriptions which state that the dead man was killed or buried. Such is the inscription on a stone from Kjølevig in Strand near Stavanger: 'HadulaikaR (*hic jacet*). [I], HagustaldaR, buried my son.' Of similar type is the inscription at Amla in Sognefjord, which contains only three words: 'N. N. [*the name is illegible*] buried here.'[1] But the formula may also be extended, as on the stone at Rö in Bohuslän, on which it is stated that the dead man was slain treacherously, and then follow the names of the two men who wrote the runes and set up the stone.[2] We give finally a very characteristic inscription,

any importance in his recent work 'Runorna', *Nordisk Kultur*, vi (Stockholm, 1933), p. 254.

[1] The reading is that of Sophus Bugge, *Norges Indskrifter med de ældre Runer*, i. 23 and 273 (Christiania, 1891–1903).

[2] Otto von Friesen, *Röstenen i Bohuslän och Runorna i Norden under Folkvandringstiden*, Uppsala Universitets Årsskrift, 1924.

PLATE 40

Specimens of Norwegian pottery of the 6th century.
After Johs. Bøe

PLATE 41

The Möjebro stone in Uppland. After Von Friesen

cut on a heavy block of stone buried in a barrow in Opedal in Hardanger; it runs: BIRGINGU BROþAR RUNOR SWESTAR MINU LIUBU MER WAGE, 'For Birging her brother cut these runes; my dear sister, be good to me.'[1]

As we see, it is not to be expected that runic inscriptions should give us historical information. They are of importance, in the first place, because the runic art in itself is an extraordinarily interesting phenomenon, and the inscriptions give occasional glimpses of the mentality and conceptions of their time; they are important also for their language, the oldest form of Scandinavian speech that is known, very nearly related to Gothic, but quite distinct and Scandinavian in character. Unusual interest is attached to the personal names, which were at the time the most important part of the inscription's content. It was noticed long ago that most of these names in the inscriptions of the fifth and sixth centuries are absolutely different from the types of personal names known in the oldest historical records in Scandinavia, and these old names which are not found again in the north in historical times often correspond to names we know among the Goths and West Germanic nations. The Swedish scholar Von Friesen has recently made a special study of this problem, and he found that the personal names of the inscriptions contain a strong West Germanic element, connected especially with the lands around the lower course of the Rhine.[2] He then points to the trade connexions between Scandinavia and the lands around the mouth of the Rhine; we have already mentioned the manufactured goods from western Europe, bronzes and glasses, which were imported into Norse lands, and a statement by Jordanes attests the export of furs from Scandinavia in the sixth century. It is significant that the word for 'skin' in Anglo-Saxon and Old German is a loan from Norse. On a Swedish runic stone in Östergötland appears the personal name Skinþa-Leubar, parallel to the Icelandic Skinna-Bjǫrn, who was so called because he used to sail to the Baltic and bring home various skins. The name Leubar itself is well known

---

[1] The reading is that of Carl J. S. Marstrander, 'Opedalstenen', *Tidsskrift for Norsk Sprogvidenskap*, iii (1929), p. 158.

[2] Otto von Friesen, *Röstenen i Bohuslän*, p. 83 f., where he gives a complete list of all the personal names which are known from the old inscriptions.

among the Franks and Anglo-Saxons (OE. *Leof, Leofa*). The foreign names which we find in the runic inscriptions must then have come in through this lively commerce with West Germanic peoples, through merchants who visited Norse lands and not infrequently settled permanently in Scandinavia. The runic inscriptions thus make an important contribution to the cultural history of the migration period.

It must also be recognized that, while the runic inscriptions in stone were produced in close contact with the culture of western Europe, they were due in part to the model of Roman monuments, even though the raised stones, the *bautasteinar*, without inscription were an ancient and well-known form of memorial in Scandinavia. An eloquent witness in this sense is the Möjebro stone in Uppland (Pl. 41), which bears an inscription in two horizontal lines, and underneath a picture of a mounted warrior, who is perhaps triumphing over a fallen enemy. The whole monument recalls distinctly a very common type of Roman grave-memorial. The combination of runes and pictures is very rare, however, though it is not uncommon to find stone monuments with pictures but no inscription. An example is the well-known stone of Häggeby in Uppland, clearly from the sixth century, which has a horse-fight depicted on one side and on the other a ship with its crew and the oars out; another is the Austreim stone in Nordfjord with a picture of a ship.[1] Traditions from the older Scandinavian rock-carvings may well have entered into the conception of such pictures in the migration period; the rock-carvings themselves were perhaps not yet a dead art at that time. But the pictures of this period have received a new impulse from contact with the Latin world.

This must in any case be true beyond all doubt of the richest and most interesting series of figured monuments ever created in Scandinavia, the sculptured stones of the island of Gotland.[2] The Gutnish sculptured stones are raised on or near the graves, the dates of which provide a means of following the origin and development of these stone monuments. The oldest, from the

[1] See Ture Arne in *Svenska Fornminnesföreningens Tidskrift*, xi (Stockholm, 1902), p. 321, and Shetelig, 'Austreimstenen', *Bergens Museums Årbok*, 1907, no. 11.

[2] Fredrik Nordin, *Till Frågan om de Gottländske Bildstenarnas Utvecklingsformer*, Studier tillegnade Oscar Montelius (Stockholm, 1903), p. 142. Also Sune Lindqvist, 'Gotlands Bildstenar', *Rig* (Stockholm, 1933), p. 97.

Roman period, are rough unhewn slabs of limestone, which are only visible for a few decimeters at most above the ground; they bear no ornament or sculpture. From about A.D. 400 the stones become somewhat larger, cut in an irregular rectangle; the upper free edge has incised ornamentation, usually a border of meanders or spirals. Later than these, precisely from the period which now occupies our attention, are still larger rectangular stones, regularly hewn, and almost entirely visible above the ground; they are higher and narrower than the older stones. They have as before an ornamental border uppermost, and in addition the front of the stone is covered with sculptured pictures. In these certain geometrical motives play a large part, sun-figures and circles filled with spirals, but some representations of actual life also appear, as a pair of horses, a ship or a boat, and one stone also bore an inscription in the earlier runes. From these simple stones the classical form of Gutnish sculptured stone was developed already before the beginning of the Viking age. The sides of the stone were swung out and the top finished off with a contour of horse-shoe form. The whole surface of the stone was covered with figures—ships, horsemen, wagons, men and animals, sometimes whole groups of pictures illustrating legend or myth (Pl. 59). At the beginning of the Christian period the pictures disappear and are replaced by runic inscriptions, though the stones retain their traditional form.

In concluding the account of stone monuments in the migration period, we have to mention finally a small group of monuments which are connected with the worship of the gods in western Norway. These are the so-called 'holy white stones' in the form of a short cylindrical pillar, the top of which swells into a hemisphere, a little wider than the shaft. The material is as a rule white marble, more rarely white quartz or granite. The height varies, reaching 90 cm. in the largest, most of them being about 30 cm. Some of these stones are found on or in grave-mounds, a few on ancient house-sites, but a striking number have come to light in the ground under churches and in present-day churchyards. As is sufficiently known, churches often stand on places which had formerly in heathen times been dedicated to the worship of the gods, and it is thus indicated that these white stones served some religious purpose. They have been explained with great probability as phallic symbols, which must have been connected with the worship of a god of fertility of the same type as the god Frey in the religion of the Viking age. But the stones belong decidedly to an older time; they are never mentioned in the old literature.[1]

The 'holy white stones' are found exclusively in the west of Norway, in the same area that is marked by the rich graves of the migration period and also possesses the greater number of runic inscriptions from that time. In this archaeological survey there is hardly room for a more detailed investigation of religious history, the sources of which must be sought primarily in place-names and the old literature.[2] But the holy stones are necessarily mentioned as an important feature characteristic of the West Norwegian area in this period. We have emphasized above the peculiar division of Scandinavia which can be observed in the fifth and sixth centuries. Denmark and Sweden are extraordinarily rich in gold hoards, but have very poor graves, while the coastland of Norway has an abundance of rich graves and little gold. As we have indicated, this dissimilarity is founded upon the divergent foreign connexions; the gold came by way of the Baltic from the continent to the south, while Norwegian civilization took its character from connexions across the North Sea with western Europe. We shall see in the following chapter that the same conditions decided the developments in the immediately following centuries.

To conclude the sketch of the migration period in Scandinavia, a word must now be added on the ruins of buildings and fortifications surviving from that time. The structural arrangement of farmsteads and houses is now well known from the extensive excavations carried out in all the Scandinavian countries, and the forms everywhere show a high degree of uniformity.[3] The

[1] Th. Petersen, *Nogle bemerkninger om de såkalte 'hellige hvide stene'*, Det kgl. norske Videnskabs Selskabs Skrifter, Trondhjem, no. 8.

[2] See Chapter XXIII below, p. 406 f. Also Magnus Olsen, *Farms and Fanes of Ancient Norway. The Place-Names of a Country discussed in their bearings on Social and Religious History*. Instituttet for sammenlignende Kulturforskning, Serie A, vol. ix (Oslo, 1928).

[3] Jan Petersen, *Gamle Gårdsanlegg i Rogaland*, Instituttet for sammenlignende Kulturforskning, Serie B, xxiii (Oslo, 1933); Sigurd Grieg, *Jernaldershus på Lista*, ibid., B, xxvii (Oslo, 1934), with a summary in German;

ground-plan is a long rectangle, and the characteristic feature of the structure is that the roof is supported by two rows of columns running parallel to the long walls and set further in towards the centre of the room. We shall return to this construction in a later chapter (XIX), to examine it in more detail. At this point it need only be added that this form of building is known in Denmark from the La Tène period onwards, in Norway and Sweden (and in Swedish lands especially on the islands of Öland and Gotland) mainly during the migration period, the fifth and sixth centuries. In many places the buildings lie close together in groups of two, three, or more, and in the immediate vicinity may be seen remains of stone walls, traces of old paths and cultivated fields, and the heathen grave monuments belonging to the farm.

Equally interesting as memorials of the past are the ancient fortifications found in very considerable numbers in Norway and Sweden, and in Finland also. By far the greater number of these fortresses are high places provided with some defensive work, 'hill forts', with ramparts of bare stone without mortar.[1] Whenever possible, the site chosen was an isolated eminence rising above precipitous mountain sides, so that the artificially constructed defences could be limited to the sides where the approach was easiest. Very often the added fortification took the form of double or multiple ramparts, one within the other, and the entrance in many such forts is protected by special defensive structures. At the present day the walls appear as ruined irregular heaps of stone, but in places it can be seen that they were originally built up to present a vertical outer face; and the entrance was always carefully built. As a rule a reservoir

Mårten Stenberger, *Öland under äldre järnålderen*, Kungl. Vitterhets Historie och Antikvitets Akademien (Stockholm, 1933); Hans Kjær, *Vor Oldtids Mindesmærker* (København, 1925), p. 132 f.; and id., *Oldtidshuse ved Gunderup i Thy*, fra Nationalmuseets Arbeidsmark (København, 1928); Gudmund Hatt, 'To Bopladsfund fra ældre jernalder', *Aarb. f. nord. Oldk.* 1928; and id., 'En Brandtomt af et Jernaldershus', ibid., 1930.

[1] Herm. M. Schirmer, *Fortegnelse over de hidtil paaviste bygdeborge*, Aarsberetning, Foreningen til norske Fortidsmindesmærkers Bevaring, 1908, (Kristiania, 1909), p. 113; Bror Schnittger, *Die vorgeschichtlichen Burgwälle in Schweden*, Opuscula archaeologica Oscari Montelio dicata, (Stockholm, 1913), p. 335, with a map; Mårten Stenberger, *Öland under äldre järnålderen* (Stockholm, 1933), pp. 213 and 269; Hjalmar Appelgren, 'Verzeichnis von den vorgeschichtlichen Schanzen in Finland', *Finska Fornminnesför. Tidskrift*, xii (Helsingfors, 1891), with a map.

is found inside the fort to contain the water supply. On the other hand there is no trace of any buildings within the ramparts. The name for this kind of fort in the old Norse tongue was *borg*.

To judge from the rather meagre finds of antiquities brought to light by systematic excavation, the hill forts in Sweden may be assigned to a comparatively short period, about A.D. 400–600. In Norway no comparable investigation has been carried out, but it may be assumed that the hill forts of Norway too belong to about the same period as in Sweden. In the Finnish hill forts the antiquities found date mainly from the eighth to the twelfth century.

While the type of hill fort just described is common to Norway and Sweden proper, the island of Öland has its own special form. The whole island is an unbroken flat plateau; there are no steep peaks such as elsewhere determined the choice of site and the plan of the fortification. A considerable number of forts from the migration age is found in Öland, but they are constructed as complete enclosures of walls, of round or oval ground-plan. The building material used was a specially suitable kind of limestone which splits naturally into parallel slabs, and the excellence of the material permitted the production of masonry worthy of the name, of far better quality than was possible with the raw uneven material in Sweden and Norway. We also find in Öland foundations of buildings, sometimes in large clusters, in the space enclosed by the defences. It is accordingly inferred that the forts of Öland were not built solely as places of refuge and defence, but also to be meeting-places for the worship of the gods. Speaking generally, such forts were mostly established in the fifth century, and remained in use until the Viking age and the Middle Ages.

These prehistoric forts of the north are of no special interest as architecture, but they are highly significant as records of the history of their time. They are now commonly called *bygdeborger*, 'clan-forts', and are thought to be places of refuge for the people of the district in time of war or sudden raids. Often too, by virtue of their position, they may have served definite military ends as strategic bases or defences against invasion. In any case these hill forts are evidence that the period round about A.D. 400 was a time of unrest and warfare in Scandinavian lands. The forts are also worthy of attention as the oldest public buildings known in the north. They are often very extensive structures such as imply a highly developed organization and discipline for military needs.

XV

PEOPLES AND KINGDOMS IN THE MEROVINGIAN ERA

IN an earlier chapter we have mentioned the first scientific discovery of Scandinavia by Pytheas in the second half of the fourth century before Christ. But Pytheas was far in advance of his time; his achievement was received with incredulity, and the Greek geographers following him have only the meagrest information about northern Europe. The Mediterranean peoples first began to take a real interest in Scandinavia after the Roman conquests, commercial and military, north of the Alps, and this interest was expressed in new geographical discoveries. In the year A.D. 5 a Roman fleet sailed around Jutland into the Baltic, as Augustus himself declares in an inscription in marble from Ancyra: 'My fleet sailed over the ocean from the mouth of the Rhine towards the realms of the rising sun as far as the lands of the Cimbri; Charudes, Semnones, and other Germanic peoples in this land sent ambassadors to ask for friendship with me and with the Roman people.' In the reign of the Emperor Nero, about A.D. 60, a Roman expedition reached the Baltic and in A.D. 84 Agricola sailed with a Roman fleet to the northernmost point of Scotland. In the same period Roman military expeditions were made into Germania on the mainland, and Roman merchants carried on trade among Germanic peoples far beyond the frontiers of the Empire.[1]

Moreover, new information now finds its way into geographical literature. This is evident in Pliny the elder, who made use of earlier writers, but also obtained information first-hand while serving in a campaign in Germania. He knows the immense mountain Saevo 'by the vast bay which stretches to the Cimbrian promontory; which bay is called Codanus and is full of islands, among which the largest is Scadinavia, of unknown extent. Some say that these regions extend as far as the Vistula.

---

[1] There is an account of Roman trade in northern Europe by Heinrich Willers, *Die römischen Bronzeeimer von Hemmoor* (Hanover and Leipzig, 1901), pp. 191 ff. Probably Roman merchants even established direct communications with Norway; see Bjørn Hougen, 'Trekk av østnorsk romertid', *Universitetets Oldsamlings Skrifter*, ii (Oslo, 1929), pp. 125–6.

. . . The Cimbrian promontory runs far out into the sea and forms a peninsula called Tastris.' We omit in this passage a series of unintelligible names of localities and tribes, in order to show clearly that Pliny had a certain grasp of southern Scandinavian topography; we recognize the entrance to the Baltic as the Cattegat, the mountains north of it as those in the south of Norway, the promontory Rusbeas as Lindesnes, Jutland with the Skaw, and under the name of Scadinavia, the Danish isles and the south of Sweden. Further on Pliny gives more information about the north, with Britain as the starting-point of his description; among the British Isles he names the forty Orcades and others, and then 'the outermost of all known isles is Tyle, where at the summer solstice there is no night, and, correspondingly, no day at the winter solstice. . . . Some authors mention yet more islands, Scandia, Dumna, Bergos, and the largest of all, Nerigon, from which the voyage is made to Tyle. From Tyle it is one day's sail to the frozen sea which some call Cronium.' Here Tyle must be understood as in Pytheas's account as a name for the northern part of Norway, and Nerigon may possibly be the name Norway, which was Norþrawegaʀ in the oldest Norse speech.[1]

The name Scandinavia thus appears for the first time in Pliny, and is there clearly a name for the southernmost part of the Scandinavian peninsula, the present-day Skåne. We find fresh information about Scandinavian peoples in Tacitus, c. A.D. 100. He knows of Angles and Jutes in Jutland, as well as the Cimbri and Harudes who were mentioned by Augustus, and he is the first to name the Swedes (Suiones), whose 'communities lie in the ocean itself', and they are 'a mighty people not only in men and arms, but also in ships'. He also describes the Finns in the most northerly regions of Scandinavia. The last of the great geographers of antiquity, Ptolemy of Alexandria, who was at work round about A.D. 150, collected in his geography the whole knowledge of his time concerning northern Europe, and he also made the first map in which Scandinavia is represented. In the northern sea, Germanikos Okeanos, we find the Cimbrian peninsula, and east of it three comparatively small Skandiai nesoi, which represent the Danish isles, and a short distance

---

[1] All these problems are discussed fully by Fridtjof Nansen, *In Northern Mists*, i. 96 f.

farther east the large Skandia (Skåne), charted as a detached and isolated island. Unfortunately there is no means of interpreting the greater portion of the tribal names which are placed in Jutland and Skandia; most of them are pretty clearly gross copying errors. Yet in Jutland can be recognized Cimbri, Charudes, and Jutes, and on the Scandinavian peninsula the Gutai, who must be the Gautar in present-day Götaland, and the Chaidinoi, interpreted as the Norwegian Heiðnir, a people whose name is preserved in the present district of Hedmark. Less accurately, however, Ptolemy has placed the island Tule close to the north of Scotland, evidently through confusion with the Shetland Islands, a confusion first introduced by Tacitus in his biography of Agricola.

As we see, the information about the Scandinavian peoples which found its way to the Greek and Roman geographers was rather meagre. To this small stock must be added some interesting facts about the peoples on the south shore of the Baltic. Here the ancient writers of the fourth century A.D. mention the Gotones (the Goths) by the Vistula, the Burgundians and the Silingi farther west. There can be no doubt that the Gotones bear a name which also forms the first element of the later Götaland and Gotland, and that the Burgundians came earlier from the island of Bornholm, which was called Borgundarholmr in Old Norse. In the same way the name Silingi can be satisfactorily derived from Selund, the old name of Sjælland, or Zealand, as the island is called in England. We must conclude that there had been a colonization of the north German coast from Scandinavia in the period immediately before the beginning of Christian chronology. A possibility, less certain, is that the Vandilii, the later Vandals, came originally from Vendsyssel in north Jutland,[1] just as the Langobardi later had a tradition that their original home was in Scandinavia. In any case it is beyond all doubt that the later celebrated nations, the Goths and the Burgundians, emerged out of an early migration from the north, and we also know that these nations during their wanderings remained conscious of their Norse origin, and that through this consciousness new connexions were established between Scandinavia and the southern lands. As has been

[1] Gustaf Kossinna, 'Die Wandalen in Nordjutland', *Mannus*, vol. xxi (Leipzig, 1929).

stated earlier, these relationships appear clearly enough in archaeological evidences, and they are also expressed in the earliest writings concerned with Germanic nations.

Theodoric the Great's Roman minister Cassiodorus wrote a history of the Goths in twelve books which has come down to us only through the epitome made by the Gothic writer Jordanes in the middle of the sixth century. There are a number of observations on Scandinavian peoples in this work, though many of the names are miswritten and are difficult to understand. Yet we recognize beyond doubt the Swedes, known for their excellent horses; from them too the Romans obtained costly furs which were renowned for their black colour. We also find in Jordanes the West Götar (?) and the East Götar, and in Norway tribes named from Romerike and Ranrike (the later Bohuslän). We learn too that both the Swedes and the Danes claimed to be the tallest of the Scandinavian peoples, and that the Danes boasted of having driven the Heruli from their home. But of similarly conspicuous height was also a group of Norwegian tribes which apparently had their home on the west coast of the peninsula, among them the Harothi and Rugi, 'over whom not many years since Roduulf was king, who, despising his own kingdom, hastened to King Theodoric of the Goths and found what he sought. These nations fight with the ferocity of wild beasts, and are mightier than the Germans both in body and soul.' In Jordanes we first meet with the Danes, settled in Denmark, from where they had driven the Heruli, an event which cannot otherwise be dated with any closer precision. In Norway we are told of a king ruling over a group of tribes whose province coincides exactly with the spread of special West Scandinavian culture described in the preceding chapter. Here we see the beginning of a political unification which is of great interest. Among these names we also find tribes which are known in the history of the migration period, the Rugi in Rogaland and the Harothi in Hordaland, and it is natural to suppose that these tribes made their way to the west of Norway about the time when the Anglo-Saxons were conquering Britain. A similar movement is supported historically by Procopius' account of the Heruli's return from the Balkan peninsula to Scandinavia in the early years of the sixth century. As we have seen, the West Norwegian culture was in many respects related to the migration kingdoms in western Europe; the new grouping of Germanic peoples around the North Sea was a powerful factor in the development of western Scandinavia after the migration period.

During this period the conditions of the new age also became prevalent in the Baltic, especially in Gotland, which from this time onward became a centre of Scandinavian trade. But the development here followed altogether different lines, since the most important connexions of the Baltic lands did not follow the sea to western Europe, but rather the land-route south into central Europe. It has already been described how gold came to the Baltic from the south, and we may now add that among Gutnish ornaments certain special forms are found which must be due to relations with the Goths in Hungary in the fifth century. The large silver brooches in Gotland have not the usual Scandinavian form with a square plate at the head, but a semicircular form, and certain details in the ornament point to the same source.[1] Two gold bracteates of Swedish type are said to have been found in Hungary. In Gotland in the sixth century unmistakable influences begin to appear from the German culture of the mainland, as we know it in the burial-places in the south and west of Germany. This influence shows itself in weapons, in certain ornaments, in belt-clasps and rich mountings on belts and riding-gear, in a taste for *verrotterie cloisonnée*, a mosaic of coloured polished stones in gold cells, which was cultivated with special predilection in South German handwork. Highly significant too is the new style of animal ornament, which developed in an altogether different direction from the first Scandinavian style of about A.D. 500.

We shall return later to the history of animal ornament; but it is certain that this new style betokens a continental influence from the Rhineland, Bavaria, and northern Italy, which affects earliest and most powerfully the islands in the Baltic, Gotland and Öland, and Finland, and grows so strong that in these regions an immigration of Germanic population from the mainland has even been suggested. This was part of the movement which from the sixth century onwards produced a rich development in the Baltic lands, especially in Gotland, which exhibits

[1] Bernhard Salin, *Die altgermanische Thierornamentik* (Stockholm, 1904), pp. 197–202.

luxurious wealth during the whole of this period; though before long a similar richness is evident on the Swedish mainland also.

At this time the kingdom of the Swedes was making immense advances, in all probability through conquests at the expense of their southern neighbours, Götaland and Gotland,[1] and their new power is exhibited in forms very striking to the archaeologist. The graves of the kings at Old Uppsala, which date from the fifth and sixth centuries, are among the largest monuments in Europe. There are three massive barrows, each about 65 metres across; they were thrown up over the place where the funeral pyre had been burned. The fire destroyed most of the grave-goods, but some remains are found of melted bronze, glass beakers, beads, gold, and other articles.

The classical and richest find of this Swedish group was at Vendel in Uppland, from which the whole period is often distinguished as the Vendel period, and the decorative style of the time as the Vendel style.[2] Excavation at Vendel brought to light the burial place of a noble family extending over the period from the sixth century to the ninth, and showing during the whole of this time a uniform structure and furnishing of the graves. In these graves the princes are always buried without cremation in a boat upwards of 10 metres in length, adorned with splendid weapons, and accompanied by horses with bridle and saddle, hounds on the leash, once also by a hunting falcon; the boats were provided with cooking gear and rich supplies of food. Among the antiquities the most notable are richly gilt bronze plates for belts and harness, handsomely ornamented swords and shields, all of which exhibit the style of decoration proper to the period, the Vendel style, in its finest flower. In addition to animal ornament in relief, inlay of garnets was also employed, and sometimes a red enamel as a substitute for cellwork (*verrotterie cloisonnée*).

Another burial place, at Valsgärde in Uppland, has been in course of excavation during the last few years, and the work is still unfinished. The graves are of precisely the same character as the Vendel graves, and they have a very rich furnishing of weapons, saddlery, glass beakers and other articles. Thanks to

---

[1] Birger Nerman, *Det Svenska Rikets Uppkomst* (Stockholm, 1925).
[2] Hjalmar Stolpe and T. J. Arne, *Graffältet vid Vendel*, utgifvet af Kgl. Vitterhets Historie och Antikvitets Akademien (Stockholm, 1912).

the perfect methods of excavation employed, Professor Sune Lindqvist has brought these rare treasures to light in a condition far surpassing that of the older finds.[1]

Among the weapons the 'ring-swords' call for special attention, handsomely turned out swords on which the pommel bears a thick ring of pure gold (Pl. 42a). But the most remarkable pieces in the Vendel graves are the helmets, made of iron with decorative mountings of bronze, including pictured bands with various figures embossed on them (Pl. 42b). These helmets are remarkable not only as Swedish metal-work of the migration period: they are also pieces of the greatest interest in the history of culture. Helmets of metal were then and later extremely rare among the prehistoric peoples of northern Europe, and even among the Anglo-Saxons in England; a certain level of culture is therefore indicated when we find that the chiefs of Vendel were thus magnificently equipped. The type of the helmets follows a certain form used by Roman cavalry under the late Empire; the classic example is a helmet decked with silver plates, found at De Peel in Brabant,[2] bearing the Latin legend *Stablesia VI*, which shows that it belonged to one of the Equites Stablesiani. This was the type which supplied the model for the Vendel helmets, evidently through the intermediary of the South Germans. Remains of similar helmets are also found in other graves of chiefs in Uppland, as in Uppsala and Ulltuna, and also in Gotland and the east of Norway. We can hardly be wrong in saying that the helmets, in themselves an innovation in Scandinavian culture, give expression to a new ambition among these chiefs who were striving after greater political power than their predecessors possessed.

The same impression is conveyed by the rich decoration of the helmets, which includes the usual animal ornament of the time,

[1] Sune Lindqvist, 'Vendel-time Finds from Valsgärde in the Neighbourhood of Old Uppsala', *Acta Archaeologica*, iii (København, 1932), p. 21; Greta Arwidsson, 'Some Glass Vessels from the Boat-grave Cemetery at Valsgärde', *Acta Archaeologica*, iii (København, 1932), p. 232.

[2] Sune Lindqvist, 'Vendelhjälmarnas Ursprung', with a summary in German (Der Ursprung der Vendelhelme), *Fornvännen* (Stockholm, 1925). Cf. also M. A. Evelein, in *Oudheidkundige Mededeelingen van het Rijksmuseum van Oudheden te Leiden*, v, 1911. Another helmet of the same type is illustrated by Lindenschmidt, *Altertümer unserer heidnischen Vorzeit*, v (Mainz, 1911), Taf. 41; Sigurd Grieg, 'Norske hjelmer fra Folkevandringstiden', *Bergens Museums Årbok* 1922–3, Hist.-ant. rekke, no. 3.

PLATE 42

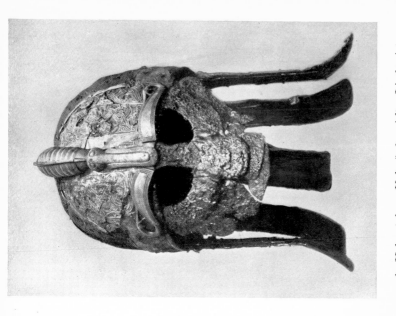

b. Helmet from Valsgärde. After Lindqvist

a. Ring-sword from Gotland. After Montelius

PLATE 43

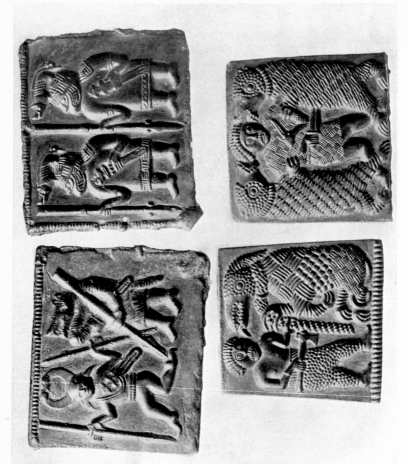

Stamps for impressing figured bronze plates. After Knut Stjerna

but motives introducing human figures as well. Along the rim of the helmet is a broad band with reliefs stamped in the bronze, and in these we see the Vendel earls as they themselves wished to be represented: the chief like Othin on horseback, accompanied by his ravens and armed with helmet and spear; or there is a duel between two young men, or a procession of distinguished warriors in full martial array. Other pictures represent legendary scenes of men in combat with supernatural beings which recall the fabulous episodes in *Beowulf*.[1] The pictures have a peculiar style of their own, and are not mere ornament; there is a distinct art of portrayal, an art, moreover, which appears very seldom in the prehistoric culture of the Germans. In this case we may assume influence of the southern Germans on the continent, where similar pictures appear in the same period, some in metal work and some as sculptures on stone, and there too we meet with the chief mounted and armed with spear and shield, and with the same fabulous animals.[2] The Norse pictures are certainly not imported pieces; on Öland have been found stamps for impressing the same kind of figured bronze plates as those on the helmets from Vendel, and work of this kind was therefore undoubtedly produced in Sweden (Pl. 43).

This Swedish culture with its richest representation on the commercial island of Gotland and its political centre in Uppland was a leading factor in Merovingian times on the Baltic and in large areas of Norway. The district around Trondhjem in the seventh and eighth centuries was strongly impressed by influences from Sweden, and in the south-east of Norway we trace similar conditions, though there they are connected by direct importation with German culture on the mainland. A famous Norwegian find, a chief's grave at Aker in Hedmark, yielded

---

[1] Knut Stjerna, *Essays on Questions connected with the Old English Poem of Beowulf*, published for the Viking Club (London, 1912), I. Helmets and Swords in *Beowulf*. The interpretation of the pictures is one of the matters touched upon by Henrik Schück, *Studier i Nordisk Litteratur og Religionshistoria*, ii (Stockholm, 1904), p. 214.

[2] L. Lindenschmidt (Sohn), *Altertümer unserer heidnischen Vorzeit*, iv (Mainz, 1900), Taf. 29; Hans Hahne, 'Der Reiterstein von Hornhausen', *Mannusbibliothek*, xxii. 171, Taf. XI–XIV; Axel L. Romdahl, *Gammal Konst* (Stockholm, 1916), in a chapter entitled 'Vendel och Bysanz' has tried to show that these pictures in Scandinavia were derived ultimately from Byzantine archetypes, which is possible; but they were in any case transmitted through South Germanic peoples.

antiquities undoubtedly continental, among them a handsome belt-clasp which has parallels in finds of southern Germany.[1] Other East Norwegian antiquities, such as ring-swords, helmets, personal ornaments, and the style of decoration too, give clear evidence of contact with Swedish culture. We should perhaps recall at this point that a branch of the Swedish royal family of Uppsala established itself in Norway in this period, according to tradition, and laid the foundation of the later Norwegian monarchy.

The Swedish influence flowing westward into Norway was balanced by a similar expansion of Swedish culture eastward into Finland and the Baltic provinces. The earlier periods of the iron age in Finland were characterized by the predominance of eastern Baltic civilization; Finnish culture had connexions to the south with Esthonia, Livonia, and Lithuania, and through these lands drew upon Prussian forms. In the following two centuries we still find the Baltic types, East European enamelled ornaments and other such antiquities, as has already been described (p. 210). But at the same time an increasing Scandinavian influence is to be observed, first in purely imported articles, later also in local work.[2] Presumably these currents in Finnish culture of the early iron age were produced by the entry of various national elements, Finno-Ugrian peoples from the south and Scandinavians from the west.

Scandinavian influence first gained the upper hand in the fifth century. In the beginning the northern line of communication across Österbotten played the most important part and introduced into Finland many features of West Norwegian culture, through the intermediary of Sweden. From this source came the large silver brooches with square plate, the migration style of animal ornament, imported weapons and many other forms. After a time relations with central Sweden become apparent, as also with continental German culture, and above all with the large islands in the Baltic. From the seventh century onward Finnish culture was stamped throughout by

[1] Sigurd Grieg, 'Akerfundet', *Oldtiden*, vii (Kristiania, 1918), p. 80. Gutorm Gjessing, *Studier i Norsk Merovingertid*. Skrifter av det Norske Videnskaps Akademi i Oslo, II. Hist.-Filos. Klasse 1934, no. 2, pl. I (Oslo, 1934).

[2] Alfred Hackman, *Die ältere Eisenzeit in Finland*, i (Helsingfors, 1905).

these Swedish influences, far more strongly than in either the preceding or the following period. A specially Finnish character, however, can be seen in some forms of weapons, as in the shield-mountings and the heads of spears, and also in ornaments and the application of decoration; but it is in this period, from the fifth century to the eighth, that the Scandinavian element prevails most strongly in the culture of Finland. One might almost infer that the greater part of Finland was politically dependent on Sweden, and that the ruling class was of Swedish origin. An example of the evidence pointing in this direction is a grave-find in northern Finland, where a chief was burned in a ship, arrayed with helmet and splendid weapons, and accompanied by his battle-charger with richly finished accoutrements. This period. is moreover the richest in the whole of Finland's iron age.

In the same period the southern Baltic lands also become subject to Scandinavian influence for the first time. The older Baltic culture at this time appears poor and stagnant, with little development and few new forms; but there is a series of antiquities quite certainly imported from Gotland, ornaments, belt-mounts, and weapons, and it is most likely (as has been generally assumed) that these finds are evidence of an immigration from the western shores of the Baltic. This early Swedish expansion eastward prepared the way for the great colonization to be accomplished in the Viking age.[1]

On the west coast of the Scandinavian peninsula cultural development during this time followed different lines.[2] In the fifth and sixth centuries the districts along the coasts of Norway developed a rich and characteristic civilization in close connexion with England and France; but with the seventh century came a striking change, expressed primarily in a marked simplification of the structure and furniture of graves. Large grave-cists of stone cease, and we find graves made quite rudely in the earth, often originally with a simple wooden coffin which

---

[1] Birger Nerman, *Die Verbindungen zwischen Skandinavien und dem Ostbaltikum in der jüngeren Eisenzeit*, Kungl. Vitterhets Historie och Antikvitets Akademiens Handlingar, Del 40, 1 (Stockholm, 1929). Professor Nerman here connects the archaeological evidence with the account in *Gutasaga* of an ancient emigration from Gotland across the Baltic.

[2] *Det Norske Folks Liv og Historie*, i (Oslo, 1930); Haakon Shetelig, *Fra Oldtiden til omkring 1000 e. Kr.*, pp. 148–53.

has now disappeared. Barrows grow fewer too, and become comparatively low and unimpressive; or the graves may be made with a flat surface and no visible memorial. Similarly, the furniture of the grave diminishes, and it is to be noted in particular that beakers, flagons, and cups are no longer found. It is at this point, the beginning of the seventh century, that we take leave of the ancient and classical conception which demanded that the grave should be supplied with food and drink for the entertainment of the dead.

There were also great changes in personal outfit—ornaments and weapons, and, quite evidently, in dress—and they were changes which broke with the traditions of hundreds of years. The large silver brooches with animal ornament disappear, as also the cruciform long brooches and whole series of other old types; they are replaced by forms altogether new, round or oval convex brooches, others cut from a plate into the form of an animal, bird, serpent or the like. These are forms which had been rare in Scandinavia before this time, but not wholly unknown, while they had always been in quite general use among the south Germanic peoples, especially within the sphere of Merovingian civilization, in central Europe and the south of England. The prevalence of these forms in Norway from the seventh century onwards must be due to new impulses which brought taste and fashion into closer agreement with western European custom.[1]

The same tendency is also manifested in forms of weapons and armour. Until and during the sixth century the Norwegians used the traditional weapons, the selfsame equipment that had been formed far back in the Roman period, consisting of a two-edged sword, two spears (both comparatively light), often an axe, and always a wooden shield with an iron boss. At the end of the sixth century great changes were introduced: the two-edged sword disappeared and the two spears were replaced by a single lance with a very heavy, wide, and thick iron head; a new weapon was added, a short, one-edged sword, the Frankish *scramasaxa*. Precisely the same changes in arms can be observed in the Merovingian burial places in the north of France but they are not carried out to the same extent anywhere else

[1] Shetelig, 'Smaa bronsespænder fra folkevandringstiden', *Oldtiden*, i, 1910 (Stavanger, 1911), p. 51.

in the Germanic world.[1] Thus we trace in the west of Norway in all spheres of which we have any knowledge, in the structure of the graves, in ornaments and weapons, new and strong impulses from Frankish Merovingian culture, while the contemporary civilization in the east of Scandinavia derived its character from continental forms traceable ultimately to central Europe.

In the Merovingian period we get a glimpse for the first time of the political and constitutional configuration of Scandinavia We have already mentioned the growth of Sweden with its political centre in Uppland, where immense monuments, the king's graves at Old Uppsala and Ottar's Barrow in Vendel, stand as memorials of a great period in the nation's development. It was in this same period that the kingdom of the Danes, with its nucleus in the district around the ancient fane at Lejre in Zealand, began to extend its power both east and west. A similar movement can also be traced in the east of Norway. The small kingdoms of older time, Raumaríki, Heiðmǫrk, and Hringaríki, before this time had always been marked by deep conservatism in burial custom and religion and still more clearly in political constitution. But in the course of the Merovingian period the graves of princes built in these old kingdoms are among the most remarkable in the whole north, such as Raknehaug in Romerike and Svenshaug in Hedmark, the former nearly 95 metres in diameter and about 19 metres high. The most impressive burial ground in Scandinavia is that of the Vestfold kings at Borre in Oslofjord, containing nine of these royal monuments. The ancestors of Harald Fairhair were laid in these barrows, the dynasty which became the basis of the Norwegian monarchy. Just as the great mounds at Uppsala are associated with the first great consolidation of a Swedish kingdom, these Norwegian monuments are witnesses to a new striving for greater political power and a stronger constitution in the east of Norway.

The political changes, which, strictly speaking, do not lie within the scope of the archaeologist, are nevertheless of the highest interest in the history of culture. The older Norse confederate groups pretty certainly had no strong political

[1] J. Pilloy, *Études sur d'anciens lieux de sépulture dans l'Aisne*, i (Saint Quentin, 1879), pp. 6 and 10, and in vol. iii (Paris, 1903), p. 25.

organization, just as among the Germanic peoples generally; the monarchy was only feebly developed, and the local tribes lived in isolation. The military movements of the migration period created a more comprehensive and stronger organization, and the example set by new Germanic kingdoms founded by conquest induced pretensions to similar powers among the chiefs of Scandinavia. From the same period come also the oldest historical traditions of Scandinavia that have been preserved for us, contained, strangely enough, for the most part in ancient Anglo-Saxon poetry. One poem represents the utterance of one Widsith, who on his past journeys had visited, among others, some Scandinavian kings; a still more important record is contained in the epic *Beowulf*, in which supernatural episodes are given a setting in actual Scandinavian history of the Merovingian period. There are glimpses of a vanished heroic age, the glory of great kings and heroic exploits, the Skjǫldungs (OE. *Scyldingas*), who are the Danish royal family, the wars between the Danes and the Heathobeardan, between the Geatas and the Swedes (*Sweon*). The historical truth of these traditions can be checked at some points; a hero in the Anglo-Saxon poem, the Geatish king Hygelac, who was slain in an expedition to Friesland (an outstanding event in the tradition about Beowulf) is also mentioned by Gregory of Tours, and from his account the expedition would appear to have been roughly about the year 516.[1] Many of the names and events of this older tradition can also be identified with names and events in later Scandinavian records, in Saxo Grammaticus and in *Ynglingatal*, a genealogical poem from the ninth century which was one of the principal sources of Snorri's history of the earliest kings, and in other Norwegian and Icelandic writings.

This is not the place to enter into a critical examination of these interesting traditions, which are often obscure and uncertain of reference. It is the whole picture of the life of the time portrayed in the poem which is of the greatest interest. The heroes of the tradition are always kings or chiefs, and *Beowulf* gives a most attractive impression of this aristocratic society, its high standard of character and loyalty, and no less of its dignity, its noble and gracious manners. Scenes are described

[1] See further Chambers, *Introduction to Beowulf* (Cambridge, 2nd ed. 1932), p. 2 f.

in the king's hall where his warriors are gathered; we hear courteous words passed between host and guest, and the singer who recites an heroic lay at the royal feast. These pictures of court life and its good fellowship bear the stamp of actual truth. Obviously one must not forget that these Scandinavian traditions are embodied in poetry that is Anglo-Saxon, and that in many particulars they may have taken form and colour from the English culture of the poet's own time, some two hundred years later than the events described. But at the same time it can be shown from archaeological evidence that the poem has preserved accurately many details of the Scandinavian society to which the tradition originally belonged; as has been mentioned several times in this survey, the descriptions in *Beowulf* can often be illustrated directly by the Scandinavian antiquities of the period. The Swedish rulers whom we know from the graves at Vendel and Valsgärde are actually the same chiefs as the heroes in *Beowulf*.

In Norse poetry too lays are preserved which may have originated in the Merovingian period. In some of the Edda poems ring-swords are spoken of as very costly and distinguished weapons, as in *Helgakviða Hjǫrvarðssonar*, where the valkyrie says:

Sverð veit ek liggja	Swords I know lying
í Sigarsholmi	in Sigarsholm
fjórum færi	four fewer
en fimm tøgu;	than fifty;
eitt er þeira	one of these is
ǫllum betra,	best of all,
vígnesta bǫl	destroyer of shields
ok varið gulli.	and mounted with gold.
Hringr er í hjalti . . .	A ring is on the hilt . . .

And in the *Sigurðarkviða* Brynhild says:

Liggi okkar	Let lie
enn í milli	once more between us
malmr hringvariðr,	the ring-adorned blade,
egghvast járn . . .	the sharp-edged iron . . .

Dr. Stjerna has pointed to these stanzas as a clear indication that some parts of the Edda poems must go back to the seventh century, and are thus somewhat older than was formerly assumed.[1] The ring-swords which are also frequently mentioned in *Beowulf* are a well-known and quite definite type in archaeology, and they belong actually to a sharply defined period. These poems then must belong to a time which still knew this special aristocratic form of weapon, and the inscription on the Eggjum stone has now removed the linguistic objections to this early date.

The Edda poetry is built upon foreign, not Norse, heroic legends, and the poems therefore make no contribution to the history of Scandinavian traditions. Yet poetry itself must be included as an element in our picture of Scandinavian culture in the Merovingian period.

[1] Knut Stjerna, *Essays on Questions connected with the Old English Poem of Beowulf.* Viking Society (Coventry, 1912), p. 19 f. Cf. O. Montelius, *Aarbøger for nordisk Oldkyndighed* (Kjøbenhavn, 1920), p. 40; Birger Nerman, *The Poetic Edda in the light of Archaeology.* Viking Society (Coventry, 1931).

XVI

THE VIKING AGE

THE Viking raids at the beginning of the ninth century first introduced the Scandinavian peoples into general European history. In the period towards A.D. 800 we stand on the threshold of that remarkable epoch when almost all coasts and lands in the whole of our quarter of the world were visited by pirates and invaders from Scandinavia. According to the chroniclers the raids came suddenly and dramatically as an undreamed-of calamity, something new and unheard of. But this Viking activity has a different aspect to the archaeologist. In the preceding chapters we have several times had occasion to mention traffic across the North Sea, begun already in the first years of the Christian era; we have seen that this sea traffic had its earliest southern centre at the mouth of the Rhine in the territory of the Frisians (p. 193), and in the following period we mentioned the communications between peoples on both shores of the North Sea, between Jutland, Norway, and England. Nor were military expeditions wholly unknown in this older period. The Geatish king Hygelac was slain during a raid on Friesland c. 516. In the same region a Danish attack was beaten off c. 565, according to Venantius Fortunatus. Here too we should observe a notice in an Irish chronicle, stating that the monastery on the island of Eigg was burned by heathen sea-rovers in 617, and in the same year Donegal was completely devastated by a fleet from overseas; some scholars believe that this must have been an early raid from Norway, while others ascribe it to heathen Picts.

It is certain that the Norwegian colonization of the Orkneys and Shetlands was in full swing before the Viking raids began,[1] and we also find traces of Danish immigration into Friesland, especially on Walcheren and at Dorestad, a town which at that time was a centre of trade on the North Sea coast.[2] On the other side of Scandinavia we have already mentioned Sweden's earlier

---

[1] This process has been exhaustively studied by A. W. Brøgger, *Ancient Emigrants, A History of the Norw. Settlements of Scotland* (Oxford, 1929).

[2] Johannes C. H. R. Steenstrup, *Normannerne*, ii (Kjøbenhavn, 1878), p. 28 f.

relations with Finland and the Baltic provinces, and traditions from the Merovingian period frequently make mention of expeditions of Swedish kings to Esthonia and Courland. They were ancient and well-known routes which the Vikings followed when setting out on their expeditions at the end of the eighth century. This moment was a turning-point in the history of northern Europe, because piratical raiding now became a permanent occupation and grew by degrees to a scale unheard of earlier.

The general history of the Viking expeditions is sufficiently well known. They began just before the year 800 as scattered and sudden raids; there was the descent on Lindisfarne in 793; a year later on the monastery of Wearmouth in Sunderland; 795 Lambay near Dublin and also on the coasts of Wales; 798 Saint Patrick's Isle, off Man; 802 and 806 Iona; 807 Inismurray in Ireland. In 799 there was a similarly sudden descent on Aquitaine. These were typical small expeditions, small bands of some few ships in concert. Somewhat later in the ninth century the Vikings began to join together in larger fleets and organize themselves, so that they were able to extend their operations inland. This stage was introduced by the Danish king Godfred's expedition to Friesland with two hundred ships in 810. In the decade 820–30 Ireland was plundered by large fleets, in the 830–40 decade it was Friesland which became the main scene of action, in 840–50 it was France and in part Germany, and 850–60 the serious attacks on England began.

During this time there were always large fleets which went out year after year; they would establish a base and spend the winters there, an ever-present menace. On an island especially or in the estuary of a river the Vikings would make a fortified camp; this they did for the first time at Noirmoutier on the Loire in 836, in England first in 850 on Thanet, and in 851 they first wintered in Seine. In 841 they built the fortress at Dublin as a base for raids into Ireland. In their winter camps the Vikings were at home, as it were, in a foreign land; from there proceeded regular conquests and colonizations on a large scale. In the course of the ninth century a series of new Viking realms was gradually set up in the west of Europe, the earldom in northern Scotland, the kingdoms of Man and Dublin, Northumbria with York as its capital, East Anglia and the Five Boroughs, and finally, at the beginning of the tenth century, the duchy of Normandy.

Viking activity in the ninth century was like a rising wave; it began as sea-roving, gradually in steadily increasing intensity passed on to conquest and finally to permanent colonization. After this follows a comparatively peaceful time in the tenth century. Viking life did not cease completely, but it fell off to something inconsiderable. There were large conquered areas where peaceful immigration was possible, and conditions in Scandinavia were more settled than before, in Norway under the rule of Harald Fairhair, in Denmark under Gorm the Old and Harald Bluetooth. This may also have discouraged the sea-rovers. But during the weak rule in England of Æthelred (978–1016) the Vikings renewed their activity in great force. This activity begins with Olaf Tryggvason's sack of Ipswich and the battle of Maldon in 991 and ends in the Danish conquest of England under Kings Svein and Knut the Great. But this was nothing more than a brief episode; England soon returned peacefully to its own royal house, and the Viking period came to an end when Christianity was introduced into Scandinavia about this time.

Not long after the earlier Viking expeditions to the west, Scandinavian colonization was begun in the east of Europe, actually recorded for the first time in the year 859 in Nestor's chronicle, though a Swedish mission had been to Constantinople twenty years earlier and had returned home through France. In the year 862 Nestor gives a further account of the founding of the Russian kingdom, when the Slavs sent a message across the sea to ask the 'Rus' for a ruler. 'Rus' in this passage is a name for a tribe in Sweden; from them Rurik was sent, and he became ruler of Novgorod and the founder of the kingdom. For this reason the men of Novgorod were called Russians, as they are in this chronicle. The name Rus is derived from Finnish Ruotsi, which was the name for Sweden. In its essentials the account in the chronicle is doubtless correct, but we lack detailed historical records of the earliest Scandinavian expansion in eastern Europe. Yet we have information of an attack on the Byzantine empire made by the Swedes of Russia. In 865 the 'Russians' sailed from Kiev down the Dnieper, plundered the islands and coasts of the Black Sea and suddenly appeared before Constantinople with two hundred ships. Renewed attacks are recorded in 907, 941, and 944. In the treaties of peace concluded we perceive that nearly all those who appear on the Russian side have Scandinavian names. These indications are supported by independent Arabian sources, which record audacious Viking raids on the coasts of the Caspian Sea several times in the tenth century.

These records agree entirely with the results of archaeological excavations carried out in Russia. From the finds one gathers that Swedish merchants from the town of Birka on Lake Mälaren found their way through Russia to the Caspian Sea already in the first half of the ninth century. The oldest Swedish colonies were planted to the south and south-east of Lake Ladoga, where extensive burial places are found containing a great quantity of Scandinavian articles; then follow numerous settlements along the great rivers, the Volga and the Dnieper, in places which were stations for trade between the Baltic and the Orient. One of the principal routes through Russia was provided by the rivers Dyna and Dnieper down to Kiev, where graves with Scandinavian furnishing of the Viking period have often been found; and from Kiev the route passed on down the Dnieper and across the Black Sea to Constantinople. By this route the Varangians were recruited as a corps in the Imperial Guard. This Swedish colonization in Russia was at its height during the tenth and eleventh centuries. The foreigners were then living as an upper class ruling a subject population; but they were soon on intimate terms with the natives, and by degrees the Swedish elements became completely Slavonicized.[1]

As we see, Viking activity had an astonishing range. Towards the east the Vikings reached the Caspian Sea and Grecian seas; to the south, northern Africa and Spain; on the other side of the world they colonized Iceland and Greenland, and were the first European explorers to tread North American soil. This is a new and astonishing display of power, which must have its origin in a similar development within Scandinavia itself, in

---

[1] T. J. Arne, 'La Suède et l'Orient, Études archéologiques sur les relations de la Suède et l'Orient pendant l'age de Viking', *Archives d'Études Orientales*, viii (Upsal, 1914); Vilhelm Thomsen, *The Relations between Ancient Russia and Scandinavia* (Oxford, 1877).

increasing population and power among the peoples in Scandinavia. The significant side of the Norse expansion in the Viking period is not so much the piratical life with the incidental raids on foreign coasts, but rather the wide conquests and colonization of new territories. The *here* of Vikings which operated in France and England was a strong military confederation, similar in kind to the Germanic military groups in the time of the Empire, and, just as in the earlier period, a considerable emigration took place in this later age to the Viking kingdoms established in the British Isles, Normandy, and Russia. We are now brought to a completely new side of Scandinavian cultural history, which we encounter for the first time, namely, the relations with the colonial kingdoms founded in foreign lands through Viking expeditions. The life in these Viking settlements, the conflict between Scandinavian and foreign culture, is an extraordinarily interesting subject, but it belongs essentially to the historian and not to the archaeologist.[1]

First claim to our attention is now made by the effects of the new age on Scandinavian lands. As we should naturally expect, they teem with evidences of connexions with foreign lands. In Norway a notably large number of imported bronzes is known, of Irish workmanship; there are buckets mounted with decorated bronze plates, saddlery with rich fittings of gilt metal and a multitude of small ornamental bronze pieces, originally ornaments on caskets, books, and similar objects, but in Norway always converted into brooches. There are souvenirs of Viking expeditions to Ireland to be found in Norwegian graves of the ninth century.[2] Among them is a great rarity which must be given special mention, a little reliquary decorated in part with enamel, from a grave in Namdal.[3] Another reliquary of the same kind, now in the museum at Copenhagen, also came from Norway, though the precise place of the find is not known; it bears as a later addition an inscription in the so-called Manx runes, which were also used

---

[1] Excellent surveys are provided by W. G. Collingwood, *Scandinavian Britain* (London, 1908), and T. D. Kendrick, *A History of the Vikings* (London, 1930).

[2] A rich selection of Irish ornaments found in Norway is illustrated by Adolf Mahr, *Christian Art in Ancient Ireland*, i (Dublin, 1932).

[3] Th. Petersen, 'A Celtic Reliquary found in a Norwegian Burial-Mound', *Det kgl. Videnskabs Selskabs Skrifter*, 1907, no. 8 (Trondhjem, 1907).

in the south-west of Norway.[1] Another unique and highly remarkable Celtic product is a round box of bronze hammered very thin, with engraved ornament; its use is unknown, but it was probably ecclesiastical (Pl. 44a). This box was found in Aurland in Sognefjord.[2] In Scandinavia these Celtic objects are found almost exclusively in Norway and bear witness to a constant and intimate contact between Norway and the Viking colonies in Scotland and Ireland. Yet some Celtic pieces also found their way to the town of Birka on Mälaren and to Finland.

From the British Isles there also came in considerable numbers the handsome hemispherical cauldrons of thin bronze with three lugs to hang them by, very often decorated with multi-coloured enamel.[3] Of similar character is an ornamented bucket mounted with bronze and enamel, from the Oseberg grave (Pl. 44b).[4] A rare piece of southern English work from c. 800 is the silver goblet from Fejø in Denmark, decorated with rich ornament nearly related to that on the Tassilo chalice and on the binding of the Lindau book.[5] Glasses of the Viking period are rarely found in Scandinavia, and those which are found have undoubtedly been brought home from western Europe. Very important articles were English weapons, especially swords, often with damascened blades, of which many bear the smith's name Ulfberht, a mark which had a wide distribution in Scandinavia and along the Baltic shores. One group of swords has a hilt adorned with silver and ornaments of Anglo-Saxon work (Pl. 45a). Other weapons are of Frankish origin, among them an interesting group of swords with richly wrought hilts all of metal.[6] In the ninth century in Scandinavia

[1] Ingvald Undset, *Norske Oldsager i Fremmede Museer* (Kristiania, 1878), p. 63.

[2] Johannes Bøe, 'An Ornamental Celtic Bronze Object, found in a Norwegian Grave', *Bergens Museums Årbok*, 1924-5, Hist.-ant. rekke, no. 4. In this work are given statistics and a map of the finds of Celtic articles in Norway.

[3] Ingvald Undset, 'Mindre Bidrag om den Yngre Jernalder i Norge', *Aarb. f. nord. Oldk.* (Kjøbenhavn, 1889), p. 291.

[4] Gabriel Gustafson, *Notes on a Decorated Bucket from the Oseberg Find*, Saga Book of the Viking Club, vol. v (London, 1908), p. 297.

[5] J. Brøndsted, *Early English Ornament* (Copenhagen and London, 1924), p. 153.

[6] A. L. Lorange, *Den Yngre Jernalders Sværd*, Ed. Bergens Museum (Bergen, 1889), with a summary in French; Jan Petersen, 'De norske Vikingesverd', *Videnskapsselskapets Skrifter*, ii, Hist.-Filos. Klasse, no. 1 (Kristiania, 1919), pp. 72-3.

PLATE **44**

b. Wooden bucket with bronze and enamel, of Celtic make, Oseberg, Norway. After Grieg

a. Irish censer found in Aurland, Norway After Johs. Bøe

PLATE 45

a. Anglo-Saxon sword with silver decoration.
Tysnes, Norway. After Shetelig

b. Set of brooches and pendants for a woman's dress. After Shetelig

ornaments of Frankish make were worn not uncommonly, sometimes excellent specimens of Carolingian work, as, for example, the famous massive brooch from Hoen near Drammen in Norway; and a silver hoard from Ribe provides a prettily decorated silver cup with Carolingian ornament. Frankish pottery, too, imported through Hedeby in Slesvig, played a certain part in Viking times. At a later period imported oriental pieces appear, ornaments of silver, silver beakers, and some bronze vases; a little cup of faïence found on Gotland is even thought to have come all the way from China.

A great amount of foreign goods we must certainly believe to have been brought to Scandinavia as booty from Viking raids, but a great quantity also came by way of peaceful commerce. We get a more direct impression of the scope and extent of trade from the finds of coins and precious metals. The current medium of valuation in Viking times was silver, usually worked into twisted or interlacing rings in all sizes, for neck, arm, and fingers, and also into ear-rings, pendants, beads, and brooches of filigree work, and ingots and bars. But only a small portion of the silver hoards consists of ornaments; the greater part is in lumps cut off and detached pieces of silver articles, owing to silver being used in payments by weight. This has been styled *Hacksilber*, and it is found in more or less uniform form over an area stretching from central Russia to the Baltic, Germany, and Scandinavia. Both the forms and the distribution show that these silver hoards are products primarily of the trade with the Orient, but in the north they are obviously mixed with silver from western Europe and ornaments of Scandinavian workmanship. The largest proportion of the silver of the Viking period in Scandinavia has been found in Gotland, which now more than ever attracted trade and wealth from east and west; but other Swedish provinces have also yielded considerable quantities of silver.[1] Denmark comes second with about thirty hoards, of which the two largest each have a total weight of about 6·5 kilograms. Most of the others are about half a kilogram in weight. Norway is comparatively poor in silver from the Viking

[1] O. Montelius in *Kulturgeschichte Schwedens* (Leipzig, 1906) gives a complete survey of the silver and gold from Viking times found in Sweden. For Gotland alone the amount is stated to be 125 kilograms of silver, for the rest of Sweden nearly 80 kilograms. The largest hoard from Gotland contains 8·75 kilograms of silver, and several others more than 7 kilograms.

period,[1] as is Finland. Some Scandinavian silver hoards found their way through the agency of Vikings to the British Isles.

A very important part of the silver hoards is formed by foreign coins, which were brought to Scandinavia in large numbers. We have at first a comparatively small number of silver coins from western Europe in the eighth century and the beginning of the ninth; these are Frankish coins of Pepin, Charlemagne, and his immediate successors, and contemporary English coins from the kingdoms of the heptarchy, and also some West Arabian coins of the caliphs in Spain and Africa. They are found a few at a time or singly, often buried in graves, and they may be regarded as booty brought home from the early Viking raids on western Europe round about 800 and in the following century.[2] The hoards of later coins date from a considerably later time, mainly from the end of the tenth century and the beginning of the eleventh. In studying these hoards we are impressed by the very large number of coins which were in circulation; first there are Arabic coins, which began to reach Scandinavia round about 900, then English and German coins, and scattered single coins from other countries, Byzantium, Italy, Hungary, Russia, and others, and finally the first coins minted in Scandinavia appear, though in extremely small number. Thus a confused mixture of nationalities is represented in the coinage which circulated in the north in the Viking period, a striking illustration of the commercial conditions of the time. The greatest number of them are Arabic and English, which are both counted in tens of thousands, and are extant in roughly equal numbers, but the Arabic coins reach a considerably higher total in weight. The largest number of the English coins belongs to the reign of Æthelred. Next come the German coins, the greatest number being minted by Otto III and his grandmother Adelheid round about the year 1000. The first Norse rulers who minted coins themselves were Svein and Knut the Great in Denmark, the contemporary Olaf Skautkonung in Sweden, and Earl Hákon Eiríksson and King Olaf the Saint in Norway.

[1] Sigurd Grieg, 'Vikingetidens Skattefund', *Universitets Oldsaksamlings Skrifter*, ii (Oslo, 1921).

[2] A. W. Brøgger, *Angelsaksiske mynter fra VIII og IX årh. i Norden.* Historisk Tidsskrift (Kristiania, 1910).

Yet these coins of the kings from the beginning of the eleventh century were not the oldest in Scandinavia. The first Norse silver coin was minted about two hundred years earlier, imitating the coinage of Dorestad in Friesland at the end of the eighth century. It is a peculiarly barbarous coin without inscription, stamped with representations of ships and animals and with magical symbols. It is commonly assumed that this coinage was minted in one of the two important trading centres in existence at that time in Scandinavia, either at the Swedish town of Birka on Mälaren, where most of the coins are found, or else at Hedeby in Slesvig, which was a centre of the trade between Scandinavia and the west of Europe. Both of these places were already actual towns with a permanently settled population quite early in the Viking age; in both of them the original ground of the town can be traced at the present day, surrounded by a rampart of earth, close to which stands the castle mound, also protected by earthworks. Outside the town wall at Birka is a cemetery containing over two thousand barrows and other graves, which have yielded an extraordinarily rich harvest of antiquities. Excavations in Hedeby and Birka have in general provided an interesting insight into the life of the oldest Scandinavian towns, about which something is also known from historical sources connected with the first Christian mission to Scandinavia. In Norway in this same period mention is made of a town called Skiringssal on the western shore of Oslofjord; but no remains of a town can be found there, and it is possible that this place was still hardly an actual town, but only a well-known marketing place where the people came together to trade at appointed times.

The Viking period was a time of immense progress in Scandinavia. Place-names and finds of antiquities alike bear witness to a clearing of new ground for farms and hamlets on a scale never known before or since. The smelting of bog-ore must have reached really large dimensions for the time, even if we judge only from the quantity of iron articles which have been preserved from Viking times in Norwegian and Swedish graves, and in Denmark from the stores of smith's implements.[1] In Norway hidden stores of iron used as a trading commodity are

[1] V. Boye, 'To Fund av Smedeverktøi fra den sidste hedenske Tid i Danmark', *Annaler for nordisk Oldkyndighed* (Kjøbenhavn, 1858), p. 191.

quite frequently found.[1] A Norwegian industry which was then, as now, of considerable importance was the making of vessels from soapstone, a material which is easily accessible in many places in Norway, and is fireproof and eminently suitable for cooking-vessels. Soapstone had been used for this purpose for a very long time, at least as early as the end of the Celtic iron age, but only for local needs and not on a large scale. With the Viking period the industry entered upon an entirely new development; soapstone wares were now produced wholesale as in factories, expressly for export from Norway. In Hedeby in Slesvig, which has just been mentioned, fragments of a large number of soapstone vessels have been found, undoubtedly imported from Norway. Thus commercial development led to progress in industry.

It is clear also that foreign imported goods such as we have described earlier were in a diminishing minority among the articles preserved from the Viking period in Scandinavia. This stands out with especial clarity in women's ornaments, which have a distinctive national character (Pl. 45b). There were large oval brooches ('tortoise brooches') which were worn in pairs, one on each shoulder, and also a third brooch of different shape fastened in the middle of the breast; it was oblong, round, or trilobate. The two oval brooches were connected by a luxurious set of beads or chains which lay as a necklet across the breast.[2] This invariable and characteristic set of ornaments was probably influential in giving a peculiarly Norse style to the costume, common to Danes, Norwegians, and Swedes, while Finland at this time followed Baltic modes more closely, as we shall describe later. There are some pictures which give us an idea of the Scandinavian women's costume in Viking times: a skirt reaching to the feet and over it a shorter cloak, the hair wound in a knot at the nape of the neck and then hanging loose down the back. We may mention also that the old laws recognize a _norrøn hárskur_, 'Norse style of hair-cut', as a distinguishing mark of the nation.

As for the men, we are unable to indicate any correspondingly

---

[1] Jan Petersen, 'Jernbarrer', _Oldtiden_, vii (Kristiania, 1918), p. 171.

[2] Jan Petersen, _Vikingetidens Smykker_, Utgitt av Stavanger Museum (Stavanger, 1928), with 240 illustrations; Peter Paulsen, _Studien zur Wikinger-kultur_, Ed. Mus. vaterländ. Altertümer (Kiel, 1933).

national costume. In pictures we recognize warriors with kirtle reaching to the knee and unarmed men clad in a large cloak, fastened in front with a penannular brooch, which is, moreover, the only ornament we find in the graves of men. Men's costume is characterized otherwise by weapons, which generally follow the international forms of the time; an exception is the battle-axe, which was specially characteristic of Scandinavia in Viking times.

The graves give the best idea of native Scandinavian culture in the Viking period. Right up to the final phase of heathendom inhumation and cremation were practised side by side, but cremation was more usual in Sweden and Norway than in Denmark. In Denmark the graves are on the whole poorly furnished, as they were in Merovingian times; even the personal equipment of ornaments and a single weapon is not frequently found, probably because Denmark was readily subject to influence of Christian burial customs. An exception is provided by a small number of rich graves of chiefs in Jutland, such as the Mammen grave at Viborg and the grave at Hvilehøj, near Randers. Under the barrow at Mammen a chamber made of oak planks was found, in which the dead had rested on a feather bed and cushions, and remains of gold-worked fabrics, embroidery, and silk were found.[1] A large wax candle stood on the coffin. The most famous of these Danish graves of princes are the two large barrows at Jellinge near the town of Vejle, which from the evidence of the runic stones set on them we know were raised over King Gorm and his queen Thyra; in the one of these which has been explored there was a large grave-chamber of oak containing remains of rich grave-goods, unfortunately much perished.[2]

In Sweden, and still more in Norway, the graves give a different picture. There a more complete furnishing of the graves is always required. We have already seen that the Scandinavian graves to a great extent show a gradual simplification during the seventh and eighth centuries. But on the Scandinavian peninsula this tendency is met by an opposite and stronger movement which required that the dead should

---

[1] J. J. A. Worsaae, 'Om Mammen-Fundet', *Aarb. f. nord. Oldk.* (Kjøbenhavn, 1869), p. 203, plates 1–9.
[2] J. Kornerup, *Kongehøjene i Jellinge* (Kjøbenhavn, 1875).

receive in the grave or on the pyre an equipment as rich and
complete as possible. Not only the purely personal belongings
are included—costume, ornaments, weapons, and the like—but
also a miscellaneous outfit of agricultural tools, implements for
handcraft and manual labour. In the men's graves implements
for agriculture, smithery, and woodwork predominate; in the
women's graves heckles for treating linen and hemp, implements for spinning, weaving, and sewing, and also kitchen
utensils, vessels, pans, roasting-spits, &c. In addition there
were domestic animals, especially horses and dogs, often also a
vessel, a boat or ship. It is this furnishing that gives the graves
of the Viking period their distinctive character. The furnishing
was supplied both in graves with cremation and in graves with
inhumation, and there is an enormous number of both types
known in Norway from the two centuries of the Viking age.

These large numbers of graves which are found, far greater
than from all the earlier periods of the iron age, are probably
to be explained in part from increasing population; there is no
doubt that in this respect the Viking period was a time of rapid
advance. But the larger number of perceptible graves is due
most of all to the rich furnishing now deposited by a population
which had hitherto buried its dead in the simplest form. This
we can see clearly from the average quality of the antiquities;
as a rule they are far from being show-pieces or specially costly
articles, but are quite ordinary everyday things such as every
man possessed. It is evident enough that a rich furnishing of
the graves was now not specially aristocratic, but the expression
of a custom and belief common to the whole people. The graves
of the Viking period, therefore, give on the one hand a remarkably
complete picture of the daily working life of the time, and at the
same time a strong and vivid impression of the spiritual nature
of the age. We perceive in these graves the conceptions and
faith of the true heathen mentality, of the heathen belief in
future life and of the cult of the dead, as deeply rooted as they
had ever been in any age of antiquity; and these conceptions
are especially impressive in the Viking period, a time which was
more than half historical and on the threshold of the Christian
Middle Ages. There was a great sacrifice demanded at the
burial; an Arabian traveller who was present at the funeral of
a Swedish chief by the Volga relates that a third part of the

dead man's property had to accompany him on the pyre, a third part was spent on the feast at the funeral, and a third fell to the heirs. This was a costly burial custom. The deep and sincere heathen religious feeling permeating the whole thought of the nation must be recognized as one of the most important elements of the age, if one is to understand the physiognomy of the Viking age as a whole.

This is one of the most significant aspects of the creed held in that age which is reflected in the graves, and its conceptions were generally widespread in all societies; every one at that time strove for means to give the dead the equipment which belief and custom found desirable. The same conception provided the motive when a farmer was buried in a boat with his horse and weapons and working tools as when a king was buried in a ship with the most luxurious furnishing. At the highest peak of society, where no economic considerations stood in the way, and pride and vanity encouraged magnificence, stand the mightiest and most remarkable grave-monuments known in the whole of northern Europe. We have already mentioned the graves of the Danish kings at Mammen and Jellinge in Jutland. A grave of the same type is also known in Norway on the farm Haugen in Rolvsøy, Østfold.[1] The grave as a whole is very similar to the Mammen grave, and in its inner chamber to the grave at Jellinge; this chamber, which was covered by a huge mound, was built of timber in cubic form, each side measuring about 3·75 metres. Inside it was found a large number of bones of domestic animals, metal mountings of saddlery, buckets, and pails, a bronze cauldron, vessels of stone, drinking horns, and a large heap of iron articles perished from rust. The dead had lain on a bed with a feather mattress and pillows; there were also remains of various woollen fabrics, silk bands, and tapestries woven with pictures. Here, too, as at Mammen, the textile fabrics were very conspicuous among the furnishings of the grave, and we shall find the same circumstance in the Oseberg ship as well. Rich costumes, a luxuriously appointed bed, cloths, and wall tapestries are the most characteristic features of the

[1] A. W. Brøgger, 'Rolvsøyætten. Et arkeologisk bidrag til vikingetidens historie', *Bergens Museums Årbok*, 1920–1, Hist.-ant. rekke, no. 1, p. 20 f. Graves of similar structure have been investigated at Bygstad in Sunnfjord and at Stod near Trondhjem; see Shetelig, 'Vestlandske Graver fra Jernalderen', *Bergens Museums Skrifter*, Ny Rekke, ii. 1 (Bergen, 1912), pp. 211 and 233.

distinguished graves in the Viking period, both in Denmark and Norway. Among these the ship-graves in Norway are the most luxurious of all, the most princely form of burial known in the Viking period.

The custom of burial in a vessel was itself not limited to royal persons, as we have already seen; on the contrary, it was very common in Norway and Sweden at this time to bury the dead in a boat, usually in one that was not very large, but not in the smallest. The custom is remarkable, and, so far as we know, without any analogue in prehistoric Europe; the nearest parallels must be sought in ancient Egypt, where examples are known of graves with ships and also a grave built of stone in the form of a boat. We have described earlier (p. 151) an interesting group of grave-monuments on Gotland, constructed with ship-formed rows of stones, which can be traced back as far as the fourth and fifth phases of the bronze age. All are agreed that this form of grave expresses the same idea as the ship-graves of the Viking period, that the symbolical rows of stones represent an actual vessel, and go back to a time when it is not inconceivable that there might be some connexion with the similar forms of grave in Egypt. In these forms we have to reckon with the belief about the dead journeying in a ship, and the function ascribed to the ship in the cult of the dead, which we have already discussed in connexion with the bronze-age rock-carvings, and we discovered from some of the Norwegian carvings and Swedish sculptured stones that pictures of this kind, representing ships, were still executed in the early iron age. Accordingly, it seems probable that the boat-graves and ship-graves, as we encounter them in the Viking period, have their roots in a very ancient Norse survival, and that the vessel in the grave has a more specific symbolism than the rest of the grave-goods. The most natural interpretation of the boat-graves must be that the vessel was to serve for the journey over the sea to the kingdom of the dead.

We have other traces also of this belief in the iron age in Scandinavia: there is a certain number of examples from the Roman period and the migration period of a gold coin or a small cut piece of gold being put into the dead man's mouth as he lay in the grave, or into the urn when the body was cremated.[1]

[1] Knut Stjerna, *Essays on Questions connected with the Old English Poem of*

These are 'Charon's pennies' following the true classical example, which also originated in the belief that mankind after death must make a journey across a river or the sea: this is clearly the same notion that is at the root of the boat-graves. Graves with vessels are also undoubtedly in evidence some time before the Viking period. In the years round about A.D. 500 some examples of boat-graves appear on the coasts of Norway in Nordland, near Bergen, and near Arendal;[1] the boat is sometimes burned on the pyre, sometimes buried unburned. To the same period belongs the only boat-grave known from Anglo-Saxon times in England;[2] it was found on Snape Common near Aldeburgh in Suffolk. The contents of this grave had not been burned; the boat was a good 14 metres long, and contained, among other articles, a gold finger-ring of fifth-century Italian make and fragments of a glass vase. Mr. Reginald A. Smith has dated the grave c. 500, and it is thus completely parallel with the oldest boat-graves known in Norway. But it is by no means certain that the oldest boat-graves which we know are the oldest that existed. In earlier times the boats were made entirely of perishable material, without even iron nails, so that they would disappear on the pyre or in the earth without leaving a trace, and it is accordingly quite possible that the boat-graves represent a much older custom than we now have evidence of.

What is certain is that graves containing vessels first become apparent in Scandinavia in the migration period, c. A.D. 500. In the seventh century they are more widely distributed through Norway, Sweden, and Finland, and are then represented with unusual richness in the royal graves in Uppland which have already been described. In the Viking period, from the beginning of the ninth century, this form of burial reached its greatest extent and popularity, and at the same time achieved its highest development in the graves of the Norwegian kings.[3] All of them

---

Beowulf (1912), p. 101 f.; Shetelig, *Færgepengen, Spor av en græsk gravskik i Norge.* Sproglige og historiske avhandlinger viede Sophus Bugge Minde (Kristiania, 1908), p. 1. Cf. Oscar Almgren, *Ett Guldmynt från en Gottländsk Graf,* Studier tillägnade Oscar Montelius (Stockholm, 1903), p. 80 f.

[1] Shetelig, 'Tidlige Båtgraver', *Oldtiden,* vii (Kristiania, 1918), p. 73 f.

[2] Described by Reginald A. Smith in the *Victoria County History of Suffolk,* vol. i.

[3] All of these are described by the present writer in the work on the *Oseberg-fundet,* vol. i, published by the Norwegian state, edited by A. W. Brøgger, Hjalmar Falk, and Haakon Shetelig (Kristiania, 1917), p. 216, with a summary

exhibit a constant arrangement which in this particular group of royal graves can be described as a general feature. The king's own ship in which he regularly made his journeys, as a rule a vessel of something over 20 metres in length, was set up in the place which had been selected for the grave (Pl. 46). A burial chamber of boards or of thick oak planks was erected amidships, but in the form of a ship's tent with a sharp gable, and there the dead man was laid to rest on a bed of down and pillows. Remains of clothing are found worked with gold and with embroidery and *appliqués* of vari-coloured silks; there are cloths woven in patterns and long friezes of tapestries woven in pictures. The personal equipment was the richest possible, we must believe, though practically all the ship-graves were plundered in ancient times, so that now very little in the way of ornaments and weapons is found. In Storhaugen on Karmøy, the only grave of this type which had not been touched, were found a gold ring, playing-pieces of glass and amber, and all the usual weapons.

The whole ship was freighted in the same luxurious fashion. We need only mention the Oseberg grave, where the conditions were so exceptionally favourable that everything was preserved complete; in addition to all the gear of the ship, the mast, oars, anchor, gang-plank, &c., there were two large tents, a four-wheeled wagon (Pl. 47), four sledges, three or four beds, a large number of chests, buckets and pails, implements for weaving and other handcrafts, and much else. There was also an offering of many kinds of animals at the burial. In the Oseberg ship were found thirteen horses, six dogs, a whole young ox, and a severed ox-head; in the Gokstad ship a similar number of horses and dogs and also a peacock. Finally there was in the Oseberg grave a very interesting feature, the remains of skeletons of two women, one elderly and one young, one of them (but it is uncertain which) in all probability a serving-woman sacrificed

in English. Some of the graves are on Rolvsøy at the mouth of the River Glommen on the east side of Oslofjord; the Tune ship in the museum at Oslo came from there. From the west side of Oslofjord come the famous ships of Gokstad and Oseberg; in a third grave at Borre the ship had perished, but a profusion of antiquities from there are to be seen in the museum at Oslo. On the west coast of Norway we have two similar graves at Karmsund, near the town of Haugesund, but only comparatively small fragments are preserved in Bergen Museum. There is a record of a grave of the same type on the coast north of Trondhjem on the island of Leka, but no remains from it have been preserved.

PLATE 46

e stem (prow) of the Oseberg ship, moored in the grave-mound. After Brøgger

PLATE 47

The wagon from the Oseberg ship. After Grieg

in order that she might accompany her mistress. When everything was disposed in order, an immense mound was raised over the grave and the ship, composed for the most part either of thick clay or of grass turf alone, a solicitude which we have to thank for several of these ships being found in a remarkably well-preserved state. The ship-graves unroll to our gaze a complete picture of the life of the time, ranging from all kinds of everyday things for household work up to the highest forms of decorative art in woodcarving and weaving. Scarcely anywhere else in Europe is the whole inventory of the early Middle Ages known in such complete detail as in Norway.

With the emigrations of the Viking period both antiquities and graves of the Scandinavian type were brought to colonies in foreign lands, from Sweden to Russia, from Norway to Scotland and Ireland. The ancient burial places around Dublin have a completely Norwegian character, and have yielded rich finds which are now in the National Museum of Ireland. On the coast of Brittany, on the Île de Groix, a large barrow containing the grave of a chief in a burned ship has been excavated, and its closest parallel is in Nordfjord on the west coast of Norway. There is hardly room in this survey for a more detailed description of the monuments of the Viking period outside Scandinavia; we refer the reader to the works already cited in which they are fully treated.[1]

In Finland the connexion with Sweden was, surprisingly, weaker in the Viking age than it had been in the preceding two centuries, most probably because Swedish expansion was now operating on a much larger scale in the colonization of Russia.[2] Weapons were imported into Finland, some Swedish, some West European (probably by way of Sweden, like the Anglo-Saxon coins).[3] But in the much more important spheres such as

[1] T. J. Arne, *La Suède et l'Orient*; Birger Nerman, *Die Verbindungen zwischen Skandinavien und dem Ostbaltikum*, &c; A. W. Brøgger, *Ancient Emigrants*; Haakon Shetelig, *Vikingeminner i Vest Europa*, Instituttet for Sammenlignende Kulturforskning, A, xvi (Oslo, 1933).

[2] A. Hackman, 'Finland. C. Eisenzeit' in Ebert's *Reallexikon der Vorgeschichte*, iii. 346; Julius Ailio, 'Karialaiset Svikeat Kupurasoljet', with a summary in German, *Finska Fornminnesförenings Tidskrift*, xxxii (Helsingfors, 1922); C. A. Nordman, 'Karelska Jernåldersstudier', ibid. xxxiv (Helsingfors, 1924).

[3] C. A. Nordman, *Anglo-Saxon Coins found in Finland* (Helsingfors, 1921), Ed. The Finnish Archaeological Society.

costume and ornaments, Finland in the Viking period was
almost untouched by Scandinavian motives. The oval brooches
('tortoise brooches') were introduced through the influence of
the Swedish colonies south of Ladoga, but they were modified
and converted into a purely Finnish national type, and the
Finnish ornaments otherwise are thoroughly Baltic in style;
they include various brooches, pins, ring-buckles, and other
forms, and show a definite predilection for chains draped
lavishly as ornaments across the breast. In Viking times there
was a local development in personal costume: the material had
spirals of bronze thread woven into it, a taste which was
common to Finland and the south-eastern provinces of the
Baltic.[1] Imports from Russia can also be traced, and connexions
with the great trade-routes from the Baltic to Mesopotamia and
Persia. The Permian forms come from this source, as also
oriental ornaments and Arabic coins found in Finland, but
otherwise the number of coins is surprisingly small. It was not
until a somewhat later period that the west of Finland again
came under a strong influence from Sweden through crusading
expeditions, the Church, and colonization.

To the four Norse lands which have occupied our attention
through the long prehistoric ages a new Scandinavian land was
added in the Viking age; this land was first settled in that period,
and it was endowed with a destiny of the greatest significance
to Norse literature and history. This was Iceland, settled by
Norwegian emigrants during a period from the end of the ninth
century to about 930.[2] We have from Iceland a considerable

[1] Hj. Appelgren-Kivalo, *Finnische Trachten aus der jüngeren Eisenzeit*, i
(Helsingfors, 1907).

[2] The Norse settlement in Greenland and the history of the colony established
there belong almost entirely to the Christian Middle Ages, and therefore lie
outside the scope of this survey. This applies likewise to the Norse expeditions
from Greenland to the mainland of America. A concise survey of these matters
is given by T. D. Kendrick in his *History of the Vikings* (London, 1930), pp. 360–
87. See also G. M. Gathorne-Hardy, *The Norse Discoverers of America* (Oxford,
1921), and Edward F. Gray, *Leif Eiriksson* (London, 1930). A more detailed
study, in which use is made of evidence from excavations and remains of the
old dwellings, is that of Daniel Bruun, *The Icelandic Colonization of Greenland
and the Finding of Vineland*, Meddelelser om Grønland lvii (København, 1918).
A number of articles describing the remains of the old colony have been published in this series, Meddelelser om Grønland. The latest account is Nørlund's
De gamle Nordbobygder ved Verdens Ende (København, 1934), describing the
author's investigations in the years 1921–32.

number of antiquities and graves from the tenth century, before
Christianity was introduced,[1] in general corresponding exactly
with Norwegian forms. The graves are dug down into the earth
and covered with low stone cairns; the women are provided
with brooches and beads, the men with a single weapon.
Skeletons of horses are commonly found in the graves, and
bones of dogs too are recorded. Boat-graves are also known in
Iceland.[2] The graves are, however, much poorer than in Norway,
and it is a most striking circumstance that cremation is absolutely not to be found. The heathen burial customs in Iceland
no longer had the same power as in the motherland, since many
of the settlers came to Iceland after a stay, long or short, in the
British Isles. On the other hand the national religion has left
visible memorials in Iceland of a kind which we cannot match
in the other Scandinavian lands, namely, the remains of heathen
temples.[3] The Icelandic *hof* consists of a large and long hall
where the people gathered together for the sacrificial feasts and,
joined to this, a smaller separate room where the images of
the gods stood.

With the close of the Viking period this survey of the prehistoric archaeology of Scandinavia reaches its end. We have
now come to the time which has the illumination of historical
documents, both the contemporary English and Frankish
authors and the fuller but more uncertain traditions recorded
at a later period in Norse sagas. Contemporary Scandinavian
records are limited to runic inscriptions, which are from their
very nature comparatively short, but yet in some degree possess
an historical content. The earlier runic alphabet with its
twenty-four letters, which has been already described, in the
eighth century underwent a complete revision resulting in a
new alphabet of sixteen letters; but the old division into three
groups and the individual names of the runes were retained.
One of the causes of this change in the runic alphabet was
undoubtedly the great shift in the sounds of the language at
that time; but the change was in part also a simplification of the

[1] Kr. Kålund, 'Islands Fortidslævninger', *Aarb. f. nord. Oldk.* (Kjøbenhavn, 1882), p. 57 f.
[2] Daniel Bruun and Finnur Jónsson, 'Dalvik-fundet. En gravplads fra
hedenskabets tid paa Island', *Aarb. f. nord. Oldk.* (1910), p. 62 f.
[3] Daniel Bruun and Finnur Jónsson, *Om Hove og Hovudgravninger på Island*
(Aarbøger, 1909), p. 245.

written symbols. The cumbrous letters consisting of two parts were replaced by simplified runes, and the change proceeded in the direction of making the greatest possible number of runes into letters of even height with projecting branches. But the smaller number of letters was capable of far fewer distinctions between individual sounds than was the older series, so that, for example, the old rune for *k* now became the sign not only for *k* but also for *g* and often also *ng*, and the rune for *u* was used for the consonant *w* and the vowels *u, o, y, ø*. Skill in writing and reading runes must have been much more generally current than in the older period, to allow of such a result without immediate dissatisfaction being felt with this ambiguous representation of sounds. With these and some other changes the later runic alphabet of Viking times was given the following form:

ᚠᚢᚦᚨᚱᚴ : ᚼᚾᛁᛅᛋ : ᛏᛒᛁᛚᛦ
f u þ ą r k : h n i a s : t b m l ʀ

This is the form which may be called 'normal' in the Viking period, the so-called Danish runes, which are actually the nearest of the new series to the earlier prototypes. This series was produced in Denmark and was always a special characteristic of Danish inscriptions, while Sweden and Norway show a variation with a more ruthless reduction of the branch-strokes:

ᚠᚢᚦᚨᚱᚴ : ᚽᚼᛁᛂᛌ : ᚴᚽᛐᛚᛁ
f u þ ą r k : h n i a s : t b m l ʀ

This latter form, the Sweo-Norwegian runes, appears to have been first developed in Gotland, and from there spread to the rest of Sweden, to Norway, and to the Viking colonies on the British Isles. A slight variation of these is the form known as 'Manx runes'. In the eleventh century, however, the Danish runes became prevalent in Sweden also; almost all the runic stones of Uppland from that time are inscribed in Danish runes. In order to complete this rapid summary of the development of runes, it must be added that the disadvantage of the incomplete representation of sounds was soon felt, and from about A.D. 1000 small modifications were introduced for the purpose of distinguishing different sounds. The result was finally the runic alphabet which was used generally in the Christian Middle Ages, and is given here in the usual Norwegian form:

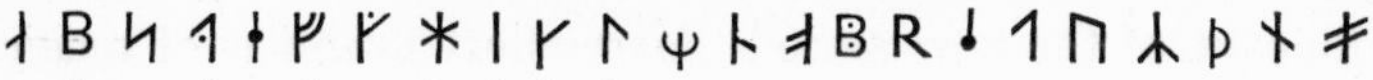

a b c d e f g h i k l m n o p r s t u y þ æ ö

The influence of the Roman alphabet produced this rearrangement of the runes; but to the very last runic writing preserved much of its original magical character.

The inscriptions from the heathen Viking period can be only glanced at here. It is comparatively seldom that we find runes written on detached objects from the Viking period, as on the well-known Hunterston brooch, now in the Scottish National Museum, a Celtic ornament with a Norwegian inscription.[1] From the ninth century we have a few inscriptions from Norwegian graves, including those from the Gokstad and Oseberg ships. The inscription on the large silver ring from the island of Senjen in the east of Norway is well known; it runs:[2]

Fórum drengja	We went forth to seek the Frisian
Físlands á vit	warriors, and we changed battle-
ok vígs fǫtum	garments with them (i.e. took their
viðr skiptum.	armour).

But the greater number and the most important of the inscriptions of the Viking period are found on stone monuments erected to the memory of distinguished persons. This kind of memorial became very common in certain districts of Scandinavia towards the end of the Viking period, first in Denmark and later even more generally in Sweden, but was never as widely distributed in Norway.[3] The content of the inscriptions is

[1] George Stephens, *The Old Northern Runic Monuments*, ii (London and Copenhagen, 1867–8), p. 589.

[2] Sophus Bugge and Magnus Olsen, *Runene þaa en Sølvring fra Senjen* (Kristiania, 1906) (*Norges Indskrifter med de yngre Runer*, utgivne for Det Norske Historiske Kildeskriftfond). The inscriptions from the Oseberg ship have been edited by Magnus Olsen, *Osebergfundet*, ii (Oslo, 1928), p. 287 f.

[3] A complete edition of the Danish inscriptions has been produced by Ludv. F. A. Wimmer, *De Danske Runemindesmærker*, i–iv (Kjøbenhavn, 1893–1908). There is an excellent and convenient epitome of this work under the same title by Dr. Lis Jacobsen (Kjøbenhavn, 1914). A corpus of Swedish inscriptions, published by the Kgl. Vitterhets Historie och Antikvitets Akademien under the general editorship of Hans Hildebrand, comprises: Sven Söderberg and Erik Brate, *Ölands Runinskrifter* (Stockholm, 1900–6); Erik Brate and Elias Wessén, *Östergötlands Runinskrifter* (1911–18), and *Södermanlands Runinskrifter*, parts 1–3 (1927–33), and still incomplete; R. Kinander, *Kronobergs läns Runinskrifter* (1935). See also Otto von Friesen, *Runorna i Sverige*, 3rd ed. (Uppsala, 1928); id., *Upplands Runstenar* (Uppsala, 1913) and 'Runorna', *Nordisk Kultur*,

significant of the new period. Mere short formulas of magical runes are no longer in use, as they were in the migration period; the inscriptions of the Viking period are full, intended to give information to posterity and preserve the knowledge of historical events. The monuments are memorials of honour, and the dead are named accordingly in laudatory terms: 'He was the best of good men', or in expressions such as 'a good hard-knit man', typical of the standards of the Viking age. It was always an important point to speak of a dead man of heroic temper as having been on an expedition, and sometimes mention is made of other exploits in his life, and from such references we get many glimpses of the history of the time, as we find men who fell 'on a Viking cruise to the north', or in England, or in Greece. Usually the information is given in general expressions of this kind, but occasionally reference is made to definite events of the time, such as the wars in South Jutland in the first half of the tenth century, and to Knut the Great's expedition to England. On several Swedish stones it is stated that the dead man had taken Danegeld in England two or three times.

In the first rank of historical runic stones stand the two at Jellinge in Jutland, erected in connexion with the kings' graves there which have already been mentioned. One was erected by King Gorm the Old for his queen Thyra, and the other about A.D. 980 by their son Harald Bluetooth as a memorial to both his parents. The latter is the most impressive memorial monument in northern Europe, in form roughly a three-sided pyramid; two of the three sides are sculptured with pictures, while the third side bears the proud inscription: 'King Harald commanded this memorial to be made in memory of his father Gorm and his mother Thyra—Harald who won for himself all Denmark and Norway, and converted Denmark to Christianity.'

It would be outside our subject to pursue runic inscriptions any farther. The pictures and ornaments which are connected with the inscriptions will be discussed in the next chapter; it remains only to mention briefly that the runic art went with the Viking expeditions and Viking colonizations into foreign lands. Many Manx crosses with runic inscrip-

vi (Stockholm, 1933); Oscar Almgren, *Sveriges Fasta Fornlämninger från Hednatiden*, 2nd ed. (Uppsala, 1923), p. 80 f. A complete edition of the Norwegian inscriptions in later runes is being prepared by Magnus Olsen.

tions are known, most of them from about 1000; they have
been published in handsome form in Mr. Kermode's book on
Manx crosses. Some few inscriptions have also been found in
Scotland and Ireland, and above all there is the richly sculptured
stone from Saint Paul's, now in the Guildhall Museum. From
Normandy no runic inscriptions of this period are known, and
on the continent generally they are extremely rare. So much
the more striking, therefore, are the inscription from Bere-
zanji and the famous monument, the Piraeus lion, now in
Venice; the inscription on it is a visible memorial of a Scandinavian visitation upon the harbour of Athens in the eleventh
century.

XVII

THE DECORATIVE ART OF THE IRON AGE

DURING the preceding account of Scandinavian archaeology in the iron age we have several times mentioned ornamental metal-work and other forms of decorative art, such as wood-carving, weaving, and stone monuments, from various periods. The decorative art exhibits a continuous development during the last six centuries of Scandinavian prehistory, from the fifth century to the eleventh, and it is without doubt one of the most interesting elements of this ancient civilization. On several occasions we have also observed that the varying styles succeeding each other in this period are intimately connected with the general culture of the whole era, and that the different phases of style are due to changing influences and contacts with other spheres of culture. The decorative art is obviously not a detached phenomenon; it has its background in all the other movements of the period. Much might be said in favour of introducing the various phases in the history of style each in its own chronological division of our cultural history, but I believe that it is a more effective mode of presentation to give the development of style a chapter by itself, so that it can be treated continuously. There is, moreover, a certain orientation of development which can hardly be followed by any other method.[1]

To present a clear conspectus, a scheme of the successive styles in the iron age is given, specifying the conventional names and approximate dates of each:

Style I. The *Migration Style* or *North Sea Style*, c. A.D. 450–600.

Style II. The *Early Vendel Style* or *Continental Style*, c. A.D. 600–700.

Style III. The *Late Vendel Style*, c. A.D. 700–800.

The *Early Viking Style*, c. A.D. 800–930. This type is sub-

[1] An excellent survey of recent literature on the subject is given by Peter Paulsen, *Der Stand der Forschung über die Kultur der Wikingerzeit*, 22 Bericht der Römisch-Germanischen Kommission (Frankfurt a. M., 1933), pp. 182–98 and pp. 244–54. Also *Nordisk Kultur*, xxvii, Kunst (Stockholm, 1931), ed. H. Shetelig, pp. 100–79.

divided into the *Early Oseberg Style*, the *Late Oseberg Style*, and the *Borre Style*.

The *Late Viking Style, c.* 930–1100. This type is subdivided into the *Jellinge Style*, the *Ringerike Style*, and the *Urnes Style*.

These successive variations in the decorative style will be described in the remainder of this chapter.

The Migration Style. I shall begin by recalling the large handsome brooches of silver belonging to the migration period, which provide the most distinguished examples in the oldest style of Norse iron-age ornament. From these early periods we have not preserved any other decoration than that in metalwork, on personal ornaments and goldsmithry of similar sort; it is, however, quite possible, perhaps even probable, that such ornament was also executed in wood on a larger scale, but no articles of this kind have survived.

We will first examine a piece of unusual magnificence, the Norwegian brooch from Fonnås in Østerdal (Pl. 48*a*), one of the largest specimens known of this kind of ornament, nearly 18 cm. long. It is made of massive cast silver heavily gilt, with raised listels of ungilt silver, stripes of niello-work, and garnets set in round sockets. All flat surfaces are filled with closely compact ornament; the outline is broken into waves of uneven ornament, partly of perforated work, and projecting corners are finished off with wide baroque masks. It is a striking and effective piece of work, even though the effect is undoubtedly barbaric.[1]

The motives which provide the details in the composition are everywhere small images of animals, extremely schematized creatures which have nothing to do with any existing zoological form; we also find birds similarly treated, and not very uncommonly human forms. The individual figures may have a somewhat varying character as they are produced with a varying technique, engraved in relief, or outlined in perforation or in filigree; but the ornamental motive is always the same. The quality of this decorative art has often been under-estimated, because the modern point of view gives prime importance to the execution of the figures in the ornament. This is a mistake: it is the whole effect which should be judged, and the decorative value of these pieces does not lie in the working out of the design, but in the modelling of the relief. This is a plastic art;

[1] Other examples of this style are depicted in Pl. 39*b* and frontispiece, *a*.

and it teems with multitudes of figures, which give it a rich and luxuriant effect. Obviously the style should not be judged by the clumsier pieces which are found among the others, but from the best and most significant work. As in all art, there is here too a wide difference in quality between original works of the first rank and the lesser imitations.

The development of this style can be illustrated from a series of ornaments from the fifth and sixth centuries. The earliest stage shows a prevailing use of engraved and stamped decoration (Pl. 39a); next comes cast work with profuse use of geometrical chip-carved motives together with animal figures, and finally, from the beginning of the sixth century, animal figures alone prevail. This is the style we call the migration style,[1] because it was developed upon the basis of the peculiar cultural conditions in northern Europe during and following the Germanic migrations. Recently the style has also been called the North Sea style,[2] a designation which better expresses its geographical distribution. It is a style which flourished almost uniformly among the three Scandinavian peoples and among the Anglo-Saxons in England, but never had any comparable development among the Germans on the continent.

The problem of the origin of this style is one of the most controversial questions in Norse archaeology. Yet most Scandinavian scholars are agreed that the animal motive which is the basis of the ornament was formed under influences from Roman industrial art, since individual forms have been copied from classical animal images. As an illustrative parallel to the history of this animal ornament the gold bracteates may be cited; they are ornaments thoroughly Norse in character, but produced originally in imitation of Roman imperial coins, as has already been related. This interpretation of the migration style is in full accord with the historical situation and the general cultural conditions in the fourth and fifth centuries. Late classical industrial art was decadent, but it was nevertheless the source of the forms adopted by the Germans; from the fifth century onward German adaptation of the motives took a new and independent course, and produced a new Scando-Germanic decorative art.[3]

---

[1] Sophus Müller, 'Dyreornamentiken i Norden', *Aarb. f. nord. Oldk.* (1880).

[2] A. W. Brøgger, *Norsk Kunsthistorie* (Oslo, 1925), p. 52.

[3] This theory was first propounded by Hildebrand, *Tidskrift för Konst och*

PLATE 48

a. Brooch of silver from Fonnås, Norway

b. Panel of a sledge from Oseberg. After Shetelig

PLATE 49

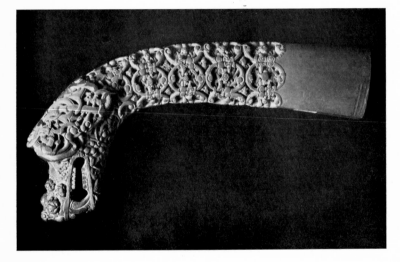

b. Animal head, wood carving from
Gokstad ship. After Gustafson

a. Animal head, wood carving from
Oseberg ship. After Shetelig

As far as we can see, this is the best and most natural solution of the problem, but it should be added that such a distinguished authority as Sophus Müller takes a different view; he presents elaborate and careful arguments to prove that the style was entirely independent Norse. Sophus Müller, it is true, knew all the existing monuments better than any one else, and he did not fail to observe that certain classical models were imitated; but he believed that no further impulse was derived from this imitation tending to the formation of a new style, and accordingly that the animal ornament must have been created spontaneously and quite independently in the north and is a purely Norse innovation in the realm of art. It was a personal aesthetic valuation which most of all decided the matter for Sophus Müller; his sense of the profoundly original in this style in its fully matured development led him to draw a sharp line between classical and barbaric form, and it is obviously a very important consideration which he has emphasized. But this estimate of the originality of the style may quite well be reconciled with the other interpretation which has just been mentioned, the interpretation which must indeed be the right one; it provides the only explanation which gives the migration style its natural place in the culture of the whole period.

Then in more recent years another possible source of this Norse ornament has been indicated by various considerations, namely, the east, or, more precisely, the ancient Scythian territory in southern Russia. The Goths who founded their kingdom by the Black Sea in the third century A.D. would come into contact with Scythian traditions and may conceivably have imbibed some elements of ancient Scythian art. Impulses from this source may then have spread northward with the cultural connexions reaching north-westward through Europe; these, as we have noticed earlier, were very lively in the third century. The distinguished archaeologists Ellis H. Minns, Rostovtzeff, and Strzygowsky have been the special champions of this theory, and it is not entirely a new idea to look to the East for this solution. The same theory was adumbrated earlier by Scandi-

---

Konstindustri (Stockholm, 1876), who was followed later by the Swedish scholars Söderberg (in 'Die Thierornamentik der Völkerwanderungszeit', *Prähistorische Blätter*, vi (Munich, 1894), pp. 67 and 83) and Salin (*Die altgermanische Thierornamentik*, Stockholm, 1904).

navian archaeologists, and more recently the interest in oriental art in general has been very much in the foreground. The scholars just mentioned in their discussion of animal ornament have laid the chief stress on psychological factors in the decoration; they believe that oriental and Norse art are unmistakably akin in spirit, and therefore must necessarily have some inner connexion.

According to our conception the problem is primarily an historical one, and in treating it as such we find it very difficult to discover links which could connect ancient Scythian art with the north in the migration period. The true Scythian art flourished at a much older period, c. 400 B.C.; southern Russia in the time of the Empire was dominated by classical Graeco-Roman forms. Local reminiscences of ancient Scythian art are found, in particular conventionalized decorative representations of reindeer and harts, but there is much more that is classical in motive, half-barbarized in treatment; and it is true that among such work there are things which are related to Germanic work of the late Roman period, as, for example, certain types of ornamental animal figures. But the kinship between South Russian and Norse forms probably rests upon a common source; the most characteristic of Scythian motives, a severely conventionalized hart, was never adopted in Germanic ornament, and it is, moreover, a point of some importance that the migration style was not developed among the Goths, but among the Scandinavian and Anglo-Saxon peoples. The basic impulses proceeded from contact with provincial Roman industrial art on the Rhine frontier and in the North Sea trade. We are thus unable to subscribe to the hypothesis which seeks an eastern origin for this Norse animal ornament.[1]

The Early Vendel Style. While the migration style was still in full flower in the sixth century, we already begin to observe a new current in Norse art, a current which was destined to be fully dominant by the beginning of the seventh century, and thus introduce a new period of style. This new style consists of interlacing lines combined with animal forms. Germanic

[1] Shetelig, 'The Origin of the Scandinavian Style of Ornament during the Migration Period', *Archaeologia*, lxxvi (London, 1927). Dr. J. Brøndsted, in 1931, again strongly emphasizes the South Russian influences as the principal inspiration of Teutonic animal ornament, in *Nordisk Kultur*, xxvii. 100 s.

style was already acquainted with the earlier interlacing in a pure form, as a borrowing from Roman ornament, but the animal figures were never set in interlacing patterns in the migration style, and the design was not founded on lines as an independent motive. This is precisely what now occurs from the beginning of the seventh century. In its new form Norse ornament continues to work on animal figures as a leading motive, and many details of their form are still derived from the migration style; yet the decoration is quite new, as the bodies of the animals are used to join profusely interlacing patterns of bands, both for borders and to fill complete surfaces. The effect is no longer dependent on the relief, but upon the lines, the delineation, and the clarity and symmetry of the composition.[1] We are thus confronted with a marked change in style, both in the trend of taste and in the treatment of the motives. The new style has sometimes been called the Vendel style[2] from the rich finds in Vendel in Uppland, and sometimes the continental style[3] in contradistinction to the North Sea style. The latter designation also correctly expresses the distribution of this style over a different geographical area from that of the migration style.

This change of style in the north accompanied a general European movement. The great interlacing bands were everywhere a leading motive in decoration at this period, in Byzantium as in Italy, and they were applied to various materials, being found in stone architecture, in carved ivories, and in wood.[4] The same decoration grew and flourished just as luxuriantly in central Europe; in England it was blended with the migration style in a very original form, and it made its way westward as far as Ireland, where the interlaced bands were combined with animal motives in forms which very often recall Germanic types. The new style came to Scandinavia, as has been mentioned, across the Baltic from the south, and attained its richest growth in the eastern districts of the north, on the islands of Gotland and Bornholm, in Uppland in Sweden (see p. 256), and in Finland. In this style there is a great wealth of magnificent work in cast

---

[1] Specimens of this style are depicted in Pl. 42 and frontispiece, *b*.

[2] Shetelig in *Osebergfundet*, iii (Oslo, 1920).

[3] A. W. Brøgger in *Norsk Kunsthistorie* (Oslo, 1928).

[4] Einar Lexow, 'Hovedlinjene i Entrelacornamentikens Historie', *Bergens Museums Årbok*, 1921–2, Hist.-ant. rekke no. 1; Françoise Henry, *La Sculpture Irlandaise* (Paris, 1933), pp. 89 f.

bronze, thickly gilt, distinguished equally in its decoration and its technical execution (frontispiece, *b*). Impulses from central Europe and northern Italy inspired a new artistic flowering by the Baltic; and yet this style too has in it a very strong cast of true native Norse.

The Late Vendel Style. The Vendel style is only meagrely represented in Norway, as in the west of Scandinavia generally. It is first in the late, more mature, phase of the Vendel style in the eighth century that we see signs of increased Norwegian production, while Sweden, and especially Gotland, produce the greatest wealth of decorated metal-work in this kind. There are certain nuances in the forms of the ornament which make it easy to distinguish between work of the seventh and eighth centuries, but there is no ground for the recognition of a definitely new style; we therefore regard these two groups as early and late forms of the Vendel style.[1] The principal motive in the ornament is still interlaced bands combined with decorative animal figures, but the composition had now dispensed with strongly geometrical designs. The ornament develops a free and capricious movement, with plentiful variation of broad and narrow bands. The technical treatment is brilliant; the decoration is usually engraved on bronze with a precision that is amazing, and the utmost care is devoted to the whole execution. The late Vendel style is found in a local Norse group, and has been developed from the older form of the style; but from the end of the eighth century we again observe features pointing to new foreign influences and leading up to the earlier Oseberg style, which introduces us to the art of the Viking period.

The Early Viking Style. The Oseberg find has provided us with an abundant wealth of large pieces of wood-carving, and it is in this find that we first become acquainted with the art of the period in its larger forms, and in a completely different monumental type, since from earlier times we have only small pieces preserved, personal ornaments and similar pieces of goldsmithry. The wood-carvings in the Oseberg find cover some fifty years, roughly the first half of the ninth century, a period which presents one of the most interesting phases in the

---

[1] The early Vendel period embraces Salin's Style II (seventh century), and the late Vendel period Salin's Style III (eighth century). See his *Altgermanische Thierornamentik.*

whole history of our ancient art, a transition from an older, highly academic and disciplined ornament to a powerful baroque modelling, which is the first real expression of a feeling for beauty in the Viking period.

The first innovations which appear in eighth-century style are unmistakable borrowings of classical forms, now derived from the Carolingian art of France. In Frankish art about Charlemagne's time we find a strong movement back to Roman forms, a tendency known as the Carolingian renascence; it was strongly influenced from Italy, and still more strongly by Byzantine art and artistic handcraft.[1] Undoubtedly the first Viking raids in western Europe made this art known in the north, and inspired a reformation of Scandinavian style. At first the character of the northern style was not seriously altered; we have the same designs as before, composed of band-formed animal figures, but now combined with newly-borrowed motives. We have remarkable examples of this kind of decoration among the older carvings of the Oseberg find. We depict here a panel from one of the sledges (Pl. 48b), where the lower portion is carved with animal ornament in the late Vendel style, while above this is inlaid a strongly geometrical moulding of true classical form. And in other pieces also this new current of classical taste can be perceived. A decorative post terminating in an animal head shows a very restrained limitation of decoration, which is foreign to all barbarous ornament. We often find purely geometrical decoration, applied especially in borders and listels, and some figures of classical form have made their way even into the animal ornamentation. We refer in particular to figures of birds represented in outline with outspread wings, which are often seen in Carolingian carved ivories.[2]

These examples are sufficient to show how Norse art at this time was reformed by contact with classical forms; and now again, as before in the migration style, westerly influences are

[1] A leading work on this and the succeeding styles is J. Brøndsted, *Early English Ornament* (London and Copenhagen, 1924); see p. 167 f. and p. 270 f. On some points we do not share Dr. Brøndsted's views, but space does not permit us to enter upon any detailed argument here.

[2] The wood-carvings from Oseberg are illustrated complete in *Osebergfundet*, vol. iii. On the Carolingian ivories see Adolph Goldschmidt, *Die Elfenbeinskulpturen aus der Zeit der karolingischen und sächsischen Kaiser, VIII–XI Jahrh.* (Berlin, 1914–22).

predominant: the Viking expeditions in the period around about 800 introduced a new movement into Norse style. The most important factors were not the individual motives which were adopted and assimilated by the prevailing Norse style; of far greater importance was a completely new form of decorative composition evoked by Carolingian models. This new form can best be studied in the Oseberg ship itself.

The stems of the ship are decorated in usual native style, an elegant design of interlacing animal figures and bands, a perfect example of the late Vendel style of *c*. 800, as this style was formed on Norse ground. But the other parts of the ship are decorated in an altogether different style. We find plump grotesque animal figures which are carved with strange clumsiness, a complete antithesis to the refined elaboration which distinguishes the Vendel style; but they are nevertheless effective and possessed of a peculiar power: especially characteristic is the modelling of the figures in high rounded relief. It is the modelling here that is of interest, while the design is negligible, in contrast with the Vendel style, in which the effect depends wholly on the lines of the artistically designed interlacing. In this new and powerful decoration on the Oseberg ship the decorative conception is the same as in the migration style, a similarity which is explained by the two styles being inspired by closely related models, comparatively late Roman art and Carolingian art. These two belong to the same world of form, and have the same powerful naturalistic treatment of relief.

The strange, extremely barbaric ornament which became prevalent at the beginning of the Viking period offers one of the most fiercely disputed problems in the history of our ancient art. Again an attempt has been made to find eastern sources for a definitely Scandinavian decoration.[1] But even before this attempt Sophus Müller had turned to the Carolingian renascence as a much closer source, and, so far as we can see, the larger pieces of decoration in the Oseberg find have greatly strengthened his theory. We can come to no other conclusion than that this ornament in Norway is due to borrowing from the Frankish Carolingian, and can rightly bear the name which Sophus Müller

---

[1] Hj. Appelgren-Kivalo, 'Om den så-k. karolingiska stilens ursprung', in *Opuscula archaeologica Oscari Montelio dicata* (Stockholm, 1913); Max Ebert, 'Der Goldring von Strobjehnen', *Praehistorische Zeitschrift*, iii (Berlin, 1903).

first gave it, the Scando-Carolingian style. There were in Carolingian art representations of lions which were the actual models that Scandinavian artists tried to imitate. At first the result was anything but successful; the animal figures are so clumsily made that they may almost be called monstrosities, and they are singularly ugly; but the power is there, and there is likewise the courage of the decorator who is striving towards an effect which he has neither the training nor the command of form to reach. This still extremely imperfect ornament now became a new ferment in Norse art and was the source of the first great flowering in the Viking period.

Already in the latest work from the Oseberg find this new development had arrived at maturity. On the sledge-runner and on decorative animal heads we have in its most developed form the luxuriant modelling in relief which was the ideal of the time, an overcrowded swarm of ornamental figures in which all the motives of the style are assembled and used together, but at the same time there is a constancy and certainty in the treatment that makes each piece a unified and finished work. He must have been a great artist who could execute such carvings as the latest examples on the Oseberg ship, one of those rare and great beings who can themselves create style for their time. These same carvings also show a quite inimitable fineness in technical execution (Pl. 49a).

Others of the late decorations from Oseberg do not stand on the same level as these, though they demand our full attention. The character of the style is uniform, an ornament modelled in high relief, of powerful grotesque effect; but the separate pieces have such individuality that they must have been the work of different artists, each of whom worked in his own personal mode. One carver has given special importance to details, and seeks his effect in a wealth of varying forms; another conveys a striking impression of completeness without troubling about accurate representation of individual animal figures. This last especially was a decorative artist of a high order.

The wood-carvings from the Oseberg find are the principal works of decorative art which are preserved in Scandinavia from the ninth century, and we accordingly call the respective phases of style in this century early and late *Oseberg style*. The small pieces, personal ornaments and similar metal objects, follow in their modest scale the same development that we perceive in the monumental wood-carving from Oseberg; we also see here an increasing predilection for powerfully modelled ornament combined with strangely distorted animal figures. The metal objects are similarly represented in the different Scandinavian lands, and they prove that the development of the style took the same course over the whole of Scandinavia. The same trend of style also prevails in the period immediately following, the close of the ninth century and the beginning of the tenth, though there are certain fine differences of form, sometimes even completely new motives introduced into the ornament; specially significant are the knots and bows of bands which are cut in strong relief, and a peculiar design of bands which we call a 'ring-chain', now produced in the north for the first time. This phase of style which follows immediately after the Oseberg style we have named the *Borre style*, after the royal graves at Borre.[1] This style is represented by part of the wood-carving from the Gokstad ship, especially in large decorative animal heads, which are very expressive, and have a peculiarly fierce and barbaric character which agrees remarkably with our notion of the Viking spirit (Pl. 49*b*). These heads adorned the gable peaks on the ship's tent, and were set there for the express purpose of frightening away evil spirits. The Borre style too is very richly represented in all Scandinavian lands in small metal pieces, cast silver or bronze with bright thick gilding.

The most striking aspect of stylistic history during the ninth century in the north is the extreme ferment of change in style and the violent conflict in tradition. Old and new forms are mixed; we see examples of definitely baroque and barbarous treatment of ornaments, and side by side with this goes a certain academic trend which works towards precision and clarity with purely geometrical decoration. Throughout the whole century there was, moreover, continual adoption of classical motives from western Europe. The many different elements could not be blended together; as a record of style this is a period of confusion. But in the first decade of the tenth century a new current is once again perceptible, a current which leads to a very decided revolution in style in the years round about 930.

---

[1] A. W. Brøgger, 'Borrefundet og vestfoldkongenes graver', *Videnskaps-selskapets Skrifter*, ii, Hist.-Filos. Klasse, no. 1 (Kristiania, 1916).

The new style then introduced is conventionally known as the *Jellinge style* from the Danish royal graves at Jellinge; it dominated the whole of the north until the end of the tenth century.

The Late Viking Style. This was a change in style just as far-reaching as that mentioned at the beginning of the ninth century, but the change is now the expression of a movement in the opposite direction. In the Jellinge style the interest in modelling and in plastic form again disappears, and once more composition and design are the important matters; the whole effect of the decoration is dependent on elegant lines and tasteful interlacing, a style which in many respects approaches the earlier forms of the seventh and eighth centuries, sometimes still showing definite reminiscences of the earlier style preserved by tradition through the ninth century (Pl. 50a). This revolution, like other changes in style, naturally has its psychological cause in the regular reactions of taste; but we can also trace certain foreign elements which have made themselves felt, and this time they come from Celtic decorations. In spite of all the close connexions between Scandinavia and the British Isles continuously from the end of the eighth century, Celtic art had not exerted any influence in the north in the ninth century, when Norse and Celtic taste were tending in diametrically opposite directions. But in the tenth century Norse taste swung round to the same ideals as had reached their most artistic form in Celtic decorative art. Ornament in Ireland was based still further back on traditions of the seventh century, on the early Christian interlacing bands combined with animal motives, joined with other elements derived from the ancient Celtic art of the early iron age. Irish decorations depend primarily on design; the illumination of manuscripts was the leading form of art, and forms which were actually evolved in the technique of coloured pen-work were also strongly prevalent in metal and stone work. Otherwise Irish handcraft stood at a very high level, especially the work in metal, which is excellent in form and execution alike. From the details it can be proved conclusively that this Irish art had an important influence on the formation of the Jellinge style.

The artistic basis of the Jellinge style was the design of lines on a surface; it is significant of this that the Jellinge style more

PLATE 51

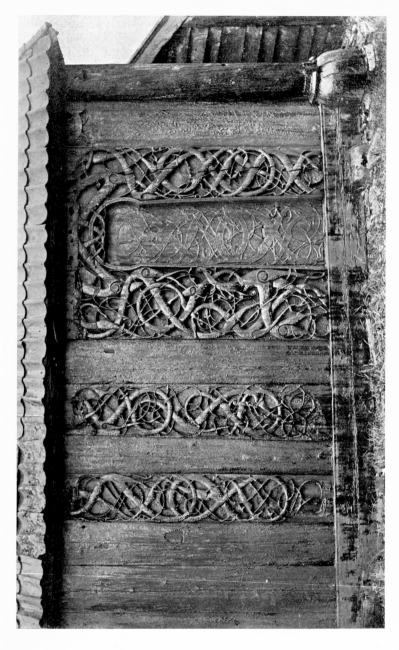

Church of Urnes, carving on north wall

its way in, the oriental. Particularly admirable examples of the Ringerike style are the symmetrical compositions of palmettes, which in the tendencies of their taste are strongly suggestive of the orient, and there are also friezes of palmettes in a form which must unmistakably derive from Arabian art. The tenth century was the very time of the liveliest intercourse with the Arabic world through Russia; decorated silver work in Arabic style is found often in Sweden, occasionally also in Norway. Apart from this we might well think of influence from decorative eastern designs such as were found in carpets and other textile fabrics. The oriental element in the Ringerike style is in any case certain enough. Connexions with the east were by no means limited to Sweden; we should remember the Norwegian kings Olaf Tryggvason and Olaf the Saint, who had both lived in Russia.

Thus in the Ringerike style the ancient animal ornament was thrust firmly into the background, even though tradition had unfalteringly preserved the motives of the Jellinge style. And the art of this period knew other depictions than the purely ornamental. The stone monuments from this time are in general rich in representation of figures, depictions of warriors, ships, and whole scenes from myth and legend; these are particularly distinctive on the Swedish runic stones, on the stones of Ringerike in Norway and on the crosses of Man. Among these pictures we often find a great monumental figure, resembling a lion most nearly (Pl. 50b), represented as a rule in combat with serpents. The Jellinge stone is the largest and most famous example (from c. 980). This is not pure decoration: it is representation with a certain narrative or symbolic content. The same is true of pictures of a large bird which also occur. Such representations were very popular; small brooches of bronze or silver were cast in these forms; we have them also on the ship's vane from the church at Heggen near Modum, which is the most magnificent piece of metal-work we have from the period; and above all, these forms have their place on grave memorials, on the Jellinge stone and on other Danish stones, on the Vang stone in Valdres in Norway, on the stone from Saint Paul's in London and on Swedish runic stones. During the period of the Ringerike style these figures are distinct from ornament; they are independent pictures. Then they become unconsciously drawn into purely decorative treatment and are turned from figures into ornament.

In this arose the change in style which distinguishes the last brief flowering of a Norse animal ornament in the early Christian Middle Ages. This is the *Urnes style*, which takes its name from the chief monument in Norway, Urnes church. It is a style which may well have been an expression of a still living craving for animal form as ornament, a taste which was ancient in Norway, though created anew in the second half of the eleventh century without direct tradition from the ornamental animal forms of the Jellinge style. It is a rich style, refined and elegant, as it appears in monumental form on Urnes church (Pl. 51), on the remains of Hemse church in Gotland and on a large number of Swedish runic stones. The Urnes style falls in the main into the second half of the eleventh century. At this point we are brought into historical times, into the Christian Middle Ages, when the original Norse style is supplanted by the art of the Roman Church.

XVIII

SUBSISTENCE

THE oldest archaeological finds in the north reveal a people under the absolute necessity of seeking their subsistence in hunting and fishing. In the oldest Danish kitchen middens[1] remains have been found of a number of molluscs, especially oysters and other edible shell-fish, of fish and of wild animals, including many kinds that are now extinct in Denmark: black-cock, pelican, beaver, lynx, wildcat, wolf, bear, wild boar, elk. In the refuse heaps of the later stone age there is evidence of oxen, pigs, and sheep. As an example from the older stone age in Norway may be mentioned the find at Viste in Jæren in the southernmost part of the country. Here were found the remains of twenty-eight kinds of birds, among them the great awk (*Alca impennis*), now wholly extinct, seventeen kinds of mammals, including a large number of wild swine, whose name *jǫfurr* (the same word as OE. *eofor*, 'boar') is preserved only in poetic language as a designation for a chief; there were also eight kinds of fish, prominent among them cod and shell-fish, chiefly oysters. As in Denmark the dog was the only domestic animal; that it was slaughtered and eaten is shown by the marks of cuts on the bones. In a refuse heap of the later stone age at Ruskenesset (see p. 86), on the west coast of Norway, remains were found of no fewer than sixty-six kinds of animals, of which seventeen were evertebrates. The animals of which there were the greatest number were the hart, which in Norway belongs essentially to the coastal districts, and the seal, an indication that this was a hunting-place used only in autumn and spring, when the slaughtered animals were dried or salted. Among the shell-bearing creatures snails and crabs preponderated. In Sweden too are found similar refuse heaps containing remains of domesticated animals, elk, roe, hart, and others, including fish from the lakes. The hare, it is worth noting, was never eaten.

Of fishing tackle from the stone age hooks of bone and flint have been found, some small ones for fishing from the shore,

---

[1] Detailed descriptions of the sites are given in Chapter IV, pp. 35 ff.

some larger for fishing at sea. From the early stone age are preserved bone harpoons, forked spears, and arrows for shooting fish. The great cod fisheries of Lofoten in the north of Norway, of which mention is made in *Egils saga* and other early sources, have undoubtedly been carried on from time immemorial, and from there—possibly already in the bronze age—large quantities of dried cod were exported to foreign countries. In Hálogaland these fisheries, together with the herring-fishing and whale-hunting (of which the Norseman Ohthere gave some account to King Alfred), afforded the chief means of subsistence to the population. The Swedish province Bohuslän, which in older times was part of Norway, also has old and rich herring fisheries.

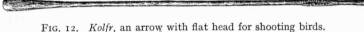

Fig. 12. *Kolfr*, an arrow with flat head for shooting birds.

These extensive annual herring and cod fisheries go back to a much earlier age, as is proved by the oldest Norwegian law-books and other early sources, which imply a definite organization of them.

Hunting of large animals, such as the bear and wild boar, was carried on with spears, especially the kind called *sviða* (see p. 387). After the spear, the bow and arrow were most used. For shooting birds a special arrow (the *kolfr*, see p. 391) with a flat head was employed; its nature is reflected in the expression *slá fugla* (literally 'strike down birds') of shooting birds. Hunting on skis in winter was specially favoured, as the tracks were then easiest to follow. The old hunting god Ull, called *veiðiáss* or *bogáss*, was also the god of skiing (*ǫnduráss*); it is related also of the goddess Skaði that she went on skis with a bow and shot animals. Clearly of primeval antiquity was the use of pits (*grǫf*) and of enclosing traps such as the *bjarnbáss* or *ulfshús*, of which some survivals can still be seen, and likewise snares (*gildra*) of various kinds. Hunting with hawks was introduced from the south in the migration period; skeletons of falcons are found in Norse graves from *c.* A.D. 500. This sport, however, was esteemed only in aristocratic society; though the export of trained hunting falcons from Norway and Iceland was of some importance. Regulations governing all kinds of hunting are set forth in the oldest Norwegian law-codes.

That even our Indo-European forefathers practised the arts of agriculture is evident from the numerous expressions for ploughing, sowing, and for kinds of corn that are descended from primeval times; ON. *arðr*, a simple type of plough, for example, is an Indo-European word which appears also in Latin *aratrum* and Greek ἄροτρον. Among the Scandinavians cultivation of the soil goes back to the later stone age: on the upper surface of earthenware vessels the impress of grains and ears of millet, barley, and wheat has been observed, and, further, a sickle with handle of wood and blade of flint has been dug up in Denmark. In the bronze age the same kinds of cereals are attested, but millet, being ill suited to the climate, disappeared entirely. To compensate for its loss oats now made their appearance in Denmark; in Norway they are first attested by the impressions on earthen vessels from the older iron age. Knowledge of rye, which in Denmark dates from the first century A.D., was perhaps introduced by the Rugians, when they entered Scandinavian regions, presumably before the beginning of our chronology; the very name of this tribe seems to mark them as cultivators of rye. Rogaland and Rygjafylki in the south-west of Norway derive their names from this people.

Barley was of the six-lined and four-lined varieties, which had no rival in the market until the appearance, in the Viking period, of the two-lined variety, known as *valbygg*, that is, barley from Valland, the north of France. The Norse word *bygg*, 'barley', means etymologically 'the cultivated (corn)', and so designates barley as the corn κατ' ἐξοχήν. Being the oldest kind of corn cultivated in the north, barley became the most important as a means of subsistence, and the corn most generally used for bread; in literature, wherever corn is named without any closer specification, barley is meant. A name for barley recorded only once, *barlak*, points to importation of barley from England in the Viking period; the word is borrowed from OE. *bærlic* (the ancestor of modern English *barley*). The first element of the name is found also in the poetic word ON. *barr*, an old special name for six-lined barley which is still preserved in the Norwegian dialect word *barlog*, 'malt water'.

Wheat was little cultivated, especially in Norway (where it

was first known in the migration period). The old Edda poem
Rígspula mentions wheaten bread as a food of chiefs. In
the Viking period, however, wheat was imported in no small
quantity from England (as is illustrated in *Egils saga* especially)
for the use of men of rank, and later also for ecclesiastical use.

Oats were undoubtedly cultivated originally for fodder: thus
their Norse name *hafri* is a derivative of *hafr*, 'goat', and
similarly both Old West Norse and Old Swedish have the name
hestakorn, 'horse-corn', for oats. In Old Norwegian literature
oats are mentioned only once, namely in the Edda poem
Hárbarðsljóð, where Thor says he has eaten herring and oats
(that is, oaten porridge or gruel) for breakfast, and it was
undoubtedly a common food in the west of Norway in the Viking
period. From the Celtic connexions of the Viking period came
the name *korki*; the Celtic source is illustrated by Gaelic *corc*,
Irish *coirc*. In Iceland, which was poor in corn, the wild oats
growing in the coastal parts, called in Norse *melr* or *hjalmr*
(*Elymus arenarius*) seem to have been used from early times as
a makeshift for breadcorn.

Rye seems to have reached Denmark first, and from there
came to the south of Sweden and finally to Norway, where the
word *rugr* is known from *c.* 1000. A common name for wheat
and rye was *hamalkyrni* meaning awnless corn for bread.

In the history of corn cultivation the development of the axe
is a landmark: with the general spread of the timber-axe it first
became possible to bring forested tracts under cultivation. The
first great period of clearing falls in the third and fourth centuries after Christ.

Beans (*baunir*) were cultivated in Norway in the migration
period, while the evidence for the cultivation of peas belongs
to the beginning of the historic period, when they appear
to have become widespread, except in Iceland. The way by
which they came to the north can be inferred from their name
ertr, which is borrowed from Old Saxon *erit*. Cabbages and
turnips were undoubtedly known in the Viking period, but
perhaps first became objects of cultivation at a later period in
monastic and communal village gardens. The names *kál*,
'cabbage', and *næpa*, 'turnip', were derived from OE. *cāwel*
and *næp*, but the Swedish and Danish name *rova*, *roe*, for the
turnip is presumably a Low German loanword. To a later

period also belongs the cultivation of the wild-growing plants called *laukr*, of which there are several kinds, as, for example, the *geirlaukr* (*Allium sativum*), the same name as English *garlic*, and angelica, called in Norse *hvǫnn* or *hvannjóli* (*Angelica arch-angelica*), which is mentioned in *Ólafs saga Tryggvasonar* as being on sale in the market-place at Nidaros. Wild apples are evidenced in the Danish and Swedish finds of the stone and bronze ages, but it is evident from the myth about Iðun's apples that other kinds were known at least in the Viking period. Hazel-nuts have been found in remains of meals from the stone age, but the walnut, together with its name *valhnot*, was derived from Valland (the north of France). Finally, among edible green plants may be mentioned *sǫl*, a kind of seaweed (*Fucus palmatus*) which in Viking times and later was used as a food, especially in Iceland.

Agriculture in ancient times was dependent on pasturage to a much greater degree than it now is; not only were draught animals necessary, but, above all, manure, even though it could be economized by letting some of the ground lie fallow. The stone age is characterized by a long transition from the more or less nomadic existence of a hunting people to a life in fixed habitations with a primitive agriculture and a stock of domestic animals. In the refuse heaps of the older stone age dogs are the only domestic animals found, but in the later stone age the cow, goat, sheep, and pig are added. The horse is attested from the final phase of the stone age; but at first horses appear in very small numbers. A rock carving of the bronze age in Bohuslän shows a man driving a plough with two horses.

Domestic fowls are absent from the Danish dwelling-sites of the bronze age, but they are found in the dwelling-sites and in graves of the older iron age. Their presence is probably due to the introduction of the classical culture of ducks, geese, and hens. It cannot be doubted that these birds were eaten, even though the people in many places still have a prejudice against such food, as they have against birds' flesh in general.

A description of the preparation of the food will also be the history of the origin and development of culinary art. At first the food was torn asunder and devoured raw. This was especi-ally general in the stone age when molluscs and shell-fish were eaten, but in the later refuse heaps they are found roasted in the embers and then crushed. Means of kindling fire had been known from the infancy of the human race. Fire-stones from the later stone age are known, flints (*tinna*), which when struck against iron-bearing pyrites produced sparks that were caught in tinder. This method is met with again in the Middle Ages in the stones worn in the belt by women, for use in the kitchen. Of still greater antiquity is the fire produced by friction (*bragðalseldr*), made by inserting a pointed stick of hard wood into softer wood and turning it rapidly; this method has been used in historic times at religious ceremonies to produce a manifestation of the holy flame. Much later still meat seems to have been eaten raw, being only made tender by beating. Mention is made in Norse legendary sources in several places of eating raw meat—in the second lay of Helgi Hundingsbani, for example. The process of roasting seems to be older than boiling, as the pottery also indicates. Usually the roasting was done by sticking the piece of meat on a spit and holding it over the fire: this is reflected in the etymology of ON. *steikja*, 'to roast', originally meaning 'to stick on a spit' and related to *stika*, 'rod'. Another primitive practice is denoted by the word *seyðir*, 'fire-pit', a hole in the ground in which the meat was placed, surrounded with hot coals and covered over with earth and stones. To this process apparently belong some remains of fire-plates found in Bornholm; and such fire-pits have also been found in excavations in Iceland. There they were possibly used for baking bread also.

Boiling was at first accomplished by placing red-hot stones in the water, where the sudden cooling caused them to split in pieces; this practice was kept up in Iceland all through the Middle Ages in the treatment of milk. Remains of rude vessels of burnt leather, which point to the boiling of foodstuffs, have been discovered in finds of the older stone age, while remains of boiling-stones from the same period have been found in Norwegian dwelling-sites. In historic times meat was usually boiled. This was certainly the method followed from ancient times in preparing the animals which had been sacrificed. The Old Norse name for sheep, *sauðr*, in the corresponding Gothic form *saups* has the sense 'sacrifice', and originally denoted the sheep boiled and eaten at the heathen sacrificial feast; the word is related to *sjóða*, 'to boil'.

Meat or fish which had to be kept for any length of time was wind-dried, smoked, or salted. Cod especially was frequently eaten dried, with butter; this is also reflected in the etymology of the name *þorskr*, 'cod', which etymologically means 'dried (fish)', and is related to *þurr*, 'dry'. Salt was obtained by boiling sea-water, or by burning seaweed, producing what was called *svartasalt*, 'black salt', or *búsalt*, 'salt for cattle'.

Milk, as a rule, was not consumed raw, but was either boiled or made into curds (*skyr*), while the whey (*mysa*) was drunk, or else buttermilk (*saup*), or milk mixed with water (*blanda*); or the whey might be boiled, producing *sýra*. Sometimes the milk was boiled until the hard curds were separated from it: this was *drafli*. In addition to cow's milk goat's milk also was used (as still in Norway), and sheep's milk (as still in Iceland). The use of butter (*smjǫr*) was in ancient times more general among the Scandinavians than in other Germanic lands, where it was regarded more as a luxury. It was made of sour cream, strongly salted and stored for some time. There are still reminiscences of the importance of butter in the old heathen cult in many place-names. In many places in Norway butter was the stand-ard of value, the unit being the *laupr smjǫrs*. The Old Norse cheese (*ostr*) was originally without doubt made of sour milk, and thus was different from the Roman *cāseus* (from which Eng-lish *cheese* and German *Käse* are derived), which was made of sweet milk coagulated by rennet. In making *ostr* the sour milk was allowed to ferment, after which the solid part was precipi-tated by heating and the whey was drawn off. In the eleventh century mention is made of a *jastostr*; in this the fermentation was brought about by yeast (*jǫstr*).

The inhabitants of the north seem to have learned much about the treatment of corn from foreign peoples, as may be seen from the several technical terms adopted from them. Thus ON. *kylna*, a drying room for corn and malt, was evidently borrowed from OE. *cylen* (modern English *kiln*), which was again a borrowing from Latin *culina*. ON. *þúst*, *súst*, 'flail', is Irish *súist*, which in its turn was an adoption of Latin *fustis*; and a borrowing of Irish *sorn* (from Latin *fornus*) has survived in Norwegian dialects as *sorn* and *torn*, a term for an apparatus used to dry corn. Beside this word both Norwegian and Swedish dialects have preserved in *tarr* 'a drying apparatus for corn and malt, made of thin boards' a genuine Norse word of great antiquity; it is cognate with German *Darre* and Greek ταρρός, ταρσός.

In the oldest times corn to be ground was placed in a shallowly concave stone and crushed there with a round stone. Historic times show a vastly improved form of the same apparatus (represented in the Oseberg find and elsewhere), which seems to have come from the south. The Edda poem *Grottasǫngr*, which relates how two giant women ground out gold for King Fróði, describes a fully-developed handmill. The bedstone in this type lies fixed in a hollowed piece of wood, the mill-stand (*lúðr*), while the grinding stone is turned upon it around a perpendicular axis by strength of hand; in this upper stone there was a round hole (*kvernarauga*) through which the corn was poured in. Water mills—in Old Norse sometimes named by the old name *kvern*, sometimes by the term *mylna* derived from Popular Latin *molina*—are mentioned in the Old Norwegian laws and were perhaps introduced as early as the Viking period. Windmills are mentioned in England as early as 833 (*Molendinum ventricium*), but not in the north until several centuries later.

Corn was probably eaten roasted and crushed before the people learned to grind it to meal and make bread. The oldest find of a loaf was in Östergötland and it belongs to about A.D. 400. This loaf is a charred object in the shape of a bun, and is made of coarsely ground barley meal with intermingled gravel. In the same place a loaf of coarsely ground field peas (*Pisum sativum*) and spruce bark was also found, dating from about A.D. 800. The oldest bread was baked in hot ashes, and this was later distinguished as *ǫskubakat brauð* (the same as the OE. *axbacen hláf* or *heorþbacen hláf*, 'subcinericius'); this method is still followed in some isolated places in Norway and Sweden. This bread was unleavened, but usually salted. How far back in time the use of a leavening agent goes is not known, but it must at least be much older than the use of yeast in making bread.

No less important than bread in the diet of the ancient Scandinavians was gruel (*grautr*, meaning etymologically 'the crushed or ground'), made of coarsely ground corn. It was made from all kinds of corn. Pliny had already referred to oaten gruel as a national institution of the Germans; according to the Edda poem *Hárbarðsljóð* Thor had it for breakfast, and it still keeps its dominant position, in Norway at least.

The Greek explorer Pytheas of Massilia, who in the time of Alexander the Great undertook a voyage on which he came to Thule (Norway), relates that beer and mead (or possibly a drink made from barley with honey added) were to be found there. In the Danish find at Juellinge, dating from about A.D. 200, there was discovered in two Roman bronze cauldrons a mass which chemical analysis proved to be the remains of a fermented drink made from barley, cranberries, and bog myrtle, and was thus a combination of beer and fruit-wine. The Old Norse word for beer, *ǫl* (the same word as English *ale*), seems to be related to Latin *alūmen*, so that the name must be derived from the addition of the bitter flavouring, hops and bog myrtle (*Myrica gale*), or, in Iceland, milfoil (*Achillea millefolia*), which gave the drink its strong taste. Another name was *bjórr*, which was used specifically of imported beer, and was presumably borrowed from OE. *bēor*. The drink found at Juellinge and in other Danish finds seems to come most accurately under the designation *lið*, a common Germanic word which often renders Greek σίκερα, and hence must have been a kind of fruit wine. The wine made from crowberries (*Empetrum nigrum*, ON. *krækiber*), mentioned once as an Icelandic makeshift for communion wine, does not seem to have been much known. A drink much older than these is mead, the name of which (ON. *mjǫðr*) is an Indo-European word for honey and for a drink made from honey. It was prepared by boiling the honey in water, and afterwards causing it to ferment; herbs too might be added, when it was called *grasaðr mjǫðr*. A high consumption of beer and mead is indicated towards the end of the heathen period by the extensive imports of hops and honey brought into Norway, according to the sagas. How far hops, which grow wild in Norway, were cultivated already in the Viking period is unknown. On the other hand it is probable that bee-culture was to be found at this period in Denmark and the south of Sweden. Imported wines, however, were even more highly esteemed than mead. Of Othin, the highest of the gods, it was said that he lived on wine alone; and wine was always included in the booty of the Vikings who made expeditions to Normandy in the ninth century.

If we look from the beginnings to the end of the developments in ways and means of subsistence which must have taken place in prehistoric times in the north, we find one essential difference: there had been a gradual transition from hunting and fishing to agriculture and pastoral husbandry as the most important means of winning sustenance. Whereas the soil had earlier been wholly free, it now became the common possession of the family, and cattle became the most important personal possession: this is well illustrated in the double meaning of ON. *fé* (and OE. *feoh*), 'cattle' and 'property'; of ON. *arfr*, 'ox' and 'inheritance', the same word as OE. *ierfe*, meaning both 'cattle' and 'heritage, property' and OHG. *erbi*, 'inheritance'. In diet a complete revolution was brought about: gruel and bread, milk and its products came into the first rank among foodstuffs. After this period the characteristic national diet becomes strongly conservative. This is natural enough, since housekeeping among this people, scattered over a wide area, has always been mainly dependent upon natural resources, and the supply of native foods never underwent any great change. Towards the end of the Middle Ages a modification was effected inasmuch as imported spices came to have a certain part in the diet, but it was not until the last two centuries that the old national institutions of the peasantry became enriched with new resources, with new means of subsistence and pleasure derived from the culture of the towns; probably the most important of these new resources were colonial produce and potatoes.

Our oldest forefathers in Scandinavia were undoubtedly omnivorous, though it is true that vegetable foods did not stand high in their esteem. The primitive people were not fastidious in their choice of food, as is proved by the kitchen middens of the stone age. In these various sorts of animals are found which are no longer regarded as edible in the north, such as sea-snails, beaver, and dog. The horse was eaten also, beyond all doubt, though many hold that this was not a practice among the heathen Germans except at sacrifices; the Christian law's strict prohibition of the eating of horse flesh—and the effects of this prohibition have retained their force up to the most recent times—points definitely in that direction. How far the inhabitants of the north were ever cannibal is a disputed question. Finds from the different prehistoric periods in all three Scandinavian lands, especially of human bones much cut and split, have raised the question, and there are in addition some indications in the oldest Norse literature of ancient cannibalism, especially of the eating of a slain enemy's heart and the drinking of his blood, in order to acquire the dead man's strength. Two cases of this sort are told of in the Edda poem *Fáfnismál*, but in *Atlakviða* the motive is revenge: Guðrún kills the sons she has borne to Atli and gives him their hearts to eat. It is not improbable that an echo of the custom of a former age is preserved in such legends.

The lack of means of communication in prehistoric times imposed on the separate districts a necessity of being self-supporting in all essentials, and on this account local ways of life came to show greater differences than in later times. This was true especially of Norway, where the population was thin and scattered, the distances great, and the roads difficult. In the northern districts fishing and gathering of sea-birds' eggs provided the principal means of subsistence: these were the more important because the corn harvests often failed. The western districts too, with their sparse areas of tillable soil, were no better able to support their population without the assistance of the sea. It was otherwise in the east, however, where agriculture, helped especially by the labour of thralls captured on Viking expeditions, advanced with gigantic strides, which can still be traced in the numerous farm-names ending in -ruð, 'clearing', and are first known in the period round about A.D. 1000.

It should not be supposed that there could be a wholly uniform diet for the whole of any local population. As far as one can look back in history, there has always been a certain differentiation of social rank; society even as early as the bronze age seems to have had an aristocratic trend, and possibly possessed a serf class also. The division into three classes is also very old in the Germanic world. Tacitus (in *Germania*, ch. 25) makes mention of *serui, ingenui*, and *nobiles*. The same classes are named among the Anglo-Saxons *þēow, ceorl, æþeling*, to which the terms *þræll, karl*, and *jarl* in the Edda poem *Rígsþula* correspond respectively. This poem also gives a graphic picture of the different standards of living among the chiefs, the free farmers, and the great mass of tenant farmers and thralls.

Ríg (the god Heimdall) comes in the way of his journeying to different homesteads, where he is entertained. Among the thralls he receives a coarse loaf, heavy and thick, mixed with bran, and meat soup in a bowl. Next he comes to the free farmer, where brimming dishes are set before him, boiled veal, and the best of food. Finally Ríg comes to the chiefs, where the table is covered with an embroidered linen cloth, and the entertainment consists of thin loaves of wheat, bacon, and roasted fowl, together with wine. Foreign influence has been at work here, as even the vocabulary shows: thus *kalkr*, 'beaker', and *skutill*, 'trencher-board', were undoubtedly introduced from England.

The suitability of the diet can be ascertained in some degree from the skeletons. Thus, while cases of dental decay appeared only rarely in the north from the stone age down to more modern times—this is to be ascribed above all to the hard bread and the absence of sugar—on the other hand the teeth had been greatly worn: gaps or defects in the sets were very frequent in the people of the iron age. This loss of teeth is thought to have been caused by scurvy, a disease whose very name (*skyrbjúgr*) appears for the first time in Old Norse literature, and is of Norse origin. The chief cause of this sickness, which is still prevalent in the north, is in the diet, the lack of vegetable food in combination with the paucity of fresh meat to relieve the constant consumption of dried and salted meat. Not until after the end of the Middle Ages is there any mention of a preventive, the plant *Cochlearea officinalis*, which was known in Norway as *skyrbjúgsgras*.

In the Viking period there were two principal meal times (*tvímælingr*): the one, *dǫgurðr*, about nine o'clock in the morning, the other, *nátturðr*, after the work of the day was finished. The old Germanic table-board was likewise a food-plate. It was intended for a single person: so Tacitus (*Germania*, ch. 22) *sua cuique mensa*. The table consisted of this wooden plate (the *bjóðr*, the same word as OE. *béod*, meaning originally 'serving board'; it is related to *bjóða*, 'to offer') placed upon a trestle. At the end of the meal the table was taken away. Such round table-boards are still preserved from the Viking period. Most food was eaten with the fingers, as forks were unknown until a much later date, and knives were used only to cut up the meat.

For gruel a spoon was used, named in ON. *spánn* or *spónn*, the same word as OE. *spōn*, meaning etymologically 'chip of wood'; of spoons there are specimens made of wood, bone, and horn from the later stone age. Gruel was served in a wooden trough (*grautartrog*), milk in bowls or in a kind of covered dish (*askr*), the side walls of which were made of pieces of wood curving together like the staves of a barrel. The usual drinking vessel, even for young infants, was the ox-horn (*dýrshorn*), and in the older iron age also the horn of the urox (*úrarhorn*); at times also metal horns are found, such as the golden horn of Gallehus, dating probably from about A.D. 400. The food was portioned out (an action denoted by the verbs *brytja, deila, skipta*) by the head of the house, or in large households by the steward (called in ON. *bryti*, villicus), who was, however, replaced later by a woman, the *matselja*. This portioning of the food developed into a complete economic system which was also applicable to provisioning for military and other purposes. It was also made the basis of reckoning food by the weight needed for given periods of time: thus *vikumatr*, 'food for a week', and *mána-ðarmatr*, 'food for a month', denoted fixed calculable amounts.

Concerning the apparatus of the kitchen, it may be remembered that water and milk could be boiled in wooden vessels by means of red-hot stones. In the Viking period vessels for boiling were generally of plates of metal welded together. Characteristic of Norway, and in some degree of Sweden, were the vessels of potstone or soapstone (called *tǫlgugrjót*, because it could be cut; cf. *talga, telgja*, 'to carve'); from the use of such material was derived the general name for a pot, *grýta* (cf. *grjót*, 'stone'). To hang the pot over the fire there was an iron handle fastened into two lugs on the pot, and it was hung on a hook which could be adjusted to bring the pot higher or lower. As another kitchen utensil the churn (*kjarni, kirna*) may be mentioned, a cylindrical wooden vessel in which the milk was churned with a dasher. For the brewing of beer several vessels were used, one in which the malt was mixed with constant stirring with warm water; next, a brewing cauldron in which the wort was boiled with hops, and finally a vessel for fermentation (*gilker*), in which yeast was added to the mixture.

XIX
DWELLINGS

AMONG the sources available for studying the history of dwellings in the north the archaeological evidences[1] must be recognized as documents of first importance. From the oldest periods, during the time of the Maglemose and kitchen-midden cultures, there is no trace of any house. On the dwelling-sites it is evident that the fire-places stood under the open sky, and for shelter from the weather we can assume with some probability that there were light rudely made roofs of green branches and leaves, or else simple structures of branches covered either with turf or, in winter, with snow. In Norway, however, even at this early stage of prehistory instances are known of men living in caves (as at Viste), or in sheltered places under rocks or cliffs (*Skibshelleren*),[2] a custom which continued throughout the stone age. But true dwelling-houses are first known from the late neolithic period. The stone-age house in Scandinavia was never more than a flimsy hut, made of upright rods inserted in wattle of twigs which was plastered with clay both inside and outside. The ground-plan is always round or approximately round. The oldest form has a wall slanting inward, so that the hut as a whole is conical in shape; but already in the stone age there appears a less simple structure with vertical walls and a separate roof. The diameter of the room varies from two to four metres. The fire-place is set just inside the entrance so that the smoke can escape through the doorway. The floor is level with the surrounding ground, or is at least at no considerable depth below it. In the north not a single example is known of this type of house where it can be said definitely that the interior room has been dug down below the surface of the ground.[3] This same structure con-

[1] A complete survey is given by Mårten Stenberger, *Öland under äldre jernåldern*, Antikvitets Akademien (Stockholm, 1933), p. 144. See also Walther Schulz, 'Das germanische Haus in vorgeschichtlicher Zeit', *Mannus-Bibliothek*, no. 11 (Würzburg, 1913).

[2] Johs. Bøe, 'Bopladsen i Skipshelleren', *Bergens Museums Skrifter*, no. 17 (Bergen, 1934).

[3] Stenberger, op. cit., pp. 144–5; Oscar Almgren, *Sveriges fasta fornlämningar*, 2nd ed. (Stockholm, 1923), pp. 13–14; Hans Kjær, *Vor Oldtids Mindes-*

tinues as the prevailing type in the north during the bronze age, but tends then to have an oval rather than round ground-plan. The classic example is provided by Professor Almgren's excavation of the hut at Boda in Uppland.[1] The room inside was a rounded oblong about 9·5 metres by 7 metres. The entrance was on a long side. The walls were of wattled branches plastered with clay. A bronze fibula dates the dwelling in the fourth phase of the bronze age. The type is excellently illustrated in the 'house-urns' mentioned above in connexion with graves of the late bronze age. These burial urns are of baked clay, and they are shaped as models of houses, sometimes of round ground-plan, sometimes oval. In some a construction of upright posts is indicated, bearing a conical roof with a smoke-vent at the top (Pl. 52a). In the oval forms the door is on a long side. Here then we find the bronze age linked directly with the tradition of the stone age. Yet there are a few sites of houses in Sweden with a long rectangular ground-plan that have been studied and also assigned to the bronze age.[2] No trace of a fire-place has been found in these houses, nor any refuse of daily life, and it has been inferred with some reason that these buildings were intended for the worship of the gods rather than for ordinary habitation. The dating, however, is not absolutely certain.

It is, in any case, in the iron age that a completely new type of building for habitation first appears. This is a long rectangular building of quite large dimensions (Pl. 52b). The length is generally from 10 to 30 metres, and the width varies correspondingly from 5 to 15 metres. But considerably larger houses are also found, up to 60 metres and more in length. The outer walls in Sweden and Norway are of stone and earth, built more or less regularly, but in Denmark they are made of grassy turves or of wattle plastered with clay. The constant characteristic feature of this type is that in the interior there are traces of two rows of detached wooden pillars, round tree-stocks which supported the roof. The structure must have been the same as that known in later times in the north, when each row of pillars supported a horizontal lengthwise course of beams, on which the roof rested.

merker (København, 1925), pp. 30–2 ; Shetelig, *Primitive Tider i Norge* (Bergen, 1922), pp. 202 and 209.

[1] *Fornvännen*, 1912.
[2] T. J. Arne, 'Hus från bronsåldern i Sverige', *Rig* (Stockholm, 1925).

This construction gave the house a very curious appearance, with its low walls surmounted by an enormous turf roof. In the interior the fire-place is found as a sunken hearth in the floor. Often a group of buildings lie close together, enclosing a central courtyard, and in Jutland whole villages of the early iron age are still in evidence. In fortunate conditions it is even possible to see that the buildings were surrounded by a cultivated stretch, and to trace fences, wells, and paths, and grave-mounds on the highest ground near the farmstead.

Several establishments of this type have been excavated in Jutland, and they are known in especially large numbers in Gotland and Öland, more sporadically in the rest of Sweden, but again in large numbers in the south-west of Norway.[1] The oldest known example was found in Jutland, and is assigned to the pre-Roman period some hundred years B.C. The houses in Gotland and Öland go back to the second century A.D., while those which have been investigated in Norway belong to the period from A.D. 400 onward. In the Viking period the same type of house was transported abroad to the new settlements, to the Orkneys and Hebrides, to Iceland and Greenland. This type has left traces even down to modern times both in Scandinavia and Scotland.[2]

From this summary account of the archaeological evidence we turn to the information gleaned from literature and etymology. The round or oval huts of wattle and clay which we have described in finds of the stone and bronze ages are also attested linguistically as the normal type of building among the Germanic peoples in primitive times. All the words for 'wall' in the Germanic languages have, etymologically, the ground-meaning 'plaited work'. Thus OE. *wāg* has both these senses, and 'to build a wall' is *windan wāg*, where *windan* means literally 'to

[1] Gudmund Hatt, 'To Bopladsfund fra ældre Jernalder', *Aarb. f. nord. Oldk.* (1928), p. 219; id., *Jernaldersbopladsen ved Ginderup i Thy*, Fra National-museets Arbejdsmark (København, 1935), and also *En Jernalders Hustomt i Troldtoft Vind Sogn* (Aarbøger, 1935), p. 47; John Nihlén and Gerda Boëthius, *Gotländske Gårdar och Byar under äldre järnåldern* (Stockholm, 1933); Mårten Stenberger, *Öland under äldre järnåldern* (1933); Jan Petersen, *Gamle gårdsan-legg i Rogaland*, Instituttet for Sammenlignende Kulturforskning, Serie B, xxiii (Oslo, 1933); Sigurd Grieg, *Jernaldershus på Lista*, same series, xxvii (Oslo, 1934).

[2] Stenberger, op. cit., p. 168; Aage Roussell, *Norse Building Customs in the Scottish Isles* (Copenhagen and London, 1934).

PLATE 52

a. Cinerary urn of the bronze age. After Montelius

b. Site of house, with remains of walls, of the migration period.
After Jan Petersen

wind'; compare also German *Wand* and *winden*, 'to wind'.
The Old Norse name for the door points to the same material:
ON. *hurð* is the same word as OHG. *hurd*, 'plaiting of branches';
compare also English *hurdle*.

Yet houses of timber were built already in primitive Germanic
times, as is shown by the common Germanic word 'timber'
(ON. *timbr*, OE. *timber*, OHG. *zimbar*), which originally and
etymologically meant 'building material'; it is cognate with
Greek δέμω, 'build', and Latin *domus*, 'house'. Remains of
houses built of timber or planks, however, are first known from
the iron age. On Öland and Gotland are found remains of
dwellings from the first centuries after Christ, as already
described. In the old Swedish town of Birka on the island of
Björkö have been found remains of dwellings of the Viking
period, some of the plastered wattle type, some of timber with
the joints stuffed with moss and clay. Of special interest are
the remains of a house from the early Viking period which have
been found at Augerum in Blekinge (Sweden). This house
was plastered with clay, oblong in ground-plan, with rounded
corners. In the middle of the floor lay a number of charred
pieces of wood from the hearth-fire. Between these and the walls
were the remains of two rows of posts which had supported the
roof. The entrance was from a gable-side, where columns had
supported an overhanging roof, an arrangement known elsewhere: indeed, from widely sundered places in the Indo-European area the projecting roof before the entrance is found; it
is held up by posts, and serves as a protection against the
weather.

With this house the picture which the sagas give of farmers'
dwellings corresponds in most features; but in the sagas the
usual material of the walls is timber, and the shape is perfectly
rectangular. There is also a closed built out structure, provided
with a door, before the main entrance. A name of great antiquity for this appears in ON. *ǫnd*, which is the same word as
Latin *antae*, 'the pillars on each side of the door'; compare also
Armenian *dr-and*, 'room in front of the door'. From this
arrangement some light is thrown on the common Germanic
word 'door', the original meaning of which was 'door-opening';
but the plural form (with singular meaning), as in Gothic
daúrons, ON. *dyrr*, *dyr*, requires explanation. The form was

originally dual (the dual ending being still apparent in the OE. form *duru*), referring, not to a double-leaved door, which was not known among the heathen Germanic peoples, but to the two door-ways of the entrance-room; both in Old Norse and in dialects of modern Norwegian the word *dyr* is used of the space between the outer door and the door of the chief room, that is, of the passage-way or lobby; compare also Greek θυρών, 'ante-room'. The word is thus valuable testimony of the great antiquity of this construction. In the Viking period the built-out vestibule had a rival in the balcony (*svalar*), open on three sides, which protected at least one side of the house. This roofed row of pillars is also to be found outside of Scandinavia: compare Gothic *ubizwa*, στόα, OHG. *obasa*, 'vestibulum' (a side-gallery supported by pillars), the same word as ON. *ups*, 'eaves', and modern English *eaves*.

Further, we find in dwellings of the saga period, just as in the iron-age houses, rows of pillars inside the large room. While in smaller houses the roofing rested on a ridge-beam which in turn was supported by a single row of pillars, in larger houses the roofing was usually supported by two rows of pillars; each row was connected above with a beam running the whole length of the roof, and cross-beams joined each pair of pillars. There was a break in the line of the roof between the two longitudinal beams, the ridge-beam resting with short supports on the cross-beams. No inner horizontal ceiling was found. The roof consisted of two coverings, an inner one of lathes, planks, reeds, or bark, and an outer one of turf. To prevent the turf from sliding off, a board was fastened at the lower edge of the roof. On the gable-sides the edge of the roof was similarly supplied with a board (*vindskið*) which was intended to give protection against the wind; this board was usually carved and its upper projections adorned with fantastic heads of animals.

The middle part of the dwelling was occupied by the flaming fire which was stretched out in a line parallel to the long walls; this was the *langeldr*. Since the name of the fire-place, *arinn*, also has the meaning 'elevation' it may be inferred that the fire-place was higher than the floor. Its framework was formed of thin upright flat stones (actually found in some of the ancient house-groups). The hearth-fire was always kept alight and was regarded as sacred; at sacrificial feasts horns filled with beer were carried around the fire, and in legal transfers of house and land, earth was taken from the four corners of the hearth. The fire-place in the kitchen (*eldhús*) had other names. No other illumination than the hearth-fire was needed. On the Gokstad ship, however, slabs of oak were found with a hole in the middle into which a resinous piece of wood was thrust to act as a torch. There are also two kinds of train-oil lamps (*kola*) known from the Viking period, both of which are open bowls, one with a ring to be hung on a post, the other with a long spiked shaft to be fastened into the floor.

Like the older house the farm-house of the Viking period had entrances from the gable-sides. The doors themselves (*hurð*) consisted in saga times of boards held together by cross-pieces. In the ground-sill or door-sill there was a groove (*gátt*) into which the door fitted when it was shut; as a result of this arrangement, which gave a firmer and more secure fastening, the door had to be lifted slightly when it was opened. The door was swung on a door-post, the lower end of which rested in a hole in the door-sill, while the upper end turned in a hole in the lintel or in a withe; the arrangement is comparable to the Roman door-pivots. The door usually swung inwards and was provided with a ring by which it could be raised. It was often supplied with a peep-hole, and sometimes an animal's head was fastened above it. Windows in the modern sense were unknown (glazed windows are first mentioned in Denmark in the year 1086), but there were openings in the wall and shuttered windows in the roof, which served to admit air and light into the hall and to let out the smoke. The smaller shuttered openings (*gluggr, vindauga*) were made in the wall or in the lower face of the roof, but the opening for smoke (*ljóri*) was placed by the ridge-beam. This latter opening could be closed by means of a pole and a piece of board (*speld*), or a frame covered over with transparent membrane (*skjár*).

The oldest and common Germanic name for the dwelling-house appears in ON. *salr* (= OE. *sele*), which in the poetic Edda is the constant and only name; it occurs also in many old place-names. Later, probably in the tenth century, the term *stofa* makes its appearance; in place-names it is found only in those of later origin. This name also is a genuine Germanic word (related to MLG. *stoven*, English *stew*), which originally signified 'steam-bath room' (compare OE. *stofa* and OHG. *stuba* in this sense) or else the fire-place peculiar to the steam-bath (cf. English *stove*). How *stofa* became the name of the Norse living-room is not clear. The *stofa* differed in its arrangement from the German *Stube*, which was heated by means of a stove, whereas the Norse *stofa* only gave up its flaming hearth-fire long after the Viking period. The new name can hardly have come from Germany, since MLG. *stove* does not seem to have been used of the living-room; on the other hand, several indications seem to point to an eastern origin: compare Slavonic *istuba*, borrowed from Germanic. The chief distinction between the *salr* and the *stofa* seems to have lain in the furnishing and use of the space on each side of the hearth. In the *salr* of the Edda the raised floor along the side wall is called the *flet*; it served during the day as a sitting-place and at night as a place for beds. It was usually floored with boards or covered with straw, at feasts with carpets. In the *stofa* the *pallr* corresponds to the *flet*; this name possibly came from Russia (Russian полъ *pol*, 'board, plank, bench'). The *pallr* from the first was only a sitting-place, and two or three steps led up to it. Common to the *salr* and the *stofa* (in its older form) was the house-owner's high-seat in the middle of the northern long bench. Its name, *ǫndvegi*, is derived from the two thick pillar-beams (*ǫndvegissúlur*) between which it is set: compare ON. *ǫnd*, 'porch', corresponding to Latin *antae*, 'pillars on each side of the door' (see above, p. 321). These pillars were adorned with carven representations of the gods and were regarded as holy. The Norwegian colonists emigrating to Iceland brought their high-seat pillars with them to their new homes.

The cause of the disappearance of the *salr* was no doubt that its functions became separated in two new rooms, the *stofa* and the *eldhús* (etymologically 'fire-room'). This latter word is not found in the Edda poems; the usage of the Edda reflects the conditions of the time when the cooking was done in the *salr*, as it was, according to *Hymiskviða*, in the hall of the giant. With the coming of the *stofa* the old *salr* seems to have been used as *eldhús*, that is, as a combined kitchen and sleeping-room. In the Norwegian laws of the Gulaþing *salhús* still occurs in the sense of *eldhús*; and in King Valdemar's Jutish laws both words are used in the same sense. Similarly in the *eldhús* we hear of a *flet* which belongs properly to the *salr*; the phrase *liggja í fleti*, 'lie on the *flet*', is used of an *eldhúsfífl* or half-wit who sits all day by the kitchen fire.

Another common Germanic name for a dwelling-house in addition to *salr* is *búr* (modern English *bower*). The *búr* was the only Old Norse house which had more than one story. The ground floor served as a storeroom for supplies of food, clothing, or tools. On the upper floor the housewife and the grown-up daughters lived by day, while at night it was the sleeping-room for the family, though usually only in the summer, as there was no fire-place in the *búr*. Around the upper story (*lopt*) went a half-open gallery (*loptsvalar*), which rested on the ends of projecting beams. A set of steps or a ladder led to the *lopt*, and another descended to the lower floor through an opening in the floor of the *lopt*, which was provided with a trap-door. In the old German house also a gallery is often found around the upper floor, sometimes called *loubia* (related to *lopt*), sometimes *soleri*, a name which points to a Roman prototype (Latin *solarium*).

The Germanic steam-bath had nothing to do with the Roman bath, which was dependent upon heated air. The Old Norse bath-house (*baðstofa*, identical in sense with OE. *stofa*) in fact corresponds rather nearly to the Slavonic type. The steam was produced by pouring water on a glowing stone stove, that is, a stove made of piled-up stones held together with clay; and in Old English too we find that *stānbæþ* and *stofbæþ* denote the same thing. A scaffolding (the *pallr*; cf. Russian полокъ *polok*, 'the sweating-bench in a steam bath', i.e. the uppermost step of the scaffolding) rising in several steps made it possible to move the body into a continually higher temperature. Lying on this scaffolding the bather slapped himself with branches. In saga times there was a bath-house in nearly every homestead. In Iceland bath-houses were also to be found built over hot-springs.

In every homestead there was a stable (*stallr*) and cow-byre (*féhús, fjós*), usually several of the latter, for the cattle, sheep, and goats; the pigs had to be content with a shed (*svínstí*), and the poultry presumably with a space in the cow-house. The byre for the larger animals was divided by two rows of posts into two spaces at the sides with stalls (*báss*) for the beasts, and a narrower space between which afforded drainage for the droppings, which were cleared out through a trap-door in the wall. A thrall had his sleeping-place in the byre on a board floor (*hjallr*) above the stalls. In Iceland horses and sheep ordinarily were free in open pasture all year; protection against bad weather was given by the *fjárborg*, a round sheep-house with dome-shaped roof.

The barn (*hlaða*) was not an absolute necessity. A roof (*hjalmr*) which could be adjusted higher or lower on a pole (*róða*) was sufficient to preserve the hay as well as the unthreshed corn. In general, however, each homestead had a barn (*heyhlaða*, *kornhlaða*), often of considerable size. The barn was divided by two rows of posts supporting the roof into deepened side-spaces (*golf*) and the threshing-place (*láfi*) in the middle, the floor of which was either clay stamped hard or a surface of boards. The threshing-floor was not always placed so that carts could be driven in; in Denmark and Sweden especially the unloading was often done through doors or other openings. Where there was no barn, the threshing-floor lay in the open.

In the later saga age, in the larger homesteads, especially in king's manors, there were still more buildings, separate tool and provision houses (*útibúr*) and also a privy, whose common Germanic name *gang* is really only an abstracted and elliptical term; compare ON. *ganga til garðs*, 'to go about one's needs'.

The buildings of a homestead never lay in haphazard confusion, but were arranged in two groups: dwelling-houses and outhouses each lay by themselves. To the former group belonged the *salr* (or *stofa*), *eldhús*, and *búr*, to which was often added the *dyngja* and usually the *baðstofa*. In the latter group were reckoned the *hlaða*, *fjós*, *stallr*, and *útibúr*. In addition there were various smaller buildings which lay outside the homestead proper, as the smithy (*smiðja*) and boat-house (*naust*). The arrangement of the two principal groups of buildings was dependent on the nature of the local settlement; in the village system the arrangement was quite different from that found in single homesteads. In the parts of Scandinavia occupied before the Viking age, namely Denmark, south Sweden, and the coastal regions of Norway, the village system prevailed, in which the parcels of cultivated land lay side by side in a medley, while woodland and pasture were undivided. The individual settlement was effected mainly in the Viking period, when great forests in the east of Norway and the south of Sweden were cleared. This difference in the form of the settlements in the different periods manifests itself in place-names: in the oldest stratum a personal name is never found as the first element, while in names originating in the Viking age this type becomes general.[1] In Sweden at the end of the heathen period a large part, perhaps the largest part, of the population lived in villages, and in Denmark as late as the thirteenth century the village-system greatly preponderated. In Norway, according to the laws of Gulaþing and Frostaþing, even after the Viking period a more or less complete community of field and pasture was the established organization of the land economy in the western and northern districts. In accordance with this organization in the west of Norway all buildings were gathered into a single group, in which the dwelling-houses formed one row and the outhouses another, which was separated from the first by a road. In the broader districts of east Norway, where the home-steads were mostly scattered, the buildings were so arranged that the dwelling-rooms were built around one courtyard and the outhouses around another. This double court we also find here and there in Sweden, especially in Öland and Gotland. It is otherwise in Denmark, where all the buildings belonging to one homestead formed a closed square around an inner court-yard. Iceland, where the settlement was the work of individuals, shows a peculiar development of its own, which brought together a joined complex of buildings without any inner court.[2]

The dwelling-house and the larger buildings in historic times were constructed of horizontal logs, unshaped, and rough-hewn, the projecting ends (*lapt*) of which crossed each other. In the lighter outhouses the walls were made of boards standing up-

---

[1] For a fuller account see Magnus Olsen, *Farms and Fanes of Ancient Norway* (Oslo, 1928), p. 29 f.

[2] The Icelandic complex houses do not appear until the eleventh century, and are therefore not treated fully here. The evidence of the sagas about Icelandic houses has been collected and studied by Valtýr Guðmundsson, *Privat-boligen på Island i Sagatiden* (København, 1889) ; the complex house is described and illustrated by Daniel Bruun, *Fortidsminder og Nutidshjem paa Island*, 2nd ed. (København, 1928). The complex house is also found in Greenland, but the Greenland houses more often show derivation from the Hebrides and Ireland: see Poul Nørlund, *Norse Ruins at Gardar*, Meddelelser om Grønland, vol. lxxvi (København, 1930), and cf. Roussell, *Norse Building Customs in the Scottish Isles* (Copenhagen and London, 1934).

right, their lower ends resting on the ground-sill, while at the upper ends they were held together by horizontal beams supported by posts, of which the four corner-posts were stouter than the others. The timber in Norway was usually fir, in Denmark spruce. In building the axe was the most important of the implements used, both the characteristic timber-axe (*viðarøx*) and the lighter axe with which the timbers were trimmed (*tǫlguøx*), as well as the axe with curved cutting-edge (*þexla*). Saws do not seem to have been of great importance. Probably wedges (*veggr* = OE. *wecg*) were used to split the timber into planks. There were several different forms of auger. Spoon-shaped augers are known from the find at Vimose in Denmark, and they are also found by the side of screw-augers in finds from the Viking period. The Old Norse names are *borr* (= OE. *bor*); *nafarr* (= OE. *nafugār*), meaning etymologically 'pointed iron for making wheel-naves'; and *þvari*, etymologically 'the turning tool'.

XX

COSTUME

NO remains of clothing from the stone age have been found. But as sheep first appear in the later part of this period, it must be assumed that before that time skins formed the only material for clothing. Moreover, pins have been found which seem to have been used for boring holes in skin so that threads could be drawn through. These threads may have been plant fibres: Danish archaeological finds show that in actual fact the making of threads and cords of this material (for use in fishing nets) was understood during the whole of the stone age; they may also have been animal sinews, or, most likely of all, of gut: the Old Norse and common Germanic name of twined thread, *garn* (the same word as English *yarn*), etymologically means 'gut' (for which the Old Norse word was *gǫrn*). Sewing needles were made of bone; animals' teeth and other roughly-worked objects of bone and amber served as ornaments.

Of the preparation of skins in this period little can be said with certainty. It is possible that the scrapers of flint and bone known from the older stone age were used to scrape the flesh from hides. To prevent the skin from shrivelling up, it was dipped in salt water, just as was usual in historical times. Probably the efficacy of rubbing grease into the skin to make it pliant was also understood, but the instrument (the *brák*) used in historical times, by which a much more thorough dressing was effected, must be of later origin. It is probable that the skin clothing of the stone age always had the hair left on it. The removal of the hair is in itself a very simple process, since it can be done by laying the skin in urine and then scraping off the hair when it has rotted. But this process has no known significance in actual practice except as a preparation for tanning, and this would imply a more advanced technique, like that derived later from Rome. The first trace of tanning in the north is in some remains of leather from the bronze age, found in Slesvig-Holstein. It is noteworthy that the method used in these remains is 'white tanning', that is, by means of alum; this has never been general in the north, where the prevailing usage has always been red tanning, chiefly with oak bark: hence ON. *barka*, 'to tan', derived from *bǫrkr*, 'bark'.

Although there is no trace of skin clothes in the graves of the bronze age that contain unburned bodies, there can be no doubt that, even apart from footwear, they were in common use. In general, this use of animals' skins for clothing has always been more highly developed in the north than among the southern Germans, partly because of the severe climate and the life on the sea, which made warm and waterproof clothing a necessity, and partly as a result of the easy accessibility of skins as material. In Old Norse literature mention is made of garments made from the skin of all kinds of domestic animals (though seldom of horse-hide), and wild animals both terrestrial (reindeer, bear, wolf, fox, lynx) and aquatic (seal, beaver, otter). The skin of the smaller sorts of animals, martin, cat, stoat, squirrel, was used for trimming and lining. A great many skins came from the Lapps of Finmark, and were exported still further to England already in the Viking period: such trade is mentioned in *Egils saga*, ch. 17, and elsewhere. The sheepskin played the most important part: where *skinn* is mentioned without any closer specification it is always the sheepskin that is meant. In the older period goatskins too must have been much used among the Germanic peoples, as is indicated by the etymology of two ancient names for a cloak: ON. *heðinn* (= OE. *heden*), which is undoubtedly related to *haðna*, 'young goat', and *hǫkull* (Gothic *hakuls*), which, with its derivative *hekla* (OE. *hæcele*), is naturally to be connected with OE. *hēcen*, 'young goat'.

The oldest finds of woollen clothes belong to the bronze age and were found well preserved in oak cists in grave-mounds of Jutland and Slesvig (see Chapter IX above). In a cist from Muldbjerg, Hind herred in Jutland a skeleton of a man was found together with the garments depicted in Pl. 21. These were a woollen cap, with a rounded crown, the outer side of which was adorned with projecting woollen threads all ending in knots. Such burled texture, produced by knotting the thread-ends on one side of the warp while the cloth was woven, has been characteristic of Scandinavian winter caps and mittens in later periods also. Further, there was a cloak, which, when spread out, was of half-round shape; it was a single piece of coarse woollen material. Then there was a kind of short skirt which was held

PLATE 53

a. Woman's woollen hair-net, bronze age. After Broholm
and Hald

b. Section of a woven shawl, bronze age. After Montelius

PLATE 54

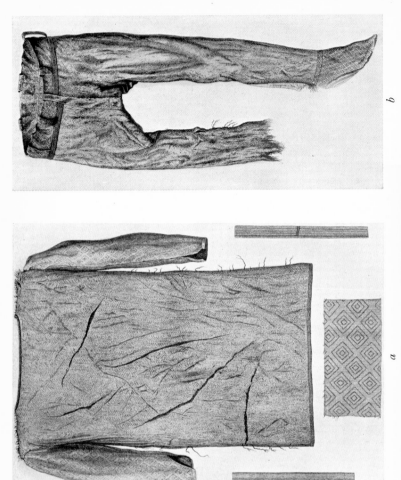

a. Kirtle and *b.* Trousers of wool, Roman period. After Engelhardt

together by a leather belt and on the shoulders by leather straps with bronze buttons. In this garment one may see the prototype of the Germanic *brók*, 'trousers': both from the etymology of the word (illustrated by OE. *brēc*, 'podex') and from the evidence of old glosses it can be seen that the word originally denoted a short covering for the hips; thus Old English has the glosses lumbare, *gyrdels*, *brēc*; femoralia, *brēc*; perizomata vel campestria vel succinctoria, *wǣdbrēc*, and in Old High German are the glosses lumbare, *bruoch*; cingulum lumborum, *bruocha*, *lumblo*. Finally, there belong to this set of clothes two joined pieces of woollen material rolled up together, forming a shawl ornamented with fringes. Some smaller pieces of woollen stuff and fragments of skin constitute the remains of the foot-covering.

A complete set of women's clothing was brought to light from a Danish barrow at Borum-Eshøi in the neighbourhood of Aarhus in north Jutland. The body was wrapped in a large mantle woven of coarse wool and cow-hair. On the head was a woollen net held in position by cords (Pl. 53*a*) and plaited in the characteristic manner known as *sprang* (see p. 333). The dress was divided into a short-sleeved jacket, ingeniously cut out from a single piece of material, and a long skirt. The structure of the weaving is seen in Pl. 53*b*, representing a piece of a shawl from a contemporary Swedish find. The material was mostly of naturally marked wool, but some of it also was artificially coloured. Another woman's costume was found more recently in a grave at Egtved near Kolding, and has been described above (p. 148). This costume has the same jacket as that from Borum-Eshøi, but the only other garment was a short skirt, consisting entirely of woollen fringes, reaching from the hips to a little below the knees. At the upper and lower edges of the skirt the fringes were bound with a woven border, and the whole piece is so long that it could go just twice round the waist. Between the jacket and skirt a belt was worn, fastened with a knot hanging loose in front, and decorated with a round ornamental plate of bronze (Pl. 16 and 22).

Upon the basis of the finds made in the Danish peat-bogs at Thorsbjærg and Nydam in south Jutland it has been thought possible to reconstruct a true picture of a Norse warrior of the first phase of the migration period. The clothes are of wool and show finer weaving than the bronze age; frequently a diamond-shaped pattern appears in the materials. The most important garments were a long-sleeved tunic or kirtle of wool (see Pl. 54*a*) and trousers which were firmly fastened around the waist with a strap, and at the lower ends were sewed onto short stockings (see Pl. 54*b*). The feet were covered by a kind of leather sandal with impressed ornamentation. On the shoulders hung a large square cloak of wool with long fringes at the lower end. In this costume influence of the south Germans is apparent, beyond all doubt. The long trousers, which closely resemble the ON. *leistabrœkr* when compared with the *brók* of the bronze age, are seen to represent something quite new, but they were well known to the south Germans, to the Lombards and Marco-manni, for example. The low sandals correspond in all respects to those used by the Romans, and were never in general popular use in the north. It seems a very likely hypothesis that here we have to do with a tribe which had immigrated from the south.

Traces of linen material are preserved from the bronze age in Denmark, where it is evident also that flax was cultivated at that period. In Swedish graves linen appears in the later iron age. Hemp was not cultivated among the Scandinavians in the archaeological period, but the nettle was gathered as a textile material.

The word 'wool' had its origin in the practice of plucking the wool from the sheep: the related Latin word *vellere*, 'to pluck', may be compared; this method has indeed been current in the north far down the ages, and is still sometimes employed in Iceland to-day. The clipping of the fleece can hardly be evidenced before the twelfth century, though it may well have been practised earlier: the shearing-knife (called *skæri* in Old Norse), consisting of two blades joined together by a spring band, is distinguished as the instrument ordinarily used for clipping sheep, and it is known from the Roman iron age. For the carding of the wool a comb-like instrument was used, called *ullkambr* (= OE. *wullcamb*,) corresponding to the Roman *pecten*. The wool was cleansed, just as in more modern times, by means of urine, the ammonia in it being effective in removing the greasy dirt; hence ON. *þvag, þvætti, þvál*, 'urine', are related to *þvá*, 'to wash'. The treatment of linen has been essentially the

same at all periods among all the Indo-European peoples, and
therefore needs no further discussion. Linen-heckles have been
found in Viking graves.

In the bronze age thread was spun on a hooked stick of the
same kind as is still used in certain districts of Sweden for making string and rope. In historical times the spinning instruments
were the same in the north as among the classical peoples in
ancient times, namely, the distaff (the rod which the wool or
hair was wound on), the spindle (a round rod inserted in a
circular disk of wood, stone, or burned leather, in the Viking
period, also of amber), and lastly a needle of bone, with which the
wool was kept in place. The distaff (*rokkr*) was so thin that it
could be easily bent when the thread was being spun from it;
during the process of spinning it was held in the left hand or
under the left arm, but might also be stuck under the belt or
fastened onto the bench. The spindle (*snælda*) had a hook at
the top which served to hold the thread firmly in position; when
the spinner with thumb and forefinger set the spindle in motion,
which received increased force and steadiness from the heavy
disk, the thread was spun. By the time the spindle reached the
floor, the spun thread had been wound round it, and the process
was repeated until the spindle was full, whereupon the ball of
thread was slipped off. Few examples of the spindle have been
preserved, but the whorl (*snáldr*), the disk used on it, appears
frequently in women's graves during the whole of the iron age.
As late as the eighteenth century spinning was still carried on
in many places in Norway by this method, which moreover had
the advantage that it could be practised while walking. In
Denmark the spindle is still used to make cord for fishing nets.
Already in prehistoric weaving yarn of several strands is
found.

The art of weaving, as is well known, was developed out of
the older plaiting. In the Swiss pile-dwellings of the neolithic
period plaited cloths have been found of such skilful workmanship that only textile experts could distinguish them from woven
materials. In transition between the two methods comes the
texture known as *sprang*, which is exemplified in the hair-net
mentioned above, p. 331, belonging to the bronze age. In the
later Middle Ages this style of textile work spread over the
whole of the north and is alive at the present day as an industry

in various parts of Norway, as also in Galicia and Croatia. The fabric is produced by simple plaiting of the threads without any other implements than a pair of needles (see Fig. 13). *Sprang* was sometimes used as a border, sometimes as the central piece of the fabric. The material was sometimes wool, sometimes silk.

The Old Norse weaving loom stood upright (whence its name *vefstaðr*), just as the oldest Indo-European loom did; compare

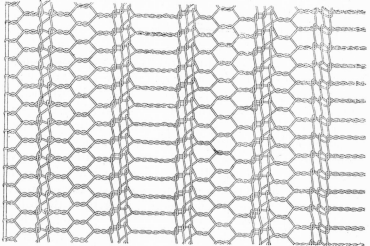

FIG. 13. The plaiting of *sprang. After Broholm and Hald.*

Greek ἱστός, 'loom', related to ἵστημι 'raise up, erect', and containing the same root as *staðr*. The Old Norse loom also agrees with the Homeric and early Roman looms in weaving from the top downwards. While several Old English and Old German glosses point to the later Roman type of upright loom in which the weaving was from the bottom up, among the Scandinavians the old type remained in use until the change to the horizontal loom; in Norway and in Iceland the old instrument disappeared only a hundred years ago, in the Faroes still later. Pl. 55 shows a Norwegian example.

During the weaving the loom was placed obliquely against a wall. The most important function in its working belonged to a shaft, called the *skapt* (in OE. *websceaft*, Latin *scāpus*), named from its resemblance to the shaft of a spear. Around this shaft

PLATE 55

Loom from Lyngen, North Norway

PLATE 56

a. The arrangement of *spjaldvefnaður*. As found in the Oseberg ship

b. Plates of *spjaldvefnaður*. After Brøgger

were fastened a series of small loops through which half of the vertical threads were drawn. Thus the warp was divided into two sets of threads, and, as the shaft was raised and lowered, first one set was brought uppermost, then the other. At each fresh movement a woof-thread was introduced into the middle space, the opening between the two sets of warp-threads. The stones hanging at the bottom were to keep the warp-threads taut; they are also found on the loom of classical antiquity. In Old Norse they bore the name of *klé*; they were usually of soap-stone, as is shown by the modern Norwegian name for soap-stone, *klebber*, descended from ON. *klé-berg*.

The fabric produced on such a loom was 'single-shaft'. The finds in graves show that by the side of such material the making of two-shaft, three-shaft, and still more complex fabrics was understood from ancient times. In addition to single-coloured materials, materials with patterns were also woven. Striped materials were made by inserting at intervals layers of different coloured threads. The diamond-shaped pattern from the older iron age, mentioned above, p. 332, was produced by manipula-tion with the fingers only, as the skein of coloured woof-threads was guided by them in each passage between the warp-threads.

In addition to the upright loom for larger fabrics, there were weaving machines for smaller pieces. The ON. *borði* was a long and narrow fabric which was used as a border for large wall tapestries, just as the OE. *borda* was a trimming for clothes. As an enlarged form of the West Germanic border-piece, the *borði* implies an enlarged version of the usual machine employed in Germany for the old border-weaving. In this machine the warp was stretched out on a horizontal frame, and the division of the threads was made by a vertical board with slits in it; a needle-shaped instrument was used as slay, and the woof was also set in with it. Nearly related to this is the border-loom which in Norway and Denmark now bears the name *spjeld*. This apparatus consists of a frame pierced with slits, and the warp-threads are alternately drawn through the slits between the ribs, and through the holes in the ribs; the opening for the woof-threads is made by the alternately rising and sinking frame. The *borðar* found in the Oseberg ship are fine pieces of average width about 25 cm., and whole scenes have been set into the weaving in coloured thread with the aid of a pointed instrument.

The Norse border used for trimming (and also as a hair-ribbon) was called *hlað*. This was produced by a large number of *spjǫld*, that is, small square cards of wood used in upright position; there were normally four holes (one in each corner), through which the warp-threads were passed (see Pl. 56). By this widely-known method of weaving a great variety of patterns were produced simply by varying the motion of the plates. This kind of border-weaving has been kept up in all the Scandinavian lands to the present day, in Iceland under the name of *spjaldvefnaður*. Cards of this sort are found in the Oseberg ship and elsewhere.

The treatment of the materials after they are woven has now to be considered. The fulling was usually done with the feet, and the mordant used for the process was either sea-water or urine. Textile material fulled by the Roman method with a kind of fuller's earth (*Creta fullonica*) seems to have first become generally known in the north in the Viking period, and then under the name borrowed from the Frisians, *klæði*. The method of fulling is reflected in the etymology: the word is related to OE. *clipe*, 'poultice, plaster'; similarly, ON. *dúkr*, 'cloth', which came from the same quarter, is related to OE. *dēcan*, 'to smear, plaster'. For detersion of the fabrics, sometimes urine was used, sometimes lye from ashes. Linen cloth was smoothed with glass or whalebone (of which specimens have been found in Viking graves), sometimes after first being rubbed with wax.

How old the dyeing of fabrics is in the north cannot be definitely stated. Dyed garments are found as early as the Thorsbjærg find, it is true, but they may have been imported. The berries of woad (*Isatis tinctoria*) found in the Oseberg ship show that dye materials were imported in the Viking period. But mention is made in the sagas of native dye-plants also, such as *jafni* (*Lycopodium alpinum*), producing a golden yellow dye, and a few varieties of moss (ON. *litmosi*) which yielded a reddish-brown or reddish-violet dye and in later times formed a commodity of export to England; moreover, the red dye from *maðra*, 'madder' (*Galium boreale*), is certainly very old. For a black dye iron-bearing mud from bogs was used, in skins as well as textile fabrics; this was called *sorta* in Old Norse.

In contradistinction to the foreign *klæði* the usual Scandinavian woollen material was called *vaðmál*, a name borrowed in

English as 'wadmal'. The etymological basis of this name is a certain measure (*mál*) of woven fabric (*váð*), with reference to the use of this measure of cloth as a standard of value and lawful unit of price. Various kinds of wadmal were distinguished, the coarser and finer, dyed and undyed, patterned, burled. In linen also there was a distinction made between the simpler native-woven kind and the imported. The coarser parts of linen which had been combed out (Danish *blaar*) were made use of from very early times, as may be inferred from the etymology of the word *blæja*, 'bedcover', derived from the base which appears in Danish *blaar* and in MHG. *blahe*, 'coarse linen material'. No trace of cotton fabric can be found in the north in the archaeo-logical period. The name which originally denoted cotton, *guðvefr* (the same word as OE. *godwebb*, and ultimately derived from Arabic *koton*, 'cotton'), was applied solely to a costly cloth of crimson or dark red colour. ON. *silki*, 'silk', like OE. *sioloc*, was borrowed from Slavonic. Richly ornamented silk fabrics were among the articles of the Oseberg find. The Edda poem *Rígspula* grades the clothing of the classes; the serf child is wrapped in coarse linen, the free child in fine linen, the noble child in silk. The hair of animals was also to some extent used in clothing. In ancient finds wool is found mixed with hart's hair in the cloth. A common Germanic word for a garment of unmixed hair is ON. *hæra* (OE. *hære*). Saint Olaf, according to his saga, wore one under his shirt, and Randalin is said to have presented Ragnar Loðbrók with a magical shirt of this sort. Several old Norwegian farm-names point to the cultivation of nettles, and in actual fact cloth made from nettles was used in older times both in Norway and Sweden. In prehistoric times belts were made from lime-bast: hence ON. *lindi*, 'belt', derived from *lind*, 'linden tree'.

The scattered references in the old sagas supply material which puts us in a position to reconstruct the ordinary popular costume of the Viking period, and shows that in the main it agrees with the ancient Germanic dress, in so far as this re-mained unaffected by Roman influences. The monk of Saint Gall (i. 34) describes the most important characteristics of Frankish dress thus: The shoes were provided with laces three ells long, which were wound crosswise round the legs (*fasciolǽ crurales*). No kirtle is mentioned; the body was covered by a

linen shirt which was gathered in by the sword-belt. A grey
or blue cloak was worn over the shoulders, four-cornered and
doubled, reaching down to the feet both in front and behind,
but barely covering the knees at the sides. The trousers were of
linen, sometimes long, sometimes short. The variations from
this account which can be observed in the everyday dress of the
lower classes in the north can be explained naturally from the
difference of climate, which required that the linen should be
replaced by woollens. The Norse farmer's costume is accordingly
characterized by the following garments: a square cloak, a
woollen shirt, short woollen trousers, and finally, leg-bands,
which were often an extension of the long shoe-laces.

While this costume remained unaltered in essentials during
the ages, the festive costume followed the higher classes' quest
for novelty. The power of fashion was as great in the north as
in the south, and in both quarters exerted its strongest influence
on the men: we hear several times in the sagas of a *sundrgǫrða-
maðr*, a man who is showy in his dress and introduces new
fashions. In no region of culture has there been a livelier interchange of customs than in matters of dress. This interchange
manifests itself in terminology, and its movements can be traced
by analysis of the words borrowed. If we leave aside the pieces
of clothing found in the Thorsbjærg bog, which may perhaps be
regarded as products of provincial Roman workshops, Frisian
modes seem to be those which were first imitated in the north.
The inhabitants of the north very early entered into commercial
relations with the Frisians living on the eastern shore of the
North Sea, the leading Germanic seafaring people before the
Viking period. The Frisians' most important commodity of
trade was woollen goods, and we have already (p. 336 above)
adduced evidence that their superior art of weaving—which
they had perhaps learned from their neighbours in Flanders,
where the Romans had introduced weavers—was known and
esteemed among the Scandinavians. From the Frisians the
inhabitants of the north probably came to know of the kirtle:
that its name (ON. *kyrtill*, OE. *cyrtel*) was originally a Frisian
word is demonstrated by the fact that the adjective *kurt, kort*
(from Latin *curtus*), from which it was derived, was found only
in Frisian. Frankish influence began somewhat later, and from
the ninth century onward brought Byzantine modes also to

the north. The names of the cloaks *møttull* and *kápa* are of
French origin, from OFr. *mantel* and *cape*. The oldest foreign
modes of which the sagas give direct evidence came from England; from there the skald Egill, among others, brought his fine
clothes; yet it was not until the reign of King Olaf the Quiet
(in the second half of the eleventh century) that English fashions
became general in Norway. From one or other of these last two
associations was derived the fashion of clothes of two or more
colours, that is, garments made up from differently coloured
pieces of material; this fashion was introduced at the end of the
Viking period, but from which of the two possible sources,
France or England, cannot readily be determined. There was
a close correspondence between the Old Norse and Old English
terminology of costume, but it is certain that this correspondence was not in the main due to the many direct connexions
with England; it goes back to a time when the Anglo-Saxons
were still living on the Continent. Finally it may be observed
that, in addition to the foreign influences just reviewed, relations with the Scandinavian colonies in Ireland and Scotland,
and intercourse with neighbouring peoples of Finnish and
Slavonic stock, also gave access to new cloth fabrics and new
forms of clothing.

We shall now examine the individual garments, beginning at
the lower end of the costume. The making of shoes for the
peasantry was in general carried on as a household industry.
As has already been mentioned, the awl (ON. *alr* = OE. *æl*)
is of primitive antiquity; with it the holes for sewing-threads
and for shoe-laces were punched. The needle for sewing shoes
was of bone with a long eye-hole in the middle; just such a
needle was used in Norway only a short time ago. The sewing
material (*seymi*) in the oldest period consisted of animal sinews,
later also of narrow thongs of skin (*seymipvengr*). The shoes were
made of untanned skin of various domestic animals or of reindeer; they had no distinct soles—the very word *sóli* is of foreign
origin—and they were sewed without the help of a last. They
were of different kinds, according as they were intended for use
in winter or in summer. If they were for winter use, the hair
was left on, and they were known as *húðskór*; if for summer use,
the hair was removed. A very old type of winter shoe, still in
use in Norway, was that called *fitskór* (from *fit*, 'foot of a skin'),

made from the skin on a cow's or reindeer's hind leg, where the sack-formed skin of the knee-joint provided a toe for the shoe. The shoes were then sewed on both sides of the instep right to the back, in such fashion that the animal's dewclaws came into position on each side of the heel, and prevented the shoes from slipping when on slippery ground. Both winter shoes and summer shoes might be provided with an additional piece of hairless skin pierced with holes for shoe-laces. Stockings were unknown, and foot and ankle were wound round with laps of cloth. Such wrappings for the feet were known also to the old Germans, but in the north they have been in popular use at all periods.

The oldest Norse trousers (*brók, brœkr*) consisted of a short skirt fastened together at the waist by a string. In the historical period the *brœkr* were short knee-breeches, and their waist-belt also served to confine the upper garments, after the ancient custom, whenever it was of special convenience to get their skirts out of the way by thrusting them down into the trousers; this action was described by the phrase *gyrða í brœkr*. Of greater dignity than these short trousers were the long trousers. These sometimes reached to the ankles, and sometimes were provided with feet which were sewed on; these latter were the *leistabrœkr*. Trousers of this kind are still used among seafaring folk in Iceland, and were found in the diocese of Bergen in the eighteenth century. Trousers were generally made of wadmal, though seafaring folk often wore trousers of skin. Long trousers of linen were sometimes worn by gentle folk as undergarments, sometimes as nightwear. The women as a rule do not seem to have worn any trousers.

When the trousers were of the old short kind the legs were covered in various ways. The poor wrapped them round after the ancient Germanic fashion with strips of cloth (*vefspjarrar, vindingar*), while those who were more comfortably situated used a kind of gaiter or legging of wadmal (*hosa*) which was fastened with a band or with the extended shoe-laces. This *hosa* was sometimes a square piece of cloth, and sometimes was sewed up like a sleeve. In the later part of the period the hose, like the long trousers, were provided with feet (*hosuleistr*). At the end of the period a kind of riding-hose, made of leather, appears, something between long stockings and long boots, and supplied the place of shoes as well. In women's dress the parallel

to the hose were the *sokkar* (probably introduced from England)
which were kept up by a band below the knee.

According to Tacitus (*Germania*, ch. 7) the Germans, women
as well as men, wore only a single garment under the mantle;
the poorer folk wore a garment of skin, and the wealthier a
close-fitting tunic of wool or linen, while the women of this class
wore a linen dress without sleeves and cut low at the breast.
There was a similar relation between the dress of men and women
in popular use among the heathen Scandinavians. The men
covered the upper body with a woollen garment which had
the form of a shirt (see Pl. 54). The old word *skyrta* has been
preserved in this application in Norway and Iceland down to
modern times. In contrast to this the woman's upper garment
(*serkr*) in the north was generally of linen, without sleeves and
cut low at the breast. With the appearance of the kirtle, as it
replaced the woollen shirt more and more, an undershirt of linen
came into use, a product of Roman culture which was at first
adopted only gradually by the lower classes of the Germanic
peoples. About the same time the custom arose among the
wealthier people of sleeping in shirt and underdrawers at night,
while the lower classes held to the old common Germanic custom
of lying naked in bed.

The ON. *kyrtill* was a closed garment, but it was always worn
over a shirt and not immediately over the body. It was provided
with sleeves and was drawn in above the hips by a belt. It was
shorter for men than for women, but the women when in the
house and in summer were customarily clad only in their linen,
that is, in the *serkr*. The kirtle was often divided into two parts,
an upper and a lower, which might be of different material, and
in women's costume they might be completely detached. In this
respect the woman's kirtle resembles the woman's dress known
from the bronze age (see Pl. 23), consisting of separate bodice
and skirt. The festive kirtle was the same for both men and
women; it was a splendid dress of costly material with various
adornments. According to *Egils saga* the poet Egill wore such
a kirtle, and according to *Rígspula* the lady of rank.

There were many kinds of mantles. The short cloak of the
bronze age mentioned above (Pl. 21), made of rough woollen
material with hanging fringes, is still spoken of in legendary sagas
under the name *loði* (the same word as OE. *lopa*). Moreover, an

open and sleeveless cloak or mantle hanging over the shoulders was common to all the ancient Germanic peoples. Tacitus (*Germania*, ch. 17) describes it as a *sagum*, that is, a short cloak consisting of a square piece of wadmal, the upper ends of which were fastened together over the breast. The Arabic writer Ibn Faḍlān, who gives a description of the 'Russians' (the Scandinavian Rus) in the years 921–2, stated that they did not wear kirtles, but carried a rough cloak which they threw over one shoulder, so that one arm remained free. The ON. *feldr*, worn only by men, was of the same character. In legal language *feldr* referred to a square skin garment sewed together from several sheepskins, recognized as a lawful medium of payment. The cloak of the same name, on the other hand, was usually doubled, and either the outer or the inner side was lined with wadmal. Like the cloak described by Faḍlān, the *feldr* was fastened with a clasp over the right shoulder, so that the right arm remained free. In addition to the generally worn *feldr*, there were various other forms of cloaks in the Viking period, as the *mǫttull* and *kápa* coming from the Franks, and further the *skikkja* (OE. *sciccels, sciccing*), *hekla* (OE. *hæcele*), *heðinn* (OE. *heden*), *olpa*. With these newer forms there was often a hood, sometimes as an independent article, sometimes attached to the cloak. The *stakkr* and *bjalfi* were varieties of sleeved cloak.

In winter the hands and the lower part of the arms had to be protected against the cold. A primitive method was to wrap them round with bands of cloth (*bandvetlingar*) corresponding to the leg-bands already mentioned. Woollen mittens (*vǫttr*) were in general use, but the much later skin gloves with fingers (*glófi* = OE. *glōfa*, or *hanzki*, from OLG. *handscō*) were proper to the upper classes.

The close-fitting round caps made of burled wool (see Pl. 21) known from the bronze age were also common in the Viking age. But often the cap (ON. *húfa* = OE. *hūfe*) was made of skin, and sometimes of linen or silk. More like the modern forms of hat was the *hǫttr* (OE. *hætt*), made of wadmal or felt and usually provided with a brim, sometimes also with a chin-strap. The *hǫttr* was taller than the *húfa* and often ended in a conical point. At the close of the Viking period various new forms of cap came into use, as the *kofri* and *kveif*, which both came from France; their names are derived from OFr. *covrechef* and *coif*. All these forms of head-gear were restricted to men, though the *kofri* is mentioned as worn by two witches.

Unmarried women wore their hair after the old fashion, hanging loose over the neck and shoulders, but married women had theirs fastened up at the back of the head or on the crown. From this arrangement of the hair various kinds of tall head-coverings were developed. In the old sagas the *faldr* (the word is recorded only in West Norse) was the housewife's only head-dress in everyday costume. It was of white linen and rose up in many folds into a conical shape. There was a fillet or a plate as foundation and on this the head-dress was made to stand more or less upright, according to its position. A variation called *krókfaldr* or *sveigr* had the top bent forward, in contrast with the usual kind standing straight up.

How far back in Germanic history the custom of veiling the face goes, we do not know. The bridal veil is certainly of high antiquity, since the common Germanic word 'wife' etymologically means 'veiling', and hence later 'veiled bride': compare ON. *vífinn*, *vífaðr*, 'veiled'. The bridal veil certainly covered the face, as can be seen in the Edda poem *Þrymskviða*, for example, which tells how Thor, in quest of his hammer, visited the giants disguised as a bride, with the veil hanging over his face. A very old word is *motr*, a name for a long bridal veil with embroidery of gold thread; its antiquity is attested by the existence of a Lithuanian cognate *muturis*, 'a white linen cloth which was fastened to the bride's head after the wedding'. The *motr* was worn together with the *faldr*, but there were other kinds of veils or linen coverings which were used without any other head-dress. Such was the *hǫfuðdúkr*, a long narrow band which was wound around the head and might be made to cover the face. The long series of names for the female head-linen, older (as *meðja*, *ísungr*, *ifingr*) as well as younger, shows how strongly fashion manifested itself in the adornment of the head. Men did not wear veils, but it is frequently related that they prevented themselves from being known by covering the face with a mask (*gríma*).

When the hair was worn long, it was usually held together by a hair ribbon or fillet. Similarly we find that in Greece a fillet was used by both men and women as long as the fashion of wearing the hair long prevailed. Women of the Viking period were not permitted to cut the hair short. Braiding of the hair is not mentioned in historical sagas; a hair-net was used instead, just as in the bronze age, and by the other Germans of the same period. Married women fastened the hair up by means of a band, but the unmarried women had long hanging hair which was held together by a fillet; the fillet was often adorned with gold thread, embroidered or inwoven or sewed on, and was then known as *gullhlað* or *gullband*. Men also might wear ornamented fillets (*gullhlað* or *silkihlað*), but only on festive occasions. Men of the Viking period in fact held to the same fashion of wearing the hair as the other Germanic peoples until the end of the tribal migrations: long locks fell down to the neck, while the fillet either bound the ends of the hair or was fastened around the middle of the forehead.

XXI

SEAFARING

THE art of rowing is as old as Indo-European speech; this much may be inferred from a group of words in the primitive language, formed on the base *ere, which denoted the action of rowing and nothing more. These words have descended into the later languages as ON. *róa*, 'to row', Latin *rēmus*, 'oar', Greek ἐρέτης, 'rower', Sanskrit *arítram*, 'oar', to choose only a few of them as examples. Perhaps the oldest manner of rowing was really paddling, but there is no early evidence of this method of propulsion in the north, though a double-bladed oar was found in a coracle excavated at Viborg in Jutland. There is conclusive proof of the existence of boats in the older stone age in the numerous finds of bones of sea-fish in refuse heaps of that period. The inhabitants of the north had extended their voyages from the coastal routes at least into the Baltic already in the later stone age; this is proved by various objects of antiquity, as, for example, the flint articles found on Bornholm, which has no flints of its own. A strong impetus was doubtless given to sea-voyaging in the bronze age by trade in bronze, gold, and amber. From this period we have in the rock-carvings the first rare evidences of the form and appearance of sea-going vessels. Characteristic of these pictures is the double prow, a device for protection in collisions of all kinds,[1] and the high stern. In many representations oars are to be seen, but mast and sail cannot be made out with certainty. The fact that the Old Norse word for mast (*viða*, *sigla*) is quite different from West Germanic *mast* (OE. *mæst*) is a strong argument against any assumption of such high antiquity for the mast. There are indeed several indications that the ships of the north were first equipped with mast and sail in the post-Christian era. Thus Tacitus, in *Germania*, chapter 44, says that the Swedes in his time had no sail on their boats; neither has the Nydam boat (from *c.* A.D. 300) any trace of a mast; no more have the ships on the oldest Gutnish carved stones, which are perhaps one or two centuries

---

[1] In the boat of spruce found at Nydam, which had a double prow, the lower one seems intended for piercing enemy ships.

later in date. The theory seems not improbable which assumes that the Frisians were the first among the Germans to learn the art of sailing from the Romans, under whose rule they came shortly before the birth of Christ, and in whose colonial army in Britain they served as mercenaries in the third century. The art of sailing and the word 'sail' (ON. *sigla*) itself must have come to the northern peoples from the Frisians, together with several other nautical terms, such as *bátr*, 'boat', *kuggr* (a type of merchant ship), *akkeri*, 'anchor', *bákn*, 'beacon-light'.

Probably the oldest form of boat in the north, as elsewhere, was a hollowed tree-trunk, a monoxylon. Several of the oldest Norse words for a boat point to this type: for example, ON. *nór*, related to modern Norwegian *no*, 'watering trough made of a hollowed tree-trunk'; *nǫkkvi*, cognate with Sanskrit *naga*, 'tree'; *beit*, related by vowel gradation to *biti*, 'beam'. All these names for a vessel had disappeared from ordinary colloquial language in historical times, but the same type has survived in several places in Norway and Sweden to the present day, as in the name *eikja*, meaning etymologically 'boat made from an oak-trunk'. Another primitive type of boat is the coracle, made of wickerwork covered with skin. In Old Norse literature the coracle is spoken of only as used by the aborigines of Greenland and Vínland (in some passages, at least, the kayak of the Eskimos is intended); moreover, the Old Norse name for the coracle, *keipull*, or *húðkeipr*, is undoubtedly of Celtic origin: the Welsh form is *ceubol*, borrowed in Old English as *cuopel*. But it seems arguable that such boats were also in use in the north in primitive times, on the ground of the nautical terms derived from the base **su*, the original meaning of which is found in Latin *suere*, 'to sew'; thus Old Norse has *súð*, 'the joining of planks on a clinker-built ship', *sýja* (verb), 'to join the planks in a ship', *sýja* (noun), 'coursing of planks in a ship's structure', *saumr*, 'nails (in a ship)'; and this base originally had reference to all kinds of skin-work, as may be seen, for example, in Latin *sutor*. The joining of planks with animal sinews, mentioned once or twice, is also reminiscent of the sewing of the hide. The folding ship of mythology, *Skíðblaðnir*, may also find its true explanation in this structure. The conclusion reached here from consideration of etymological evidence finds some support, too, in the oldest actual vessel preserved in northern Europe, the boat from Hjortspring bog on the island of Als in Slesvig, which can be dated in the earliest phase of the iron age, some hundred years before the beginning of Christian chronology. This find has been described in Chapter XI. It is a flat-bottomed boat with an interior length of about 10 metres, made of very wide thin boards of linden wood. The whole hull comprises a single broad floor-plank and two planks on each side. The planks are sewed together with slender cords in wide stitches, and the holes pierced for the stitching were afterwards caulked with resin. The inner framework of the boat is a system of slender ribs made from hazel branches, fastened to the planks by lashing them through broad projecting clamps attached to the inner side of the boards. It is characteristic of the primitive technique that every part is made, to the utmost possible extent, of un-divided pieces of wood. There is no trace of any arrangement for holding oars in position on the side of the boat, and it must accordingly have been paddled like a canoe. The rudder is shaped like a broad oar and fastened to the side. There is no indication that this boat had a sail. The construction of the prow and stern are especially characteristic, in that both floor-plank and the bulwarks project in the form of beaks inclined sharply upwards—the very shape that is so well known from the pictures of ships in rock-carvings of the bronze age.

In connexion with this question of the oldest mode of con-struction, we should take special note of the extraordinarily light structure of the Hjortspring boat, and of the characteristic method of joining all the parts with stitching and lashing. These features point clearly to the skin-boat as the original of the type.

The sources of our knowledge of the nautical science of the Norsemen during the migration period and the Viking age are of many kinds. In the first rank are the finds of ships, especially the Nydam ship (from the fourth century A.D.), the Kvalsund ship (from the sixth or seventh century), the Oseberg ship (c. 840), and the Gokstad ship (850–900), the first Danish, the other three Norwegian. Then there are representations of ships on the pictured stones of Gotland, and on old coins. Old Norse literature is also rich in material, the sagas, the laws, the poetry and the versified lists of nautical terms.[1] These terms are often

---

[1] The literary and philological evidence has been fully studied by Falk in *Altnordisches Seewesen* (Heidelberg, 1912).

fully understood only when compared with the modern senses; just as the type of ship which the archaeological finds have made known to us still survives in all essentials in the northern parts of Norway, in the western islands and in the Faroe Islands, so also do the names of the different parts of the ship. Again providing fruitful material for comparative study, a large number of nautical expressions occur in one or more of the other Germanic languages, which are in part the survival of an ancient common ancestry, and in part the result of a lively intercourse and exchange between the Germanic coastal tribes. This association was extended even to non-Germanic peoples. A number of maritime terms passed from Norse into the Lappish and Finnish languages. The Irish learned from the Norsemen all that pertained to navigation; their ancient manuscripts teem with nautical words from that source. The French derived from the Germans, and especially from the Scandinavians, terms for the points of the compass, for boat and ship, mast and keel. While the origin of these loanwords is explained through their Norse prototypes, their application frequently throws light on the use of the original Germanic word.

Life on Board Ship

Every ship had a captain (*stýrimaðr*), who was often the owner himself, though on warships he was appointed by the king. On certain occasions the crew would be gathered round the mast to receive the captain's communications and orders, or to decide questions of doubtful policy. Of the words of command a few have been preserved, as for example: *meir á stjórn*, 'more to starboard', *betr á bakborða*, 'more to port', *lát síga til*, 'let the ship drift' (i.e. cease rowing), *lát víkja*, 'turn the ship', *halt svá fram*, 'hold this course'. The crew had to do all the necessary work by turns, such as working the sail, tending the helm, rowing, bailing out, and keeping watch. The bailing, owing to the elasticity of the ship's structure, played an important part; in low-sided vessels it was carried on with buckets, which might be of considerable size, but in high-sided ships tubs were used which were drawn up on a spar; one man in the bailing-well saw to the filling and a second on deck to the emptying. Boats might also be emptied after being drawn up on land, by pulling out a plug in the bottom. The watches kept were of various kinds. In journeys along the coast and in the fjords it was necessary to look out specially for submerged rocks, and in time of war for the enemy, to keep informed of his movements. For this last purpose a man of ready tongue was usually chosen, and his place was at the prow.

Towards the close of the Viking period special ship's cooks were carried, but they functioned only when the ship was near land, as there was no fire-place on the ship itself. As a rule only gruel was cooked, and vessels used for this purpose have been found in the ships from Tune, Oseberg, and Gokstad. The usual fare on board ship was meal and butter, dried fish, and sometimes bread. The customary drink was water, which was stored in large casks, but not infrequently whey or beer was used. When provisions ran short, it was allowable to slaughter strange cattle; such slaughter was known as a *strandhǫgg*. No general ship's provisions were carried. Often, however, two or three sailors had a common store; this custom, known as *mǫtuneyti*, was recognized in marine law, and later the name of such mess-mates, *mǫtunautar*, became the general designation for a seaman in several languages, as in Dutch *matroos*, French *matelot*.

As a rule the men slept under the deck. In harbour they also slept under a canvas covering, which was sometimes spread over the whole deck, sometimes only over part of it. This awning was held in position by a pole which ran the whole length of the ship with its ends resting on two upright stanchions; where the long pole and the stanchions met, the long pole supported two boards from the side, which were fitted together upon it, intersecting at that point, while the lower ends of these boards fitted into a socket in the ship's gunwale (see Fig. 14);[1] thus the awning could be fastened across the ship over the deck. There are indications, too, that there were sometimes actual cabins. Thus the Old Norse term *vængi* answers to modern Norwegian *veng*, which in some places is used of a cabin at the back of the ship that can be set up and taken down at convenience; the word has also passed into Lappish. There are also doubtful traces of an erection for the captain. In warships the *viða* built behind the mast was used in later times both as a

---

[1] The illustration (Pl. 49*b*) represents the barge-boards found in the Gokstad ship. Both these and the portions of tent-structure (Fig. 14) found in the Oseberg ship, however, belong to tents used on land.

commander's bridge and as a 'castle' or tower of vantage. The name *viða*, which properly means 'mast', must be an abbreviated expression for *viðuhús*, which was borrowed in Irish as *idús*, 'castle'. That in the ancient period there was sometimes a *viðuhús* on ordinary merchant ships seems to be a fair inference

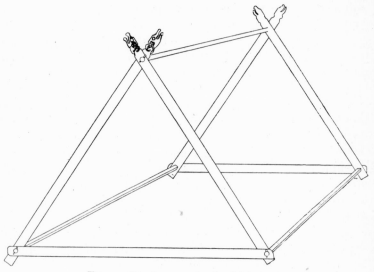

FIG. 14. The framework of a ship's tent.

from the frequent mention of the ship's ornament *húsasnotra*, which in modern Icelandic means 'ornament on the gable of a house'.

When a storm was approaching certain preparations were made immediately. When it was feared that the movement of the mast would force the timbers apart and make the ship leak, the mast was taken down or cut shorter. On large and heavily laden merchant ships boards were placed on the sides above the bulwarks, called *vígi* (related to Dutch *weger, weiger*, French *vaigre*) or *víggyrðill*. When this term is used in connexion with war-ships, it denotes a strong breastwork, and the boards intended for protection against the waves then have the name *hlýða* (cf. OE. *hlīewþ*, 'protection'). Since the comparatively loosely joined planks had to withstand great stress from violent rolling, sometimes the stays known as *þvergyrðingar* were used;

these were ropes thrown across the middle of the ship, drawn round under the keel and tightened by means of spars of wood.

The art of navigation was obviously in a primitive stage. In journeys along the coast or in the fjords directions were ascertained from the natural landmarks, and there were also artificial harbour-beacons (*hafnarmark*). In each locality the member of the crew who was most experienced and best acquainted with the lie of the land acted as pilot (*leiðsǫgumaðr*). Strangely enough, the lead-line and sounding-rod (in OE. *sundline, sundgierd*) are never mentioned. When sailing on the open sea it was important for the voyagers to know the directions . The horizon was regarded as divided into eight equal portions (the *ættir*): four of the points between these divisions were the directions of north, south, east, and west, while the other points midway between these were named from their relation to the mainland: thus midway between north and east was *landnorðr*, since the land lies to the east of any ship sailing off Norway; similarly *útnorðr* was north-west (*út*- meaning 'out to sea'). Even the Norwegians who emigrated to Iceland retained this terminology. To determine the directions there was no other means than observation of the sun and stars. Like other Germanic peoples the Norsemen steered by the Pole Star, but its usual Old Norse name, *leiðarstjarna* (literally 'way-star', the same formation as English *lodestar*) was comparatively late in making its appearance. In summer navigators were wholly dependent on the sun, and when it was hidden for any considerable length of time they could only steer by fortune and chance. In this way they sometimes went astray off their course: this accident was known as *hafvilla*. The standard measure of distance was the *vika sjávar* (from *vika*, 'change', 'spell', in this application 'spell of rowing'), which seems to have been about 10 kilometres. The longer distances were described in *dœgr-sigling*, 'half-day's sail', the *dœgr* being twelve hours. Thus the distance from the promontory Stad in Norway to the Horn in the east of Iceland was given as seven *dœgr-sigling*, which implies an average speed of more than 1·6 geographical miles an hour. In other instances voyages are described of two to three geographical miles an hour. That this speed is not exaggerated was proved by the experiment made with a copy of the Gokstad ship which was sent from Norway to America in 1893.

The voyagers of old time were dependent on the direction of the wind to a much greater degree than are modern sailing-ships. Since the square-sail was the only type of sail known, the ship could only sail before a breeze that fell directly or obliquely behind it. The navigator did not venture to tack or beat up into the wind. The difficulties involved in sailing along the coast through the numerous bends in the channel are indicated by the many Norwegian promontories bearing the name *Staðr*, meaning etymologically 'stop', i.e. a place where it was frequently necessary to wait because of the direction of the wind. The Norseman Ohthere, according to his own account to King Alfred, only knew how to sail before the wind, and he had to wait for the wind to change whenever his course was altered. Yet already in *Hávamál* we come upon terms for tacking or taking a zigzag course (*beita*), and elsewhere a contrivance to facilitate the shifting of the sail for a new tack is mentioned: it is a long pole or yard (*beitiáss*) attached to the lower side of the sail.

The circumstances just mentioned explain why the ancients would rather wait for days, however inconveniently, for clear weather and a favouring wind than sail out into the unknown. Spring and autumn were most favourable for long voyages, when the stars were visible in the heavens. From the beginning of October sea-voyaging ceased until the beginning of April. The long nights, the dark skies, and the storms forbade winter-voyaging. In autumn the vessels were drawn up by means of rollers and ropes over a slipway on to the shore and put under the shelter of a shed (*naust* or *hróf*), where they were repaired and freshly tarred. The Old Norwegian laws contain special regulations about the strictly limited right of such laying up of ships (*uppsát*), and about the help which the neighbouring farmers were bound to give in certain circumstances.

Where a promontory lay in the way of a direct course, the obstacle could often be overcome by dragging the smaller and lighter ships over the lowest point. The dangerous voyage around Jutland, for example, was avoided in this way, the ships being conveyed from the River Eider to the Sli estuary in the Baltic; this communication was at that time effected by means of a water-system which required haulage overland for only a short distance. In the same manner waterfalls and rapids were avoided in voyages on rivers. The place-name Drag, which is especially frequent in Norway, remains still as a memorial of the old practice. Voyagers on rivers also had recourse to another device. When the current was too strong for the vessel to be rowed against it, it was often pulled upstream from the banks by means of poles; the expression for this was *leiða skip*.

The Structure of Iron-Age Ships

While the Hjortspring boat from the earliest iron age still has the primitive character proper to bronze-age vessels, we have in the Nydam ship the first example of a large and strong vessel built entirely to meet the requirements of the new age. This ship came to light in 1863 in Professor Engelhardt's excavation of Nydam bog in south Jutland, and is now kept in Kiel Museum.[1] Thanks to skilful excavation and handling it is still preserved practically complete. The Nydam ship is a very large row-boat with fifteen pairs of oars, constructed entirely of oak, clinker-built, without external keel, pointed at both ends, with sharply projecting stems.[2] The length from stem to stem is 22·84 metres, the length of bulwark 21·38 metres, the maximum width 3·26 metres, and the depth, measured from the under surface of the keel-plank, 1·09 metres. Despite the impressive dimensions the method of building is extremely simple. The whole vessel consists of keel-plank, five planks on each side, the stem-posts, ribs, and thwarts. Moreover, every part is as far as possible made of single pieces: the keel-plank and the side-planks are each undivided pieces of wood from fore to aft, except the two uppermost strakes, the longest of the five, which have each a piece added forward. The stem-posts and ribs are similarly single pieces. Apparently it was also important to make the side-planks as wide as possible, in order to reduce the number of seams in the ship's sides to a minimum. This preference for heavy solid material is without doubt a primitive characteristic, but at the same time it sets on the ship a stamp of high quality. From the painstaking treatment of the wood and the resourceful craftsmanship of the whole construction it

---

[1] Haakon Shetelig and Fr. Johannessen, 'Das Nydamschiff', *Acta Archaeologica*, i (København, 1930).

[2] 'Stem' is used in the old sense in this chapter, referring to the timber at *either* end of the vessel, to which the ends of the side-planks were fastened.

A a

is evident that the Nydam ship provides a specimen of the best that the shipbuilding of the time could achieve. By means of the many other antiquities associated with the ship the find can be satisfactorily dated in the fourth century A.D.

Though it was a triumphant achievement for that age that men had reached the stage where they could build a sea-going vessel of such impressive dimensions, they were still confronted by many unsolved problems of construction; yet the advance was enormous, when we compare the smaller and lighter vessels of earlier times. The stem-posts are fastened firmly and solidly to the keel-plank, the bulwark-strake of massive dimensions and thickened at the upper edge effectively stiffens the structure longitudinally, the inner framework of ribs lashed to clamps on the side-planks, thwarts nailed to heavy clamps under the bulwarks, all together impart to the hull sufficient resisting strength against pressure from the sides. In addition there is the clinker structure with rivets of iron, an extraordinary advance beyond the sewing of the plank-seams found in the earlier age, and a wholly necessary development in building vessels of such heavy and extensive timbers as there are in the Nydam ship.

The weak point of the ship is its bottom. The keel-plank, in spite of its size, has not the strength required to withstand the pressure a ship of that length is subjected to when out at sea. The weakness is overcome by making the ship's sides rise comparatively steeply from the bottom to the bulwark. By this formation the pressure on the bottom is relieved and thrown in part on the sides, but there is a corresponding loss in stability. The Nydam ship must necessarily have carried ballast whenever it was in use. Through this necessity of avoiding pressure on the keel-plank the ship was also built disproportionately narrow in relation to its length; and so it is not specially elegant in shape, nor would it be easy to row.

The Nydam ship is interesting primarily as evidence of a stage in the development of shipbuilding; it shows an ambition which aims high, and at the same time numerous imperfections that have yet to be overcome. This can be seen in the rudder, for example, which is in transition from the steering oar to the fixed side-rudder, but is not yet satisfactorily attached to the side of the ship. Moreover, there is no possibility of using a sail, because the building of the time was unable to produce the special devices needed to bear and support the mast. The propulsive power in the Nydam ship was limited to the fifteen pairs of oars, pulled in rowlocks on the bulwarks, but these, too, so far as we can make out, were not happily designed, in consideration of the ship's height above the water.

These weaknesses which still vitiate Scandinavian shipbuilding in the fourth century A.D. are seen to be completely overcome in the ninth century, when the Gokstad and Oseberg ships were built. A more recent find has also made known an intermediate stage in this development. At Kvalsund in Møre were discovered remains of two vessels,[1] undoubtedly an offering of the same kind as the finds at Hjortspring, Nydam, and other sites in the Danish bogs. One of the boats at Kvalsund was quite small, having two pairs of oars, while the other was, by the standards of the period, a biggish vessel with ten oars on each side. They are constructed in the same fashion, but we shall confine the discussion here to the larger one, which has a special historical value when studied in comparison with the Nydam ship and the two Viking ships. The full length of this vessel was 18 metres, the maximum width 3·20 metres, the depth from the underside of the keel 0·885 metre. The whole construction of the hull follows the same principle as that of the Nydam ship. The ribs are single pieces which extend from one bulwark to the other, and they are fastened to clamps in the side-planks; in this ship, however, there is one clamp on the edge of each board. The keel is attached to the stem-posts by means of an overlapping joint fastened with wooden nails. The gunwale is formed by a thickening of the uppermost strake of planks. But other features show a more developed mode of construction; thus we find more and narrower strakes in the sides, namely, eight, though the eight do not reach the height of the five in the Nydam ship; and further, each strake consists of several pieces. Experience is beginning to overcome the primitive belief in whole-piece materials as the sole source of strength. We also perceive greater freedom of design, in that the planks above the water-line are fastened with wooden nails, while the lower planks are lashed to the ribs; here we see the beginning

---

[1] Haakon Shetelig and Fr. Johannessen, 'Kvalsundfundet og andre norske myrfund av fartøier', *Bergens Museums Skrifter*, Ny rekke, bind II, no. 2 (Bergen, 1929).

of a differentiation of the bottom and sides according to their function, a principle which was consistently turned to good account in the Viking age. Finally, the new system of fastening the rudder has been worked out completely, precisely in the form which we shall see on the Gokstad ship.

Perhaps the most interesting feature of the Kvalsund ship is the keel, which, as we have seen, was the weak point in the Nydam ship. In the Kvalsund ship the bottom ends in a solid plank 20 cm. wide, with clamps to support the ribs; but it is also provided with a keel on the under side, the whole consisting of a single piece of wood. This external keel is still of modest dimensions, 10 cm. high, 5 cm. thick, but is strong enough to allow the bottom a fuller, wider form, and so give the vessel greater stability. This is a very important advance in the development of Scandinavian shipbuilding, an advance which we shall see more fully established in the Viking ships. It is possible, too, that the Kvalsund ship carried sail; it would be strong enough for this, but among the pieces which survive there is none that gives any positive evidence on the point. It should be said, however, that the rudder seems to indicate that the ship was intended for sailing as well as rowing.

The find at Kvalsund afforded no certain indications of date. From the construction of the boats alone, however, we can infer that they belong to a later time than the Nydam ship, and are certainly much older than the Viking ships of the ninth century. The Kvalsund boats are more nearly related to the primitive construction; the Viking ships present a far more developed and serviceable structure.

We now pass on to description of the vessels of the Viking period, as we know them from archaeological and literary sources.

The Ship's Hull

The ship was built either under the open sky or under a roof (*hróf*) on a slope near the water, so that it could be launched easily down a slip-way. The building-slips (*bakkastokkar*) were raised above the ground, and they must have been solid beams, as is shown by Snorri's statement that those used for the building of the Long Serpent were still to be seen in his time, two hundred years later, so that the length of the keel could be reckoned from them. The material in the oldest period was mostly oak, which was always used for the keel. In the Viking period a variety of woods was used, but fir most frequently. The parts which were carved were often of beech, the spars always of spruce. In Iceland there was no timber other than driftwood for shipbuilding; when it is related in one saga (*Svarfdæla saga*, chaps. 15 and 19) that a sea-going ship was built of native timber with a keel of oak, the accuracy of the statement may be doubted.

For the conception 'keel' the old Germanic languages had no word in common: English *keel*, German *Kiel*, French *quille*, &c., were derived from ON. *kjǫlr*. Probably the oldest vessels had no independent keel, but, like the Nydam ship, had the bottom plank made thin at the edges. The after end of the keel was called the *hæll*, meaning etymologically 'heel'; from this word English *heel* (in the nautical sense) was derived, together with the verb *to heel*.

Like the keel the outermost timber at the prow and stern (the stem-post)—made, like the keel, of oak—was sharpened towards the outer edge, while at the inner edge there were grooves which the planking of the sides fitted into. The old ships were remarkable for their high stems, which were often adorned with carvings, and not infrequently carried over from an old vessel to a new. Pl. 57 shows the stem of the Oseberg ship richly carved with animal designs. On large ships both stems, prow, and stern usually consisted of three pieces, *undirhlutr* (below the surface of the water), *barð*, and *stál*, of which the last was an upright beam surmounted by the figure-head. On some warships the *barð* was covered with iron as a protection against collisions of various kinds; thus King Knút's dragon-ship was provided with *aerata rostra*. Such a ship was called *járnbarði* or *barði*; and the name was borrowed in Old English, appearing in the glosses: navis rostrata, *barda*, *barþa*. In smaller vessels the stem was either undivided or consisted of two pieces. The top piece as a rule was pointed and curved out from the vessel, a form which may still be seen in Faroese fishing-boats (see Fig. 15); this point in the Shetlands is called the *horn*, with which the Old English terms *hornscip*, *hyrned cēol*, 'beaked ship', are comparable. The Oseberg ship had the top piece carved in a whorl like that of a snailshell, as also had

the ships of several of the Gutnish pictured stones (see Pl. 58);
this form of figure-head is also the basis of the ON. term *hringr*
for a ship, of the name of the god Baldr's ship *Hringhorni*, and
of OE. *hringedstefna*, *hringnaca*, 'ship'. A peculiarity of the
whorl on the Oseberg ship is that it is finished off with a serpent's
head (see Pl. 57); thus we have in this ship something between
a ring-ship and a dragon-ship.

Of primeval antiquity is the custom of fastening figures,
especially figures of animals' heads, to the stems of the ship.
Swedish and Danish carvings on stones show an animal head

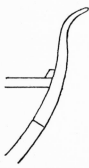

projecting from both prow and stern. The
dragon-ship was always, the *skeið* usually, and
the large merchant-ship often, of this type,
which was called *hǫfðaskip* or *hǫfuðskip*. The
most frequent ornament of the prow was the
carved and often gilded dragon's head with
gaping mouth, and it was this head which
gave to a group of warships the name *dreki*,
'dragon-ship'; of this type the most famous
is King Ólaf Tryggvason's *Ormrinn Langi*, 'the
Long Serpent'. Very often both stems had one

FIG. 15. The stem
of a Faroese fishing-
boat. *After Falk.*

or more dragon's heads; sometimes only the
prow had this decoration, while the stern
ended in a curving point (*krókr*) or a dragon's

tail (*sporðr*). Less frequently heads of other animals are mentioned in Old Norse literature, such as the ox, bison, and the
legendary bird *gammr* (apparently a gryphon), and once a man's
head. Of Knút the Great's ship a Latin source (*Cnutonis Regis
Gesta*) relates that it had lions, dragons, oxen, and human
images at the prow. In two passages there is mention of an image
of Thor at the prow, which indicates that in heathen times ships
might be consecrated to a god, just as in later times to the
Virgin Mary or the Apostles, whose name the ship would bear.
Above the prow there was very often a gilded weathercock
(*veðrviti*, from which French *girouette* was derived).

On the inner side of the prow the Oseberg ship has two
beautifully carved cross-pieces, one of beech and the other of
oak. These splendid pieces are separated by a space, and they
extend across the whole width of the prow. The former bore the
name of *tingl*, and both together composed the *ennispænir* (from

PLATE 57

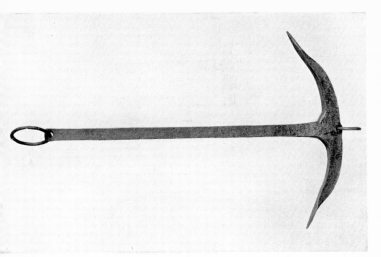

b. The anchor of the Oseberg ship

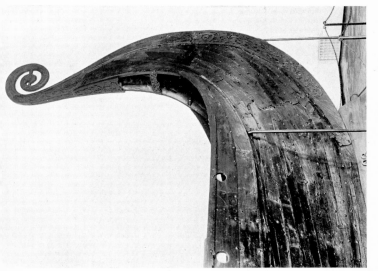

a. The stern of the Oseberg ship, terminating
in a serpent's head

PLATE 58

Picture of ship on sculptured stone from Stenkyrka, Gotland

enni, 'brow', and *spænir*, 'pieces of wood'), or *gullspænir*, as they are often called in the old literature, and under this name they were not restricted to the prow. On the Oseberg ship on both sides at each end a beautifully carved plank ran from the same position on the gunwale up to the stem, and was at first rather narrow, but broadened out towards the stem. It formed a continuation, as it were, of the abruptly ended *meginhúfr* (the main strake of planks, see below, p. 361). This carved plank is the *brandr*, properly meaning 'sword'; the same application is found in OE. *brandstæfn*, adj. 'having blade-shaped planks on the stem'. It was often gilded and was in general regarded as a treasure.

On the Nydam boat and on the ships of Oseberg and Gokstad, the ribs rested on cleats which projected from the planks of the ship's sides, and they are fastened to these cleats by bands (in the Oseberg ship of whalebone), which are drawn through a hole in each cleat and through a corresponding hole in the narrow underside of the ship's rib. This loose fastening of the ribs was an inheritance from an older age, and was not used on boats. It gave the hull greater elasticity, and is in character with the light structure of the ship and its thin covering of boards. The name of such a rib was *rǫng* (older *vrǫng*, meaning etymologically 'something curved'); but when, in the middle of the historical period, the ribs were usually made up of several parts, and not, as in the vessels just mentioned, of a single piece, the name *rǫng* became more or less restricted to the lowest part of the rib, that which lay across the keel and was most acutely curved (French *varangue* similarly has this meaning), while the complete ribs became known as *innviðir*, meaning properly 'interior beams'.

On the Oseberg and Gokstad ships the ribs are clenched with their curved upper ends upon the projecting inner edge of the heavy strake of planks called *meginhúfr* (see p. 361). The two ends of each rib were joined by a thick plank (*biti*) which braced the hull athwart. These transverse planks or deck-beams provided a foundation for the deck, acting as a support for the boards (*pilja*), which rested in a hollowed space cut in the surface of the deck-beams. On the upper side of the deck-beams at each end a bracket was fastened, one arm of which lay horizontal and was let into the deck-beam, while the upright arm acted as a brace for the two uppermost strakes of planks in the side of the ship. The deck-beams were supported by one or more upright stanchions (*snælda*, properly 'spindle'), which in the Oseberg and Gokstad ships have a hollow rounded space in which they gripped the rib, while the upper ends are mortised into the deck-beam (see Fig. 16). The boards of the deck on the Gokstad

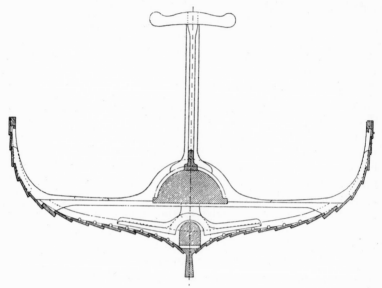

FIG. 16. Section of the Gokstad ship. *After Shetelig.*

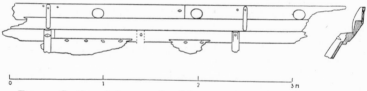

FIG. 17. Section of the gunwale of Gunnarshaug ship. *After Shetelig.*

ship are all loose, while a certain number of those on the Oseberg ship are fastened to the deck-beams with nails of yew. In the fore and after parts of the ship there was an elevated half-deck (the *stafnlok* and the *lypting*), both of which are preserved in the Oseberg ship. Merchant-ships and cargo-ships had an open hold for cargo amidships. In boats boards were laid on the bottom, where they formed a flat floor. There were only one or two cross-beams (*bitar*) in boats: their place was taken by rowing seats (*popta*).

The structure of the planking in the ship's sides was of two kinds. The clinker-built style was the more frequent, known as *skarsúð* (from *skǫr* 'step'; for *súð* see above, p. 346); each plank was placed with its lower horizontal edge fastened over the upper horizontal edge of the plank below. Rarer, but more highly esteemed, was the *fellisúð*, used in King Ólaf Tryggvason's Long Serpent, in which the rows of planks were mortised into each other in such a way that the sides of the ship present a smooth appearance. A mixture of the two methods may be seen in the remains of the ship found at Gunnarshaug in Norway (see Fig. 17). Another method had to be used if it was important that the ship's sides should be smooth both inside and outside; the joining of the planks was then practically that illustrated in Fig. 18. The means of joining were partly iron rivets, partly wooden pegs, the latter mainly on smaller vessels; the iron rivets had round heads and were riveted inside over a small square iron plate. For caulking between the planks cows' hair or wool loosely spun into thread (*síþráðr*) was used, being driven into the sutures with a hammer and painted over with tar. Usually the whole ship's hull was tarred. Warships, however, were very frequently painted above the water-line, sometimes completely, sometimes in part, and often with a variety of colours.

FIG. 18. Joining of planks in carvel-built ship. *After Falk.*

The number of strakes varied. The Nydam boat has five, the Oseberg ship twelve. They all have their own names, of which eight have been preserved in the old literature. The stoutest strake was the *meginhúfr*, to which the upper ends of the ribs were fastened and on which the brackets mentioned above (p. 359) rest. In the Oseberg and Gokstad ships this is the tenth strake from the keel. Where the gunwale begins to rise up to the stem, the *meginhúfr* is continued by the much thinner *brandr* from the point where the upper strakes disappear (see above, p. 359). The gunwale is formed in the Gokstad ship of a beam (*borðstokkr*) fastened to the inner side of the topmost strake, and shields were tied with cords of bast to a moulding with holes bored in it, fixed under the gunwale. The lighter built Oseberg ship has no beam at the gunwale, but only a moulding nailed to cleats which are attached to the outer side of the topmost strake. This moulding afforded a slight strengthening of the ship's gunwale, but it was also useful to hang shields on. This row of hanging shields, characteristic of certain types of ships, might thus be arranged in two ways, either turned outwards or inwards. It might pass round the whole ship, or only part of it; it was especially frequent to have only that part of the bulwarks supplied with shields which sloped up to the stems. On the Gokstad ship the shields cover the holes for the oars, and must therefore have been taken down when the ship was to be rowed; this arrangement, however, was by no means universal.

The Rigging

The mast consisted of a single stem of fir or spruce, and was usually tarred. It was sometimes placed in the middle of the ship (as in the Gokstad ship), sometimes a little farther forward (as in the Oseberg ship), and it was either set vertical or slanted back. The latter position was evidently more usual, as is shown by the common use of a forestay and the absence of any backstay. In boats the mast passed through a hole in one of the thwarts (*siglubiti*), and the foot of the mast stood on the bottom of the boat in a socket in the rib lying below the thwart. In larger vessels the mast-socket was in a heavy block (*kerling*, properly meaning 'old woman'; it is borrowed in English as *carling* and in French as *carlingue*), which rested on the keel and was fastened to at least two ribs, being fixed in a space cut into them. On the side of this keelson which was turned towards the prow there was a strong upright brace which clasped the lower part of the mast on three sides; its top was carried through the massive *siglubiti* and mortised into the mast-partner. This last was made of a single block of oak and rested on several thwart-beams. It had a convex formation round the mast, and the ship's deck was considerably raised up at that point. In front of the mast the partner was undivided, and it enclosed the mast on three sides; behind the mast there was an opening in it, in the form of a long cleft (whence its name *klofi*, related to *kljúfa*, 'to cleave') of the same width as the mast. When the mast was raised, the space between the arms of the partner was filled by a fitted block (*keili* = German *Mastenkeil*). To lower the mast there was no need to lift it out of the socket (which would often be impossible): the rounded shape of the socket and mast-end in the Oseberg and Gokstad ships shows that a partial lowering of the mast would be quite possible without lifting it at all. According to one reckoning the mast when resting on the after gallows-frame formed an angle of 40 degrees with the horizon. The operation was performed with the aid of the mast's tackle, without the use of a windlass. It is mentioned as carried out especially on warships in violent storm; in merchant-ships and cargo-ships the mast could not be lowered, but only removed entirely. This was always done when the ship was stowed away for the winter.

At the top of the mast was a kind of knob, which on the bigger vessels took the form of a square box. In this knob (*húnn*, meaning etymologically 'cube') was a hole (*húnbora*; in Old English called *húnþyrel*) through which the halyard ran, probably over a pulley. The *húnn* was often gilded, just as it was elsewhere outside the north. At the masthead there was sometimes a little pennon or a wind-vane (*flaug*).

A variety of rope-tackle was attached to the mast. From the top the forestay (*stag*, the same word as OE. *stæg*, 'stay') ran to the prow. From the sides the mast was stayed by the mainstays (*hǫfuðbenda*, borrowed in French as *hauban*) fastened to the gunwale, two or more on each side. These ropes were usually made of walrus skin or sealskin, which for this purpose was cut from the beast in a long spiral-shaped strip from the head to the tail, after which the strip was twisted round itself into a rope. Ohthere's narrative to King Alfred may be recalled, according to which the Lapps paid the Norsemen as tribute ship-ropes of such skin 30 metres long. On the Oseberg ship the rougher tackle was mainly of bast, the finer of hemp; on this ship were also found various kinds of spars and knots similar to those used in later times.

The sail-yards comprised the mast, the yard, and the spar used to spread the sail out. This last was used only for sailing close to the wind, and was accordingly named *beitiáss* (cf. *beita*, 'to sail near the wind'); it was made fast with a line (*ásdrengr*) to the foremost sail-sheet, and when it was not in use it was stowed (as was the yard) on a rack above the deck. The yard (*rá*, meaning etymologically 'pole') was a round stock of spruce, thickest in the middle. To hold the yard firmly to the mast a parrel (*rakki*, etymologically 'cord', from which French *raque* was derived) was used; this was either a collar of rope slung round the mast, or a knee-timber, as in the Oseberg ship. To hoist and lower the yard there was a halyard (*dragreip*), a rope fastened to the middle of the yard; it ran through an opening in the *húnn* and was made fast aft of the mast, which it supported as a kind of backstay. The sail was fastened to the yard by a rope (*ráband*, whence English *robbin*) which was passed through holes in the upper border of the sail. The hoisting was described as *draga segl*, or, when it was done with the help of a windlass, as *vinda segl* (French *guinder*). The windlass (*vindáss*, older *vinda*) was a round horizontal beam which was turned between two supports by a handle; in the Gokstad ship these supports are found in front of the mast. A related form of windlass seems to be denoted by the name *volt* (etymologically 'cylinder'), from which is derived French *virevau*, 'windlass'.

FIG. 19. Ship figured on a coin from Dorestad. *After Falk.*

In saga times the sail was ordinarily made of wadmal, but on a royal ship of linen. Sometimes it was made of variously coloured pieces, or else it was white with coloured stripes that crossed each other more or less at right angles, as can be seen in the representations of ships on the Gutnish stones (see Pl. 58) and on ancient coins (see Fig. 19). From the end of the period comes an account of a sail adorned with purple and embroidery of gold thread.

The sail was always a four-sided square-sail. On the smaller vessels it was comparatively narrow at the top and very wide at the bottom, which made the ship steady and secure against squalls. On large fast-sailing sea-ships on the other hand long yards appear. To the edges of the sail a bolt-rope (*lík*) was attached, which in ancient times was made of walrus hide or sealskin. In the Gokstad ship some peculiarly formed blocks of oak (see Fig. 20) were found, which are assumed to have been tackle-blocks used for the sail-sheets. Braces, by which the yard could be turned on its vertical axis, were not necessary, but had been in use from ancient times (as is shown by the Roman name *versoria*). Their Old Norse name is *aktaumr*, a derivative based on *aka segli*, 'to set the sail'. They stretched from the ends of the yard obliquely down to the after deck, and were used, like the *beitiáss*, to negotiate winds from the side. As a further aid to close-sailing there was the bowline (*bóg-lína*), a rope made fast at the fore end to the bow (*bógr*), while the other end was divided into two lines which were fastened to the foremost points of the sail's bolt-rope. By means of this rope, which is still used in Norway with a square-sail, the sail could be pulled tautly forward, which was of importance when it began to lose the wind. In addition to these devices for close-sailing there are traces of others which correspond to what is related of ancient Greek methods, and which explain how the old Norsemen could sail with the yard nearly parallel with the keel (*sigla alpveran byr*).

Sail was slackened always from the deck, and by two different methods. One was called *heflaskurör*; the second element of this term is related to the verb *skera*, 'draw a rope through a hole', and the first is *hefill*, 'lifting rope', that is, a vertical rope by which the sail was raised and furled to the yard, a process described as *hefla* or *hefla upp*. By loosing this rope (*láta síga* or *hleypa ór heflum*), which was done by means of a pole with a hook on it (*hefilskapt*), the reduced sail-surface was

FIG. 20. Tackle-blocks for the sail-sheets of the Gokstad ship. *After Falk.*

lengthened again. We must suppose that there were rows of holes in the sail at regular intervals, and the ropes attached to the sail's lower bolt-rope passed through these alternately on the fore side and back of the sail right up to the yard. When one pulled on these ropes, the sail was laid in horizontal folds. A parallel procedure is known also on ancient Greek vessels. Fig. 19 shows a sail furled in this way with a single hauling-rope. In strong winds this operation was impracticable, because of the danger of the wind pressure causing damage to the top of the mast. In such a case the sail-surface was reduced by lowering the yard (*lægja segl*, or impersonal *lægir segl*, or reflexive im-

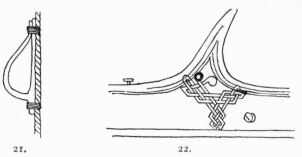

21.   22.

FIG. 21. The 'claw' of a ship's sail. *After Falk.*
FIG. 22. Rowlock (*keipr*) of a boat from Gokstad. *After Falk.*

personal *lægisk segl*), after which one or more reef was taken in the sail below (*svipta segli*). By 'reef' is meant the part or strip of sail-surface which lies between two horizontal rows of reefing ropes (*sviptingar*). In this operation the sail-sheets were unfastened, and the sail's new corners were made fast to the ship's sides; this was done by passing ropes through loops (*kló*, etymologically 'claw'; see Fig. 21) attached to the side bolt-ropes, and then making the ropes fast. This procedure is also mentioned as a device used in time of war, to deceive the enemy by an optical illusion, as the gradual lowering of the yard makes him believe that the pursued vessel has the start of him. In close-sailing the different terminology points to some distinct process, which is called *halsan* or *halsaskurðr*, that is, lowering of the foremost sail-sheet (*hals*).

Oars

The oars had a form similar to that usual now. They were planed smooth and usually tarred. In boats they were set when in use under a beak-shaped rowlock (called *keipr* or *hár*: see Fig. 22) which was plugged into the gunwale; a cord (*hamla*) was drawn through a hole in this *keipr*, and the oar fastened in its loop. A simpler device was the vertical pin (*þollr*) inserted into a horizontal base; or the oar might be laid between two such pins. On large vessels the oars were operated through holes (*húnbora*) in one of the upper strakes of planks. This strake, the *róðrahúfr*, was of marked stoutness and strength. In the Oseberg and Gokstad ships the holes for the oars were placed midway between the deck-beams, and they have a little cleft at the back which the oar-blade can be drawn through. When the oars were withdrawn, the oar-holes could be closed by small shutters attached to the inside (as in ancient Greek ships). The oar-holes were generally made along the whole length of the ship, but in merchant-ships and freight-vessels only fore and aft.

In boats the rowers sat on thwarts (*þopta* = OE. *þofte*). Very small boats had only one fixed plank, while the larger ones had several loose thwarts resting on a moulding which passed over the heads of the ribs. In vessels in which each oar was served by its own man, each rower sat on a short rowing-bench or on a ship's chest, so that there was free passage along the middle of the ship.

The Rudder

Originally the rudder (*stýri*) was an oar, as it is on the Nydam boat; this is reflected in OE. *stēorrōþor*, 'rudder' (properly 'steering-oar') as compared with *rōþor*, 'oar'. Even in historical times a loose steering-oar was used in smaller boats. The Germanic rudder, like the Greek, was fastened to the right side of the ship, which has accordingly the name *stjórnborði*, 'starboard', properly 'steering side'. The name *bakborði* for the port side is less clear, since the first element is *bak*, 'back', whereas at the usual rudder of the Middle Ages the steersman always faced the prow. Probably the name goes back to the time of steering-oars, which the steersman faced, with his back to the port side of the ship. The arrangement of the rudder in the Viking period is seen in Fig. 23, which is taken from the Gokstad ship. The rudder was fastened to the ship's side on an axle (*stjórnvið*, from *við*, 'withy', 'fastening'), which passed through a round hole in the rudder-blade and also through a wedge-shaped block (*varta*) nailed to the outside of the ship, which held the rudder at the proper distance from the ship; the axle then passed on farther through the side of the ship and one of the planks nailed to the inside at this point. The rudder was controlled by a shaft (*hjalm* or *hjalmvǫlr* = OE. *helma*) which extended from a square opening in the head of the rudder athwart over the gunwale. The *stjórnvið* had to possess some elasticity —on the Oseberg ship it is made of a strong piece of fir-root— to allow movements of the rudder on its vertical axis. It was

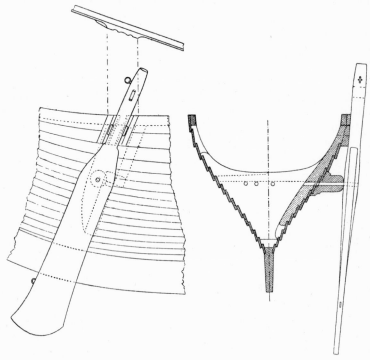

FIG. 23. The rudder of the Gokstad ship. *After Nicolaysen.*

in such movements that the rudder had its effect: if the steersman pushed the helm away from him, the rudder-blade turned its inner side forward and the ship swung to port; if he pulled the helm towards him the outer side of the blade came forward and the ship swung to starboard. The principle was thus the same as with the rudder fastened at the stern. The lower part of the rudder's neck was bound by a rope, which in the Gokstad ship passed through a block nailed to the side of the ship and on through the ship's side and through the extra planking which has been mentioned, nailed to the inside to strengthen the side here. This rope (*stýrihamla*) served to hold the rudder in correct position. When the rudder was to be raised, which was done by swinging the blade up around the *stýrivið* as centre, the *stýrihamla* had to be untied. Such raising of the rudder was resorted to in shallow water, where the bottom might be dangerous to it, since it extended deep down below the keel. The rudder was also raised when the ship was allowed to drift before the wind and waves, and most usually when it lay at anchor. For the purpose of raising the rudder there was a rope, the ends of which were fastened to rings, one at the top of the rudder-neck and one at the lower end of the blade (see the illustration). When the ship was under sail, this rope (*hjalpreip*, properly 'auxiliary rope') was drawn taut from the upper end, but when the rudder was raised it was pulled up from the lower end. It was proved that such a rudder was practical for this type of vessel, when the copy of the Gokstad ship in 1893 sailed across to America, often at a speed of ten to eleven knots.

The Anchor

To moor a vessel in the water a heavy stone was used in the oldest times, especially one with a hole in the middle, such as is still often used for boats. An anchor of this sort was called in Old Norse *íli*. Another sort was the *stjóri*, which may be roughly described as a wooden anchor with four flukes and stones fixed between them. The Scandinavians learned at an early period, however, to use the Roman iron anchor, and they adopted the Latin name at the same time. The anchor found in the Oseberg ship (Pl. 57*b*) shows a close similarity to the type used in the Mediterranean. The anchor-shaft attached—a necessary adjunct to the old anchors with two flukes—was of oak. Instead of the rigid eyes of the Mediterranean anchor this anchor has loose rings to accommodate the anchor-cable and the buoy-rope. The buoy-rope, together with the buoy attached, was called the *hnakkmiði*, composed of *hnakki*, 'anchor-shank', and a derivative of *mið*, 'mark', because of its function of showing the anchor's position. At times the rope also served another purpose: when the anchor was fixed firmly in the bottom, it could be freed by jerking at the *hnakkmiði*, and, if necessary, the anchor could be pulled up by it, as when the anchor-cable had broken. The anchor-cable was usually of walrus hide or seal-skin; it was called *svǫrðr*, from which Dutch *zwaartouw*, 'anchor-cable', was derived. The anchor, which was kept at the prow, was lifted by strength of hand. No windlass for this purpose is mentioned until after the Viking period. As the ancient anchors, like those on the Oseberg ship, were ordinarily comparatively small, one very often finds references to several anchors on one ship.

The Divisions of the Hull

Various divisions of the hull (*rúm*) were marked by the deck-beams (*bitar*). On the long-ships (war-ships) the following are mentioned: (1) *Lypting*, the poop, a raised deck in the after ship, where the chief and his nearest associates had their station, and the steersman had his seat. (2) *Fyrirrúm*, the space in front of the poop, where the most distinguished persons took their station in battle, and where the ship's chest of weapons stood. (3) *Krapparúm*, the next of the larger divisions forward from the *lypting*; here the rank and file of warriors stood in battle, among them the rowers. (4) and (5) *Austrrúm*, the two well-spaces, one in the after part and one forward, probably one on each side of the division just named; they are never mentioned as a position for men. (6) *Sǫx* (properly a name for the part of the gunwales rising up to the prow), the space between the forward *austrrúm* and the prow. (7) *Stafn* or *stafnrúm*, the space in the prow occupied by the forecastle guards, the *stafnbúar*, among them the standard-bearer and the look-out; it was a raised floor of small area. On merchant-ships the divisions were quite different. Such vessels are mentioned without *lypting*, but they have a *stafnlok* and two *hǫfuðbitarúm*, one on each side of the chief deck-beam; the space for cargo was called *klofarúm* (from *klofi*, the mast-partner). In boats the number of divisions varied according to the size of the vessel; it is to be noted that in them the *fyrirrúm* lay in the foreship.

Types of Ships

The Old Norse language possessed a large number of names of vessels. Some of these are of general signification, but most of them denote specific types of ships. Of these, however, many belong to a later period than archaeology is concerned with. The vessels of the saga age fall into the following classes:

1. The boats (*bátr*) named according to the number of oars, the larger forms of which are also called *skip*. The following names of individual types are recorded: *feræringr*, 'four-oared boat', *sexæringr* (with six oars), *áttæringr* (with eight oars), *teinæringr* (with ten oars), *tolfæringr* (with twelve oars); they may also be named in the form *feræror bátr*, &c., and *tolfært skip*. The form *teinæringr* is striking, as its first element is not Norse, but corresponds to MLG. *tein*, 'ten'. In Iceland it is now usual for each oar on a *sexæringr* and bigger boats to be operated by one man. Boats were without deck, though they had fairly large half-decks fore and aft. They had rowing-seats athwart and floor-boards. The larger sorts, at least, carried sail as well.

Every sea-going ship carried at least one, and usually two, boats (*skipsbátr*), of which the smaller one on a cargo ship was placed athwart on the cargo behind the mast (hence its name *yfirbátr*), while the larger one was towed on a rope (*eftirbátr*). The merchant-ships not well equipped for rowing were often towed short distances by means of the ship's boat.

A special variety of row-boat was the ferry (*ferja* or *eikja*), which was used for crossing rivers or bays. An *eikja* operated by a *ferjukarl* is mentioned in the Edda poem *Hárbarðsljóð*. Originally the *eikja* was undoubtedly a monoxylon of oak, but in later times was usually a small boat without keel.

2. Between boats, of which the largest variety carried six pairs of oars, and war-ships, the smallest of which (*prettánsessa*) had thirteen pairs, stand vessels whose size is indicated neither by the number of oars nor by the number of rowing-benches, but by the number of rowers on each side of the ship (*róa á borð*). The ground for this difference in terminology seems to have been this: in these vessels the individual rower could never have operated a pair of oars, as in boats, and there were no fixed rowing-benches as in war-ships; when these ships were rowed, each rower seems to have sat on his own low ship's chest. This supposition is confirmed by the fact that the Oseberg and Gokstad ships, belonging to this class (with fifteen and sixteen rowlocks or rowing-holes on each side), have no fixed rowing-benches. In all probability both of these vessels are to be assigned to the group which in literary texts has the name *karfi*,

a combined sailing- and rowing-vessel intended for journeys on fjords and lakes. When the *karfi* was the private vessel of a chief it was often painted or otherwise ornamented. Though the *karfi* might equal the smaller war-ships in number of oars— mention is made of one, for example, in which *sextán menn reru á borð*—it had less carrying power and was of lighter build; moreover, its crew was smaller and did not exceed the immediate needs of the journey. It is repeatedly related of a *karfi* that it was carried overland from one body of water to another. The source of the name is in Medieval Latin *carabus*, Medieval Greek κάραβος, which is often used by Byzantine authors, though also by Hesychius in the fifth century A.D. The Old Russian корабль *korablĭ*, корабь *korabĭ*, 'ship', is the same word; it appears in numerous accounts of the Scandinavian Varangians' journeys by way of the Dnieper to Constantinople. It is evident also that the *karfi* represents an ancient type of ship used for coastal defence, as is shown by a royal ordinance of 1315, by which the inhabitants of Hálogaland (in the north of Norway) were permitted to use this vessel according to ancient custom for naval defence.

Apart from the *karfi* there was still another type of ship whose size was reckoned by the number of rowers on each side, namely, the *skúta*. This ship also carried both sail and oars, but, unlike the *karfi*, was specially designed for use in war; the fast-sailing smaller *skútur* made excellent scout-ships or dispatch-boats, while others served as supply tenders to the fleet. Like the *karfi*, the *skúta* was often carried overland, and, again like the *karfi*, it was also used for river voyages. The name *skúta*, and the same type of vessel, is found outside the north, and phonological considerations indicate that it originated in north Germany, or perhaps in Friesland.

3. In long-ships (*langskip*), or in war-ships in proper conception, the size was reckoned by the number of rowing-benches (*sess*) on each side of the ship, or in Sweden possibly by the total number. The smallest was the *prettánsessa* with thirteen benches on each side, the normal size *tvítugsessa*, with twenty, while the *prítugsessa*, with thirty, and still larger specimens of the kind were rare. This reckoning does not give any absolute standard of size, as may be seen from this fact, among others, that the number of men in each *rúm* (by which is meant in this case the space belonging to one *sess*) varied greatly in the different ships.

The ships regularly designed for naval defence, the *leiðangrsskip* or *landvarnarskip*, of which each coastal district (ONorw. *skipreiða*, OSw. *skiplagh*, ODan. *skipæn*) had to equip one, were in Norway for the most part *tvítugsessur* with a crew of 100 men, four to each bench and the rest in the prow and stern. The great dragon-ships which were fitted out by the king and his nobles seem to have had on the average seven men on each bench and a corresponding strength of other men.

As regards the structure of the long-ship, its name alone proclaims its length to be great in relation to the width, and this relation was especially striking in comparison with the broad cargo-ship. The long-ships also differed from other sea-going ships in the height of the sides; since the battle in naval warfare was concentrated around the stem, the height of the bulwarks was of little importance in comparison with the height of the stem. Only the great dragon-ships, which projected out beyond the battle-rank of ships, seem often to have been distinguished by the great height of their bulwarks.

That the word *langskip*, which is not recorded in Old Swedish or Old Danish, is a translation of the Latin name for a war-ship, *navis longa*, cannot be doubted. Outside Norse the name appears only once in Germanic ground, in the *Anglo-Saxon Chronicle*, annal 897, where it is said that King Alfred had *langscipu* with sixty oars or more built against the Danish *æscas* (ON. *askar*). Since the long-ship, as well as the dragon-ship, had been in use in Norway before this time, neither the name nor the type of ship could have come to the north from England.

To the long-ship class belonged the *leiðangrsskip*, *dreki*, *skeið*, and *snekkja*. The last was the usual term in Sweden for a war-ship, but the meaning of the term in Old Danish is not clear. In Old French *esneque* was the term applied to the Norsemen's fast rowing-ships. In Old Norse literature also the *snekkja* was often a Viking ship, and was, moreover, an established term for a Wendish ship. Most examples had twenty benches, and were distinguished from war-ships of the same size by a narrower shape, intended for greater speed.

The typical long-ship of the larger sort was the *skeið*, a name which is also found in Old Swedish and Old Danish runic inscriptions. It was borrowed in Old English as *scegþ*, where it was originally used of the ships of Scandinavian sea-rovers, but later also of the heavy 43-bench ships which King Æþelred had built in the year 1008. The word was also adopted in Old French as *escei*, which is especially frequent in the twelfth century. Little is known of the structure of the *skeið*, though it seems to have been smaller than the true dragon-ship. The source of the name was probably Medieval Greek σχεδία, evidently a Byzantine word; it appears also in Nestor, the Russian chronicler, as *skedija*.

The dragon-ship, *dreki*, is not mentioned by name in Danish and Swedish sources, but in Norway it was older than the foundation of the kingdom. In the winter of 868 King Harald Fairhair had a great and magnificently equipped *dreki* built, and in the year 872, according to *Egils saga* (chapter 10) a ship with a dragon's head was built in the north of Norway, and this was probably the ship which in chapter 11 is expressly termed a *dreki*. There can be no doubt that this heavy and wide type of ship derived its name from the ornamentation of the prow; less clear is the difference between the dragon head and the *hofuð* 'heads' which are spoken of in various other types of ships: it may be noted especially that even the Oseberg ship, which was a *karfi*, had a serpent's head at the prow. It is probably best to assume that *dreki* was originally the name of a definite type of ship which was adorned with a dragon's head, but later became the common name for all heavy war-ships built on the model of this type; dragon-ships had at least thirty benches, and the largest was King Knút's with sixty benches. Just as the origin of the name is to be found in Latin *draco*, a gaping dragon-head appears at the prow of a ship in a wall-painting at Herculaneum; there is also a dragon's tail at the stern (ON. *sporðr*, *krókr*, see above, p. 357).

4. The size of the merchant-ship, *kaupskip*, was usually indicated merely by such general expressions as 'large'. The *knǫrr* was generally understood to be a *kaupskip*, but that did not prevent it from being used in war also, especially in the older period. The *knǫrr* was the usual sea-going ship (*hafskip*), and it was used as such for voyages to distant lands such as England, Iceland, and the Faroes. The much less seaworthy long-ships could not be used for voyages to Iceland or the Faroes, according to the express words of one saga, because of the roughness of the seas. A special group is formed by the smaller *austrfarar-*

knǫrr, which was restricted to the Baltic trade and was not reckoned to be a *hafskip*, though it was a *stórskip* (large ship). There was no necessity for a large crew on a merchant-ship, since the oars were only employed for special needs, and were few in number: they were rowed only from the half-decks forward and aft, while the middle space, occupied by the cargo, was free from oars. As compared with long-ships, merchant-ships were wider and had higher sides; they were more seaworthy and easier to sail. The name *knǫrr* is also known from Swedish runic inscriptions and from Old Danish records; OE. *cnear* and OFr. *canar(t)* were borrowed from Norse, but an old German glossary has 'mioparo', *gnarren*, evidently a Saxon pirate vessel. Several indications point to the name having arisen from the shape of the prow: thus a Norwegian glossary of about 1700 has *knorr* in the sense 'prow' of a boat. The word may be related to Middle English *knarre*, 'gnarl', 'knot' (cf. English *gnarled*), and may have referred originally to a gnarled tree-root used as a prow. This form of prow is found in Gutnish ships (see Pl. 58, where the figure-head carved in spiral form may have descended from such a gnarled piece of wood). Just as other Gutnish pictures of ships show an animal's head at the prow, the Old Norse *knǫrr* in the oldest times often had the same adornment there. The old form of the prow seems to have disappeared at the same time as the definiteness of the name.

The *búza* or *bussa* in the twelfth century was mostly a merchant-ship, though the earliest record (in the year 1026) referred to it as a war-ship, and a second example, too, one with thirty-five benches, had a dragon's head at the prow. In England there is mention of *butsecarlas*, 'men of a *búza*', in 1052 and 1066, as the name of Norman seamen in Yorkshire and at Hastings. The source of the name, also found in German and Old French, was Medieval Latin *buza*, which probably had the double sense of 'a kind of galley' and 'transport ship'.

5. Freight ships were of greatly varying sizes, according as they were used on the open sea or not. The most important type was the *byrðingr*. In Norway this was used especially for carriage of freight along the coast, and, among other purposes, to bring the product of the great cod and herring fisheries to the market-places; but also to ship it to other countries. It resembled the merchant-ship in most respects, but was

distinguished by still higher sides. To judge from the etymology—the word is derived from *borð*, 'side of a ship'—the
name *byrðingr* must originally have denoted a monoxylon with
planking raised up at the sides: such auxiliary planks at the
sides are called *bort* in Old Low German documents. While
the Norse *byrðingr* included vessels of very different dimensions,
the MLG. *bordinc* was always comparatively small.

While the smaller specimens of the *ferja* belonged to the boat
class, the larger ones were cargo-ships, though never used on
the open sea. The Norwegian *ferja* had no sail, whereas the
Icelandic type usually had.

XXII

WEAPONS

The Sword

THE precursor of the sword was the dagger. Examples of undoubted daggers of flint from the later stone age have the form illustrated in Pl. 7, in which the handle and blade are hewn out of a single piece of flint. Their edges are often provided with small saw-teeth, and the handle adorned with zigzag lines. This form is characteristic of Scandinavia and the north of Germany, and is of varying length up to a third of a metre. Of other specimens it is doubtful whether they are daggers or spearheads. No longer blades could be made from stone.

The oldest sword which has been preserved is of bronze, and it can hardly be distinguished in length of blade from a dagger; that is, it was a two-edged stabbing weapon: the pointed bronze blade was not well suited to hewing. But the bronze sword (see Pl. 14) belongs only to men's graves, while numerous bronze daggers are found in women's graves. The handle of the bronze sword was short and often likewise of bronze, and not infrequently it was inlaid with gold and adorned with settings of amber or resin. In other examples only the pommel is of metal and the handle itself is of horn. Scabbards also have been found, consisting of two thin strips of wood fastened together with bands of leather, or covered with leather and lined with furred skin.

In the pre-Roman iron age a one-edged sword appears. This was designed specially for hewing, though the contemporary two-edged sword also is proved by the rounded end of the blade to have been used in the same way. A specimen of the one-edged sword is shown in Pl. 29*b*, while Pl. 29*a* shows a two-edged sword with a scabbard made of two thin plates of iron.

The finds in the Danish bogs, dating from the third and fourth centuries A.D., sometimes brought to light the short broad-bladed type of sword, sometimes and more generally the long and narrower sort. The latter often has a damascened blade with the mark of the maker and a non-Roman name. The handle is usually of wood covered with bronze and silver hammered thin, or adorned with broad-headed nails of these metals; other handles are of bone, ivory, or iron. From other parts of Scandinavia come magnificent sword-hilts with pommel, and boss by the side of it (see Pl. 42*a*). The pommel was either gilt or made of pure gold, and was often adorned with filigree work and set with garnets or enamel. The round knob by the side of the triangular pommel was often of solid gold. The mounting and chape of the scabbard, too, were often magnificently ornamented. These are the ring-swords already described in Chapter XV.

The numerous finds and the accounts in Old Norse literature show that the swords of the Viking period were of numerous and varying types.[1] Some specimens of swords found in graves of this period may be seen in Pl. 59*a*, *b*, the latter being the one-edged type. The finds from graves and the old literature alike prove that the sword was the Viking's most important weapon. These two sources of information supplement and explain each other, though the correspondence of their evidence is not quite complete. Swords were handed down from generation to generation, just as oral tradition often handed down descriptions of old swords, and the strength of these traditions is sufficient to explain the similarity which can be observed between the descriptions of literature and the swords of an older time, when the finds from graves contemporary with the literature show nothing that corresponds. A long series of terms preserved in the old literature were first interpreted with certainty through the finds in graves, though some of them, it is true, are not yet wholly clear. The most important to be considered at this point are the chief names for the different forms of swords: *sverð*, *sax*, *mækir*, *skǫlm*.

Skǫlm is a term preserved only in Old Norse literature, and it denoted a short one-edged type of sword. According to etymology (the basic sense is 'piece split off') the word must originally have signified either a flint dagger or a wooden sword of a kind similar to those found in the Danish bogs. Relationship with Greek (Thracian) σκάλμη, 'sword' or 'knife', is doubtful. In the historical sagas it is never the name of a man's weapon, but it often appears in legendary narratives, especially when female supernatural beings are introduced, and also in Edda poems. In the Viking age it played no practical part.

[1] Jan Petersen, 'De norske Vikingesverd', *Videnskapsselskapets Skrifter*, ii, Hist.-Filos., 1919, no. 1 (Kristiania, 1919).

PLATE 59

a. Viking sword; *b*. One-edged Viking sword; *c*. Spearhead of the
Vendel type. Sogn, Norway

PLATE 60

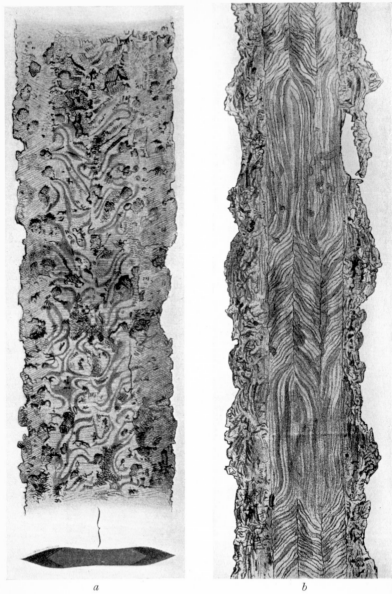

a   *b*

Damascened blades of Viking swords. After Lorange

The name *mækir* is common Germanic (Gothic *mēkeis*, OE. *mēce*, OS. *māki*). But in what the distinctive character of this type consisted has not been determined with certainty. There are indications which speak for ON. *mækir* having been the special name for the two-edged sword with sharp point (*oddr*), as distinct from the usual type with rounded end (*blóðrefill*), which had a prior right to the name *sverð*, in so far as this was not the common term for this whole species of weapon.

Sax was originally the name of the one-edged sword, and it continued to be used in this sense when applied to the larger type (known by archaeologists as the *scramasax*), but the smaller type, the *handsax* might also be two-edged (*tvíeggjat handsax* = OE. *twíecge handseax*). The long *sax* of the Viking period was generally of the same length as the two-edged long-sword, having a blade of about 80 cm. While the *handsax* was intended to be a thrusting-weapon, the long *sax* was mostly used for hewing. There was also another kind of *handsax* which, like the small *sax* of the South Germans, was especially made for throwing; this action was spoken of as *kasta handsǫxum*.

The one-edge *sax* sometimes had deep grooves (usually three) along the back of the blade. The two-edged blades of the Viking period always had a broad shallow depression running down the middle on each side. This type in particular often had damascening in the middle of the blade. The so-called 'false damascening' was produced by welding and forging together pieces of iron or steel of different hardness, which gave the blade greater elasticity and a surface with a pattern of serpentine or wavy form; the variegated flame-pattern was brought out even more strongly by corrosion with acid, as the softer parts were more affected by it than the harder parts. Such blades are known in great numbers from Norse grave-finds and belong to the period A.D. 300–1000. The Arabic writer Ibn Faḍlān, in his famous account of his travels, mentions the wavy ornamentation of the Russian (i.e. belonging to the Scandinavian Rus) swords, which he supposes to be of Frankish origin. This pattern is the basis of the poetic name for a sword, *vægir* (compare *vágr*, 'the billowy sea'), and of the term *wǽgsweord* (literally 'wave-sword') used in *Beowulf*. In Pl. 60*b* the damascening is strongly suggestive of eddies in a stream; this pattern is called *blóðiða* in Old Norse ('blood-eddy': *iða* means 'eddy'). In Pl. 60*b* there is a manifest likeness to rows of mown hay or corn where the series of parallel sloping lines form angles with each other; the Old Norse name for this form of damascening is *ánn* (the same word as MHG. *jān*, 'swathe of mown grass or corn'). Or the pattern might consist of parallel stripes lengthwise down the blade. The mysterious terms *blóðvarp* and *iðvarp*, occurring in a versified list (*þula*) of the parts and features of a sword, are probably to be explained as names for this type of pattern; *varp* means 'warp in weaving', and the long lines down the blade are regarded as a warp of a web which is complete when the sword is thrust into blood (*blóð*) or the vitals (*iðr*). The iron of the blade was of widely varying quality. When it was inferior, a steel edge welded on to it made up in some degree for its deficiencies. The hardness of the iron could be proved by testing it with a file, and the strength of the blade by tests of its elasticity; it was a demonstration of perfection when the point could be bent back right to the handle.

Between the blade and the handle a cross-piece was fixed, generally of iron, but on the *sax* of wood. At first this guard projected only slightly beyond the blade, but later increased in size and sometimes had each end bent down towards the blade; a special name for the long, pointed, and slender guard of the later Viking age was *gaddhjalt* (from *gaddr*, 'spike'). On the older form of *sax* the point of the iron tang was bent down over the wooden grip or over a thin iron plate covering the end of the grip. The two-edged sword had always a second cross-piece parallel with the guard; on this upper hilt[1] a knob was fastened by a pair of rivets. Later these two parts formed a single piece, when the end of the iron tang was bent over the knob; only a groove cut into the knob remained as a vestige of the older form. This knob or pommel had different forms, triangular, hemispherical, or having three or five rounded projections. Both guard and pommel were often covered with copper, bronze, gold, or silver plates, or were wound round with gold or silver wire. Hilts made of walrus-ivory or horn are also mentioned in the sagas. The grip was usually of wood, preferably, as is

---

[1] 'Hilt' is here used as in Scandinavian and Old English. In Old Norse it was the cross-piece that was called 'hilt' (ON. *hjalt*); the guard was the lower hilt (*fremra hjaltit*), the pommel the upper hilt (*efra hjaltit*). The handle was called *meðalkafli*, 'middle-piece'. Except when loosely applied to the handle and guard together, *hilt* in English corresponds normally to ON. *meðalkafli*.

indicated by a number of sword-names, of the resinous, yellow-ish Norway pine. It was often wound round with gold or silver wire or inlaid with gold. The common Germanic name for the inlaid figures of silver or gilt bronze on the guards and handle appears in Old Norse as *mál*, in Old English as *mæl*, though the word *mál* is also, and perhaps more fre-quently, applied to the damascening of the blade. As in the Roman period and in the finds of the Danish bogs from the migration period saxes with curved handle and slightly arched back edge are still known in the Viking age: some Old Norse sword-names are based on this form, and Saxo speaks of a *gladius incurvus* (see Pl. 29*b*).

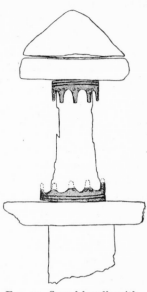

On some old swords a small ring is found attached to the pommel. This ring was originally open, but later, when it had become a mere ornament, closed. Allusions to this ring occur in a few sword-names and in Edda poems, as also in the poetic use of *hringr*, 'ring', as *pars pro toto*

FIG. 24. Sword-handle with *véttrim. After J. Petersen.*

in the sense 'sword'; compare also *hringīren*, 'ring-adorned sword', in *Beowulf*. Probably the ring served originally as a fastening for a cord attached also to the scabbard, which pre-vented the sword from slipping out. Such cords (called *friðbǫnd*, meaning literally 'peace-bands') are mentioned many times in the old literature and were certainly prescribed at thing-assemblies (see p. 265, Pl. 42).

Some Viking swords had metal rings between the handle and the guard, sometimes also between the handle and the pommel (Fig. 24). These casings or sockets are mentioned in literature under the name *véttrim* (meaning etymologically 'lid-formed rim'). In one Edda poem, *Sigrdrifumál*, direction is given to cut runes *á véttrimum ok á valbǫstum*; in another, *Helgakviða Hjǫrvarðssonar*, there is said to be a serpent-sign on the *valbǫst*. The etymological sense of this last word is 'foreign covering';

bast originally denoted any thin membrane covering an object, and in this application it first referred to the thin covering of skin which was sometimes laid on the round wooden grips of Norse swords in the migration period. Later this name was applied to the thin metal plates with which Viking swords were so often adorned. The same sense-development is seen in the synonymous OE. *scenn*, which etymologically meant 'membrane', 'bast'.

Every sword seems to have had its name. This was most frequently derived from peculiarities of its appearance, but sometimes some adventure or other would supply the name. Not infrequently the name of a Germanic tribe or nation occurs as a sword-name, as *Flæmingr*, *Langbarðr*, &c. The numerous animal names may have either of two origins: sometimes they contain a nickname of the original owner, sometimes they are derived from pictures on the hilt. Such animal pictures are found at least on Swedish swords. Serpent names are especially frequent. These may allude to the damascening of the blade, which is often compared to a crawling serpent, as when it is said in the Edda poem *Helgakviða Hjǫrvarðssonar*: 'Along the edges lies a blood-stained serpent.' Such names might also be derived from a representation of a serpent on the hilt: compare the epithet *wyrmfāh* applied in *Beowulf* to the handle of a sword of which the blade had been burned away. Often magical power was ascribed to these representations of animals. An inscribed magical formula seems to be the basis of the sword-name *Atti*, a word which appears elsewhere with the meaning 'quarrelsome'.

It is remarkable that the historical sagas never mention a sword made in the north, whereas it is expressly stated of a number of swords that they were obtained in a foreign country; 'Valsk' (i.e. French) swords are named with special frequency. Foreign origin is indicated also by the sword-names which are derived from names of other peoples. The best and most prized swords of the Viking period thus seem to have been imported into the north. The mythical sagas allege mythical origin for the best blades, and their tempering likewise (in venom or blood) is surrounded by dark mystery.

Like the Romans and Greeks, the ancient inhabitants of the north wore their swords in two fashions, sometimes girded around the waist, sometimes on a shoulder-belt. Examples of both these types of sword-belt are preserved in the finds of the Danish bogs, and Old Norse literature affords evidence of both fashions. Several passages in the sagas show that the sword was worn on the left side, but on the other hand the opening in the chape of the swords found in the Danish bog shows that these swords were worn on the right side after the Roman fashion.

Although it was only in the later period that the sword-handle was long enough to be gripped with both hands, the sagas often mention a sword being wielded with both (*tvíhenda sverði̇t*). By this is meant only that the left hand was placed over the right to increase the force of the blow. It was an accomplishment of those who were most adroit in the use of weapons to be able to hew equally well with either hand, and be ready to change the weapon from one hand to another at any advantageous moment, so that an opponent was never secure against feints. Often accounts are given of a fighter using two weapons at the same time, especially sword and spear. Like the Romans of the Empire the Norsemen frequently carried two swords, usually one two-edged long sword and a *sax* as an auxiliary weapon; these same weapons are ascribed in the epics to Beowulf and Waldhari.

The sword was used by the ancient Germans in various symbolic acts. As in other literatures, there is mention in Old Norse mythical sagas of the custom of a man laying a naked sword between himself and a woman who was not to be married to him. There is mention of the sword as a symbol of investiture in the reign of King Harald Fairhair. By means of a similar ceremony, too, the Anglo-Saxon king Æþelstan maintained that he had made this same King Harald his vassal.

Superstitious beliefs gathered round the sword more than any other weapon. A kind of personal life was ascribed to the sword which expressed itself among other ways by giving forth sounds on certain occasions. The most famous swords of legend were endowed with definitely supernatural powers and qualities (*álǫg* or *atkvæði*, spells laid on the sword) and they had to be treated accordingly. According to a widespread superstition persons skilled in magic knew how to blunt a sword by a glance or by blowing on it; for this reason the opponent in a duel often carried two swords, of which the magician only knew of one.

The Spear

Numerous spearheads of flint are known from the later stone age, of beautiful workmanship and often large and long (up to 45 cm.). Spearheads of slate or bone belonging to the so-called Arctic type have been found in Norway, in Swedish Norrland, and on Gotland.

The spear blades of the older bronze age are broadest at the base, and they have a high and broad ridge down the middle. Later they become slenderer and more elegant. The Swedish rock-carvings show spears of double or three times the height of a man.

From the pre-Roman period come spears with two-edged blade, normally comparatively small in size and of no very definitely established form. In the Roman period we observe that each warrior carried two spears as a rule, one a lance with two-edged blade, the other a throwing-spear with barbs. Over 1,500 spears of these forms have been collected from the great finds in the Danish bogs, which have already been described (above, p. 204). The lance-heads from this source are often adorned with incised lines and dots, or with rings of inlaid thread of silver or gold. The shafts are usually of ash and up to three and a half metres in length; at the centre of gravity a firmly nailed throwing-band is found. About A.D. 600 the two types, lances and throwing-spears, are succeeded by a large spear with heavy leaf-shaped head, exemplified in the finds from Vendel (Pl. 59c).

FIG. 25. Viking spearhead adorned with silver. *After Montelius.*

In the graves of the Viking period various forms of spears appear, often adorned with silver or gold, as in Fig. 25. The spears of the Vikings fall into two main classes:

one type was for lancing (whether thrust or thrown), the other also for hewing (*hǫggspjót*). The former, the most widely used class, included both thrusting-spears (*lagvápn*) and throwing-spears (*skotvápn*); these last were lighter and had a shorter blade. The whole class of thrusting- and throwing-spears is divided according to the form of the head into the following groups:

1. The *geirr* had a triangular blade (compare *geiri*, 'wedge-shaped piece': see Fig. 26). This common Germanic name (OE. *gār*, OS. and OHG. *gēr*, Germanic groundform **gaiza-*) for a throwing-spear was probably borrowed in pre-Roman times from Old Gaulish *gaisos*, *gaison* (Irish *gae*) from which Latin *gaesum* and Greek γαῖσος were also borrowed. As the archaeological finds show, the Germans adopted the Celtic type of spear, and in fact a number of spear-heads seem to have been imported direct from Gaulish makers. The name *geirr* does not occur in historical sagas, but is frequent in poetry.

FIG. 26. Spearhead *geirr. After Rygh.*

2. *Fleinn* (the same word as OE. *flān*) was a name given to both a light throwing-spear and a kind of arrow. Like *geirr*, this name does not occur in historical sagas, but is found in poetry. Etymologically *fleinn* means 'prong' (of a fork or the like), and it must have been a spear with a long and very narrow bayonet-shaped iron head; it is significant that *fleinn* could also mean the same as *járnteinn*, 'iron spike'. In the legendary sagas we read of a *tvíangaðr* (or *tvíoddaðr*) *fleinn*, which is described as an iron spike split at the point into two prongs (compare the arrow *fenja*). A special type of *fleinn* is mentioned in *Grettis saga* (chap. 66) under the name *heptisax*. This weapon consisted of a sword-like blade fixed at the end of a wooden shaft, and differed from the other types of *fleinn* in not being a throwing-spear, but was used as a *hǫggspjót*, for hewing and thrusting. It must have been similar to the *kesjufleinn*, or, more probably, identical with it; this was evidently a *kesja* (see below, p. 388) with a longer blade than usual. It was doubtless by reason of the long narrow blade that the *heptisax* was classed by *Grettis*

saga as a *fleinn*. The same sort of weapon was known in other Germanic lands, too: OE. *stæfsweord*, glossing 'dolo' and OHG. *stapaswert*, 'framea', must also have consisted of a sword-like blade on a wooden shaft. The *hæftmēce* of *Beowulf* (line 1457) has been compared with the *heptisax* of *Grettis saga*, and special significance has been attached to the assumed identity of these weapons, since the episodes in which they appear are believed to be closely related. The *hæftmēce*, however, is not described as a wooden-shafted spear, but rather as a sword with a decorated hilt similar to those described above, p. 380. It is *hringmæl* and *wundenmæl* and *wrǣttum gebunden*, that is, it has a hilt adorned with interlacing rings[1] and ornamental plates. Yet in the original form of the legend the *hæftmēce* may well have been like the *heptisax*; it had at least a wooden handle, as is indicated by its name Hrunting, in which the first element *Hrunt-* is an extended form of the base seen in OE. *hrung*, 'long piece of wood', 'rung'. The related Norse sword-name Hrotti must also have been given to swords with wooden handles. The term *hæftmēce* is only once recorded, and may have been known in Old English only in connexion with the monster-slaying story used by the *Beowulf* poet. It would not be unnatural then if he had only a vague idea of the nature of the weapon, and he might well assume from the way in which it was used that it was a kind of sword.

3. *Broddr* was similarly a name for a light throwing-spear (also called *broddspjót*) and for a kind of arrow, but the iron point had four edges. In the Viking age this type seems to have been rare.

4. The *krókspjót* was a throwing-spear which was provided with barbs (*krókar*). This form was also used in Viking times, as is evident from a description in *Grettis saga* (chap. 19). Even after the medieval period barbed spears continued to be used in Norway in hunting bears, walrus, and whales; the hunting spears in *Beowulf* were similarly barbed, as shown by the description *eoforsprēot heorohōciht*.

5. The *fjaðrspjót* takes its name from the long broad blade:

---

[1] *Hringmæl* and *wundenmæl* might refer to the damascened pattern on the blade, but that the blade is described earlier in the poem as *atertānum fāh*, 'decorated with poison-twigs', which implies the pattern named *ánn* above, p. 380. (Pl. 60).

fjǫðr, 'spear-blade', properly means 'feather'. It was a heavy thrusting weapon, and its long shaft was often encased in iron. The name is also found in Old High German and Middle Low German.

6. The *blaðspjót* (from *blað*, 'blade') takes its name from its leaf-shaped form. In Old Norse literature the word is found only as a man's nickname.

7. The *sviða* was originally a wooden shaft with a point scorched and hardened in fire; the name is related to the verb *sviða*, 'to scorch, burn'. Tacitus refers to such spears in his *Annales* ii. 14, where he writes of the Germans' *praeusta tela*. Weapons of the same kind are mentioned in Old Norse literature, and seem to have been used, among other purposes, for hunting bears, though the *bjarnsviða* described in the sagas was provided with an iron point. Characteristic of the *sviða* were the two projecting points at the base of the head, from which the weapon was also called *króksviða*; the purpose of these was to hold the animal or opponent at a distance, as they prevented the spear from passing further into the body. See Fig. 27, which comes from the grave of a Norwegian Viking; but there are precisely similar projections on some of the Gutnish spears of the same period. This weapon is also common in German graves, and in the later period it was called *Knebelspiess*. Both this German spear and the Norse *sviða* might have the shaft covered with iron, and some specimens had ornamentation on the cylindrical part of the head. This type is frequent in graves of the Viking age, but is absent in the older period.

FIG. 27. *Króksviða*, winged spearhead. *After Rygh.*

8. *Gaflak* is a borrowing from Celtic which is also met with in other Germanic languages (e.g. OE. *gafeloc*) and in French (whence English *javelin*). It was a short and light throwing-spear, a kind of hand-thrown arrow, probably having feathers

at the lower end and a head-socket connecting the head and shaft. This weapon is first mentioned in use at the battle of Svǫlðr in 995.

In addition to these names Old Norse literature contains a number of poetic terms for the spear. As a rule, however, these do not designate any special type, or else its characteristics cannot be ascertained. Some of them allude to the shaft and its material, such as *skapt* (= OE. *sceaft*, 'spear'), *askr* (= OE. *æsc*, 'spear of ash wood'), *lind* and *lindi*, properly 'spear of linden wood'. A few names of throwing-spears point to foreign origin: *peita* (i.e. spear from Poitou), *frakka* (= OE. *franca*, 'the Frankish weapon'), *sváf* ('the Swabian spear'); the spear called *vigr* and described as 'western' was perhaps the OE. *wigar*; *darr*, as well as the equivalent OE. name *daroþ*, may be ultimately derived from Greek δόρυ, plural δόρατα.

A weapon for throwing which resembled a spear was the *skeptifletta* or *flettiskepta* (*fletta* meaning 'flint'); this consisted of a shaft split at the end, where a sharp piece of flint was inserted in the cleft. This weapon must be regarded undoubtedly as an inheritance from the stone age; from the stone age itself arrow- or spearheads have been preserved which are made of bone with sharp pieces of flint fastened in slots on both sides by the application of a resinous substance.

The second of the two main classes is formed by the *hǫggspjót*, by which is meant spears that could be used for hewing. The hewing-spear can be most concisely described as a strengthened, long, and broad sword fixed at the end of a shaft. The shaft was sometimes long, sometimes short, according as the spear was designed primarily for thrusting or for hewing.

The *kesja* is named as a kind of *hǫggspjót*, though there is no hewing done with it in any of the places where it is mentioned. It is described sometimes as a rather light throwing-spear with a short shaft, sometimes as a heavy long-shafted thrusting weapon. The *kesja* was in use over the whole of the north, and was long used as a hunting spear. If the name is rightly derived from a Germanic name for 'stone' (*kes-, *kas-), this weapon, like the *flettiskepta*, must go back right to the stone age.

The *brynþvari* is mentioned as a variety of *kesja*. The name means 'mail-piercer'. It had a very long blade, broad at the base, with a four-edged point which could be stuck into the rings of the mail. Other characteristics of the *brynþvari* were a long socket on the head and a short shaft cased in iron. No example has been found in Viking graves.

The *atgeirr* also belonged to the hewing-spears. This weapon is very seldom mentioned in historical sagas or the sagas of Icelandic families, but frequently, on the other hand, in scaldic poems and legendary sagas. The name itself was common Germanic (OE. *ætgār*, OFris. *etgēr*, OHG. *azigēr*). The Old Norse *atgeirr* was sometimes a lightish throwing-spear, sometimes a heavier spear held in the hand for thrusting and hewing. Nothing more is known of its appearance.

In the Viking period the iron head of the spear was as a rule fastened to the shaft by means of a socket, rarely by a tang at the lower end of the head; in literature only the socket is mentioned. The two parts were held together by two nails driven in opposite one another or by one which passed right through the shaft. The nails were often driven only a short way into the shaft, so that they could be taken out before the spear was thrown; this rendered it more difficult to pull the iron out of a wound or hurl the spear back. In order that the spear might be easily stuck in the ground, which was sometimes of practical value, the lower end was often provided with an iron ferrule (*aurfalr*) just as on the Roman *lancea*; this iron covering was also of use when the spear was used as a walking staff. The throwing-spear of the Viking period, like that of the preceding age, was provided with a band to hold it by, placed at the centre of gravity.

Since the throwing-spear was seldom a lifelong possession of its owner, there was not the same magnificence lavished on its adornment as on swords and thrusting-spears. The ornament consisted sometimes of engraved lines, sometimes of inlaid silver or gold, and it did not extend beyond the socket, while the blade was occasionally damascened. In Old Norse literature the inlaid socket is called *gullrekinn falr* or *silfrrekinn falr*, while a spear with damascening is a *málaspjót*.

Bow, Arrow, and Quiver

Many arrowheads of flint are preserved from the later stone age, some of them provided with a tang to fix into the shaft, others with a notch for the shaft to fit into. The long spear-like arrows, some with projections (to act as barbs) on one side cut in the same piece of bone, others with pieces of flint fixed in both sides, were no doubt used only as hunting weapons.

Arrowheads of bronze are very rare. It is certain that in the bronze age bone or flint was still used.

From the migration period long arrows with heads of iron or bone have been found in the Danish bogs. They have four rows of feathers fastened on with waxed thread, and they occasionally bore the owner's mark, sometimes in runes. The bows that have been preserved are about 1·80 metres long, tapering in thickness towards the ends, which are sometimes provided with points of iron or bone. Wooden quivers have also been found, and among them one with mountings.

The bow of the Viking period consisted of a bent piece of wood which was held upright with the left hand, on which the arrow rested, gripping it by the middle. It was flat on the inner side and rounded on the outer. The middle, the thickest part, was strengthened by an additional strip which increased the elasticity. The material of the bow was generally yew or elm: hence ON. *ýr* means either 'yew' or 'bow', and *almr* either 'elm' or 'bow'; the compounds *ýbogi* and *almbogi* were also used. This use of yew in bows is ancient, as is shown by the tendency of words for 'yew' to develop the sense 'bow' in other ancient languages, e.g. Greek τόξον, 'bow', cognate with Latin *taxus*, 'yew'. Caesar mentions yew, which is indeed well known for its hard and tough wood, as the material of the Gaulish bows. Bowstrings in historic times were mostly made of hair, and were twisted from several strands. When the bow was not in use, it was unstrung at one end or both, so that it should not lose its elasticity. It was strung by placing the loop at the end of the bowstring in the notch near the end of the bow, while the other end was braced against the ground; the technical expression for this was *benda boga* (= OE. *bogan bendan*), meaning etymologically 'place a band or bond on the bow', and thus was different from later English *bend a bow*, which corresponds in sense to Old Norse *draga (upp) boga*.

The base of the arrowhead generally had the form of a spike which was stuck into a hole in the shaft. The juncture with the shaft was usually strengthened by a band wrapped around the end of the shaft. The lower part was feathered, and at the end there was a notch to take the bowstring. As a rule arrows were marked only for hunting, especially for hunting walrus.

The quiver (*ǫrvamalr*, *ǫrvamæli*) is often mentioned in the accounts of the sagas. In one passage a quiver of buckskin is referred to, and in this the usage of an older time is apparent: compare ON. *malr*, 'leather sack'. Possibly the quiver was normally carried on the back, which would account for the statements that arrows for immediate use were stuck into the ground where they could be easily caught up. On the Bayeux tapestry the Normans are carrying quivers. Part of a cylindrical quiver of wood was found in the ship burial at Gunnarshaug in Norway.

As the arrow (*ǫr*) and spear are often described by the common name *skot* or *skeyti*, it is natural that the various types of arrows should be distinguished in the same way as spears and to some extent should bear the same names.

1. The *fleinn*, like the spear of the same name, had a long iron head, and it was of the same shape. In historical times this type seems to have been no longer in general use.

2. The *krókǫr* was provided with barbs. Since an arrow of this kind could not be pulled out, it had to be cut out and, as the body was disfigured by this, death received from it was accounted a disgrace. Possibly this explains why barbed arrows are not found in Viking graves.

3. The *broddr* or *broddǫr* is much more frequently mentioned. Like the spear of the same name this arrow had a four-edged (or sometimes two-edged) head, which had a socket. Medieval Latin *quadrellus* (French *carreau*, English *quarrel*) is a corresponding name.

4. The *bíldǫr* or *bílda* was an arrow with a leaf-shaped head: compare ON. *bíldr*, 'lancet'. This arrow is well known as the type most frequent in Norwegian finds from the Viking period (Fig. 28).

5. The *kolfr* (see Fig. 12) was a heavy arrow with a thick and blunt head of wood or iron which gave it its name: compare ON. *kylfa*, 'club'. It thus corresponds to the OE. *bolt*, OHG. *bolz*. The thick feathering seems to have been characteristic of this type. Originally the *kolfr* seems to have been intended only for fowling, and it was so used in the only place where it is mentioned in Old Norse poetry (in *Rígsþula*). The variety known

as *bakkakolfr* derived its name from its use in target-shooting: compare *skotbakki*, 'shooting-butts'.

It is not known whether the *tundrǫr* denotes an arrow of special construction. The term denotes an arrow which carried

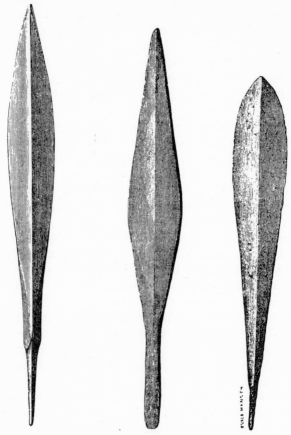

FIG. 28. Leaf-shaped arrowheads. *After Rygh.*

tinder (*tundr*) with consecrated fire. In *Landnámabók* a man appropriated a piece of land by shooting a *tundrǫr* over it, and in a late and unhistoric saga this was even done in time of war. The *ǫr finsk*, 'Finnish arrow', mentioned in *Landnámabók* was probably made of slate, like the arrows which were ascribed to the Finnish king Gusir, and the stone arrows mentioned in

Qrvar-Odds saga: both Snorri and Saxo describe the Finns as master archers. The arrow-names peculiar to poetry are as a rule poetic epithets of the arrow in general; a few of them, however, seem to denote special forms of arrows. Thus there is the *fenja*, a name which must be derived from *fǫn*, 'whalebone'. These whalebone arrowheads have a swallow-tailed shape which is reminiscent of a variety with a cloven head not infrequent in the Viking age.

The so-called *herǫr*, 'war-arrow', had only a symbolic use; it was an arrow of iron or wood which was sent from house to house as a token summoning men to war-service. Extraordinary assemblies of the Thing might also be summoned in this manner.

The Battle-Axe

The axe is known from the oldest times, both as a tool and as a weapon, though it is not always possible to decide whether a particular form has served in only one of these capacities. The material of the axe-blade in the later stone age was as a rule flint, the only kind of stone that was capable of a sharp and durable edge. An account has already been given of the earliest types of axe in Chapter V, and also in Chapter VIII, of the forms found in the bronze age; we have therefore nothing further to add here about the axes of stone and bronze.

Axes of iron do not appear in the north until the Roman period. The finds in the Danish bogs from the third and fourth centuries A.D. include many axes, of which a good proportion must have been weapons, especially the finer specimens with a hole for the haft and a modern appearance, while the forms resembling celts were primarily working tools.

Both the finds in graves and the evidence of Old Norse literature show that the battle-axe in Viking times played nearly as large a part as the sword and spear. For the numerous forms that have been brought to light the terminology and descriptions of the sagas provide a rational classification.

1. The *handøx* (which was borrowed in OE. as *handæx*) is the Scandinavian battle-axe well known in other countries under the name 'Danish axe'. The name *handøx* itself shows that it was a light manageable weapon (like the *handsax*). The blade was of moderate width, the haft was long and comparatively

slender and had an iron point at the lower end (i.e. the opposite end from the blade); for the *handøx* served also as a walking-staff, the hand grasping it by the narrower part of the blade. While the broad-axe was wielded with both hands, the hand-axe needed only one hand. Its chief use was as a hewing weapon, though the back of it might also be used as a hammer. Being a tool useful for various purposes, the hand-axe was readily taken up whenever a man went to work outside the house. Sometimes it had costly adornments: for instance, Earl Godwine gave Harðaknút a ship with eighty men who carried Danish axes over their left shoulders, and the axes were adorned with silver and gold. (See Pl. 61, from the grave of a Danish Viking.)

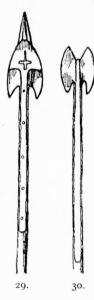

29.   30.

FIG. 29. *Bryntrolls-broddr*. After Falk.

FIG. 30. *Bryntroll*. After Falk.

2. The *breiðøx* (= OE. *brādæx*), 'broad-axe' was distinguished by a broad blade which narrowed considerably towards the socket for the haft. The broad-axe was undoubtedly the axe in commonest use over the whole Scandinavian area, while in Norway it was a choice between this axe and the sword as the favourite weapon. There was a distinction between the variety known as a *punnslegin øx*, in which the whole side of the blade was hammered out into an even flatness, and the *veggslegin øx*, which was thickest where the steel edge was welded on to the iron blade, as was the *halfpynna* likewise; Fig. 31 shows a Norwegian example of the last variety.

3. The *snaghyrnd øx* or *snaga* (from *snag*, 'projecting point') had a blade of half-moon shape. This axe could be used both for thrusting and hewing. Some mention is made also of *snǫgur* having the haft covered with iron, and of some that were adorned with gold and silver.

4. The *skeggøx* or *skeggja* was distinguished by a nearly rectangular projection of the lower portion of the blade, which was the origin of the name ('beard-axe'; compare the German name *barde, barte*) (see Fig. 32). This axe is frequent in graves of the

Viking period. In *Konungsskuggsjá* a long-hafted *skeggøx* is
recommended for sea-fighting, evidently because of its useful-
ness when it came to boarding or grappling the ships of the
enemy.

5. The *taparøx* came from the east, as its name shows, being

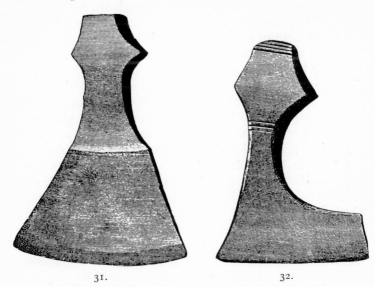

31.   32.

Fig. 31. The battle-axe *halfpynna*. *After Rygh*.
Fig. 32. Bearded axe, *skeggøx*. *After Rygh*.

identical with Old Slavonic топоръ *toporŭ*, 'axe'; OE. *taparæx*
was borrowed from Norse. Just as in England the distance
which a *taparæx* can be thrown serves as a rough measure of
length, the passages in Norse literature also where this type is
mentioned show that it was a small short-handled axe; its
blade might be of various forms, and the back of it was useful
for hammering.

6. The *bryntroll* is shown by the poetic form of its name
(meaning properly 'ogre of the byrnie', that is, its destroyer)
to be of foreign origin; it is without doubt the axe which first
appears in finds of the later Viking period, and it is identical
with the double-edged axe known from antiquity, the Greek
δίστομος πέλεκυς, Latin *bipennis*, Medieval Latin *bisacuta*. In
the north in the period treated here it exists only in the form

with the haft passing through the blade, just as it is described in the literature. The variety having a sharp iron point projecting beyond the blade is first mentioned at a later period under the name *bryntrollsbroddr* (Figs. 29 and 30).

7. The *sparða* is mentioned many times as an Irish battle-axe which was also used by the Scandinavians. As Irish *sparth* or *sparra* is not a native word, it has been conjectured that it is a modified form of ON. *barða*; if this is right, it must be the same kind of axe, that is, a type of *skeggøx*, which was less commonly known as a *barða*.

The implement known as *refði* was a combination of axe, hammer, and walking-staff. It was reckoned as an axe, but in all the passages where it was used as a weapon it was wielded in the manner of a mace. Like the hand-axe it was provided with an iron spike which made it a handy walking-staff. It was probably like the ancient miners' staves, a pike-staff with a small axe-blade and a prominent hammer at the back of the blade. It was indeed intended to be a practical tool or an insignium of rank rather than a weapon: thus King Ólaf Tryggvason carried a *refði* which was adorned with gold.

Axe-blades inlaid with gold and silver are often spoken of. Possession of gold-adorned axes and sword-hilts formed one of the conditions of admission to the bodyguard of King Knút the Great. Such ornamental axes seem to have been introduced from England in the later Viking period. Yet the ordinary Norse axes were of excellent quality, and the Irish accordingly obtained their battle-axes from the Scandinavians.

Clubs

Some of the clubs of the stone age were naturally rounded stones or stones cut into rounded form with a groove running round the middle, while others were stones hewn into the form of a disk with a hole in the middle for a handle. Doubtless clubs of hard wood were also used in the same period. No bronze clubs appear to have been made in Scandinavia. The clubs preserved in the finds of the Danish bogs (from the third and fourth centuries A.D.) were all of wood, but of various forms.

The *kefli* of the Viking period was a round stock of wood tapering towards the handle; it was sometimes used in a special

PLATE 61

Battle-axe with gold ornaments. After Lindqvist

PLATE 62

a. Shield from the Gokstad ship

b. The god Othin from a Vendel
helmet. After Montelius

form of single combat. A club which consisted of a black head with a haft of varying length was called a *kylfa* or *klumba*. The head was often made from the root of a tree, which was either charred in fire to harden the wood, or else bound round with iron. The club was not a weapon in ordinary use; it is mentioned mostly in legendary sagas, very often as a giant's weapon. When an actual Viking used a club, it was usually against a 'wound-proof' person, i.e. one protected by spells against the bite of iron weapons.

The Shield

The earliest traces of the shield are found in the rock-carvings of the bronze age, most of them round. No genuinely Norse shields of the bronze age have been found, though there are some specimens of foreign workmanship, made of thin sheets of bronze, with chased ornamentation.

From the pre-Roman iron age generally only the iron bosses of the shields have survived; though one deposit of this period, discovered in the Hjortspring bog in Als, has yielded a number of wooden shields with wooden bosses (see p. 186). A typical specimen of the migration period is shown in Pl. 30. It was made of thin boards of wood held together by a single cross-piece which served as a grip for the hand, and by a thin rim of metal bent around the edges of the wood. The boss of the shield was as a rule of iron or bronze, sometimes in the form of a hemisphere, sometimes having a projecting spike or knob in the middle. Swedish graves belonging to the latter part of the migration period contain some magnificent shield-bosses.

The simplest type of shield in the Viking age was of the same kind as those found in the Danish bogs (see Pl. 62*a*, which is taken from the Gokstad ship). It is made of a single layer of spruce, with a rim of leather and a cross-piece which serves as a handle. The material, at least in the older period, was generally linden wood, as is proved by the common Germanic name *lind* (properly 'linden wood') for the shield. In Old Norse literature *lindiskjǫldr* occurs as a term for the simplest kind of shield, which does not seem to have been approved as a regular weapon for national defence. To be recognized as a lawful weapon of war the shield must, according to the Old Norwegian law, have three bands of iron across one side. A better sort was that called *tvíbyrðingr*, which had a double layer of boards. This shield was also called 'red (i.e. brown from tar) shield', as contrasted with the 'white' or 'yellow' shield which retained the natural colour of the wood. The round red shield came to be regarded in foreign countries as a characteristic emblem of the Scandinavians. Yet shields actually painted in colours were also common. The shields that hung along the bulwarks of the Gokstad ship were painted yellow and black, and the frequently mentioned red and white shields were in many cases certainly painted with these colours. Possibly, too, the known colour nicknames, as in Ólafr Hvíti and Þorsteinn Rauði, are sometimes to be explained from the colours of their shields, as also the designations 'white strangers' and 'black strangers' used by the Irish to distinguish Norwegian and Danish Vikings. Shields with painted decorations are described almost immediately below.

The common Germanic name for the boss of the shield is represented in ON. *baugr* (etymologically 'ring'); Old English has *randbēag* in the same sense. Another common Germanic technical term is ON. *rǫnd* (etymologically 'rim'), which sometimes designated the flat ring around the convex shield-boss, sometimes the metal rim of the shield. As *pars pro toto* the word was also used of the shield itself in several Germanic languages. In the same way a certain type of shield with an iron rim was given the name of *targa* (= OE. *targe*, modern English *target*), a word which originally referred specifically to the metal rim: the OHG. form of it, *zarga*, retains the original sense. The bosses of the surviving Viking shields have a form that is peculiar to them; the ring, which was smaller than in the older period, was fastened to the wood with nails. Immediately under the boss the wood was cut away to make room for the hand to grasp the handle. In the shield prescribed for national defence the laws make no mention of the boss, but they require a hand-grip, which is to be fastened on with iron nails.

Costly and decorated shields are often mentioned in literature. An Edda poem tells of a shield with a rim of gold. The shield which the skald Egill celebrates in his *Skjaldardrápa* had a crosspiece of gold set with precious stones; it was a present from a chief to another skald. Two other old scaldic poems, Bragi's *Ragnarsdrápa* and Þjóðolf's *Haustlǫng*, were composed about shields on which scenes from myth and legend were depicted. The use of an emblem (*herkuml*) on the shield seems to have been ancient in the north. It is true that history cannot point to any definite example earlier than the device of the cross which King Ólaf the Saint told his men to mark on their shields; but many constantly recurring phrases, such as *vera eins skjaldar* and *skipta um skildi sínum* must be based on the use of emblems on the shield. Animal figures on the shield are also to be inferred from one place-name of saga-times and from two shield-names. Colouring the shield was an ancient practice among the Germans; Tacitus, among others, bears witness to it (in *Germania*, chap. 6): *scuta lectissimis coloribus distinguunt.* This usage was also well known among the inhabitants of the north; blue and green shields are often mentioned, while others were partially or completely gilded.

Reference is made among several Germanic peoples to the shield being strengthened by an outer covering of hide. The finds of the Danish bogs show only one example of this, and Saxo is the only Scandinavian source which gives evidence of the practice. The shield was, however, strengthened sometimes by attaching iron plates to it: at least this seems a possible inference from the man's nickname *járnskjǫldr*, 'iron shield', which occurs in several passages, though it is also possible that the whole shield was made of iron, like that described in *Beowulf*, 2338 ff.

The light round shield was common Germanic: already Tacitus in *Germania* (chap. 43) speaks of the Germans' *rotunda scuta*. Yet several Germanic peoples, including the Anglo-Saxons, also had a curved shield of oval shape, the lower end of which in course of time became more pointed. From the evidence of the sagas it appears that the curved shield with the pointed end (*sporðr*) was known in the north as early as the Viking period. As a rule it seems to have been long and heavy; sometimes the warrior fixed it in the ground in front of him. It was in general use in Iceland in the saga age, as may be perceived from the numerous accounts of persons wounded or dead being carried away on a shield. It was also used in battles at sea.

When the shield was not in use, it hung by a thong around the neck on the left side. When the left hand had to be freed—as when a weapon was wielded with both hands—the shield was thrown on to the back; the same was done when in flight. The right use of the shield was an important point in the art of using weapons. If it were directly opposed to a blow the thin wooden shield could only afford a feeble protection, and its part was still more important when it was a question of parrying both cut and thrust; the iron rim in particular had then to be brought into play. It is often told how deft and vigorous parrying turns the sword or spear in another direction, or breaks the weapon, or knocks it out of the opponent's hand. There was a special accomplishment in suddenly changing shield and sword, which implied that the fighter was able to wield his sword with the left hand as well. In duels each of the two combatants usually had a second who held the shield for him (*halda skildi fyrir e-m*). This custom apparently had a double purpose, as the second might, in certain situations, assist in parrying the blows, and he could also replace the fighter's broken shield with a fresh one.

An ancient Germanic formation in battle was the 'shield-wall' (ON. *skjaldborg*, OE. *scieldburh*), which consisted of a ring of shield-bearers around their leader. A shield-wall was also used in a wedge-shaped formation (*svínfylking*).

When the shield was not being carried, it hung, together with the other weapons, over the owner's seat or sleeping-place; on board ship shields were fastened to a moulding on the topmost strake of planks in the ship's side. Resplendent shields like those mentioned above, the pictured shields sung by the skalds, were only for show; they were carried on festive occasions or adorned the walls of the festive hall.

According to Tacitus in *Germania* (chap. 3) the ancient Germans increased the sound of their battle-songs by holding the shield before the mouth; the sound thus produced, he says, they called *barditus*. With this Othin's statement in *Hávamál* has been compared, that he helps his followers by singing under their shields. But in this there is hardly any question of a battle-song; the reference is rather to the battle-cry with which the ancient men of the north heartened themselves and tried to terrify their enemies. When the warriors thought they heard the voice of the war-god mingled with their own, it was taken as an omen of victory. Even in Christian times echoes of this heathen superstition are still heard.

The white shield was raised up as a token of peace, and in this function was called *friðskjǫldr*, 'peace-shield'; this is first mentioned in the description of the battle of Svǫlðr (995). Its opposite was the red shield, which was fastened up as a declaration of hostility (*herskjǫldr*), as is mentioned in one of the Edda poems and elsewhere. On the other hand, according to Saxo and Ordericus Vitalis it was the peace-shield which was red. Possibly at first a shield of any colour was hung up as a token of peace; this would harmonize with the account of the Norsemen's appearance at Aschloh in the year 882. The later distinction, which was not adopted everywhere in the north, was due to Christian symbolism.

The Helmet

The oldest helmet found in the north comes from Denmark and belongs to the older bronze age. It is a fragment, a chinpiece of gold-plated bronze. Two bronze statuettes from Skåne with conical helmets belong to about the same period. Then there is a long gap until the next find, which was brought to light in the bog of Thorsbjærg and consists of a fragment of Roman workmanship and a well-preserved helmet of Norse manufacture. This last consists of a round skull-piece with openings in it, and a kind of mask for the face attached to it, made of partially gilt silver. The Swedish graves of the latter migration period contain some magnificent helmets. In the famous Vendel helmets (Pl. 42) the skull-piece is of plate iron in the form of a hemisphere, while the broad bands of bronze plate are only for decoration. The pictures stamped into the rimband give these helmets a special value far above the technical. Bronze plates have been found in Öland which were probably used as stamps for unpressing such helmet decorations.

Although the common Germanic name 'helm' provides perfectly valid evidence of the high antiquity of this piece of armour, its use in antiquity may have been very limited, since in the north it never became generally used by all ranks of the people. The ornamental helmets just mentioned obviously belonged to chiefs. In the graves of Norse Vikings not a single helmet has been found. The poets give the distinction of wearing the helmet to chiefs only; compare, too, the poetic term *hilmir*, 'chief', which etymologically means 'the helmeted one'. The war-god Othin is called *hjalmberi*, 'helm-wearer', with which the picture of him on a Vendel helmet agrees (see Pl. 62).

The helmet of the Viking period was of iron or steel, often gilded. A bronze helmet (*árhjalmr*, from OE. *ār*, 'bronze') is mentioned once (in the year 961), and is ascribed to King Hákon the Good, who was fostered in England. It is related of King Harald Fairhair's poets that they wore helmets adorned with engraved rings, obviously gifts from the king. The most characteristic adornment of the ancient Germanic helmet was an image of a wild boar set on the crest. The remains of such a helmet have been found in an English barrow. The boar is found in full figure on two helmets depicted on the silver vessel from Gundestrup in Jutland (from the second century B.C.), and on a bronze plate from Öland (Pl. 31 and 43). In historic times in the north the boar-helmet was only known from old tradition, but it had a continued life in nomenclature. Thus the helmet which King Aðils took from the dead Áli was called variously Hildisvín, 'Swine of battle', and Hildigǫltr, 'Boar of battle'. This latter name was used by the skalds as a general term for 'helmet', while Hildisvíni, according to one of the Edda poems, was the name of the boar owned by the goddess Freyja. Similarly Sýr, 'Sow', was one of the by-names of Freyja, and the god Frey's by-name Vaningi was also used as a name for a boar. The boar-helmet evidently reflects a divine symbol, as is further demonstrated by the poetic expression *enn gollbyrsti valgǫltr*, 'the boar of slaughter with golden bristles', for the helmet, which may be compared with the name Gollinbursti given to Frey's boar. *Beowulf* also (in line 1111) speaks of a *swīn ealgylden*, 'boar all of gold', in a description of a helmet. That the boar of the helmet had a protecting power is seen from *Beowulf*, and Tacitus also, in *Germania* (chap. 45), says, in speaking of the Æstii, to whom Germanic customs are ascribed: 'matrem deûm venerantur. insigne superstitionis formas aprorum gestant: id pro armis omnique tutela securum deae cultorem etiam inter hostis praestat.' Several poetic terms for the helmet have their origin in the boar emblem, such as *Hildisvín, Hildigǫltr, Valgǫltr, Valhrímnir, Valbassi*, all meaning 'boar of battle'.

As to how the helmets of the Viking age were constructed, the sagas leave us in uncertainty. It seems a fair inference from the poetic expression *hjalmr hringreifðr*, 'ring-encircled helmet', however, that the portion specially characteristic of the period was the lower metal-work. There were several types in use, as is shown, among other indications, by the names *valskir*, 'French', or *peitneskir hjalmar*, 'Poitevin helmets', which the men on the king's ship wore at the fight near Nesjar in 1016. Of the face protections known from the older period, nose-bands, chin-pieces, and neck-pieces (see Pl. 42), only the nose-protectors (*nefbjǫrg*) are mentioned in the historical sagas dealing with the Viking period. It is several times related that a hood was laid over the helmet to prevent the wearer from being recognized or to conceal his hostile intent; thus a hood was placed over King Hákon's golden helmet at the battle of Fitjar. The *huliðshjalmr* (= OE. *heolophelm*) of legend may be compared, which rendered its wearer invisible.

The Corslet

The word *brynja*, 'corslet', according to a not improbable theory, is of Celtic origin; cf. Old Irish *bruinne*, 'breast'. But even if the Germans first learned of the use of iron breast-armour from the Celts, they did not make use of it themselves until long afterwards. The fragments found in Scandinavia from the first century A.D. are Roman work. One well-preserved ring-corslet from the find of Vimose in Denmark is a close-fitting shirt about a metre long, having short sleeves and an opening for the head. The rings of this mail-shirt are in part riveted, and in part welded together. In one specimen from the Danish bogs all the rings were riveted with bronze, which must have given the corslet a handsome appearance. At that period the mail-shirt, like the helmet, was evidently a rare piece of equipment which was used by chiefs and was bought from provincial Roman workshops.

In graves of the Viking period corslets are very rare, and they are not mentioned in the historical sagas dealing with this period. Though they are frequently mentioned in the Edda poems and by the skalds, nothing can be concluded from this about their use as a piece of popular equipment. The poets' frequent comparison of the byrnie to a kirtle of skin, together with the expression *sýja*, 'to sew' (cf. Latin *suere*, 'to sew', but also used of linking mail), used of the process of joining the links, seems to point to a time when a skin kirtle was used instead of a byrnie.

A reminiscence of this survives in historical times in the names *berserkir* and *ulfheðnar* (originally men clad in bear and wolf skins respectively). As late as the time of King Ólaf the Saint the inhabitants of Hálogaland wore reindeer skins in battle which were believed to make their wearers invulnerable.

The corslets of the Viking period were of the same kind as those known from the finds of the Danish bogs, in which every ring is linked with four others. While *Beowulf* refers to the rings as fastened by hand, the Norse skalds emphasize the activity of the hammer in the work. Riveted corslets are mentioned only once, in one of the Edda poems. Gilt or gold-adorned corslets appear only in legend; but costly specimens did actually exist, as is inferred from the recorded special names given to certain byrnies. The ringed corslet (*hringabrynja*) seems still in the eleventh century to have been the only breast-armour used in the north.

The length of the corslet varied; the shortest kind was called *brynstakkr*. The corslet was generally provided with wide short sleeves. It was always put on like a shirt over the head and it was taken off by turning it inside out. Above the hips it was gathered in by a sword-belt or a special byrnie-belt. At times it was covered with a light sleeveless tunic.

Machines of War

While Saxo mentions war-slings in use as early as the battle of Brávellir, nothing is said in the Old Norse literature dealing with the Viking period of either the little hand-sling or of the large sling constructed of wooden beams. Instead, there was in use, as a throwing weapon, a stick with a flint stone set in one end (the *skeptifletta*, see p. 388 above), or else the stone was thrown from the hand. Such hurling of stones is mentioned both in land and sea battles. Quite different from these slings was the *valsløngva*, a siege machine by which stones or burning objects were slung by the attacker or defender of a beleaguered town. The Norsemen learned the use of this catapult on their Viking expeditions in the Frankish empire, as appears from the name itself, which means 'French sling'. According to Abbo of Fleury the Norsemen used catapults (*mangana*) at the siege of Paris in 885–6. No doubt the type known as 'lever-sling' is meant, in which the lever is swung on a bolt between two posts;

the Norse name is *vág*, which means etymologically 'lever'. The first historical account of the use of this machine among the Scandinavians is associated with the Norwegian king Ólaf Tryggvason (995–1000) who threw blazing matter by this means onto the wall of the Danavirki. The machine did not come into general use until the twelfth century.

Abbo also ascribes to the Norsemen battering-rams (*aries*), wall-bores (*terebra*), mines and several other war-machines, all of which they must have learned to use during their expeditions in foreign lands, and at that time were not used in Scandinavia. Among these machines seems also to be the wall-breaker mentioned in one passage of Gaufred Malaterra; similarly, trenches and fall-pits are mentioned on several occasions when the Scandinavians were fighting in foreign countries.

A considerable part was played in the military art of the Vikings by the wattle protection known as *fleki* or *flaki*, a strongly-made roof of branches. Ólaf the Saint covered his ship with such a roof in the attack upon Southwark, and under the same sort of cover the Vikings broke through the walls of Chester in 909.

A kind of breastwork was formed by the *víggyrðlar* (etymologically 'battle-belts'), planks which were fastened before a battle to the inner side of the ship's bulwarks, so as to increase their height; they are mentioned, for example, among the preparations for the battle of Svǫlðr in 995. In this same battle there is an account of a primitive castle of beams set up for the occasion. Knút the Great's ship had a castle at the stern.

XXIII

RELIGION[1]

The Soul

SIR JAMES FRAZER, in his work *The Golden Bough*, has demonstrated from an elaborate collection of legends, derived from widely differing races of men, that savages believe the motion of life in men and beasts to be caused by a living being inside the outer covering. A man lives and moves about because within him is hidden a being which has control of the outer frame. As a rule this inner being is conceived as a true image or reduced counterpart of the outward man, but less substantial; less frequently it is conceived as having the form of a beast or bird. This is the only 'soul' that the savage knows. In dreams he believes that the soul is temporarily absent, and in death that it has left the body for ever. He tries to safeguard himself against death by various rules of conduct which are intended to prevent the soul from leaving the body, or to induce it to return. In dreams the soul is believed to wander away from the body and visit all the persons and perform all the actions which the sleeper dreams of. If the soul is prevented from returning, the sleeper will die. If it is necessary to wake him, it should be done gradually, so as to give the soul time to return to him.

[1] The chief sources of our knowledge of Norse myth and religion are: the Edda poems (for editions and translations see p. 212); Snorri's *Edda*, of which Bishop Percy's translation is accessible in Mallet's *Northern Antiquities*, and there is also a translation by A. G. Brodeur, *The Prose Edda*, American-Scandinavian Foundation (New York, 1916); *Ynglinga saga* in Snorri's *Heimskringla*, translated by Morris and Magnusson in their Saga Library, vol. iii, 1893; and numerous passages in various Icelandic sagas and poems. There is a famous description of a temple in *Eyrbyggja saga*, cap. iv, translated in Morris and Magnusson's Saga Library, vol. ii; and *Egils saga Skalla-Grímssonar* (translated by E. R. Eddison, Cambridge, 1930) is especially rich in descriptions of magical practice. The best modern manual of Norse mythology is P. A. Munch, *Norse Mythology*, revised by Magnus Olsen and translated by S. B. Hustvedt, American-Scandinavian Foundation (New York, 1926). Two short but useful works on Old Norse religion are: W. A. Craigie, *The Religion of Ancient Scandinavia* (London, 1906); H. M. Chadwick, *The Cult of Othin* (Cambridge, 1899). The evidence of ancient Norwegian heathendom to be found in place-names has been admirably studied by Magnus Olsen, *Farms and Fanes of Ancient Norway*, Instituttet for Sammenlignende Kulturforskning, Serie A, ix (Oslo, 1928).

This primitive conception of the soul is still found among civilized peoples in historic times, though usually in modified forms; very often the soul has acquired greater independence. Of the highest interest is the close correspondence between the Roman and Norse conceptions of the soul.

The *genius* of Roman belief is the individual man's higher ego. It is born with every man, follows him through his whole life, influences his character and behaviour and controls his destiny. According to the belief of the people it is always a beneficent being. After death it continues to live in the world of shades. Offerings are made to this departed soul, now known as the *manes*, as to other divine beings, sometimes privately, sometimes in public worship ordained on appointed days. The conception of the *genius* was extended so that each family, and similarly each tribe and nation, was believed to have its guardian spirit.

The heathen inhabitants of the north had no word for the soul in our dualistic sense. The various powers of the soul were denoted by the word *hugr* (mind, disposition, thought, way of thinking, desire, aspiration, perception, or courage), which was not well fitted to express the Christian conception of the soul. Missionaries overcame the difficulty by introducing a foreign word which took different forms in Norse according to the nationality of the missionary—ON. *sála* and *sál* from OE. *sáwol*, and OSw. and ODan. *sial*, *siæl* from OLG. *siala*. Or else, imitating the ecclesiastical and monastic use of Latin *spiritus* for the vital principle, they employed *ǫnd* or *andi* (properly meaning 'breath') in the same sense, a usage which has not been adopted in popular speech to any great extent, except in Iceland. Instead of distinctions between the body and the soul one finds among the heathen Scandinavians a peculiar division of personality, which evidently has one of its roots in dream-life, and the other in suggestions emerging from the subconscious or instinctive life, which were regarded as coming from an inner voice. Belief in such a second ego dominates the whole of the ancient psychology, and, as has been mentioned already, it is very nearly related in conception to the Roman *genius*. In both cases we have a being of divine nature which is born with the individual man— or, more accurately, the individual person—accompanies him during the whole course of his life, and continues to live after the death of the body. Already the *hugr* which has been mentioned stands on the verge of this conception, in that the *hugr* is said to advise, urge, or warn; such expressions as *mér segir hugr um*, 'my heart tells me concerning this', are frequent in the sagas. At times apparently the *hugr* even took the form of an animal corresponding to the character of the person concerned. In Norwegian dialects *hug* is used of a sign or presage of a person's coming, as a kind of distant effect of his thought. The names for the personal genius in general Old Norse use were *hamingja, fylgja* (which is still in living use in Norwegian dialects and in Icelandic), and *dís*; to these *vǫrðr* (etymologically the 'watcher') should be added, for although it does not occur in this sense in the old literature, it is used both in Norwegian and Swedish dialects. These names were not employed without distinction; each had its own particular sphere of usage.

The guardian spirit might show itself in dreams to the person who belonged to it; if this happened when he was awake, it was a sign that his death was near at hand. The *fylgjur* or *genii* of other persons also frequently showed themselves in dreams; otherwise they were ordinarily invisible to all except those who had second-sight or were skilled in magic. Often the *fylgja* gave warning of the coming of some person, and in this character is still well known in popular belief (in Norway under such names as *vord, vardøger, fyreferd, foring, framfare*). The guardian spirit's bodily form was usually that of a woman, but it might also— like the *fylgja* which still lives in popular belief—have the form of an animal, generally corresponding to the character of the person associated with it. The form of a bear, among others, is told of in sagas; thus the *fylgja* of Bǫðvar Bjarki fought in the shape of a bear, but he himself lay asleep, and the *fylgja* disappeared again when Bjarki awoke. Hostile *fylgjur* usually took the form of a wolf (compare ON. *ulfshugr*, 'wolfish or savage disposition'). When savage warriors were called *berserkir* and *ulfheðnar* (etymologically 'bear-shirts' and 'wolf-coats'), these names originally referred to the forms taken by the *fylgjur*; and the expressions *hamask* (properly 'to take the form of an animal') and *hamrammr* (properly 'capable of taking such animal form'), denoting their warlike rage, are also founded on the same conception. From this shape or *hamr* the spirit received the name *hamingja*, etymologically **ham-gengja*, meaning 'one who goes about in

an (alien) form'. Once or twice *hamr* is used in the old literature
clearly in the sense of *hamingja*, just as *hamn* in Swedish and
ham in some Norwegian dialects may still designate the ghost
of a dead man or the phantasm of an absent one. Any one who
for any time loses his *fylgja* loses his understanding with it; this
is reflected in the Old Norse words *hamstolinn* and *hugstolinn* =
vitstolinn, 'out of one's wits', and in Norwegian dialect *vord-
stolen*, the explanation of which is found in some of the old
Norwegian 'black-book' charms, which attest the belief that if
the *vord* after leaving the body is prevented from returning, the
person will go mad. After a man's death his guardian spirit
might pass to a son or a dear relative (in a kind of metem-
psychosis), and there were also *fylgjur* attached to a whole
family (*ættarfylgja, kynfylgja*). A single person might accordingly
have several guardian spirits. The nature of the conception was
such that, when the reference was to only one person, the
hamingja was always spoken of in the singular, but the *fylgja*
and *dís*, on the other hand, mostly in the plural. Characteristic
is the case of Gísli Súrsson, who had two *draumkonur*, 'dream-
women', one good and one evil, like the ἀγαθοδαίμων and κακο-
δαίμων of the Greeks.

Like the *genius* of the Romans, the *fylgja* had a determining
influence on a man's destiny. This is natural enough: the *fylgja*
in truth represents the man's character, which, in the belief of
the old Norsemen, decided his destiny. When the *fylgja* is no
longer willing to help, but is angry with the person to whom it
belongs and abandons him, he must die. When the *fylgja*
appears at a person's birth, decides the length of his life (ON.
skapa aldr), and foretells his destiny, it appears to be the
emissary of the norns; in this connexion a passage in *Vaf-
prúðnismál* (stanza 49) should be noticed, where the three norns
are called *hamingjur*. Similarly, in a few passages the *nornir*
seem to be identical with *dísir* and are regarded as man's
personal guardian deities. This close connexion between the
guardian deities and the powers of fate is evident also in the
frequent use of *hamingja* in the sense 'luck', especially luck as a
constant quality or possession attached to an individual, who
is then called *hamingjumaðr*, 'lucky man'.

It may be seen from the foregoing that the Norse conceptions
of the soul have in many respects passed a long way from their

origin. In the description of the divine beings mentioned above, stress has been laid primarily on their character as guardian spirits of men. The thread which connects them with the primitive conception may be perceived in this, that the accompaniment of the *fylgja* is necessary for the maintenance of life in the individual, and reflects his spiritual nature; and it has maintained its close connexion with the life of dreams. As we have seen, indications are not lacking that the *fylgja* was conceived of as living in the body, which it left during sleep. This conception appears clearly in connexion with Othin, of whom *Ynglinga saga* relates that he often changed his shape, and, while his body lay as if asleep or dead, he was a bird or beast, fish or serpent, and went in the twinkling of an eye to far-off lands. Wizards and witches especially were believed to have the power of changing their form at will, while their body lay entranced.

What may have been the Norseman's conception at the end of the heathen age of the close relation between the living man's spiritual double or *alter ego* and the nameless shade which took up its abode after death in one of the many realms of the dead, is not clear, obscured as it is by the various independent developments which the original conception has passed through. Yet we may assume in all circumstances that the inhabitants of the realms of the dead did not live in alien shapes, but kept their human form. That the soul set free by death was regarded as a divine being like the *manes* of the Romans there are several indications; for example, the Edda refers to the dead as 'sons of the gods'.

Magic

Older than the personal gods is a conception which provides the basis of magic and enchantment. This is the belief in a force or power ('mana'),[1] which is possessed in differing degree by every living thing, by every natural object, and even by natural phenomena, sicknesses and the like—a power which evades man's control and therefore comes to be regarded as divine. This mysterious power could be transferred; by eating bear's flesh, for example, a man could get a share of the beast's strength

[1] On the general conception of 'mana' among various peoples see Frazer's *Golden Bough*, i ('The Magic Art'), p. 227 f.

and savagery. In the daily life of the people the innumerable powers and the agents of these powers with which men had to deal certainly had a larger part than the gods themselves. Dangers threatened from all sides; even in food and drink dangerous forces lurked which had to be guarded against (see, for example, *Hávamál* 137). For this purpose there were many observances which every one had to bear in mind. Though less known from literature, these can be traced in all sorts of customs and magical ceremonies practised by the mass of the people, which seek to guard against perils and obtain help from good powers or centres of power.

The Old Norse name for 'mana' is *megin*, 'power'. Of the earth's *megin* we hear in several Edda poems, and of the moon's *megin* in *Vǫluspá* (compare *mōnan miht* in the Old English poem *Be Domes Dæge*). Thor's famed strength, his *ásmegin*, was not a constant attribute, but sometimes he prepared himself for special need by girding on the 'belt of strength' (*megingjǫrð*). Othin's magical strength and his power to give victory were attached to his spear, which in scaldic poetry is called his *megináss*, 'rod of power'. Through charms and *blót* (that is, sprinkling with blood) an object could be filled with 'mana' and become a centre of power. The technical expression for this was *magna*, 'to endow with *megin*'. In this way stones could acquire protecting power and become amulets (*magna steina*). In *Grettis saga* there is an account of a tree-root which became *magnat* because a witch cut runes on it, rubbed blood into them, and recited charms over them, after which she cast the wood into the sea and gave it directions as to where it should float. Of an image of Thor it is said that it was so *magnat* by sacrifices that it became quite alive and could walk. The head of Mímir was *magnat* by Othin, who recited charms over it until it was able to speak to him. Animals, too, such as an ox or cow, could be *magnat* by sacrifice so that they became holy and acquired supernatural qualities. A thing which has received such an addition of power is said to be *aukinn*, 'increased': thus the god Heimdall was *aukinn* with earth's *megin* and other things, the gods worshipped by the ardently heathen Earl Hákon are said to have been *rammaukinn*, and of a horse's penis which was honoured as a kind of deity the expression *aukinn* was similarly used. By the power of sacrifices and charms both living and dead men could be transformed into noxious trolls; such a person was said to be *trollaukinn* or *trylldr*. Thus it is told of the magician Ǫgmund that he became invulnerable through charms and sacrifices, and so *trylldr* that he was not like a man.

An object's 'mana' extended also to its double, that is, any reproduction of its form. A consequence of this was that by conjuring the image one could influence the original. It was believed, for example, that by piercing the image of a person one could wound the person himself. A rock-carving from Nordfjord, Norway, pictures about four hundred harts running towards the sea; the significance of this emerges from a statement that 'when the harts here in the autumn went westwards towards the sea, the inhabitants drove herds of them out on the steep crags of the mountains, so that the beasts fell headlong and became an easy prey'. The rock-carving contains a magical compulsion which will secure good hunting.[1]

A wheel with four spokes or ring containing a cross is often found cut in grave-stones of the stone age, and is also met with in the rock-carvings of the bronze age. The significance of the sign as a sun-image is not to be doubted in view of the numerous analogies from other primitive peoples. From a later period come sun-disks on wheels, or in a wagon provided with a horse, and also golden boats with the sun-token.[2] Clearly this sun-image, in conjunction with the appointed magical formulas or ceremonies, served to speed the sun on its course. Yet the sun has never been worshipped as a personal god among the Germanic peoples (though Sól in Old Norse mythological literature has become an *ásynja*).

Small hammers or axes of amber, bone, or stone were worn in the stone age as amulets. They clearly symbolize lightning. And when hammer-shaped pendants of silver are found in graves of the Viking period, these are undoubtedly Thor's symbol, also found cut in runic stones, where it has the same meaning as the inscription 'Thor hallow these runes' on other stones. Some connexion has been assumed between this hammer of Thor and the short-handled double-bitted axe with which

[1] A. W. Brøgger, *Kulturgeschichte des norwegischen Altertums* (Oslo, 1926), pp. 94-5.
[2] See above, pp. 155-157.

Jupiter is armed in carvings from Caria, and the double-bitted axe of Zeus in Crete. This revival of the ancient magical sign is to be explained as due chiefly to the antithesis of the Christian cross. One assumes that the hammer-symbol or thunderbolt at first had a completely independent meaning, and its development must have been similar to that of the sun-symbol in that, in conjunction with a magical incantation, it served as a protection against lightning. When connected with a god conceived as a person, the protector of men against evil powers, the symbol acquired a much wider use as an apotropaic or averting talisman.

Images, especially of stone, in the form of the phallos are known from nearly the whole of the world; among primitive peoples the phallos-image was a magical device by which the fruitfulness of nature was invoked. The rock-carvings show that the phallos in the bronze age played a significant part in Norse magic. From the finds of the Danish bogs wooden figures are known which have an unnaturally large *penis erectus*. Shaped marble stones ending in a head which is marked off by a deepened ring are found in considerable numbers in graves and in the old places of worship in Norway; they are believed to come mainly from the migration period.[1] Of a private cult of an embalmed horse's penis (called Vǫlsi) there is a detailed account in *Ólafs saga helga*. The word *tjǫsnublót* also points to the worship of a phallos-figure; compare *tja(r)sna*, a wooden peg with a head at the end, which was put into each of the four corners of the holmgang hide.[2] This word is related to Old English *teors*, 'penis'. That this originally impersonal symbol of fertility became attached to Frey appears from Adam of Bremen's description of the image of Frey at Uppsala *cum ingenti priapo*, and he adds that offerings were made at weddings to this god. It may be mentioned as a parallel that in Norway in modern times a phallos was hung up on a post at weddings. High-spirited stallions were often hallowed to Frey, and this is not unconnected with the worship of the horse's phallos already mentioned.

Related to image-magic is rune-magic. The oldest known runes of the North belong to the beginning of the third century

---

[1] See above, pp. 247–248.
[2] *Kormáks saga*, chap. 10; trans. Collingwood and Stefánsson, p. 65 f.

A.D. Runes were believed to have been devised by the god of magic, Othin, whose worship seems to have come to the north about the same time as the knowledge of runes. The similarity with the ancient letter-magic indicates that rune-magic also came from the south. Since the alphabet of Wulfila shows knowledge of the runic alphabet, it has been suggested that runes came to the north from the Goths, perhaps through the Scandinavian people known as the Heruli, of whom a part in the third century lived as neighbours of the Goths by the Black Sea. In the earliest times in the north runes had undoubtedly a wholly magical character.[1] Old Norse *rún* means etymologically 'secret communication', 'mystery', and in its origin points to associated formulas of magic. Each rune had its own name, and its application depends on the meaning of the name: the rune ↑ (Týr, the war-god) gave victory, ↓ (*nauð*, 'need'), protected against poisoned drink, þ (*þurs*, a subterranean being) was the cause of women's menstruation, and so on. With the cutting of runes was associated an invocation of the higher powers; on cutting runes of victory the god Týr should be named three times, with ale-runes the cup must be hallowed with Thor's hammer-symbol, with runes for delivery in childbirth the aid of the *dísir* was invoked. Such use of single runes, however, does not seem to have been frequent; usually whole words or formulas were employed. They were cut on stones to safeguard the peace of the grave, on weapons to obtain victory, on amulets to increase their magical power, on household articles, and on tools. Very often the runes were coloured with blood or red dye.

Like other magical figures the runes were usually associated with charms (*galdr*), the recital of rhythmic formulas of magic, sometimes fixed formulas, sometimes improvised for the occasion. In charms certain numbers with magic significance, and verse-forms based on these numbers, played a great part, as among the ancient Indians. Such magic songs were used for various purposes: to make a man invulnerable, loose bonds, heal wounds, abate fire or storm, rouse love, wake the dead in order to find out future events (*valgaldr*), and many others.

The strongest form of magic was the *seiðr*. This included two things: the art of enchantment and the art of prophecy, the

---

[1] See above, pp. 212–214.

latter with some suggestion that it actually exercises an influence on destiny. The first kind was regarded as an ignoble art, because it usually aimed at causing harm to fellow men, as in producing disease, death, or madness. It was practised in great part by men, and there are various indications that it was associated with phallic worship and homosexuality (*ergi*); it was often punished with death. Prophecy, on the other hand, was practised mostly by women, and the prophetess was given the name *vǫlva* from her magic staff, the *vǫlr*. The prophetess stood or sat on a high platform in the midst of her audience. The spell was worked at night and was introduced by beautiful songs (*seiðlæti*), by which spirits were attracted, or else by recitation of formulas (*frœði*). Precisely what were the instruments for making spells (*taufr*), which the *vǫlva*, according to Þorfinns saga Karlsefnis, kept in her skin purse, is not known; possibly they were of a kind similar to those mentioned in the early Christian law of Norway: hair, human nails, frogs' legs. Such magic-bags are found already in graves of the bronze age.

The most important magical rites were those with which men sought to exercise mastery over the forces found everywhere in nature, in objects as well as phenomena. But the list of magical arts is by no means complete under this head. The person learned in magic could transform himself or others into the shapes of beasts, evoke optical illusions (*sjónhverfing*), produce invisibility (*gera huliðshjalm*), prick with the sleep-thorn (*svefnþorn*); those who possessed the evil eye could by a mere glance blunt a sword or make their enemies insane from terror. Magical drugs (*lyf*) were also much used. The commonest Old Norse word for magic was indeed *fjǫlkyngi*, 'knowledge of many things'.

The master of magic was Othin; he made spells, was invoked as *galdrs faðir*, and was held to be the originator of rune-magic. His name (ON. *Óðinn*, OE. and OS. *Wōden*, Langobardic *Wōdan*, OHG. *Wuotan*) is a derivative of the adjective ON. *óðr*, OE. *wōd*, Gothic *wōds*, OHG. *wuot*, 'possessed, frantic', and is also related to Latin *vātes*, 'seer, prophet, god-possessed singer'. The name referred originally, therefore, to that ecstatic condition which in every age has been regarded as the effect of a supernatural force giving the person possessed by it a supernatural power; this is well known in the Greek oracles, the

Siberian shamán, and the Indian medicine-men. As magician Othin had the nature of a giant; he was originally of the same kind as the giants of the Edda poems, and he was not worshipped. Reminiscences of Othin the daemon are preserved in his descent —his mother was a giant's daughter—and in Snorri's statement that before heaven and earth were created Othin lived among the frost-giants; on one occasion, when he was travelling in disguise, he called himself by a giant's name. Othin the magician we know best from *Hávamál* (where is quoted a series of his charm-verses which he had learned from a giant) and Snorri's *Ynglinga saga*. In this character Othin has a close association with the dead in that he was leader of the storm-procession of the dead, and the Lappish god of death, Rota, is thought to have acquired most of his characteristics in early times from Othin. In the north and west of Germany Othin was raised above daemonic rank and became a god of war and victory and intellectual accomplishments. In the course of the migration period the cult of this culture-god made its way into Scandinavia also, principally from the Saxons (compare the epithet *Saxa goð*). According to the current interpretation, the myths about the war of the Æsir with the Vanir and their final reconciliation[1] reflect the introduction of the Othin cult and its union with the native worship of the gods of fertility. In the Viking age Othin was the principal god of the higher ranks of society and of the skalds; only in Iceland did his cult remain unknown. Othin as he is represented in the two Eddas has attracted to himself and assimilated characteristics which originally belonged to a god of fruitfulness whose cult he displaced. For example, the famous myth in *Hávamál* (stanzas 138 f.) relating that the god was sacrificed to himself in order to arise in a new life is undoubtedly a blending of old ideas of a consecration to sorcery with a Frey-myth; even the wording *þá nam ek frævask ok fróðr vesa*, 'then I became fertile and luxuriant', shows this. There is a wide-spread rite in which the deity who brings about the annual awakening of life is offered to himself in the form of an imper-sonator chosen for the purpose, in order that the god may be reborn with renewed youth. The change from magician to god is perceptible in the symbol of Othin's power: where he appears as a master of magic he carries a magic wand, the *gambanteinn*,

---

[1] *Ynglinga saga*, chap. 4.

with which he deprives men of their wits and performs other feats of magic (compare the nine *wuldortánas*, 'glory-twigs', with which the Anglo-Saxon Woden conjures), and he is named Gǫndlir from this wand (*gǫndull* or *gandr*, 'rod of enchantment') ; where he is a war-god the rod has become the spear Gungnir, which a skald terms his *megináss*, 'rod of power'.

The Gods

From the conception of 'mana' was evolved in the course of time a belief in personal gods as bearers of this power or force. Yet very slowly. No personal god can be shown to be of Indo-European origin. Attempts have been made, it is true, to identify the ancient Germanic god of war (ON. *Týr*, OE. *Tíw*, OHG. *Ziu*) with the sky-god, Sanskrit *Dyaus pitar*, Greek *Zeus pater*, Latin *Jupiter*, but this equation is, formally, unsatisfactory. In actuality *Týr* is simply a singular form of *tívar*, 'gods', and corresponds exactly in form to Sanskrit *dēva* and Latin *dívus*, 'divine' (etymologically 'shining', 'heavenly'), while the related Sanskrit *dyaus* formally corresponds to Latin *dies*, 'day'. From this group of words no more can be inferred than an original distinction between heavenly powers and men, whose old Germanic name, *gumi* in Old Norse (= Latin *homo*), originally signified 'earth-being' (cf. Latin *humus*), just as Sanskrit *Dyaus pitar*, 'father sky', had a complementary counterpart in *Pṛithvī mātar*, 'mother earth'.

The Old Norse names for these heavenly powers are *goð*, *tívar*, *regin*, *ráð*, *bǫnd*, *hǫpt*, all of which in the heathen age occur only in the plural, while the neuter gender of all except *tívar* represents impersonal conceptions: *ráð* and *regin* were originally abstractions with the sense of 'guiding powers', *bǫnd* and *hǫpt* mean 'bonds', while the etymology of *goð* is uncertain.[1] The first two of these names must be terms given to the impersonal

---

[1] *goð* and the cognate Germanic forms of the word, such as English *god*, are now usually derived from an Indo-European root *ghau-* meaning 'call', 'invoke': see Walde and Pokorny, *Vergleichendes Wörterbuch der indogermanischen Sprachen*, i (Berlin and Leipzig, 1929), pp. 529–30. *goð* represents an original verbal adjective in the neuter gender, and its etymological sense is therefore 'that which is invoked', with reference to the power called upon in religious or magical rites. The neuter gender represents, as Professor Falk states, the impersonal conception of this power, not, as Walde and Pokorny suggest, an application to both male and female personal deities.—*Translator's note.*

forces of fate, while the next pair indicate a notion of an organized universe, with a universal obedience to law; these are the forces which hold the world together, just as the end of the world at Ragnarøk is described in the phrase *regin rjúfask*, 'the powers are riven asunder'.

A phenomenon of nature and the being which was dimly felt to be behind it were not easily distinguished from each other. Where powers and forces were attached to a definite phenomenon, as the sky, the sun, the dawn, wind, rain and the like, their bearer had difficulty in developing into a really personal god. Personality was at first developed only by powers that had an unlimited range, such as strength and fruitfulness.

Undoubtedly Thor (ON. *Þórr*), in spite of his name, which means 'thunder',[1] originally represented strength, and the 'mana' of the hammer-symbol was given to him later. When he wished to swing his hammer he had to resort to a special source of strength, his *megingjǫrð*, 'belt of power'. His natural strength he derived from another centre of power, the earth (compare the phrase, referred to above, *jarðar megin*): his mother was Jǫrð, 'Earth', or Fjǫrgyn[2] (the same word as OE. *firgen*, 'wooded mountain'). The Norse Thor is so strongly reminiscent of the Indian god Indra, who is strength and might conceived as an independent power, that one can scarcely refrain from assuming a relationship between them of some kind. Like Thor, Indra is more strongly characterized as a person than the other gods; Indra, too, has red hair and beard, is a mighty eater and drinker and a smiter of tremendous blows; he, like Thor, is the central figure in the body of stories and myths of the gods. He also is blended with the thunder-daemon and equipped with thunderbolts. He is a slayer of serpents, even as Thor slays the serpent coiled around the world. He is the most important protector of the Indians in battle against the enemies who resisted their advance in India, just as Thor is mankind's

---

[1] The suggestion that the name OE. *Þunor*, OS. *Thunar*, OHG. *Donar*) is a borrowing from Celtic at a very early period is of dubious value; the only evidence supporting it is an inscription at Chester from the year A.D. 154 dedicated *Jovi optimo maximo Tanaro*. On the whole it seems likely that Thor was originally a by-name; Jupiter was similarly worshipped at Rome as a thunder-god under the name Fulgur, 'lightning'.

[2] The equation of Fjǫrgyn with Lithuanian *perkúnas*, 'thunder; the thunder-god', cannot be sustained. Consequently the name of Frigg's father Fjǫrgynn cannot be taken to be an older name for Thor.

protector against the primeval giants. Behind these two figures we seem to discern the hero of an Indo-European folk-story.

The oldest known Germanic deity of fertility is the goddess Nerthus, of whom Tacitus gives an account; she is said to be 'mother Earth' (*Terra mater*), and to be worshipped in a holy grove on an island by seven associated tribes on the Jutish peninsula. At certain times the goddess drove around the land in a tilted wagon drawn by oxen, and wherever she went there was feasting and peace. At the end of this tour the goddess was washed in a mysterious lake, which swallowed up the slaves who tended the goddess. What Tacitus tells of Nerthus agrees most remarkably with certain ritualistic customs connected with another goddess of fertility, the Phrygian Cybele, who was similarly called the 'great mother' or 'mother of the gods'. The Romans' great spring festival of Cybele and Attis also ended with a procession to the stream Almo, and in this procession the silver image of the goddess was conveyed in a wagon drawn by oxen. On reaching the stream the image and wagon were washed by the goddess's chief priest, who bore the name of Attis. The explanation of this close correspondence is, without doubt, that the higher forms of fertility worship in the north were derived from the peoples around the Ægean Sea, where similar rites were in widespread use.

The name Nerthus means 'power'; compare ON. *njarðgjǫrð* = *megingjǫrð*, Thor's belt of strength. The word clearly goes together with Celtic **nerto-*, 'power' (Irish *nert*, Welsh *nerth*), and has been taken by several investigators to be a borrowing from Celtic. The same name appears in ON. *Njǫrðr*, god of fruitfulness, prosperity, and peace, originally the earth-goddess's heavenly spouse. Njǫrð's son is Frey, who is likewise a god of fruitfulness and good seasons, wealth, and peace. As god of the corn Frey has the servant Byggvir (from *bygg*, 'barley'). As god of the weather he sails through the heavens in his folding ship Skíðblaðnir, a symbol of the clouds (compare *veðrmegin* as a name of the clouds). The Edda poem *Skírnismál* contains an ancient myth about Frey, the earth's delivery from the might of the giants and union with the sky-god. The same myth is found also in *Fjǫlsvinnsmál*.

Of the worship of Frey at Uppsala it is told in a Norse saga that the god's image was alive and had a young and fair woman as wife. In winter they drove around the country in a wagon, and brought with them everywhere good weather and good season. According to Adam of Bremen and Saxo the Frey-image with the huge *priapos* was worshipped in orgies and licentious ceremonies, such as are found elsewhere, both in Europe and Asia Minor, associated with the gods who have nature's fruitfulness and generation in their care. That the Swedes were in a great degree worshippers of Frey appears among other indications, in the god's appellation *Svía goð* or *blótgoð Svía*. In Uppsala he was known as Yngvi-Freyr, the first element of which (ON. *Yngvi* = OE. *Ing*) is the name of the national hero of the Ingvaeones and the eponym of the Yngling dynasty of kings in Uppsala and Norway. As the name Freyja given to the sister shows, Frey was regarded as meaning 'the lord' (cf. Gothic *frauja*), although no such word is preserved in Norse. Possibly this by-name was chosen through its formal similarity to the adjective *fróðr*, still used in Swedish dialects (and one Norwegian dialect) with the sense 'capable of germinating, strong in generation'. Frey has also the epithet *enn fróði*, 'the luxuriant', and indeed the King Fróði of Danish legend is an ancient god of vegetation and clearly no other than Frey himself.

Of the Norse gods and goddesses only Týr, Thor, Othin, and Frigg (with perhaps Eir, the goddess of leechcraft) appear to be common Germanic. The inhabitants of the northern Olympus—according to Snorri there were, without Othin and Frigg, twelve gods and twelve goddesses—were of widely differing age: Forsete, for example, was clearly adopted from the Fosite of the Frisians (cf. Fositesland = Helgoland), and Bragi was the apotheosized skald Bragi enn gamli, who died in the ninth century. Not many of them, especially of the goddesses, are named in the sagas, nor were many the object of worship or generally known among the whole people. The limits of the various deities' provinces of authority, moreover, were not always clearly marked. Often one deity would push another aside, taking over part of his power; thus one finds that Thor is invoked for a good season's crop and for favourable wind as well as Frey and Njǫrðr. In the conception of the nature of the gods widespread anthropomorphism prevails. In appearance they are wholly human: Othin is a tall and aged greybeard,

Thor a red-bearded man in the prime of life, while Frey is in his youth. The gods were born, and they were destined to die. They could propagate their kind, and did this often outside their own race, especially with the daughters of their enemies the giants. They needed sleep, and they loved recreations: games, betting on races, love adventures, and above all entertainment with good food and drink. Like human beings they were subject to the laws of fate. Of their being omnipotent, even within a limited province, there is no question, and just as little of their being omniscient: to discover Balder's fate Othin has to consult a witch. There is no one god recognized by all as the highest: worshippers of Frey called him 'the world's god', worshippers of Thor called him 'the almighty god', and worshippers of Othin called him 'allfather'. None of the official sacrifices was given to one god only, but usually to a trinity of gods.

Images and Temples

The oldest images of the gods seem to have been posts of wood. Under the name *stafr* such idols are mentioned both in the Gotland laws and in the oldest Norwegian Christian law, which forbid men to have them in their houses or to worship them. Possibly also ON. *áss* (the same word as the *anses* of Jordanes), the name of one kind of god, is to be connected with *áss*, 'beam' (Gothic *ans*). In the literary accounts of temples there are many descriptions of images of gods made of wood and ornamented with gold and silver, usually three gods together, and among them always Thor; in private temples were also images of goddesses (Frigg, Freyja) or of female tribal deities (as Irpa and Þorgerðr). Carvings representing the gods often adorned the high-seat pillars and the prow of a ship. For household use there were small images of clay or paste. Miniature images of silver or bone were worn as amulets.

A common Germanic word for a place where worship of the gods was held was *alh* (Gothic *alhs*, OE. *ealh*), of which remains are preserved in Scandinavia in old place-names. Another common Germanic name for the same thing is seen in ON. *hǫrgr* (OE. *hearg*, OHG. *harug*), the original significance of which is 'stone-pile', 'crest of a rock'. It accords with this etymology that the Old Norse word may also mean 'an altar of stone'. This stone altar seems often to have been brought into a grove

and surrounded by a fence or hedge. In its final stage of development, however, the temple appears as a timbered building containing the altar. The usual term for the temple in historic
times is *hof*,[1] a specifically Norse name identical with OE. *hof*,
German *Hof*; the original sense of the word seems to have survived in Norwegian dialect *hov*, 'hill': both farm-houses and
temples were usually built on a hill. The temples of the Viking
period, like the early Norwegian timbered churches of the following period, were planned on distinctively Christian models,
probably Irish and Anglo-Saxon churches. The arrangement
of the temple is known in detail from accounts in literature and
from excavations made in Iceland (Fig. 33). The temple consisted of a longish *skáli* (hall), to which the crowd of worshippers
was restricted; in the middle of the floor were fires, and along
the walls were benches which were fixed in position. In this
hall the flesh of animals sacrificed was cooked and the sacrificial feast was held. The hall was divided by rows of posts
into a middle space and two side-spaces. At the end a low wall
divided off a rounded *afhús* which contained the altar and the
images of the gods; this *afhús* corresponds to the chancel of a
Christian church with the altar. On the altar lay the holy ring
on which oaths were sworn, and also a bowl for the sacrificial
blood and a brush of twigs with which the blood was sprinkled.

According to Snorri the Swedes had two chief temples, one at
Sigtuna for Othin, one at Uppsala for Frey. Of the latter Adam
of Bremen, writing in the eleventh century, gives a fairly detailed account. According to his description there were images
in this temple of Thor, Frey, and Othin, but by the side of these
were worshipped various dead men who had been made into
gods. A general sacrificial feast of all the Swedes took place
every ninth year. In Denmark the chief temple was at Lejre in
Zealand. The German historian Thietmar of Merseburg, writing
about the year 1000, relates that at this temple were sacrificed
every ninth year in the month of January ninety-nine men and
the same number of horses, hounds, and hawks, or instead of
hawks, cocks. This heathen cult, which is not known from any
other source, must have been abolished by about 930. The most
important Norwegian temples were at Trondenes (in Nordland),

[1] On *hof* see further Magnus Olsen, *Farms and Fanes of Ancient Norway*
(Oslo, 1928), p. 267 f.

FIG. 33. A temple (*hof*) excavated at Hofstaðir, Iceland.

Lade, and Mære (both in Trøndelagen) ; the saga historians also tell of a great temple at Skiringssal (in Viken).

The Worship of the Gods

The ancient rites of worship consisted of sacrifice and prayer. No prayer had any power unless introduced by a gift (*fórn*), or promise of a gift, or reference to an earlier gift, in the form of an object, living beast or human being, or corn or beer for use at the sacrificial feast. Each gift, according to the ancient belief, had a binding force, if it was accepted. Accordingly we often hear that the offerer prays the gods for a sign that his offering is accepted. What was desired from the gods was worldly advantages, such as long life, wealth and good seasons, progeny, victory over enemies, or peace, or one might desire an answer to a question ; sometimes, too, a gift was made to avert the anger of the gods or to win their favour. Thank-offerings are not heard of. That on the other hand encomia belonged to the heathen cult is shown by *Hyndluljóð* (stanzas 2 and 3), where favour is asked from Othin with an enumeration of his good deeds to persons named or to his worshippers in general.

The technical term for sacrifice is *blót*, properly only the name for the slaughter of the sacrificial beast and the sprinkling of its blood. While in magical practice sacrifice in conjunction with charms of compelling power gives objects and persons a supernatural power, in the worship of the gods the magical element with its incantations disappears: the gods stand quite free as to whether they will accept the strengthening of their power. Best known is the ceremonial of the sacrificial feasts (*blótveizla*). When the blood of the victim had been gathered in a bowl, the sprinkling brush (*hlautteinar*) was dipped in it, and the blood was sprinkled on the altar, the images of the gods, the temple's walls, and also on those who took part in the feast. Through the sprinkling of the blood was realized the communion, the contact with deity which constitutes the religious relation. The common Germanic origin of this hallowing is to be inferred from various indications, among others, the Germanic word which appears in OE. *blĕtsian*, Northumbrian *bloedsia*, 'to bless', originally 'to hallow with blood'. This word has descended into modern English as *bless*. Moreover, the eating of the sacrificial animals created a mutual bond between the god and the worshipper : the sacrificial beast was the property of the offerer and thereby a part of himself, but it had also been consecrated to the god and thus received a share of his power. As among the South Germans, ale was the constant sacrificial drink, a use descending from the time when the gods of fertility were the only gods worshipped. The sacrificers hallowed the ale with the sign of the hammer and recited the formulas which each cup's purpose and content required; according to Snorri the first cup was signed to Othin for victory, the next to Njǫrðr and Frey. Thus the sacrifice was similar in a general way to the Christian sacrament. Those who took part were bound by it into a single body. Attendance at sacrifice was a duty to the members of the worshipping unit, while strangers were not admitted. The ceremonial vows which were uttered there (at the *bragarfull*) were holy and binding.

In addition to the toasts drunk to the gods at the great yearly sacrifice, cups of remembrance to the dead were also drunk, as Snorri tells us. This side of the ceremony seems to have been strongly emphasized at the midwinter or Yule sacrifice, which moreover was the most important one, and this emphasis gradually gave the feast an altered character. The Yule sacrifice is sometimes said to have been held to ensure the coming of spring, sometimes for peace and good weather. Both accounts indicate that the feast was sacred to Frey; it speaks in favour of this, too, that the vows of the *bragarfull* on this occasion were made over a boar which had been consecrated to Frey. Many customs from a later time also indicate that it was a fertility feast, while others tend to show that it was a feast for the dead, for the souls of the departed, and so in this respect most closely associated with Othin, whose by-name Jólnir is said to be due to the consecration of the Yule to him. At Yule-time, according to popular belief, the spirits of the dead and the hosts of the underworld had free play and craved entertainment, and the leader of their procession could only be Othin.

When need arose for finding out the will of the gods or for obtaining an answer to a question, one might *ganga til fréttar*, 'institute an inquiry'. This might be done in two ways. One could resort to a *vǫlva* who would prophesy with the aid of a spell; but it was considered more honourable to *fella blótspán*, 'let fall the blood-marked chip' (in sortilege). The latter practice has been compared with what Tacitus tells (*Germania*, chap. 10) of the Germans, who prophesied by means of marked chips which were scattered out over a white cloth; the priest, after praying to the gods, interpreted their answer from the chips. The Norse gods, however, made no communication gratis; for a ceremonial sacrifice the use of blood was necessary. According to *Hymiskviða* (stanza 1) even the gods themselves sought enlightenment by observing the sacrificial blood, which was sprinkled with *hlautteinar*. Even the name of the sacrificial blood, *hlaut*, in its etymology (it meant originally 'casting of lots'; cf. *hlutr*, 'lot') points to the necessity of having it for oracles of this kind. In an account of the great sacrifice in which Earl Hákon *feldi blótspán*, the earl is named in the scaldic verses belonging to the passage *Týr teinlautar*, that is, in the ordinary prose form of the words, *Týr hlautarteins*, 'a Týr (i.e. lord) of the bloodtwig'; and *blótspánn* in *Vǫluspá* is called *hlautviðr*, 'sortilege-wood'. That the blood-oracle existed among the ancient Scandinavians is shown by Strabo's account of the white-haired priestesses who followed the Cimbrian host and foretold the future from the prisoners' blood. The principle of interpretation in such auguries cannot be ascertained, however. Of Earl Hákon's sacrifice, already mentioned, it is related that two ravens (the birds of Othin) came flying and shrieking aloud, from which Hákon perceived that Othin had accepted the sacrifice, and that the time was favourable for battle. The same conception, that the gods give the sacrificer a sign in answer to a question, is expressed again in one passage thus: 'He made a great sacrifice and looked for omens (*leitaði sér heilla*) of his destiny; the inquiry (*fréttin*) directed him to Iceland.' In both these cases it may have been a question of a positive or negative answer to an inquiry, as also when it is stated that 'The chips fell out as if he would not live long'. In other cases it seems necessary to suppose that bolder interpretations were taken by the conductor of the sortilege. Thus it is told of King Dag that he asked for information as to what had become of his wise sparrow,[1] sacrificing for his inquiry a boar which had been hallowed to Frey (*gekk til sonarblóts til frétta*), and he received the reply that it had been killed in a place that was named. At another time men *feldu spán* to obtain a favourable wind,

---

[1] See *Ynglinga saga*, chap. 21.

and the chips fell out so that Othin demanded three men who should be hanged in sacrifice to him. On another occasion when the blood-chips were cast the interpretation went that there would not be a good season until the foremost prince in the land was sacrificed.

Ancestor Worship

Together with the conceptions of the mystical power or 'mana' which formed the basis of so many of the oldest religious forms went the belief in spirits of the dead. Wherever this belief was prevalent, a worship of the dead developed naturally. Finds of animals' bones and shells in the graves of the late stone age seem to point to sacrificial feasts at the grave. In the megalithic graves there are traces of a fire having been lighted in the central space to cheer and warm the *manes* of the dead. From the beginning of the iron age vessels of food and drink were set in the grave, containing supplies to be used in the future life. All this comes very near to a kind of ancestor worship. In historic times ancestor worship can be established with certainty. If a person in his lifetime had been specially revered by society, it was believed that his soul after death had more than ordinary power and would help those who turned to him with sacrifices and invocations. This was most readily believed of kings and chiefs, who according to ancient Germanic tradition were descended from the gods: thus the royal family of the Goths was said to be descended from demigods called *anses*—the same word as ON. *Æsir* and OE. *ēse*, 'gods'. There are many examples of such 'sons of the gods' being worshipped after death as divine. Even Iceland apotheosized some of its inhabitants; for example, Bárðr Snæfellsáss was honoured as guardian spirit of the western quarter. The body of the Norwegian king Halfdan the Black was even divided into four parts so that the four quarters of the land might sacrifice to him and thus share in his luck (*hamingja*).

Especially widespread was the worship of the *dísir* (in *dísablót*), the souls of the dead who acted as guardian spirits to their family and appeared at critical junctures in the life of their descendants (see above, p. 409). Such family guardians were worshipped by Earl Hákon among others, the Þorgerðr Hǫlga-brúðr and Irpa mentioned in sagas, who had been daughters of a king of Hálogaland. Freyja, a goddess of the dead, was regarded as the ruler of the *dísir*; she was given the appellation Vanadís, and a Swedish and a Norwegian temple bore the name Dísarsalr in her honour. In the Edda poem *Hyndluljóð* Freyja says of her favourite Óttar that he has built her a temple and sprinkled it with fresh ox-blood. It is stated of Alfhild, a king's daughter, that she sprinkled the temple with blood every night in sacrifice to the *dísir*. The *dísir* in Norway were the object of both public and private worship. In Uppsala a national *þing* was associated with the worship of the *dísir*, the Dísaþing, of which the memory is still preserved in the name of the annual fair Distingen.

Further, the less frequent sacrifice to the elves (*alfablót*) must undoubtedly be regarded as worship of human souls. Thus we hear of sacrifice made after death to a petty king buried at the manor of Geirstad, who is given the name Ólafr Geirstaðaalfr. In the Edda poem *Lokasenna* the inhabitants of the kingdom of Rán and Ægir, to which came those who had been drowned, are called elves. Just as the gods and the elves here feasted together, so the words *æsir ok alfar* were combined in a frequently occurring alliterative phrase.[1] According to an account in *Kormáks saga* the elf-sacrifice consisted in smearing the mound inhabited by the elves with ox-blood. Elsewhere elf-worship in Sweden is spoken of, and is there perhaps associated with the prevailing worship of Frey, who is called lord of the elves and is said to live with the light-elves (*ljósalfar*) in Alfheimr.

Priests

While the arts of magic were surrounded with mystery, the worship of the gods was open and public. Indeed, the priest in the Viking age was not strongly differentiated by his position from the rest of the people. Only the ritual which was used in the worship of the gods of fruitfulness seems to have been surrounded with a certain secrecy and to have been practised by a limited priesthood. Otherwise no initiation was necessary to become priest and perform sacrifice: any landholder could have his own temple on his estate, where he himself sacrificed to whatever gods he honoured most. At the regular general

[1] The gods and elves are similarly associated in an Old English charm, Grein's *Bibliothek der angelsächsischen Poesie*, i. 318, l. 23.

sacrifices the chief performed the office and was known as the *goði*. Several indications point to an original preference for women to perform the offices of sacrifice, and such *gyðjur* are still heard of in the Viking period; to them belonged especially the sacrifice to the *dísir*, the sacrifice to the elves, and the cult of the spirits of the land. Of the Icelandic *goði*, who was also civil administrator in his district, it is recorded that he was hallowed to his office by dipping his hands in a slaughtered wether's blood (*i goða blóði*).

The Abodes of the Dead

Of the conceptions which the inhabitants of the north entertained at different periods of the places where the dead had their dwelling, only the manner of burial can give us information. We have seen above how the Scandinavians at all periods must have believed that death consisted in the desertion of the man by the spiritual being which controlled him, in order to live elsewhere. The mode of burial may be judged to be very near the base of this belief. From the early stone age no graves are known; but in the Danish kitchen middens the bodies lie among the remains of provisions. The significance of this can hardly be anything else than an intention that the soul, which was believed to require sustenance, might find it as near as possible and remain in a dwelling-station near the survivors. The open tombs of the late stone age with their furnishing were undoubtedly regarded as a place of resort or refuge for the soul, in the same way that a house is for men. At the close of the stone age the dead were placed in completely closed stone tombs or coffins. The explanation of this form of burial must be that men now had the notion of a kingdom of the dead to which the soul went immediately after death. The same idea must lie beneath the cremation of the bronze age, which for a long period went side by side with burial in closed graves. In both of these methods of burial, however, there seems to have been another motive present, a precaution due to the belief, so strongly developed in the north, in the hauntings of the dead. Both the tightly closed graves and, still more, cremation (which was introduced from the south) gave security against the dead man's walking again. In heathen society it was a duty to give certain attentions to corpses immediately after death; these offices to the dead were called *nábjargir*, the most important of which seems to have been the closing of the nostrils, a custom which must be regarded in the light of the ancient belief that the soul passes through the nose and mouth. When these openings were stopped the soul was prevented from returning to the body, that is, the dead man was prevented from walking again as a spook. From the same motive the body of any one who walked after death was dug up and burned.

The megalithic graves of the stone age may be regarded as the starting-point of the belief in larger realms of the dead. And just as the megalithic tomb must have been the burial place of a family, we know examples from Iceland of noble families who had a special hill which they entered after death. The common Germanic name for the subterranean abode for all the dead appears in Old Norse as Hel (etymologically 'Covering'). Common Germanic also was the belief that the dead must wander a long way before they find their appointed resting-places. When in Norse sources a journey over a river or the sea is indicated, this may be connected with the mighty river Gjǫll which divided the realm of Hel from the world of the living, or it may be a poetic tradition from the Skjǫld story, in which the hero also comes as an infant in a ship to this world.[1] These myths are undoubtedly connected with the idea that the dead had to make a journey over the sea to the other world. The same conception finds expression in the custom of burying the dead in a ship, described in an earlier chapter.[2] We may also recall Balder's funeral, where his body was actually placed in a ship that was launched out to sea. The same sort of ship-funeral appears again in Snorri's account of King Haki in Uppsala (*Ynglinga saga*, cap. 27) and in Scyld's obsequies in *Beowulf*.

The description which Snorri gives of the realm of Hel as an evil and joyless place cannot be accepted as authoritative; it is coloured by the Christian conception and its natural antithesis to Valhall. When Balder, god of purity and justice, came after death to Hel, he received, according to *Vegtamskviða*, the

[1] The coming and departure of Skjǫld (Scyld in Old English) is described at the beginning of *Beowulf*. It is usually held, however, that this arrival and departure by boat belonged originally not to Scyld but to the culture-hero Sceaf; see Chambers, *Introduction to Beowulf*, pp. 68–86.

[2] See Chapter XVI, pp. 280–281.

same festive welcome that the fallen King Eirík, according to *Eiríksmál*, received in Valhall; the benches were adorned with rings, the floor beautifully paved with gold, and mead, the brightest of drinks, was brewed. Elsewhere (as in *Ynglingatal* and Saxo's history) it is said that the dead chieftain enjoys the love of the goddess Hel. In contrast to the continual life of battle (or sports of battle) of the Einherjar in Valhall, Hell was a peaceful place where the dead rested after the labours of life. This is reflected in expressions such as *hvílask í helju*, 'to rest in Hell', and Saxo's *placidae sedes* applied to the dwellings of Hell.

The belief in Valhall was a product of the Viking age. Just as in battle the warriors were grouped around their king, so the war-god Othin gathered his best men around him after death to form an army which was to follow him to the last great battle at Ragnarøk. Aristocratic military society professed this belief, though not without exception: the worship of both Thor and Frey was also known among the Vikings. Nor do the story-tellers of the Edda poems represent their most famous hero, Sigurðr Fáfnisbani, as coming to Valhall, but to Hell, and Brynhild exults in the notion that she is to live there with her hero. The later origin of Valhall is proved by its having borrowed part of its equipment from Hell, such as the river forming its boundary, the gate of bars, and the cock. Other elements of the beliefs attaching to Valhall also have their origin farther back. The valkyries (ON. *valkyrja* = OE. *wælcyrige*) who fight in battle and carry the fallen to Valhall and attend them there are probably the old Germanic amazons of whom Tacitus speaks, blended with a mythological conception of the raven as a blood-drinking demon: the word is related to OE. *wælcéasiga*, 'raven', etymologically 'devourer of the slain' (cf. OHG. *kiosan*, 'partake of, eat').

The list of abodes of the dead named in Old Norse literature is not ended with Hell and Valhall. On the contrary, one finds a rather complicated mixture of ideas about the home of the dead. By the side of Othin, god of death, stands Freyja as goddess of death; she, according to the Edda, has the right to choose half of those who have fallen in battle for her dwelling, Folkvang. According to *Egils saga* the women came to her after death, but Snorri says they came to the goddess Gefjon.

And according to some evidences the worshippers of Thor had their final dwelling with Thor in Þrúðvang. Possibly it was also believed that worshippers of Frey became elves and came to Frey in Alfheim. According to Snorri and *Halfs saga* those who were drowned were taken by the sea-giant Ægir and his divine wife Rán into their brilliantly lighted dwelling on the sea-bottom. Finally, *Eyrbyggja saga* relates of certain Icelandic families that after death they took up their abode in a fell which lay near by, and this belief is one that has very ancient roots, and has parallels also in other Norse lands. By no means rarely have men imagined a connexion between the grave and the realms of the dead.

In the heathen period thoughts of the future life did not play nearly so great a part as in Christendom. Though death might come as a release, the next life was only a colourless copy of earthly life. Moreover, destiny in the future life was fixed beforehand: from a very early time a person's existence after death was held to be dependent on the position which he held in this world; a king or thrall remained king and thrall. Yet in the Viking period there were some who believed in punishment for the worst criminals, as appears from *Vǫluspá*, where perjurers, secret murderers, and those who seduced the wives of others were visited with terrible vengeance. Elsewhere it is said that perjurers became thralls in Valhall. A more original belief appears in Earl Hákon's words about a man who had seduced his benefactor's daughter and burned the temple: 'The man who has done this will surely be rejected from Valhall.' Exclusion from the common kingdoms of the dead is also indicated in the belief in hauntings, the belief that wicked men, such as wizards and wild berserks, walk again and do evil.

Piety and Fatalism

The extent to which we can rightly speak of religion before the coming of the personal gods must depend on the definition which we give to the conception. It seems just to assume that in the growth of personal gods, as with all other human beliefs, a continuous development has taken place, though currents from without have made some modifications in the tradition. The primitive picture-magic implies a kind of impersonal godhead on which man felt himself dependent, and for whose superhuman power he felt awe. The offerings to the dead, which can be shown to be as old as this magic, may also be said to have a religious character. And since magical power became attached to personal deities, or to dead mortals raised to the divine rank, their worship must in great part be based on evolution from the older conceptions. We can therefore postulate from the oldest times a religious spiritual life which has continually assumed higher and higher forms.

The gods were believed to be good powers, who were on the whole well disposed to men. Through religious rites mutual relations were established between the god and his worshipper, based on service and return for service. That feelings of friendship and gratitude could be developed in this pact of self-interest there are many proofs. Thus the aged Egil Skalla-Grímsson says (*Sonatorrek*, stanzas 22–3), when the sea has robbed him of his favourite son: ' I was friendly with the lord of spears (Othin), and became trustful in putting my faith in him, until he broke friendship with me. Therefore I cannot with a fond heart honour the Chief of the gods, though he gave me as compensation for my grief an art without defect (poetry).' Such a feeling of friendship on equal terms as Egil expresses would obviously be rare. Earl Hákon, an enthusiastic worshipper of the gods, undoubtedly followed the usual custom when he threw himself in humility on the ground before the image of the god. Although the ancients were polytheistic, there was usually one god, the *heitgoð* or *fulltrúi* of the person concerned, with whom relations assumed a peculiar warmth. This was especially likely to happen when a man was dedicated to a particular god from birth. It is said of the Danish king Harald Hildetann that from childhood he was dedicated to Othin, who on that account always gave him victory. The numerous personal names having *þor-* as the first element often had their origin demonstrably in dedication to Thor. Of the sacrificer Eyvind Kinnrifa it is related that he was given to the gods from birth, and he had himself often renewed his consecration 'so that he no longer had the nature of men'. He defiantly ignored all Ólaf Tryggvason's promises of gifts and rewards and the vessel of glowing coals which was set on his belly, and died a martyr for his faith.

Religion set its seal on all festive functions. Births, deaths, and betrothals were solemnized with libation in the gods' honour (*barnsǫl*, *erfiǫl*, *festarǫl*). The procedure of the law-courts was closely connected with religion, though it is not recorded that the *þing* stood under the protection of any special god. The oath was a sacred ceremony, and was sworn either at the temple or at the *þing*, the swearer taking the altar-ring in his hand and calling the gods to witness. The *holmganga* or single combat was also holy and therefore combined with sacrifice and other religious ceremonies. That its result was regarded as divine judgement, however, is not so certain. Belief in divine judgement is more evident when a person sought to clear himself from an imputation by passing under a strip of turf (*ganga undir jarðarmen*)—if it did not fall, he was declared innocent. A similar ceremony was used in connexion with the swearing of oaths when two or more swore fosterbrotherhood (*fóst-brœðralag*). A woman cleared herself from a charge by taking stones out of a boiling cauldron with bare hand without being injured; this ordeal was called *ketiltak*. The close connexion between legal ceremonies and religious belief is illustrated also by the custom of summoning ghosts with all formality for the harm they had done, and banishing them by decree of the court from the house where they were at large.

What the gods required from their worshippers was fidelity in observances and trustiness in the fulfilment of vows. This religion did not comprehend any moral teaching. The strophes of *Hávamál* which are didactic are merely practical rules of life which at most aim at securing fame after death for those who follow them. The religion of the Æsir includes, it is true, such a pure and just character as Balder, but also his opposite, who, moreover, was representative of the highest intellectual life of the time: Othin was often treacherous, unjust and cruel, and he appears frequently as a seducer of women. In him is expressed the moral corruption of the military life of the Viking age. If it is desired to learn the ideals of men in the older heathen age, one should study especially the heroic poems, which with their excellent characterization show us a series of personages of unusual nobility, for whom the conception of honour, together with the unswerving loyalty which is its natural companion, is the leading motive in all conduct (as in the duty of vengeance). The fate of these men is tragic, as a consequence of their strong uncompromising personality, but in death they raise themselves morally above their fate and keep their spirit unconquered. We find the same salient traits in most Germanic heroic poetry, and we may assume for them a common Germanic origin.

Among the inhabitants of the north belief in the gods was conditioned by belief in fate. Like the ancient Germans, the Scandinavians of the Viking age were fatalists. This fatalism was not dependent on their religion—unlike that of the Mohammedans and Calvinists. In tracing the conceptions of fate and fortune (ON. *Urðr* = OE. *wyrd*, 'fate'), we must start with the spinning of the Norns, as is shown by a common Germanic group of words: ON. *auðna*, 'fate', 'fortune', *auðinn* (= OE. *ēaden*), *auðr*, 'wealth' (= OE. *ēad*, 'riches', 'fortune'), the basic sense of which appears in the Lithuanian cognate *audmi* 'I weave'; compare also OE. *gewif*, 'fortune', and *me þæt wyrd gewæf*, 'fate spun for me that destiny'. One's fate was fixed at birth, but it was not decided blindly. The career in life which the Norns determined for the new-born man had a near connexion with his character. In the poem about Helgi Hundingsbani (ii. 2) the expression *skapa aldr* refers to his winning of fame in his career, but also to the nobility of his character as a condition of his success. Thus the old heroic poems are not mere tragedies of fate, but character-tragedies of a higher type.

INDEX

In this index *æ* has the alphabetical place of *ae*; *ø*, *ǫ*, and *ǒ* are treated as *o*, and *þ*, *ð* as *th*. Foreign words are italicized, and the language to which each belongs is usually indicated by a following abbreviation. Old Norse, classical Latin, and Greek words, however, have no such designation, except in positions where ambiguity is possible. Greek words occupy the alphabetical position of their transliteration into Roman letters.

PRINTED IN
GREAT BRITAIN
AT THE
UNIVERSITY PRESS
OXFORD
BY
JOHN JOHNSON
PRINTER
TO THE
UNIVERSITY